The Art of Writing

Canadian Essays for Composition

Fourth Edition

Ronald Conrad
Ryerson Polytechnic University

McGraw-Hill Ryerson Limited
Toronto Montreal New York Auckland Bogotá
Caracas Lisbon London Madrid
Mexico Milan New Delhi San Juan
Singapore Sydney Tokyo

The Act of Writing
Canadian Essays for Composition
Fourth Edition

ISBN: 0-07-551829-5

2 3 4 5 6 7 8 9 0 TRI 4 3 2 1 0 9 8 7 6 5

Printed and bound in Canada

Publisher: Dave Ward
Developmental Editor: Laurie Graham
Production Editor: Gail Marsden
Cover Design: Dianna Little
Cover Illustration: Christopher Griffin
Printing and Binding: Tri-Graphic Printing (Ottawa) Limited
Text set in: Baskerville

Canadian Cataloguing in Publication Data

Conrad, Ronald, date
  The act of writing

4th ed.
ISBN 0-07-551829-5

1. English language - Rhetoric.   2. Canadian essays
(English).* I. Title.

PE1429.C65 1995   808'0427   C94-932719-0

For
Francisco Barco Solleiro and Lina Serrano Pardo

CONTENTS

And then. . . .

CHAPTER 1: NARRATION   21

"There were cheers and laughter as Tivadar hit me in the nose
before I got my jacket off. It was not the first time I had tasted my
own blood, but it was the first time a Christian had made it flow."

For example. . . .

CHAPTER 2: EXAMPLE 51

It's large and yellow and. . . .

CHAPTER 3: DESCRIPTION   75

wrench my eyes away from the clutch of those empty sockets. The power that I felt was not in the thing itself, but in some tremendous force behind it, that the carver had believed in."

Here's why. . . .

---

obliging me to question so many received ideas. About Germans. About my own monumental ignorance of the world. About what novels were."

It's just the opposite of. . . .

CHAPTER 5:
COMPARISON AND CONTRAST   153

In a way, it's like. . . .

CHAPTER 6:
ANALOGY AND RELATED DEVICES   187

There are three kinds of them. . . .

CHAPTER 7: CLASSIFICATION   217

Here's how it's done. . . .

CHAPTER 8: PROCESS ANALYSIS   243

prevent a whole generation of young men from following in
his path."

Therefore. . . .

CHAPTER 9: ARGUMENTATION AND PERSUASION   279

CONTENTS BY SUBJECT

CHILDHOOD AND OLD AGE

WOMEN IN SOCIETY

OUTSIDERS

THE CITY

THE ENVIRONMENT

WORK

LEISURE

VIOLENCE IN SOCIETY

SCIENCE AND TECHNOLOGY

BUSINESS AND INDUSTRY

THE MEDIA

THE ARTS

LAUGHS

PEOPLES AND PLACES

MAINLY CANADIAN

ACKNOWLEDGEMENTS

Alison Acker: "Tito" from *Children of the Volcano*, 1986. Reprinted by permission of Between the Lines.

Doris Anderson: "The 51-Per-Cent Minority" from *Maclean's* magazine, January 1980. Reprinted by permission of the author.

Margaret Atwood: "Canadians: What Do They Want?" from *Mother Jones* magazine, © January 1982. Reprinted by permission of Mother Jones, Foundation for National Progress.

Russell Baker: "A Nice Place to Visit" from *The New York Times*, © 1979. Reprinted by permission of The New York Times.

Collin Brown: "A Game of Tennis" from an interview with Collin Brown by Catherine Dunphy, p. C-8, *The Toronto Star*, May 15, 1994. Reprinted by permission of The Toronto Star Syndicate.

June Callwood: "Making a Difference" from *Homemakers Magazine*, pp. 40–46, April 1989. Reprinted by permission of the author.

xxii   *ACKNOWLEDGEMENTS*

Stevie Cameron: "Our Daughters, Ourselves" from *The Globe and Mail,* p. A-20, December 6, 1990. Reprinted by permission of The Globe and Mail.

Emily Carr: "D'Sonoqua" from *Klee Wyck,* © 1941, by Emily Carr. Reprinted by permission of Stoddart Publishing Co. Ltd.

Dian Cohen: "The Commodities Game" from *Money,* pp. 213–217, by Dian Cohen, Prentice-Hall Canada, 1987. Reprinted by permission of Prentice-Hall Canada.

Amy Willard Cross: "Safety First, Fun a Distant Second" from *The Globe and Mail,* p. A-14, January 8, 1991. Reprinted by permission of the author.

Robertson Davies: "The Decorums of Stupidity" from *A Voice From the Attic,* by Robertson Davies, McClelland and Stewart Inc., 1960. © Robertson Davies. Reprinted by permission of the author.

Wendy Dennis: "A Tongue-Lashing for Deaf Ears" from *Maclean's* magazine, November 1981. Reprinted by permission of the author.

Kildare Dobbs: "The Scar" from *Reading the Time,* by Kildare Dobbs, 1968. © Kildare Dobbs. Reprinted by permission of the author.

Phil Edmonston: "Dealer Tricks" from the *Lemon-Aid Used Car Guide 1994,* by Phil Edmonston, Stoddart Publishing Co. Limited. Reprinted by permission of Stoddart Publishing Co. Limited.

Garry Engkent: "Why My Mother Can't Speak English." Reprinted by permission of the author.

Sylvia Fraser: "My Other Self" from *My Father's House,* © 1987 by Sylvia Fraser. Reprinted by permission of Doubleday Canada Ltd.

Robert Fulford: "Where, Exactly, Are This Book's Readers?" from *Crisis at the Victory Burlesk* by Robert Fulford. © Oxford University Press Canada 1968. Reprinted by permission of Oxford University Press Canada.

George Gabori: "Coming of Age in Putnok" from *When Evils Were Most Free,* 1981, by George Gabori. © George Gabori. Reprinted by permission of the author.

Carol Geddes: "Growing Up Native" from *Homemakers Magazine,* pp. 37–52, October 1990. Reprinted by permission of the author.

Ray Guy: "Outharbor Menu" from *That Far Greater Bay,* by Ray Guy, Breakwater Books Ltd., 1976. © Ray Guy. Reprinted by permission of Breakwater Books Ltd.

Charles Yale Harrison: "In the Trenches" from *Generals Die in Bed,* by Charles Yale Harrison, 1930. Reprinted by permission of Potlatch Publications Ltd., Hamilton Ontario.

Martin Hocking: "Capping the Great Cup Debate" from *The Globe and Mail,* p. D-10, February 16, 1991. Condensed from papers which appeared in Science *251* (4993), 504–505 (1991), and Environmental Management *15* (6), 731–747 (1991). Reprinted by permission of the author.

Ann Ireland: "Never a Cowgirl" from *Language in Her Eye,* eds. Scheir et al., Coach House Press, 1990. Reprinted by permission of the author.

Captain Thomas James: "Our Mansion House" from *The Dangerous Voyage of Capt. Thomas James,* in *His Intended Discovery of a North West Passage Into the South Sea,* published in 1633.

Basil Johnston: "Modern Cannibals of the Wilds" from *The Globe and Mail,* p. A-13, August 1, 1991. Reprinted by permission of the author.

Reza Kiarash: "A Story of War and Change" from *The Eyeopener,* p. 4, January 16, 1991. Reprinted by permission of the author.

W. P. Kinsella: "How to Write Fiction" from *The Globe and Mail,* April 27, 1985. Reprinted by permission of the author.

Joy Kogawa: "Grinning and Happy" from *Obasan* by Joy Kogawa, Lester & Orpen Dennys Ltd. c/o Key Porter Books Ltd., Toronto. © 1981 Joy Kogawa. Reprinted by permission of Key Porter Books Ltd.

Bonnie Laing: "An Ode to the User-Friendly Pencil" from *The Globe and Mail,* p. D-6, April 29, 1989. © 1989 Bonnie Laing. Reprinted by permission of the author.

Michele Landsberg: "West Must Confront Anonymous Misery of the World's Children" from *The Globe and Mail,* p. A-2, November 7, 1987. Reprinted by permission of the author.

Margaret Laurence: "Where the World Began" from *Heart of a Stranger* by Margaret Laurence, McClelland & Stewart Inc., 1980. Reprinted by permission of McClelland & Stewart Inc.

Margaret Laurence: "A Fable — For the Whaling Fleets" from *Dance on the Earth: A Memoir,* pp. 291 and 292, originally published in *Whales — A Celebration,* ed. Greg Gatenby, Lester & Orpen Dennys, 1983. Published by permission of the estate of Margaret Laurence.

Gary Lautens: "Man, You're a Great Player!" from *Laughing With Lautens,* by Gary Lautens, McGraw-Hill Ryerson Ltd., 1964. Reprinted by permission of McGraw-Hill Ryerson Ltd.

Stephen Leacock: "How to Live to Be 200" from *Literary Lapses,* by Stephen Leacock.

Félix Leclerc: "The Family House" excerpted from *Pieds nus dans l'aube,* 1946, pp. 9–14. Collection "Bibliotheque Canadienne-Francaise," Montreal. Reprinted by permission of Gaetane M. Leclerc. Translated by Philip Stratford. Permission to reprint translation granted by Philip Stratford.

Thierry Mallet: "The Firewood Gatherers" from *Glimpses of the Barren Lands* by Thierry Mallet, 1930. Originally published in *The Atlantic Monthly,* March 1927.

Christie McLaren: "Suitcase Lady" from *The Globe and Mail,* January 24, 1981. Reprinted by permission of The Globe and Mail.

Stuart McLean: "The Shocking Truth About Household Dust" from *The Morningside World of Stuart McLean.* © Stuart McLean, 1989. Reprinted by permission of Penguin Books Canada Ltd.

John McMurtry: "Education for Sale" from the *OCUFA Forum,* Volume 6, Number 16, p. 3, November 1989. © John McMurtry. Reprinted by permission of the author.

Mavor Moore: "The Roar of the Greasepaint, the Smell of the Caucus," from *The Globe and Mail,* August 2, 1986. Reprinted by permission of the author.

Naheed Mustafa: "My Body Is My Own Business" from *The Globe and Mail,* p. A-26, June 29, 1993. Reprinted by permission of the author.

Michael Ondaatje: "Tabula Asiae" from *Running in the Family,* by Michael Ondaatje, McClelland and Stewart, 1982. © Michael Ondaatje. Reprinted by permission of the author.

Nathalie Petrowski: "The Seven-Minute Life of Marc Lépine" from *Le Devoir,* p. C-12, December 16, 1989. Reprinted by permission of Le Devoir. Translated by Ronald Conrad.

Catherine Pigott: "Chicken Hips" from *The Globe and Mail,* p. A-14, March 20, 1990. Reprinted by permission of the author.

Mordecai Richler: "1944: The Year I Learned to Love a German" from the *New York Times Book Review.* © 1986 Mordecai Richler. Reprinted by permission of Creative Management, Inc.

Erika Ritter: "Bicycles" from *Urban Scrawl* by Erika Ritter, Macmillan Canada, 1984. Reprinted by permission of Macmillan Canada.

Rita Schindler: "Thanks for Not Killing My Son" from *The Toronto Star,* p. D-3, December 30, 1990. Every effort has been made to contact the owner of this copyright material. The publishers will gladly accept any information that will enable them to rectify any reference or credit in subsequent editions.

Judy Stoffman: "The Way of All Flesh" from *Weekend Magazine,* September 15, 1979. Reprinted by permission of the author.

David Suzuki: "Hidden Lessons" from *The Globe and Mail,* February 7, 1987. Reprinted by permission of the author.

Catharine Parr Traill: "Remarks of Security of Person and Property in Canada" from *The Female Emigrant's Guide* by Catharine Parr Traill, 1854.

To the Student

Reading and writing are two sides of the same coin. If you read one book a year like the average Canadian, you will never really learn to write. But perhaps 80 or 90 percent of those who read habitually will become much better writers than those who don't, and because of this will succeed more easily in school and career — not to mention leading a fuller life because of what they have learned while reading.

All this is why you are using *The Act of Writing*. If you meet the challenges that a book like this poses, you can do a lot for yourself. Among these challenges:

■ Read the essays with attention, and sometimes reread them, to understand each topic and the techniques the author has used to present it.

■ React to the argument, thinking critically, agreeing or disagreeing — and in discussion tell your classmates and teacher why. Be forceful: if you have reasoned well, your opinion is as good as anyone else's.

■ Write a strong response to the topic or choice of topics suggested by your teacher. Using the essays you have studied as models, organize clearly, choose strong examples, argue well, and polish your own language to the most powerful level you can achieve.

- To do this, reject those writing habits of the past that are inefficient or even harmful; exert yourself to learn and use the "process" approach explained and encouraged throughout this book. It is based on today's research, but it is also how most good writers have always written.
- Finally, read more. See the biographical introductions, which tell what else our authors have written. See the "Further Reading" suggested after each essay. And when a particular author or subject strikes your interest, choose the books you will read now, or over the holidays, or next summer. Improve your writing and enlarge your world by reading now and for the rest of your life.

R. C.

P.S. Do you have suggestions for improving this book? Send them to me c/o the publisher, or by E-Mail to: rconrad@acs.ryerson.ca

TO THE TEACHER

Naheed Mustafa was on the phone to me, telling her life story so I could introduce her essay "My Body Is My Own Business" (p. 118 of this book). After a while she said, "There was a book I studied in school — called *The Act of Writing*."

I realized she had confused me with another anthologist who had also noticed her essay in *The Globe* and had sent a permission contract.

"What colour was the cover?" I asked.

"Blue. It had lightning on it."

"That's my book," I said.

There was a silence on the other end of the line, then she said, "It was *The Act of Writing* that inspired me to be a writer."

Now it was my turn to be silent. What, indeed, could express my feelings on seeing a young writer enter the fourth edition of the very book which she had learned from in its first? The Atwoods and Kogawas and Richlers were still there, and now she was starting to take her place beside them.

It is with humility that an anthologist begins each revision, knowing the need of all the Naheed Mustafas who will be either helped or not helped, depending on how the book turns out. Like drafts of a student essay, each edition must be clearer, more accessible, more useful, more inspiring. The moment of satisfaction at putting a new manuscript on the publisher's desk soon turns to uneasiness as the flaws of even the improved edition begin to surface. As with all writing, the job is never done.

Though new editions must be better, the path to that goal varies. In their requests for improvements to the third edition, users had focused on features; so we added cross-referencing between chapters, suggestions for "Further Reading" and a "Process in Writing" assignment after each essay, "Process in Writing" guidelines tailored for each unit, and a new final chapter, "Argumentation and Persuasion." Now that our recent survey of users has approved these additions, they stay.

By contrast, as we planned this fourth edition our readers' suggestions and our own perceptions identified challenges in other areas, imposed by the increasing rate of change in Canada and the world:

1. Reflecting Changes in Society

■ Our one totally new section, "Process and the Computer," was inevitable. Most students now routinely use word processing, but not all have yet understood the startling correlation between its capabilities and their own work of writing essays. This brief section gives step-by-step suggestions for applying the software more fully to prewriting, the first draft, further drafts, and formatting.

■ We have added new voices. As the Rushdies and Ondaatjes with roots in the Third World move to the centre of English-language literature, as Carlos Fuentes of Mexico hails the cultural *mestizaje* of North America, and as we see around us in Canada the interpenetration of several dozen cultures — this edition follows suit with the addition of Naheed Mustafa, Reza Kiarash, Garry Engkent, Collin Brown and many other new Canadian voices. We also present two First Nations writers, and two authors from French Quebec. (Translations may be second-best, but they do relay voices of the other Canadians we need more than ever to hear.)

■ Paradoxically, as world cultures interpenetrate, the hamburger and Hollywood movie model of American popular culture is still standardizing the world. Canada is fast losing voices of other places, other times. For this reason we stubbornly continue to present regional, period, idiosyncratic, or downright quirky writers to keep us real: Ray Guy, Amy Willard Cross, Stuart Mclean, Catharine Parr Traill, Stephen Leacock, Félix Leclerc, Captain Thomas James, Nathalie Petrowski and more.

■ Women have not been fully represented by anthologies, including this one. The fourth edition changes that, now offering full gender parity: 25 essays by men and 25 by women. If the proportion seems arbitrary, it was also necessary, to change old habits. In the end, I had collected so many good selections by women that the short list had to be rebalanced towards a fairer split. Is it my imagination or have all these voices changed the collective "voice" of the book? Let me know what you think, c/o the publisher or by E-mail to the address at the end of this introduction.

2. Heightening Overall Quality

■ Since the fourth is this book's first edition done on computer, changes to the text are more thorough. Retrieving a passage from the typesetter's disk of the previous edition, then dissecting and rebuilding it on screen, has meant fuller editing of every part of the book — except of course the essays themselves. On average I have trimmed about 15 percent off each set of discussion questions — mostly by phrasing more directly, pruning a word here and there. On the other hand, the same technology has helped me amplify chapter introductions with fuller explanations, examples and references to essays in the chapter.

On the whole, I have tried to exercise an editorial humility in slightly reducing my own share of the writing, to leave more space for the real writers. On the other hand, new entries to the Instructor's Manual are fuller, since their length does not inflate the size or cost of the text, itself.

■ This time it was a major search, over several years, through many linear feet of periodicals and books, that found the present essays. Our new roster is the tip of the iceberg — a small selection from hundreds on the short list. The essays come from periodicals as diverse as *The New York Times Book Review* and *Homemaker's Magazine*, *Mother Jones* and the *OCUFA Forum*, *The Globe and Mail* and *Le Devoir*. Almost half come from books, one is an interview and one a CBC broadcast. The new pieces join a "core" of selections that have proven themselves through the first three editions, though each time the ones teachers and students use least are dropped. Apologies, by the way, to those who love "The Cat" by Gregory Clark. We had decided to reprint it, but could not find the new copyright owner. If in future we do, we will bring it back.

The acknowledgements to the 1983 first edition thanked "the person who said that in Canada this book could not be written, because that's why I wrote it." Today no one who reads much would say there is too little good writing in Canada to build anthologies. This book and all the competitors that followed it have made the point. My only regret is having to leave out so many pieces that deserve reading and discussing. But then, that's how the next edition always begins. . . .

If You Are New to this Book

The Act of Writing, fourth edition, offers flexibility and encourages individualization. The combination of four to nine essays per chapter with several more identified in cross-references will yield more selections per unit than you are likely to use. Thus you can individualize, choosing readings that best suit the needs and interests of your particular class. This book also offers a range of difficulty, from essays that are easily accessible to almost all students to others that are frankly challenging. (*Note:* The "Table of Contents and Difficulty Ranking" of your instructor's manual ranks all selections by level of difficulty, so if you are new to this book you can more easily tailor a syllabus to your class.) The numerous discussion topics after each selection offer a choice of theme and emphasis in classroom debate. And finally, the "Process in Writing" topic after each essay, the 30 essay topics at the end of each chapter, and the process "Guidelines" tailored for each chapter give a latitude of choice for the individual teacher, the individual class, the individual student.

Note the two tables of contents. The first lists all selections in their chapters arranged by *form of organization* (you can choose from six essays, for example, that all demonstrate organization through comparison and contrast). The second table of contents lists all essays by general *subject,* to help you choose selections of interest to your particular students.

An introductory essay, "The Act of Writing," starts the book off by putting to rest a number of widespread misconceptions about writing that plague students in the classroom, then attempts to describe what it is that an essayist actually does. It emphasizes the individuality of the writer, the importance of motivation, the role of intuition as well as logic, and a balance of spontaneity and revision in the process of writing. The next section, "Process and the Computer," then applies word processing to these concepts.

The 50 essays are all by Canadians or persons with Canadian experience, but the scope ranges widely: some are about Canada, many are about other countries, and most express such universal themes as childhood, aging, work, technology, violence, the environment, sport and war. The focus on Canadian essays is not a statement of nationalism. In fact, it is an attempt to provide in Canada the kind of anthology taken for granted in other countries: a collection of works that are mostly universal in theme but that, naturally, draw a good part of their content from the country in which the book will be used. There is no contradiction between this goal and the fact that the fourth edition is our most international so far.

As we have seen, the essays are arranged in chapters that each demonstrate a fundamental pattern of organization. "Narration" starts the book off, because no approach is easier or more motivating for a first assignment than writing a story, in chronological order, about oneself. "Example" and "Description" follow, because these tools of development are used to some degree in almost all writing. "Cause and Effect" and the following chapter, "Comparison and Contrast," are at the centre of the essayist's organizational repertoire. "Analogy" and "Classification" follow "Comparison and Contrast," for they are both varieties of comparison. "Process Analysis," an approach used widely across the curriculum, follows. After all these *forms*, our largest chapter, "Argumentation and Persuasion," explores more fully the writer's most common and basic *purpose*: to make a point. It examines the dualities of deduction and induction, and of argumentation and persuasion, then illustrates their application with nine model essays.

Throughout the book each selection is prefaced with an introduction to the author, designed to interest the student, sometimes to present the author as a role model, and to encourage further reading of the author's works. Then each selection is followed by pedagogical material entitled "Further Reading," "Structure," "Style," "Ideas for Discussion and Writing," and in Chapter 9 "Argumentation and Persuasion." Note that in this material different questions serve different purposes. Some are directive, calling attention to major features of the essay. Some are technical, for example focusing on a specific point of language that illustrates a technique. Still others are exploratory, encouraging open-ended response. The instructor's manual offers answers to those questions that are not open-ended and suggests responses to some that are. Read the manual's introduction: it gives more suggestions for using *The Act of Writing*. For each essay, the manual also lists vocabulary that may need attention.

Each of the nine chapters begins with a discussion of how and why to use the form at hand, and ends with a selection of 30 essay topics which complement that form. These topics have been chosen with care, to tap some of the students' deepest concerns and channel them into motivation for writing. The reason for this attention to topics is that no one problem is more destructive to the performance of both student and teacher than dull or superficial subject matter. How can writing be important if its content is not? And how can a teacher enjoy or even tolerate marking without an interest in what the students are saying?

A further "Process in Writing" topic is given after each essay. If class members have had a good discussion about the selection, their motivation and writing performance may be greatest if they explore these topics, which draw upon both the subject and the underlying form of the essay preceding them. And at the end of each chapter are given the process guidelines mentioned earlier, individualized for the specific pattern of development in that unit.

Finally, a glossary at the end defines literary terms often used in the discussion questions; when one of these terms is a key part of a passage, it appears in SMALL CAPITALS.

The instructor's manual has been revised and amplified for this edition, and will be sent gratis upon request.

If You Are Teaching Interdisciplinary, Theme-based Courses

This anthology is appropriate for interdisciplinary, theme-based courses with teaching goals such as cultural and intercultural understanding, social issues, personal development, or appreciation of the arts. In teaching literature, for example, some teachers draw upon this anthology's introduction to an author such as Margaret Laurence, then her essay(s), as background for a study of one of her novels. Note also the "Further Reading" list which suggests works, either by the same author or thematically related to the author's subject, which students can then pursue in developing an independent study.

To see which of this book's essays will connect with the theme of a course or module you are planning, look over the Table of Contents by Subject. Note also the high proportion of discussion questions that deal with the subject(s) of the readings, and particularly issues.

As a book of Canadian readings, this text can support Canadian Studies courses: note the balance it seeks between content focussed directly on Canada, on content by and about New Canadians who are shaping the Canada of today, and content that expresses our relation to the world. With half the essays by women, and with many of these focussing directly on women's issues, the text can also play a part in women's studies. Again, check especially the Table of Contents by Subject.

Finally, I would like to thank all those who, in one way or another, helped with this project: students and colleagues who reacted to essays, teachers who gave of their time to answer our survey, and friends and family who suggested readings to include. Special thanks to many of this edition's authors who supplied me with information for their biographical introductions: Reza Kiarash, Amy Willard Cross, Robert Fulford, Naheed Mustafa, Garry Engkent, Alison Acker, Doris Anderson, Catherine Pigott, Ann Ireland, John McMurtry, Collin Brown, Judy Stoffman, Martin Hocking, Kildare Dobbs and Bonnie Laing. Thanks also to Doris Anderson and Kildare Dobbs for revising their selections for this fourth edition. Norma Christensen and Laurie Graham of McGraw-Hill Ryerson did excellent detective work tracking down permissions. Thanks also go to the following reviewers for their helpful comments: Stephen Campbell, University of Moncton; Gary Corscadden, New Brunswick Community College; Sharon Winstanley, Seneca College. And above all I thank my wife Mary who, with her good judgment, helped me through every stage of this edition.

NOTE: Let me know your reactions — suggestions, criticisms, favourite essays you'd like to see next time, or anything else you think I should hear. Write me c/o the publisher, or by E-mail to: rconrad@acs.ryerson.ca

R.C.

INTRODUCTION:
THE ACT OF WRITING

Writing is one of the most widely misunderstood of human activities. It is odd that after all the years we have spent in school, after all the hours we have spent reading other people's writing and producing our own, most of us cannot say what really happens when we write. We can describe other complex tasks — driving a car, baking bread, building a radio or programming a computer. But to most people the act of writing is a mystery. Not that we don't have theories, either those told us in school or those we have arrived at ourselves. But many of these theories are misconceptions that actually hinder our efforts to write. Let's look at some of them.

MISCONCEPTION: Writing is like following a blueprint: I figure it all out in advance and then just fill in the details. Of course an outline, used sensibly, will help. But our parents were taught in school that their best thinking should go into a logical and detailed outline — and that the writing itself was secondary. Thus they were reduced to carpenters or plumbers of the written word, who merely sawed, cut and fit pieces in place once the master plan was established. The problem with this reassuringly logical approach is that it views writing as a technology, not as the art that all our practical experience tells us it is. How many of us have given

1

up on a required outline, done our thinking mostly as we wrote the essay itself, then later produced the outline by seeing what we wrote? Or how many of us have painfully constructed a detailed outline in advance, only to find while writing the essay that our real message does not fit the plan?

Writing is exploring! We know which way we are headed and the main landmarks we hope to pass, but not every twist and turn of the path. What a dull trip that would be! Let's leave room for discovery, because our best ideas may occur in the act of writing. One of Quebec's major poets, St.-Denys Garneau, actually said "I cannot think except when writing." Many teachers now reflect the fact of writing as discovery by calling a first draft the *discovery draft.*

But while avoiding the rigor mortis of overplanning, let's not go to the opposite extreme, like Stephen Leacock's famous horseman who "rode madly off in all directions." We do work best with an outline, five or ten or fifteen lines that define the main point and how we intend to support it. But our outline should be a compass on a journey, not the blueprint of a construction project.

MISCONCEPTION: If I don't hit it right the first time, I've failed. It's not hard to see where this idea came from: in school we write so many essays and tests within the limits of one class period that writing in a hurry begins to seem normal. But under such conditions, merely producing enough is hard; seriously revising it is even harder. Few people can "hit it right the first time." Professional writers know this; most of them take longer to write than we do. They tinker with words and sentences, they cross out and replace sections, they go through two or three or even five or ten drafts — and sometimes they throw the whole thing out and start over. These writers know by experience that writing is not a hit-or-miss affair with only one try allowed, but a *process.* They know that revision can yield astonishing results.

MISCONCEPTION: When I write, I am speaking on paper. If you have heard a tape of yourself speaking, you were no doubt surprised at all the filler words you used. "Uh," "um," "well" and "hmmm" fill the gaps between your thoughts very well, but hardly help to carry the message. And if you listened closely, you may have been surprised at the number of incomplete statements — fragments that by themselves made little or no sense. Fillers and fragments are tolerated in speech because, after all, we make up our message on the spot. There is no chance to plan, revise, edit or proofread.

But in writing there is, and this fact increases the expectations of your reader far beyond those of your listener. Language in written form can be planned. It is complete. It is precise and concise. It uses standard words. It is punctuated. It follows all the rules. In short, it is a product of the time that its written form allows you to give it, not a spur-of-the-moment, hope-for-the-best effort like the speech that comes so easily from your mouth.

MISCONCEPTION: The best words are the biggest words. Variations on this theme are *If my writing looks scholarly it will impress the reader,* and even *If I make my essay so difficult that no one knows what I'm saying, everyone will believe me.* At the roots of these widespread ideas is a notion that writing is a kind of competition between writer and reader. A writer who is obscure enough will make the reader feel like a dummy and will thus win the game. But ask yourself: In real life do you *ambulate* or walk? *Expectorate* or spit? *Interdigitate* or hold hands? *Cogitate* or think?

Avoiding this game of writer vs. reader is not easy when so many leaders in business, education and government play it. The first step toward open communication, though, is to think of your reader not as an opponent but as a teammate. You are both moving toward the same goal, which is the reader's clear understanding of your ideas.

Another step is to admit that words small in size can be large in meaning. The best-loved writings in our language (think of the lines from Shakespeare you may have memorized for school) are filled with short words. Writing made of them is more concise, more vivid, and usually more profound than writing made of the elephantine words that some of us ransack the dictionary for. When a long word conveys your meaning best — perhaps like "elephantine" above — by all means use it. But often the writer, like the architect, finds that *less is more.*

MISCONCEPTION: I don't like to write. For some unfortunate people this statement is true. But for most who say it, the truth is really "I don't like to *begin* writing." Who does? Staring at that blank page is like staring from a diving board at the cold water below. But a swimmer and a writer both gather the courage to plunge in, and soon they both feel a new sensation: they don't want to come out. Teachers whose students write journals in class see the process at work every day. As class begins, the writers are filled with stress: they chew their pens and frown as they stare at the page to be filled. But in a while they are scribbling furiously away, recording in an almost trance-like state their latest experiences, feelings and insights. If the teacher asks them to stop, in order to begin the next activity, they are annoyed: they sigh and *keep on writing* till asked a second or third time to stop.

Let's admit that most writers — and that includes professionals — dread the beginning. Let's also admit that most writers enjoy the rest of it, hard work though it may be.

With some of the most widespread misconceptions behind us now, let's take a fresh look at the act of writing. First, allow for personal differences. *Know yourself!* If you are a person whose desk is piled high with papers and books, whose closet is an avalanche waiting to happen, and whose shoes have not been shined in two years, you may write best by planning little and relying on your spontaneity. If you are a person who plans an August holiday in January, keeps a budget right down to the penny, and washes the car every Wednesday and Saturday whether it needs it or not, you may write best by planning fully.

On the other hand, your natural tendencies may have caused you problems and may therefore need to be controlled. If your spontaneity has produced writings that can't stay on topic, plan more: make a careful outline. If overorganizing has sucked the life out of your writing, free yourself up: leave more room for discovery as you write. Whatever the case, try to determine and use the approach that works for *you.*

Let's allow also for differences in assignments. If you are dashing off a short personal sketch, your planning may be no more than an idea and a few moments of thought. If you are writing a long research essay, the product of days in the library, you may need an outline two pages long. No one approach works for every person and every assignment. Keep in mind, then, that the process we are about to examine is a *starting point,* a basis but not a blueprint for your own writing.

THE BEGINNINGS OF AN ESSAY CAN BE FOUND IN THE ANSWERING OF SEVERAL QUESTIONS:

1. Why *am I writing?* This most basic of questions too often goes unasked. If the answer is "to fill up five pages," "to impress" or "to get an 'A'," you begin with a severe handicap. The immediate reason to write may be a class assignment, but the real reason must be to communicate something of value. Otherwise your motivation is lost and so is your performance. Therefore, choose from a list of topics the one that means the most to you. If no topic seems significant, devise a way to *make* one significant. Probe the topic through the exercise of freewriting explained later on. Look at it from a new viewpoint or approach it in some unusual way. If that fails, and if your teacher is approachable, voice your concern and suggest an alternative topic. One teacher always made students analyze the relative merits of chocolate and vanilla ice cream, on the theory that a dull subject will not distract a writer from the real goals: grammar and style. He was wrong. Research shows motivation to be the single greatest factor in writing performance — and motivation comes largely from writing about things that matter.

    When you write on your own, as in a private journal, you may still need to answer the question *Why am I writing?* Simply recording events can be dull. Record also your feelings, your perceptions, and your conclusions about those events. If you have personal problems, as most people do, confront them on the page. The more you discover yourself and your world through writing, the more important the writing becomes.

2. *How big is my topic?* Classroom essays are shorter than most people realize. A book may contain 100,000 words; a magazine article 2000 or 5000; a classroom essay as few as 500 or even 250. Therefore narrowing the essay topic is more important than most people realize.

One student, who had been a political prisoner, decided to write about economic systems. He knew the subject well and was committed to it. But what he attempted was an analysis of communism, socialism and capitalism — all in two pages! A lack of focus spread his very short essay so thin that it approached the state of saying nothing about everything. It was the barest scratching of the surface, a summary of basic facts that everyone already knows.

If the same person had focused on his arrest and imprisonment — or even on one day in his cell — he might have said far more about the system he opposed. It is in specifics that we best see generalities. Think of writing as photography. Putting aside the wide-angle lens that includes too much at a distance, look through the telephoto lens that brings you up close to a small part of the subject. Select the part most meaningful to you, perhaps the part most characteristic of the whole, then take the picture.

Nearly all the essays in this book are closeups: they explore one situation, one incident, one person or one process. Yet most of them are longer than the essays you will write. Therefore, when you choose a topic, judge its size — and if you have to, *change* its size.

3. *What message am I sending?* You may know your topic well. But unless you send a message concerning it, your reader will think *what's the point?* A message is often a value judgement: Are robots dangerous? Will they take away our jobs or someday even rule over us? Or do they help us? Will they free us at last from the dehumanizing tyranny of manual labour? Most of the essays in this book take such a stance, either pro or con, toward their subjects. Some avoid judging their subjects directly, but send other messages: one shows what it's like to be down and out; one shows the tricks of dealers selling used cars; another shows how aging is a lifelong process.

If you have chosen a topic because it seems meaningful, you will no doubt have a message to send. What do you most feel like saying about the topic? Once you know, get it down in writing. This THESIS STATEMENT, as it is often called, normally comes at or near the beginning of an essay. It is an introductory sentence or passage that does more than just tell what the topic is; it clearly states, as well, what you are saying *about* the topic. It lets your reader know what is coming — and, in the process, commits you to a purpose that all the rest of the essay must in one way or another support. It is your guide as you write.

4. *Who is my audience?* Do you talk the same way to a friend and a stranger? To an old person and a child? To a hockey coach and a professor? Probably not. Neither would you write the same way to all readers. In a private journal you can write as freely as you think, for you are the reader: omissions and excesses of all kinds will be understood and forgiven. In letters to a close friend you are nearly as free, for the reader knows you well enough to supply missing explanations or interpret remarks in the light of your personality. But your freedom shrinks when you write for others: a business person, a public official, a teacher. Now you must fight a misconception shared by many people: *Everyone is like me.*

This idea is seldom articulated but may lurk as a natural assumption in the backs of our minds. It is a form of egotism. If you assume everyone is like you, many readers will not accept or even understand your message — because they are *not* like you. They did not grow up in your family, neighbourhood or even country. They are older or younger, or of the opposite sex. They have had different life experiences, so now they have different knowledge and temperaments and values.

Accept these differences as you write. You will never prove your point by quoting Marx to a capitalist, the Bible to an atheist, or Gloria Steinem to a male supremacist. Any argument built on a partisan foundation will collapse if the reader does not accept that foundation. Instead, build from facts or ideas that your reader probably does accept: killing is bad, government is necessary, women are human beings, and so on. Is your topic controversial? Then avoid an open display of bias. Calling intellectuals "commies" or abortionists "hired killers" will appeal only to those who shared your view in the first place. (For more on these matters, read the introduction to Chapter 9, "Argumentation and Persuasion.")

Does the reader know what you know? If you write about statistics for a statistics teacher, use any technical terms customary to the field, and avoid the insult of explaining elementary points. But if you write on the same subject for a class exercise in English or a letter to the editor, your reader will be very different: avoid most technical terms, define those you do use, and explain more fully each step of your argument.

The more open you become to the individuality of your reader, the more open your reader becomes to your message. It is a matter of mutual respect.

Prewriting

How do we begin the act of writing: by putting those first words on a page? The philosopher Lao-Tze said, "A journey of a thousand miles begins with the first step." In a way he was right: if we never take that official first step, we will certainly never arrive at our destination. But how much daydreaming and planning do we do beforehand? Do we set out on a journey without consulting the map or the calendar or the tourist brochure or the travel guide — not to mention our bankbook? And do we write an essay without in some way resolving the questions we have just asked:

> **Why am I writing?**
> **How big is my topic?**
> **What message am I sending?**
> **Who is my audience?**

The process of writing, then, begins in thought. But thoughts do not come on command. Like the diver, we look down at the cold water and dread the plunge. Some writers try to "break the ice" by manipulating their environment: finding a quiet spot, a particularly soft or hard chair, good lighting or a favourite pen. Others fortify themselves with a good night's sleep, food or coffee. Some have to have music. Any of these tricks may help, but they all avoid the real issue: How do we begin to *think?*

One direct approach, a variation on the old technique of outlining, is *brainstorming*: once you have roughly identified your subject, just write down words or phrases that relate in any way to it, in a list going down a page. Put down anything that comes, letting one thought lead to another. Some entries will seem off-topic, trivial or even loony, but others may be just what you need: the keys to your essay. Circle them. Put them in order. As crude as this primitive outline may seem, it has served a purpose: your thoughts have begun to arrive. The process is in motion. You have taken that first "step" before even starting the first draft.

A similar but even more powerful "icebreaker" is *freewriting*. Put a blank page on the desk with your watch beside it. Think of your topic. Now write! Put down anything that comes: sentences, phrases, words — logical thoughts, hasty impressions, even pure garbage. Do not cease the physical act of writing, do not even lift the pen from the page, for at least five minutes. (Freewriting at the keyboard works even better, because it is faster. For details see the following section, "Process and the Computer.") If your next thought doesn't come, write the last one over and over till the next one does come. What you produce may surprise you.

Like brainstorming, freewriting is an exercise in free association: the flow of your thoughts, the sudden leaps of your intuition, will "break the ice" so you can write. They may do even more: as in brainstorming, you may end up with a page of scribbling that contains the main points of your essay. Try to find them. Circle them. Put them in order. See if your intuition has led the way in answering the questions: *Why am I writing? How big is my topic? What message am I sending? Who is my audience?* If all goes well, you have already begun your journey.

The First Words

Once your thoughts are flowing comes the next step, the opening passage of your essay. In a very short composition your THESIS STATEMENT may serve also as the first words. In most longer essays it comes at the end of an introduction. Only about one-fourth of the selections in this book start right off with what could be called a thesis statement. What do the others start with?

Background information: About half the essays in this book lead off by relating the circumstances in which the topic is set. For examples, see the beginnings of our selections by Gabori (p. 24), McLean (p. 122), Richler (p. 142), Hocking (p. 286), Dobbs (p. 292) and Schindler (p. 318).

Anecdote: A brief story, usually of a humorous or dramatic incident, can lead into the topic. See Cross (p. 59), Pigott (p. 160), Leacock (p. 246), Callwood (p. 265) and Atwood (p. 306).

Quotation or allusion: The words of a philosopher, of a news report, of a recognized specialist in the subject, or of anyone with close experience of it can be used to break the ice. See Kogawa (p. 312), Cohen (p. 259) and Dobbs (p. 292).

Sense images: Vivid description can attract a reader's interest to the topic. See Fraser (p. 27), Kiarash (p. 40), McLaren (p. 82) and Dennis (p. 332).

A striking comparison or contrast: Showing how things are like or unlike each other is a dramatic way to introduce a topic. See Kiarash (p. 40), Moore (p. 235), Cohen (p. 259) and Atwood (p. 306).

Narrative: Several selections in this book begin by telling a story upon which the essay is based. See Harrison (p. 93), Engkent (p. 128), Pigott (p. 160), Ireland (p. 173) and Dennis (p. 332).

An unusual or puzzling statement: Such an opening appeals to the reader's curiosity. See Kiarash (p. 40), Fulford (p. 68) and Kinsella (p. 225).

Figures of speech: A striking METAPHOR, SIMILE or PERSONIFICATION can spark the opening. See Leclerc (p. 209), Stoffman (p. 250) and Cohen (p. 259).

Most of these introductions are short: a couple of sentences or a paragraph or two at the most. And virtually all are designed to *interest* the reader, for an apathetic reader may not even finish the essay, let alone like or understand it. Writing is fishing. You throw in the line. Your reader tastes the bait (your introduction), bites, is pulled through the waters of your argument, and — if the line of thought doesn't break — lands in your net.

You, the writer, may also be "hooked." Once you have hit upon a strong introduction, one that shows off the drama or importance of your topic, the beginning may carry you along with it. And once you get going, the idea embodied in your thesis statement may pull you through the essay, enabling you to write freely as one passage leads to another. You may become less and less aware of your surroundings as you become more and more immersed in your subject. By the time you develop a good beginning, you may experience the act of writing the way one student described it: "At first I couldn't start, but then I couldn't stop."

The Body

An introduction is like a head; it may decide to go someplace but it needs a body to take it there. The "body" of your essay has the main work to do: following the direction set by your introduction, and especially by your thesis statement, it explains, illustrates, and sometimes attempts to prove your point. But if it ever ignores the direction set by the head, it ceases to do its job. Even the best of explanations, without a sense of direction, is like one of those unfortunate football players who complete a 90-yard run to the wrong goal. On the other hand, we know that writing is discovery. The acts of writing and revising will sometimes take us in a direction better than the old one decided by the introduction. When that happens, correct not the body but the "head" — so the two can move together in the new direction.

The easiest way to keep a direction is to base your essay on a particular form — and that is what most of this book is about. As you read and discuss the essays that follow, and as you write your own essays using the forms on which other writers have based their organization, you will explore a range of choices:

Narration: In simple time order, from the first event to the last event, tell a story that illustrates the point.

Example: Give one in-depth example that explains the point, or a number of shorter examples.

Description: Recreate for your reader, through the most vivid language possible, your own or someone else's experience with the subject.

Cause and Effect: Explain by showing how one situation or event causes another.

Comparison and Contrast: Explain by showing how two things are like or unlike each other.

Analogy and Related Devices: In comparing two things, use the one to explain the other.

Classification: Make a point by dividing the parts of your subject into categories.

Process Analysis: Show how something happens or how something is done.

Argumentation and Persuasion: Using any pattern that works, make your point through logic and/or emotion.

Seldom does one of these methods appear alone. A *process analysis*, for example, is usually told as a *narrative*. Here and there it may use *examples*, *description* or any of the other patterns to help make its point. But these combinations occur naturally, often without the writer's knowing it. In most cases the only form deliberately chosen by a writer is the main one on which the whole essay is structured.

How do you choose the right form? Let the subject be your guide. In architecture, form follows function. Rather than cram an office into a pre-selected structure, a designer likes to begin with the function of that office. How much space best serves its needs? What shape? What barriers and passageways between one section and another? What front to present to the world?

An essay is much the same: the needs of its subject, if you are open to them, can suggest a form. If the main idea is to explain what something is like, you will tend to choose *examples* and *description*. If the subject is unusual or little known, you may *compare* or *contrast*, or make an *analogy* with something the reader does know. If its parts seem important, you may discuss them one by one through *classification*. When some other need is greater, you may use still another form. If you stay open to the subject, whatever it is, this process can be so natural that you *recognize* rather than *choose* a form.

If the process is natural, then why study the forms in this book? Think again of the architect: Why does she or he study design in school? For one thing, knowing how each form is constructed assures that the building will not collapse. For another, in those cases when the choice is not easy, a conscious knowledge of all the possibilities will help.

Consider the longer essay — perhaps a report or research paper. A stack of notes sits on your desk. They are in chaos. Even with brainstorming or freewriting, knowing your purpose, having the facts, and completing a thesis statement, you can't think how to coordinate all those facts. First give the natural process its best chance: sort all your notes into groups of related material, using a pair of scissors if necessary to divide unrelated points. When everything is in two stacks, or five stacks or ten, let your mind work freely. How do these groups relate to each other? Does one come before another in time? Does one cause another? Does one contradict another? Are they all steps in a process or parts of a whole? Now add your conscious knowledge of the forms: Do you see narration, example, description, cause and effect, comparison and contrast, analogy, classification or process analysis? It is the rare case when one of these forms cannot supply the basic structure to support your argument.

If you use the essay topics at the end of each chapter in this book, your choice of form will already be made. This process may seem to bypass the ideal method of letting form follow function. The topics, though, are selected to go well with the form studied in that chapter. And just as the architect practices standard designs in school to learn their forms and functions, so can the writer deliberately practice standard essay designs to learn their forms and functions. Both architect and writer will then be ready when the choice is truly open.

Transitions

We have mentioned the passageways inside a building. Without them an office would be useless: no one could move from one room to another to have meetings. Yet some essays are built without passageways. One point ends where another begins, without even a "then" or "therefore" or "however" or "finally" to join them. Readers then have to break down walls to follow thoughts from one room to the next.

Help your readers. *You* know why one point follows another, but do *they*? Make sure by supplying transitions: say "although" or "but" or "on the other hand"; say "because" or "as a result" or "since"; say "first" or "next" or "last"; say "for example" or "in conclusion." And when moving readers from one main part of your essay to the next, devote a full sentence or even a paragraph to the job (one good example is paragraph 10 of Doris Anderson's essay).

Your plan may already be the right one, setting your points in their most logical order. Now let that logic show: give your readers a door between every room.

The Closing

We've discussed the beginning, the middle, and transitions between parts. What remains is of course the ending. Every essay has one — the point where the words stop. But not all endings are closings. A closing is deliberate. In some clear way it tells the reader that you have not just run out of time, ink or ideas, but that you have chosen to stop here. If you end at just any convenient spot, without engineering an effect to fit your ending, the essay may trail off or even fall flat. But as preachers, composers, playwrights and film directors know, a good closing can be even stronger than a good opening. How do the essays in this book come to a close? They use a variety of devices:

Reference to the opening: Repeating or restating something from the opening gives a sense of culmination, of having come full circle. See the openings and closings by Kogawa (pp. 312 and 315), Stoffman (pp. 250 and 257), Atwood (pp. 306 and 309) and Cameron (pp. 327 and 329).

Contrast or reversal: This ironic device exploits the dramatic potential of the closing. See the openings and closings by Fulford (pp. 68 and 70), Moore (pp. 235 and 237), Stoffman (pp. 250 and 257) and Cameron (pp. 327 and 329).

Question: A question and its answer, or a question calling for the reader's answer, is a common means of closing. See Landsberg (p. 65), Davies (p. 191), Leacock (p. 248) and Dennis (p. 334).

Quotation: A good quotation, of either prose or poetry, can add authority and interest to a closing. See Stoffman (p. 257).

Transition signals: Words, phrases or sentences of transition commonly signal the closing. See Gabori (p. 25), Landsberg (p. 65), Pigott (p. 162) and Johnston (p. 202).

Revealing the significance: Showing the implications or importance of the subject makes for a strong closing. See Gabori (p. 25), Landsberg (p. 65), Suzuki (p. 116), Johnston (p. 202), Dobbs (p. 298) and Petrowski (p. 324).

Summary: About a fourth of the essays in this book give a summary, either alone or in combination with other closing techniques, but one that is always short. See Mallet (p. 80), McLean (p. 126), Anderson (p. 158) and Hocking (p. 289).

Conclusion: Although "conclusion" is often a label for the closing in general, more accurately it is only one of many closing techniques — the drawing of a conclusion from the discussion in the essay. See Geddes (p. 37), Landsberg (p. 65), Suzuki (p. 116), Mustafa (p. 119), Richler (p. 147), McMurtry (p. 181) and Callwood (p. 270).

Prediction: A short look at the subject's future can very logically close a discussion of that subject's past or present. See Geddes (p. 37), Cross (p. 61), Landsberg (p. 65) and Suzuki (p. 116). Sometimes discussing the future takes the form of a call to action (see Dennis, p. 334).

You have probably noticed that some authors are named more than once; like openings, closings can exploit more than one technique. In fact, the more the better. Stay open to techniques that appear while you write, even as you construct a closing on the one technique you have deliberately chosen.

Any of these choices will be stronger, though, when used with the most fundamental technique of all: building your whole essay toward a high point or *climax*. Put your points in order from least important to most important, from least useful to most useful, or from least dramatic to most dramatic. (Sometimes you will not know this order till late in the writing. If you are computerized, use your "move" function to re-arrange sections without retyping; if you write by hand, cut drafts apart with scissors to rearrange them.) When everything leads up to that climax, you have set the stage for a closing that applies all the dramatic power of the final position.

When you get there, apply the force of that closing to a real message. Techniques used just for their own sake are cheap tricks. Do not waste them. Instead, use them to underline your basic message, to impress upon your audience one last and most convincing time that what you have to say is significant. Your closing, more than any other part of your essay, can send the reader away disappointed — or moved.

The Process: How Many Drafts?

We have discussed the act of writing as a process in which, rather than trying to "hit it right the first time," we follow a number of steps in the journey toward a good essay. The rest of this book develops that approach. After each selection you will find an assignment called "Process in Writing" that draws on the essay you have just read, suggesting a related topic for an essay of your own. The main steps of the process are given, individualized for the particular topic.

Then at the end of each chapter you will find a whole page of essay topics, designed for practice in the form of organization you have just studied. After them, in each chapter, appear sections called "Process in Writing: Guidelines" which give the steps of a process designed for the organizational form you have just studied. Whether you write from a topic given just after an essay or choose a topic from the end-of-chapter list, remember that these steps are only *guidelines* to the process; use the ones that seem best for each case.

Our "process" of writing is flexible; it is not a blueprint like the elaborate outlines our parents were made to construct. Above all, the process is "recursive" — that is, while you may begin with brainstorming or freewriting, go on to a discovery draft, revise your argument in a further draft or drafts, and finally edit for spelling and grammar, you may also double back or jump forward at any time. Studies show that professionals writing all kinds of documents in all kinds of fields do this. While generating their "discovery draft" they may stop here and there to improve a word choice or fix punctuation — changes that normally occur later. Or, while they are in the middle of editing or even proofreading, a fine new idea may come thundering out of their mind; so they may back up a few steps, write it out, and add it to their argument, perhaps junking something else they had thought was good. All this is consistent with the reality that *we think while writing.*

Do feel free to transgress the process "guidelines" in these ways, but not so often that you undercut the advantages of the process itself. For example, in writing your discovery draft you may detect a spelling error or a piece of dubious sentence structure. If you must, stop here to edit. But better yet, why not just circle the spot and come back to fix it later? (Or if you are word processing, insert a signal such as several asterisks in a row.) For now, let the material keep rolling out uninterrupted. Then later on, while you are editing or even proofreading, a whole new idea may come. You could go back even now to fit it in — but this means work, maybe even reorganization. Proceed only if it is a real improvement and if you have the time.

Finally, how many drafts are we talking about? The "guidelines" later on are sometimes vague on this point — because what do we mean by a draft? Is every new copy a draft? No, unless it incorporates many improvements that you wrote between the lines and in the margins of the previous draft. (Be sure to double- or triple-space in the first place, to make such revision possible.) Very seldom can you write a good essay in only one draft.

On the other hand, a total of four or five or six drafts may be a sign of time wasted just recopying, not revising. You can often reach a point at least close to your best writing performance in two or three real drafts. In practice you might produce a discovery draft, cover it with revisions, then recopy all this into a second draft, cover it with editing, then recopy all this into your good version to hand in (but not until you proofread even it). Of course these suggestions are for writing by hand. If you are computerized, see the discussion of on-screen editing and drafts in the section that follows, "Process and the Computer."

When do you reach the journey's end? You will know when you get there. It is the point where your response to a significant topic has become so direct, so exact, so forceful, that at last you know exactly what you think. It is clear that you were writing for others, but at this moment it is even clearer that you were writing for yourself.

Process and the Computer

A few years ago only a minority of students wrote by computer; today it is a majority. Why the change? After all, school computer labs are often crowded, and having your own computer and software costs money. Learning word processing from a 600-page manual is daunting. Accidents happen ("My cat jumped on the keyboard and my essay disappeared!"), and hardware can break down. Read "Ode to the User-Friendly Pencil," by Bonnie Laing (p. 301 of this book) to hear more objections.

However, the growing supremacy of computers as writing tools has a cause so clear it cannot be ignored: as the term implies, word "process-ing" fits the *process* approach to writing. It is hard to imagine a tool that could better empower us to get our thoughts out in the open, then later to so easily revise and edit them.

This is not the place to discuss details of computer use; these are available in a thousand books, including your own computer manual if you have one. *What the following short summary does, though, is point out strategies: ways the computer can help you apply the process of writing explained and encouraged in the previous pages and throughout the book.* Let's look now at the act of writing by computer, step by step.

1. PREWRITING. We have discussed how freewriting can shake your thoughts loose, get them flowing, get them out in the open — where you can then look them over to find the beginnings of essays. Freewriting by hand, though, is slow; it can resemble those night-mares in which a monster is chasing you but your feet are stuck in the mud. Since people think faster than they write, the best way to capture thoughts before they disappear is through the keyboard. (Be sure to master touch typing, either in class or at home using instructional software. If you do not, you may be driving the fastest computer in town, but still producing text at a snail's pace. Remem-ber that with good technique, most people can keyboard three to four times faster than they can handwrite.)

If you do freewrite at top speed on a computer, a rush of thought lasting only a few minutes can result in a page or two of material, which, since it was done so fast, may contain spectacular connections of thought — as in free association exercises. It can be a real search of what's on your mind, what you know about the subject, what you really want to write about, and what your point of view — thus your THESIS — may be. Go for it. At the worst, suppose none of this works out at all. What have you lost? Five or ten minutes of your time.

2. DISCOVERY DRAFT. What is the difference between freewriting and your first draft? Sometimes not much. See what you come up with in step 1; it may be so close to a first draft that you will just begin with it on screen and revise from there.

Other times freewriting just sets a direction, so then it is your discovery draft that begins to establish the text itself. Again, the speed of the computer eases the task. Just as in freewriting, thoughts can come fast. They need to be trapped as they occur, so they are not lost. If you know touch typing, you can do it.

Above all, remember that the task of this first draft is to *generate material.* You are extracting ore from the mine. Sometimes it comes out fairly pure, but usually it needs refining. The time to do that is later: at this stage do not slow down the flow by fixing sentence structure or spelling. Just keep right on to the end, *extracting the ore.*

Another option: if you are really at home with the speed of touch typing, try this: actually write about three discovery drafts of three different topics or three angles of one topic. Of these, one will surely be better than the others. Keep it to develop, and just discard the others — as a photographer may discard the extra photos taken in the process of getting the good one.

3. FURTHER DRAFTS. Our introductory overview on the previous pages suggests that we do not move from one "draft" to the next until the first one is covered with revisions and corrections. With word processing, though, all this can happen on screen. You go through the discovery draft, using commands to delete words, lines or even pages; move passages around; move a troublesome paragraph off the screen in order to try a new version; and add further examples or explanation at any point, while the surrounding text moves away to make room. Though you can still print out "hard copy" of your first draft on paper, double-spaced, and write on it as you always have before, many people prefer editing right on the screen.

At some point, no one knows exactly when, we might say you have arrived at a second "draft." When you are done for now, "save" it to your hard drive and to a backup "floppy disk," either to the same file (so that the first draft is erased), or to a new file in order to keep both.

The next day or so, after your mind has processed things while you thought you were only going about your other tasks, come back to it: "retrieve" the file and continue with the new perspectives of a new day.

How many "drafts" do you need? Usually two or three, if each is revised and edited thoroughly. This varies, of course, depending on how much time you have and how important the document is. As the previous part of this book suggests, you are done when "your response to a significant topic has become so direct, so exact, so forceful, that at last you know exactly what you think."

4. SOME TECHNIQUES OF EDITING ELECTRONICALLY. If you have been computerized for a while, you might skip this section. If you are new to word processing, though, see below whether there are any new tools you have not used. Try them out, especially late in the writing as you put the final polish on your essay. Learn the keystroke or mouse commands that tell your system, whichever it is, to do these moves:

- Delete a letter backward or forward, delete a word, delete a line or a page.
- Move the cursor word by word forward or backward, or to either end of a line, to the top or bottom of a page, or to the top or bottom of the document.
- Move a passage, or a whole section, to another place without retyping.
- Search a word (for example if you overuse "and," as most people do, have the computer show you each "and", so you can decide which to omit or replace with more exact connections).
- Use the speller. (Remember, though, that it catches only misspellings, not wrong words; continue checking to prevent using words like "to" for "too" or "there" for "their".)
- Use the "count" function of your speller at several points during editing, to track gains in conciseness.
- Use the thesaurus often, since it is so fast, bringing alternative word choices to the screen, to find stronger, clearer, shorter or more exact choices.

5. FINAL FORMATTING. With the computer you could have done this at any stage, but now is the time when most people do it — after the work of generating and shaping their thoughts. Now apply the keystroke or mouse commands that tell your system to do the following: select the margins you wish all around, if they are different from your system's "default" settings; select the "justification" (whether the right side of the text is even, as the left side is); do any special effects such as italics or boldface for emphasis; number the pages; select line spacing (usually double for essays handed in); and select font and size of type.

Though you probably used "draft" mode, which saves time and ink, to print any "hard copy" used in editing, now for your good copy you will select your highest quality of print. It is widely believed that a better looking essay makes a better impression on the reader. While we might question the psychology behind this concept, we cannot ignore it. With today's ink-jet and laser printers, here is one last fact of computing that operates in our favour.

In summary, then, the computer's speed and flexibility help us explore our thoughts, then its many editing tools help us shape and polish those thoughts. Both these acts of writing are at the heart of the process. In fact, the computer may be your best companion on your writing journey.

"I remember a lot of togetherness, a lot of happiness while we lived in the bush. There's a very strong sense of family in the native community. . . ."

—Carol Geddes, *"Growing Up Native"*

CHAPTER

NARRATION

And then....

Telling a story, or *narrating*, is an appealing and natural way to convey information. Every time you tell a joke, trade gossip, invent a ghost story or tell a friend what you did on the weekend, you are narrating. In both speech and writing, telling a story can be the most direct way to make a point. If your idea or opinion was formed by an experience, a clear account of that experience will help others understand and believe your point.

How could a soldier explain the terrors of a shelling attack better than by sharing the experience? In this chapter Reza Kiarash *narrates* his life at war: how he crawled on his belly as shells were exploding, how he argued with an officer who was afraid to help rescue a wounded man, how the man turned black as Kiarash tried to save him in the ambulance, how the man's blood tasted in the attempt at artificial respiration. Could Kiarash have argued better using the points and logic of a standard essay? Would we have as easily seen war for the hell it is, or understood the author's self-esteem at meeting this challenge six months out of high school?

Narration is such an all-purpose tool that many authors in other chapters use it. Charles Yale Harrison *narrates* his own life at war ("In the Trenches," p. 93), although his use of *description* — an important ingredient of many narratives — is so strong that his selection appears in that chapter. Read his passage; see how the blast threw him into the air, how the ground heaved, how he breathed the smoke and tasted his own blood. As readers we tend to identify with him, share his experience, understand his point.

Note how the examples used by all writers are often bits of narrative. When June Callwood tells us on page 267 how a woman on welfare fought developers to save a park, she *narrates* even while showing us how to "make a difference."

In some ways narrating is easy. The only research Kiarash required was his own experience. And his basic plan of organization was no more complicated than the chronological order in which the events occurred. (A flashback to the past or a glance at the future may intervene, but basically a narrative is the easiest of all writing to organize.) Yet a narrative, like any form of writing, is built on choices.

Choice of scope: Time stretches infinitely toward both the past and future — but where does your narrative most logically begin and end? Include only parts that develop your point. Do you need to dwell on getting dressed, eating breakfast, brushing your teeth and catching the bus, on the day you became a Canadian citizen? Or did the event really begin when you opened the courthouse door? When facts about the past or future are needed, sketch them in briefly so you interrupt the least you can.

Choice of details: Which details count? Reject random or trivial ones and seek those that convey your main impression or idea. When on page 27 Sylvia Fraser tells us that "the ice at Gage Park is best in the morning when it's flint-hard and glass-smooth," that "all is possible" and that "you carve out circles and eights, and nothing exists until you put it there," she is not just making small talk as she begins her narrative. Rather, the cool fresh start of skating on new ice prepares a deadly contrast to the rage that later erupts when her "other self" confronts old problems. Which details are most vivid? Reject weak ones and select those that help the reader *see, hear, feel, smell* or *taste* — in other words those which, by appealing to the senses, help readers live the event.

Choice of connections: Readers love to be "swept along" by narrative. How is this effect achieved? Partly just through a good story. Time signals, though, increase the impact of any story. Like road signs for the driver, terms like "at first," "next," "then," "immediately," "suddenly," "later," "finally" and "at last" show the way and encourage progress. Use these road signs, and others like them, at every curve. Choose carefully, so signals speed your reader in the right direction.

So far we have discussed only the first-person narrative. There are many advantages to writing about yourself. You know your subject well (in fact, is there any subject you know better?), yet in writing about yourself you may better understand your own ideas and actions. Your vital interest in your subject will motivate the writing. And finally, readers appreciate the authenticity of a story told by the very person who lived the event.

But of course it is not always possible or desirable to limit the subject to oneself. A third-person narrative, which tells the actions of others, opens up many more possibilities. Only by writing about others can one discuss past eras, places one has never visited and events one has never experienced. Kildare Dobbs does this masterfully in his narrative "The Scar," on page 292 of a later chapter. He was not in Hiroshima the day it crumbled beneath an atomic blast, but his research and his imagination almost make it seem so; more importantly, reading his narrative almost makes us feel we were there too.

Finally, at the end of our present chapter, Gary Lautens consults his imagination to invent a hockey-playing friend and produce the freest form of narrative, fiction.

Note: Many authors in later chapters combine narration with other ways to develop their material. For more examples, see these selections:

Charles Yale Harrison, "In the Trenches," p. 93
Russell Baker, "A Nice Place to Visit," p. 165
Judy Stoffman, "The Way of All Flesh," p. 250
Kildare Dobbs, "The Scar," p. 292

George Gabori

Coming of Age in Putnok

Translated from the Hungarian by Eric Johnson with George Faludy

George Gabori (pronounced Gábori) runs a cab company in Toronto. Like many immigrants to this country, though, he has a past that he will never forget. Gabori was born in 1924 to a Jewish family in the village of Putnok, Hungary. His childhood was happy but short, for when the Germans occupied Hungary and threatened the existence of the Jews, he joined the resistance. He led daring sabotage raids on railyards and docks until the Gestapo sent him, still a teen-ager, to a concentration camp. Things did not improve when the Russians drove out the Germans; soon after his release from a Nazi camp, he found himself breaking rocks in a notorious Soviet labour camp. Always outspoken, Gabori played a part in the 1956 revolution, then escaped from Hungary and eventu-ally wrote his memoirs in Hungarian. With the help of Hungarian poet George Faludy, Eric Johnson condensed and translated the enormous manuscript, and in 1981 it was published. Since then, When Evils Were Most Free *has become a minor Canadian classic. Our selection is its opening passage.*

1 When I was nine years old my father, victorious after a long argu-ment with my grandfather, took me out of our town's only *cheder* and enrolled me in its only public school. Overnight I was transported from the world of Hebrew letters and monotonously repeated texts to the still stranger world of Hungarian letters, patriotic slogans and walls covered with maps.

2 Grandfather rolled his eyes and predicted trouble, but it seemed he was wrong. I sat beside a boy my own age named Tivadar, a gentile — everybody was a gentile in that school except me. Tivadar and I got along famously until, after two or three weeks, he approached me in the schoolyard one day and asked me if it was true what the others were saying, that "we" had murdered Jesus.

3 Strange to tell — for this was 1933 and we were in Hungary — I had never heard about this historical episode, and I left Tivadar amicably enough, promising to ask my father about it. We met again the next morning and I told him what I had learned: that the Romans had killed

24

Jesus, and that anyway Jesus had been a Jew, like me, so what did it matter to the Christians?

"That's not true," said Tivadar menacingly.   4

"My father does not lie," I replied.   5

By now a crowd had gathered around us and there was nothing for it   6
but to fight it out. There were cheers and laughter as Tivadar hit me in the nose before I got my jacket off. It was not the first time I had tasted my own blood, but it was the first time a Christian had made it flow. Tivadar was flushed with pleasure and excitement at the applause and not at all expecting it when I lashed out with my fist and sent him sprawling backward on the cobbles. The crowd of boys groaned and shouted to Tivadar to get up and kill the Jew, but poor Tivadar did not move. Frightened, I grabbed my jacket and shoved my way through the crowd stunned into silence by this overturning of the laws of nature.

They were silent at home too when I told them what had happened.   7
My father sent for me from his office in the afternoon, and I entered cap in hand. He always wore a braided Slovak jacket at work and looked more like a peasant than a Jewish wine merchant.

"Well, who started it?" asked my father, wearing an expression I had   8
never seen on his face before. I was not at all frightened.

"He did. I told him what you said about Jesus and he challenged me."   9

My father clamped his teeth on his cigar and nodded, looking right   10
through me.

"Jews don't fight," he finally said.   11

"Then why did you put me in a Christian school?" I asked in a loud,   12
outraged whine.

"That's why I put you there, my son," he said at last, then swept me   13
up and kissed me on the forehead. "You're learning fast; only next time don't hit him quite so hard."

Then he sent me out quickly and I stopped on the landing, startled   14
to hear loud, whooping, solitary laughter coming out of my father's office.

Δ Δ Δ Δ Δ Δ Δ Δ Δ Δ Δ Δ Δ Δ Δ Δ Δ Δ Δ Δ Δ Δ Δ Δ Δ Δ Δ Δ Δ Δ Δ Δ Δ Δ Δ Δ Δ Δ Δ Δ Δ Δ Δ Δ

Further Reading:

George Gabori, *When Evils Were Most Free*
George Faludy, *My Happy Days in Hell*

Structure:

1. What overall pattern organizes this selection?
2. Point out at least ten words or phrases that signal the flow of time in this narrative.

3. Scrutinize Gabori's opening paragraph: has he prepared us for the selection? Name every fact revealed about the setting and about the author.

Style:

1. How economical of words is this opening passage of Gabori's life story? How clearly does it reveal the author and his times? Would you predict with any confidence his character or fate as an adult? Do these pages tempt you to read the whole book? Why or why not?
2. *When Evils Were Most Free* is translated and condensed from the Hungarian original. Does this act separate us from Gabori's thoughts? How exact can translations be? If you are bilingual or multilingual, how precisely can you put sayings from one language into another? Can translator Eric Johnson even be seen as a co-author of these pages?
3. In paragraph 6 Gabori states, "It was not the first time I had tasted my own blood. . . ." Why is this image so strong?

Ideas for Discussion and Writing:

1. What exactly is the "overturning of the laws of nature" at the end of paragraph 6?
2. Was Gabori's father right to move the boy from a Hebrew *cheder* to a public school? In disproving the STEROTYPE that "Jews don't fight" (par. 11), has the boy learned a worthy lesson? Or does he merely copy the worst traits of his opponents, thereby becoming like them?
3. Every ethnic group in Canada — including English Canadians — is a minority. Has your minority been persecuted here? If you have been a victim, *narrate* an actual incident, including your own reaction. Like Gabori, give many specifics.
4. What are autobiographies for? What do you think writing your own life story would do for you? For others?
5. **PROCESS IN WRITING:** *Write a chapter of your own autobiography. Select one key incident in your life, then freewrite on it for a few minutes. Look over what you have produced, keep the best of it, and from this write your first draft. Have you begun and ended at just the right places, narrating the event itself but omitting parts that don't matter? Enrich the next draft with more IMAGES and examples, following Gabori's lead. Now share your* narrative *with a group of classmates, and adjust whatever does not communicate with this audience. Finally, read your narrative aloud, with expression, to the whole class.*

Note: See also the Topics for Writing at the end of this chapter.

Sylvia Fraser

My Other Self[*]

"Writing is healing," says Sylvia Fraser. Born in 1935 in Hamilton, Ontario, Fraser by the 1980s had become an award-winning journalist and the author of five novels (Pandora, *1972;* The Candy Factory, *1975;* A Casual Affair, *1978;* The Emperor's Virgin, *1980; and* Berlin Solstice, *1984). But signs of trouble had also appeared. Her seemingly happy marriage had fallen apart. Her fiction grew darker in vision and increasingly filled with sexual violence. Then the dam broke. In 1983, Fraser consciously recalled what her other self had never forgotten: that from her kindergarten year until almost the end of high school, her father had abused her sexually. Now it was clear how her novel* Berlin Solstice *had acquired its intimate and chilling insight into Nazi Germany. As Fraser put it, "Being victimized and essentially tortured by my father, I identified with the Jews. In trying to understand how the Germans could have done what they did, I was trying to understand my father — and I was preparing myself for my own truth"* (The Globe and Mail, *June 4, 1988). The memoir that followed,* My Father's House *(1987), startled both the critics and the public with its honesty, clarity of style, and emotional force. The book not only helped to "heal" its author, but ignited public debate on a hidden social problem, encouraging many other incest victims to deal with their past. From this book comes our selection, which dramatizes the victim's "other self" trying to emerge.*

The ice at Gage Park is best in the morning when it's flint-hard and glass-smooth. All is possible. You carve out circles and eights, and nothing exists until you put it there. Sometimes you just race around the rink, your legs sliding like they're on elastic bands, with your breath whistling through your teeth like steam from a locomotive, faster and faster. 1

Soon it's noon. The rink fills with kids in red and blue parkas playing tag or crack the whip. 2

"Hi!" It's Joe Baker from school. "Wanna skate?" 3

I prefer to play tag, but I don't want to hurt Joe's feelings and, besides, if I say no to him, maybe Perry Lord won't ask me. Such delicate weights and balances are the stuff of predating, as I am coming 4

---

*Editor's title.

to know it. Giving my hand to Joe with a bright paste-on smile, I slow my racing pace to his stodgy rhythm. The sound system squawks out "Oh, How We Danced on the Night We Were Wed" as we skate around and around, like the needle on the record. Joe's silence rattles me. I make chattery conversation. "Did you see The Thing from the Deep?"

5   By bad luck, the record never ends. The needle hits a crack, repeats "we vowed our true love we vowed our true love we vowed our true love," then jerks into "Don't Fence Me In." Now Joe links arms, forcing me to even greater intimacy and an even slower beat, *and making my other self very, very nervous. She cannot bear to be held or confined.* The game of tag is breaking up. Joe speaks his only sentence, and it is a lethal one. "Can I ah take you home if ah you're not doing anything?"

6   At the word "home" a cold shiver passes through me. I ransack my head for an explanation for the unpleasant way I am feeling and, failing that, an excuse. "I'll check with Arlene. We came together."

7   The clubhouse is crowded and noisy and steamy, as always. We jostle for a place on the splintery benches closest to the wood stove. The air stinks of charred wool — someone's icy mittens left too long on top. Joe helps me off with my skates, then unlaces his own while I inform Arlene. "Joe wants to take me home."

8   "He's cute. You have all the luck."

9   I study Joe through the lens of Arlene's enthusiasm: brown cowlick in wet spikes from his cap, earnest face bent over the task of knotting skate laces. Cute? Now that I know how I'm supposed to feel, I am reassured. Well, maybe.

10   We leave the rink just as the gang takes off in a gossipy pinwheel for the Kozy Korner. I think about suggesting we go too, but I'm afraid Joe doesn't have any money and I don't want to seem like a gold digger. Perry Lord tosses a snowball at Cooky Castle but hits Arlene instead. Tonya Philpott zings one back overhand, the way a boy would. I yearn to take up the challenge, but being with a boy obliges me to conform to more ladylike standards. Trapped, I stick my fists in my pockets.

11   Crunch crunch crunch. Skates knotted over Joe's shoulder, we trudge through the chalky snow. I've already told Joe the plot of The Thing from the Deep, and since I saw it uptown it wasn't a double feature. The silence lengthens with the shadows. Joe doesn't seem to mind. I do.

12   "Arlene says you got a hundred in arithmetic."

13   "Yeah. So did you."

14   "Yeah. But our test was easier."

15   I make the mistake of taking my hand out of my pocket to brush a snowflake. Joe commandeers it. *My other self panics.* How long before I can brush another snowflake and get it back without seeming rude? As I am working out the etiquette of this, two dogs rush the season by attempting to "do it" on the path in front of us. *My other self slips toward*

hysteria. I burst into giggles. The blood rises up Joe's protruding ears. He fumbles with his backside: "Are you laughing at the rip in my ski pants?"

"No, it isn't that." But I can't stop giggling.   16

"Joker Nash cut it with his skate."   17

"Honest, I didn't even notice." I stifle more giggles in a sneeze.   18
"Ah-choo!"

We are approaching my house. The giggles stop. Now my anxiety   19
grows so intense I'm afraid I'll faint. Snatching my hand from Joe's, I pick up a stick and drag it ping ping ping along the fence around St. Cecilia's Home the way I used to as a kid, pretending this is the most important thing in the world. How can I let you hold my hand when I am busy doing this?

We turn the corner. Now I see it — a sour-cream frame listing with   20
snow like a milk bottle with the cap frozen off. *Home.* I stop, rooted to the spot. For reasons I can't explain, it's essential that Joe go no farther. I reach for my skates. "I live only a couple of doors away."

"I don't mind. I'll carry them to the —"   21

"No!" I yank the skates from Joe's neck, almost beheading him. "I've   22
got to go — by myself."

Again Joe blushes from his neck through his ears. "Is it because of the   23
rip in my ski pants? You don't want your parents to see — "

"No!" Then more humanely: "Honest. It has nothing to do with you."   24
Pushing past him, I sprint for my father's house, clearing the steps in a single bound. As I open the storm door, the wind catches it.

"Don't slam the door!" roars my father from his armchair.   25

My other self bursts into hysterical weeping.   26

"What's wrong?" asks my mother.   27

Again, I find myself overcome by an emotion for which I must find a   28
reason. Hurling my skates at her feet, I shout: "Why do I have to wear these old things? They hurt my feet."

Wiping her hands on her apron, my mother rallies. "Those skates were   29
new last winter."

"Secondhand from Amity. You said I could have new skates for   30
Christmas."

"You needed other things." By now I'm racked with weeping I can't   31
control. Not about the skates, though I hear a voice I hardly recognize go on and on about them. "I hate these skates." Rage pours out of me like lava, devastating everything in its path. It flows around my father, implacable in his asbestos armchair.

It's a relief to be sent upstairs without supper. Flinging myself onto   32
my bed, I pound the pillow till my body is seized with convulsions, *releasing the rage my other self can no longer control.*

△△△

Further Reading:

Sylvia Fraser,
> *My Father's House*
> *Pandora*
> *Berlin Solstice*

Ruth Kempe, *The Common Secret: Sexual Abuse of Children and Adolescents*
Judy Steed, *Our Little Secret: Confronting Child Sexual Abuse in Canada*

Structure:

1. Does Fraser *narrate* "My Other Self" in straight chronological order?
2. This sequence begins with ice (par. 1) and closes with lava (par. 31). Explain how Fraser's progression of IMAGES parallels her progression of emotion. How do these progressions add force to her narrative?
3. What does Fraser achieve by putting all references to her "other self" in italics?

Style:

1. If the events on these pages occurred when Fraser was young, why does she narrate in the present tense? Would "My Other Self" have been stronger or weaker in the past tense? Why?
2. Where does Fraser use IMAGES that appeal to our senses of sight, touch, hearing and smell? Point out one of each.
3. In paragraph 9 our narrator says, "I study Joe through the lens of Arlene's enthusiasm. . . ." Point out two more METAPHORS in this selection. In paragraph 31 she says, "Rage pours out of me like lava. . . ." Point out two more SIMILES. What do these FIGURES OF SPEECH contribute to the total effect?

Ideas for Discussion and Writing:

1. Fraser stated in an interview, "I think of child abuse as being the AIDS of the emotional world. You cripple that child's emotional system so it can't deal with life" (*The Globe and Mail*, June 4, 1988). Point out all the ways in which our selection dramatizes her comment.
2. Why does Fraser refer to her "other self" in the third person as "she"? What does this usage seem to imply about young Fraser's mental state?
3. Some studies suggest that sexual abuse is an epidemic, with as many as one of every three or four children victimized (*The Globe and Mail*, April 15, 1989). What could be done to decrease these crimes? To rehabilitate the victims? To rehabilitate the offenders?

4. Fraser traces her fascination with the Holocaust to her feelings about her father (see the introduction to this selection). How fully does our relationship to our parents become a model for our relationship to the world? For example, do children of authoritarian parents grow up to resent authority in the form of employers or government?

5. Have you shared Fraser's experience of writing as healing? Analyze how the process might occur when we write an angry letter to tear up, when we send a letter to the editor, when we write a poem, or when we keep a personal journal.

6. **PROCESS IN WRITING:** *Think of a time when you got carried away by your own emotions. Experience it again by freewriting, never stopping the motion of your pen for several minutes. Use the present tense, as Fraser does, to heighten the immediacy of your account. Now* narrate *a first draft, incorporating the best of your prewriting. In the next draft add more* SENSE IMAGES *and* FIGURES OF SPEECH *(remembering the "ice" and "lava" of "My Other Self"). Have you moved the action along with time signals such as "then," "next," "suddenly" or "at last"? Have you trimmed out deadwood? If you report dialogue, have you used quotation marks, and have you begun a new paragraph for each change of speaker? Finally, test your prose aloud before writing the final version.*

Note: See also the Topics for Writing at the end of this chapter.

Carol Geddes

Growing Up Native

Since Carol Geddes tells her own life story in the narrative that follows, there is no need to repeat it all here. Born into the security of her Tlingit First Nations family in the wilds of the Yukon, she was six when she first knew her country's majority culture and began to see the problems it can make for Native people. Since then she has spent her life integrating these two worlds. She celebrates the current "renaissance" of interest in Native culture, yet also values the rest of North American life. "We need our culture," she writes, "but there's no reason why we can't preserve it and have an automatic washing machine and a holiday in Mexico, as well." Hers is a success story. Despite the obstacles, she completed a university degree in English and philosophy, did graduate studies in communications at McGill, and is today a successful filmmaker and spokesperson for her people. Our selection is from Homemaker's Magazine *of October 1990.*

1 I remember it was cold. We were walking through a swamp near our home in the Yukon bush. Maybe it was fall and moose-hunting season. I don't know. I think I was about four years old at the time. The muskeg was too springy to walk on, so people were taking turns carrying me — passing me from one set of arms to another. The details about where we were are vague, but the memory of those arms and the feeling of acceptance I had is one of the most vivid memories of my childhood. It didn't matter who was carrying me — there was security in every pair of arms. That response to children is typical of the native community. It's the first thing I think of when I cast my mind back to the Yukon bush, where I was born and lived with my family.

2 I was six years old when we moved out of the bush, first to Teslin, where I had a hint of the problems native people face, then to Whitehorse, where there was unimaginable racism. Eventually I moved to Ottawa and Montreal, where I further discovered that to grow up native in Canada is to feel the sting of humiliation and the boot of discrimination. But it is also to experience the enviable security of an extended family and to learn to appreciate the richness of the heritage and traditions of a culture most North Americans have never been

32

lucky enough to know. As a film-maker, I have tried to explore these contradictions, and our triumph over them, for the half-million aboriginals who are part of the tide of swelling independence of the First Nations today.

But I'm getting ahead of myself. If I'm to tell the story of what it's like to grow up native in northern Canada, I have to go back to the bush where I was born, because there's more to my story than the hurtful stereotyping that depicts Indian people as drunken welfare cases. Our area was known as 12-mile (it was 12 miles from another tiny village). There were about 40 people living there — including 25 kids, eight of them my brothers and sisters — in a sort of family compound. Each family had its own timber plank house for sleeping, and there was one large common kitchen area with gravel on the ground and a tent frame over it. Everybody would go there and cook meals together. In summer, my grandmother always had a smudge fire going to smoke fish and tan moose hides. I can remember the cosy warmth of the fire, the smell of good food, and always having someone to talk to. We kids had built-in playmates and would spend hours running in the bush, picking berries, building rafts on the lake and playing in abandoned mink cages.

One of the people in my village tells a story about the day the old lifestyle began to change. He had been away hunting in the bush for about a month. On his way back, he heard a strange sound coming from far away. He ran up to the crest of a hill, looked over the top of it and saw a bulldozer. He had never seen or heard of such a thing before and he couldn't imagine what it was. We didn't have magazines or newspapers in our village, and the people didn't know that the Alaska Highway was being built as a defence against a presumed Japanese invasion during the Second World War. That was the beginning of the end of the Teslin Tlingit people's way of life. From that moment on, nothing turned back to the way it was. Although there were employment opportunities for my father and uncles, who were young men at the time, the speed and force with which the Alaska Highway was rammed through the wilderness caused tremendous upheaval for Yukon native people.

It wasn't as though we'd never experienced change before. The Tlingit Nation, which I belong to, arrived in the Yukon from the Alaskan coast around the turn of the century. They were the middlemen and women between the Russian traders and the Yukon inland Indians. The Tlingit gained power and prestige by trading European products such as metal goods and cloth for the rich and varied furs so much in fashion in Europe. The Tlingit controlled Yukon trading because they controlled the trading routes through the high mountain passes. When trading ceased to be an effective means of survival, my grandparents began raising wild mink in cages. Mink prices were really high before and during the war, but afterwards the prices went plunging down. So, although the mink pens were still there when I was a little girl, my father mainly worked on highway construction and hunted in the bush. The Yukon was then, and still is in some ways, in a transitional period — from living off the land to getting into a European wage-based economy.

6   As a young child, I didn't see the full extent of the upheaval. I remember a lot of togetherness, a lot of happiness while we lived in the bush. There's a very strong sense of family in the native community, and a fondness for children, especially young children. Even today, it's like a special form of entertainment if someone brings a baby to visit. That sense of family is the one thing that has survived all the incredible difficulties native people have had. Throughout a time of tremendous problems, the extended family system has somehow lasted, providing a strong circle for people to survive in. When parents were struggling with alcoholism or had to go away to find work, when one of the many epidemics swept through the community, or when a marriage broke up and one parent left, aunts, uncles and grandparents would try to fill those roles. It's been very important to me in terms of emotional support to be able to rely on my extended family. There are still times when such support keeps me going.

7   Life was much simpler when we lived in the bush. Although we were poor and wore the same clothes all year, we were warm enough and had plenty to eat. But even as a youngster, I began to be aware of some of the problems we would face later on. Travelling missionaries would come and impose themselves on us, for example. They'd sit at our campfire and read the Bible to us and lecture us about how we had to live a Christian life. I remember being very frightened by stories we heard about parents sending their kids away to live with white people who didn't have any children. We thought those people were mean and that if we were bad, we'd be sent away, too. Of course, that was when social workers were scooping up native children and adopting them out to white families in the south. The consequences were usually disastrous for the children who were taken away — alienation, alcoholism and suicide, among other things. I knew some of those kids. The survivors are still struggling to recover.

8   The residential schools were another source of misery for the kids. Although I didn't have to go, my brothers and sisters were there. They told stories about having their hair cut off in case they were carrying head lice, and of being forced to do hard chores without enough food to eat. They were told that the Indian culture was evil, that Indian people were bad, that their only hope was to be Christian. They had to stand up and say things like "I've found the Lord," when a teacher told them to speak. Sexual abuse was rampant in the residential school system.

By the time we moved to Whitehorse, I was excited about the idea of living in what I thought of as a big town. I'd had a taste of the outside world from books at school in Teslin (a town of 250 people), and I was tremendously curious about what life was like. I was hungry for experiences such as going to the circus. In fact, for a while, I was obsessed with stories and pictures about the circus, but then when I was 12 and saw my first one, I was put off by the condition and treatment of the animals.

Going to school in Whitehorse was a shock. The clash of native and white values was confusing and frightening. Let me tell you a story. The older boys in our community were already accomplished hunters and fishermen, but since they had to trap beaver in the spring and hunt moose in the fall, and go out trapping in the winter as well, they missed a lot of school. We were all in one classroom and some of my very large teenage cousins had to sit squeezed into little desks. These guys couldn't read very well. We girls had been in school all along, so, of course, we were better readers. One day the teacher was trying to get one of the older boys to read. She was typical of the teachers at that time, insensitive and ignorant of cultural complexities. In an increasingly loud voice, she kept commanding him to "Read it, read it." He couldn't. He sat there completely still, but I could see that he was breaking into a sweat. The teacher then said, "Look, she can read it," and she pointed to me, indicating that I should stand up and read. For a young child to try to show up an older boy is wrong and totally contrary to native cultural values, so I refused. She told me to stand up and I did. My hands were trembling as I held my reader. She yelled at me to read and when I didn't she smashed her pointing stick on the desk to frighten me. In terror, I wet my pants. As I stood there fighting my tears of shame, she said I was disgusting and sent me home. I had to walk a long distance through the bush by myself to get home. I remember feeling this tremendous confusion, on top of my humiliation. We were always told the white teachers knew best, and so we had to do whatever they said at school. And yet I had a really strong sense of receiving mixed messages about what I was supposed to do in the community and what I was supposed to do at school.

Pretty soon I hated school. Moving to a predominantly white high school was even worse. We weren't allowed to join anything the white kids started. We were the butt of jokes because of our secondhand clothes and moose meat sandwiches. We were constantly being rejected. The prevailing attitude was that Indians were stupid. When it was time to make course choices in class — between typing and science, for example — they didn't even ask the native kids, they just put us all in typing. You get a really bad image of yourself in a situation like that. I bought into it. I thought we were awful. The whole experience was terribly undermining. Once, my grandmother gave me a pretty little pencil box. I walked into the classroom one day to find the word "squaw" carved on it. That night I burned it in the wood stove. I joined the tough crowd and by the time I was 15 years old, I was more likely to be leaning against the school smoking a cigarette than trying to join in. I was burned out from trying to join the system. The principal told my father there was no point in sending me back to school so, with a Grade 9 education, I started to work at a series of menial jobs.

12   Seven years later something happened to me that would change my life forever. I had moved to Ottawa with a man and was working as a waitress in a restaurant. One day, a friend invited me to her place for coffee. While I was there, she told me she was going to university in the fall and showed me her reading list. I'll never forget the minutes that followed. I was feeling vaguely envious of her and, once again, inferior. I remember taking the paper in my hand, seeing the books on it and realizing, Oh, my God, I've read these books! It hit me like a thunderclap. I was stunned that books I had read were being read in university. University was for white kids, not native kids. We were too stupid, we didn't have the kind of mind it took to do those things. My eyes moved down the list, and my heart started beating faster and faster as I suddenly realized I could go to university, too!

13   My partner at the time was a loving supportive man who helped me in every way. I applied to the university immediately as a mature student but when I had to write Grade 9 on the application, I was sure they'd turn me down. They didn't. I graduated five years later, earning a bachelor of arts in English and philosophy (with distinction).

14   It was while I was studying for a master's degree in communications at McGill a few years later that I was approached to direct my second film (the first was a student film). *Doctor, Lawyer, Indian Chief* (a National Film Board production) depicts the struggle of a number of native women — one who began her adult life on welfare, a government minister, a chief, a fisherwoman and Canada's first native woman lawyer. The film is about overcoming obstacles and surviving. It's the story of most native people.

15   Today, there's a glimmer of hope that more of us native people will overcome the obstacles that have tripped us up ever since we began sharing this land. Some say our cultures are going through a renaissance. Maybe that's true. Certainly there's a renewed interest in native dancing, acting and singing, and in other cultural traditions. Even indigenous forms of government are becoming strong again. But we can't forget that the majority of native people live in urban areas and continue to suffer from alcohol and drug abuse and the plagues of a people who have lost their culture and have become lost themselves. And the welfare system is the insidious glue that holds together the machine of oppression of native people.

Too many non-native people have refused to try to understand the   16
issues behind our land claims. They make complacent pronouncements
such as "Go back to your bows and arrows and fish with spears if you
want aboriginal rights. If not, give it up and assimilate into white Canadian culture." I don't agree with that. We need our culture, but there's
no reason why we can't preserve it and have an automatic washing
machine and a holiday in Mexico, as well.

The time has come for native people to make our own decisions. We   17
need to have self-government. I have no illusions that it will be smooth
sailing — there will be trial and error and further struggle. And if that
means crawling before we can stand up and walk, so be it. We'll have to
learn through experience.

While we're learning, we have a lot to teach and give to the world —   18
a holistic philosophy, a way of living with the earth, not disposing of it.
It is critical that we all learn from the elders that an individual is not
more important than a forest; we know that we're here to live on and
with the earth, not to subdue it.

The wheels are in motion for a revival, for change in the way native   19
people are taking their place in Canada. I can see that we're equipped,
we have the tools to do the work. We have an enormous number of
smart, talented, moral Indian people. It's thrilling to be a part of this
movement.

Someday, when I'm an elder, I'll tell the children the stories: about   20
the bush, about the hard times, about the renaissance, and especially
about the importance of knowing your place in your nation.

△ △

Further Reading:

Daniel David Moses and Terry Goldie, eds., *An Anthology of Canadian Native
    Writers in English*
Penny Petrone, ed., *First People, First Voices* (anthology of writings by First
    Nations people in Canada)
Julie Cruikshank, *Life Lived Like a Story* (interviews with Native Canadian
    women)
Basil Johnston, *Indian School Days* (memoir)
Hugh Brody, *Maps and Dreams* (anthropology)

Structure:

1. "I remember it was cold. . . ." says Geddes in her opening sentence,
    and "Someday, when I'm an elder. . . ." she says in her closing
    sentence. Most *narratives* in this chapter relate one incident, but
    "Growing Up Native" tells the highs and lows of a whole life. Has
    Geddes attempted too much? Or has she got her message across by

focusing on the right moments of her life? Cite examples to defend your answer.

2. Did you have the impression of being *told* a story, rather than reading it on the page? Cite passages where "Growing Up Native" comes across as oral history, as a tale told in person. Why does Geddes take this approach?

3. Does Geddes *narrate* in straight chronological order? Point out any flashbacks or other departures from the pattern.

4. Read paragraph 12 aloud. Analyze its power as a TRANSITION between Geddes' past and present.

Style:

1. Geddes' paragraphs are well organized: most begin with a topic sentence, then clearly develop it with examples. Identify five paragraphs that follow this pattern.

2. Why are paragraph 10 and several others so long? Why is paragraph 20 so short?

3. In paragraph 2 Geddes tells of "the sting of humiliation and the boot of discrimination." Find other good FIGURES OF SPEECH in paragraphs 9, 12 and 15.

Ideas for Discussion and Writing:

1. Despite the hardships of living in the bush, does Geddes' childhood sound like a good one? If so, why? Give examples.

2. Geddes exposes various ways in which First Nations People have been STEREOTYPED. Point out the worst of these.

3. The white high school of paragraph 11 routinely put native students in typing instead of science. How do the high schools of your province advise minority students as to course selection and career? Is a minority or working class student shut out from opportunity, or encouraged to try? Give examples from your own observation.

4. Geddes envisions First Nations People keeping their culture, yet also having washing machines and holidays in Mexico (paragraph 16). Discuss techniques for achieving such goals in the urban setting where most native people now live.

5. **PROCESS IN WRITING:** *Interview someone who either grew up long ago, or who is from a culture very different from yours, to hear her or his life story. Tape record the interview, then at home play it back, taking notes. Now choose either one main event of this narrative (such as the scene in which Geddes realizes she too can go to university), OR choose to give the overall sweep of the story. Also choose whether to just assemble the best excerpts from the tape to put in writing, OR to summarize the key events in your own words. Load your first draft with the best examples you have. Stay mainly in time order, but do use a flashback or*

flashforward if they enhance the story. Finally edit your version for things like spelling and punctuation. Read it aloud to the class. If there is time, also play the interview so the class can see how you chose and arranged the material of your narrative.

Note: See also the Topics for Writing at the end of this chapter.

Reza Kiarash

A Story of War and Change*

Like many Canadians, Reza Kiarash learned English only when he came to this country. It is his third language. Born in 1965 in Shushtar, Iran, Kiarash was the youngest of 12 children. After completing high school he was refused entry to university, so joined the Iranian army as a paramedic. His services were in demand, for the brutal war between Iran and its neighbour Iraq was in full sway. Of the 100 men in his platoon, says Kiarash, in two years only 10 were not killed or wounded. He was one of them. The narrative that follows may seem shocking, but he lived events like this "every day." Even after the war, Kiarash could not enter university or secure a good job, so he emigrated to Spain and learned Spanish. Soon, though, he continued to Canada, where after studying ESL he worked in a Toronto supermarket, then drove cab. It was in 1990 that he entered Ryerson Polytechnic University, where in a first-year English class he wrote "A Story of War and Change." His teacher helped to edit it, then a student newspaper, The Eyeopener, published it. Looking back on his war years, Kiarash says "Sometimes you blame yourself because you cannot help people the way you want, because you don't have enough knowledge in the field." After his studies in chemistry and biochemistry are completed, he therefore hopes to enter med school. His advice to student writers from other countries: "Don't translate; think in English as you write." His advice for learning English faster: "Find friends who speak English as a first language."

1   It's New Year's Eve, and everyone is waiting for the radio to announce the moment. I am with a small group of soldiers. The table we prepared is very odd. The New Year's table is supposed to have sweets, greens and fruit, but ours has bullets, guns and grenades. Finally the radio says it: the New Year has begun. Everybody is screaming and shooting into the air, but this doesn't go on long because now a heavy bombardment begins. It is the enemy's New Year's gift for us. Our side is silent now. There is no movement, and everyone is in his refuge and shelter. Some soldiers are on duty in trenches or at posts made of wooden rails and sandbags. These men are in more danger than the

---

*Retitled by *The Eyeopener*. Original title: "New Year's Eve."

others. They are not ready for this kind of fire attack. Suddenly the phone rings, and my heart starts pumping faster and faster. I know it's for me. That's my job — it comes in fire attacks when someone gets wounded. I pick up the phone. They need me at the third post, so I call the driver. We take the ambulance and move to the front, where we reach the "Death Furrow," so named because several men had been killed there. This part of the front is the worst I've seen so far. I leave the driver with the ambulance because the fire is too heavy. Now I run — no, not exactly run — sometimes run, and sometimes go flat on my belly to protect myself against fragments of bombs and shells. I am getting closer and closer. I can see the light, a huge light. It can't be fire. Yes, it is. Soldiers are calling for help, so I follow the voices. The first soldier tells me that the third post is on fire and three soldiers are trapped inside. I ask for help to go there, but everyone refuses. They are afraid, because the two front lines of war are so close together that soldiers can talk to enemy soldiers. Again I ask them to come with me to the third post, which by now is like a theatre screen with everybody watching. Then I give up trying to get help, and go alone. I can see the three soldiers. Two of them seem dead. They must be dead, because they are burnt. Another one has fallen beside the post. I go over to him. I try to talk to him, but there is no response. I find out why: he is wounded badly in the head. I try to carry him but he's so heavy I can't, so I go back to the soldiers. First of all I ask the sergeant of the group for help. He refuses. He says that's my problem, not his. I insult him because the wounded man is his own soldier. I remember how the day I joined the platoon this sergeant talked to the new soldiers about the war, and especially his boldness at war. He seemed brave to me then, but now I leave him with his boldness. Two other soldiers finally come to help me, and we carry the wounded man through the trench to the ambulance. I put him inside, then try to stop his bleeding. I find his vein and inject him with a serum to replace his lost blood. He can't breathe anymore, because his nose and mouth are full of blood. There is no way for air to get in, so I use the oxygen tank and suction tube to open his windpipe. We are halfway to the hospital when suddenly the suction stops working. There is something wrong with it. I can't fix it now, and he is turning black. Time is going fast for him and for me. Now I make my decision. I put my mouth on his bloody mouth. I am exhaling air into his mouth. I can taste the salty blood. I am thinking about home, my mother and my friends, though I don't know how I can think about these things at this time. I exhale the air. I put my mouth on his mouth, but before I give it to him, he throws up on me or, I should say, in my mouth. I don't stop. I clean my mouth, his mouth, and start all over again. The driver is watching me in the mirror and asks if I'm all right. I tell him "Yes, just drive fast. This is no time to be disgusted." I get the man alive to the hospital. I know he is not going to live, but this is my job — to keep soldiers alive and help them. I am surprised that a person who was in high school six months ago can change that much in this short a time. I am proud of myself and glad that I've not changed like that sergeant.

ΔΔΔΔΔΔΔΔΔΔΔΔΔΔΔΔΔΔΔΔΔΔΔΔΔΔΔΔΔΔΔΔΔΔΔΔΔΔΔΔΔΔΔΔΔΔΔΔ

Further Reading:

Dilip Hiro, *The Longest War: The Iran-Iraq Military Conflict*
Stephen Crane, *The Red Badge of Courage*
Erich Maria Remarque, *All Quiet on the Western Front*

Structure:

1. Why does Kiarash open with the New Year's celebration? Examine all the IRONIES of this event and its context.
2. Some *narratives* have a message, even a THESIS. Does this one?
3. Does Kiarash *narrate* in pure chronological order? Point out any exceptions such as flashbacks.
4. Why are there no paragraph breaks at all? Does this fact create difficulties, strengths, or both?

Style:

1. Why are the sentences so short? Is the resulting style accidental, or is it designed to complement the action?
2. "I can taste the salty blood," writes Kiarash near the end. What device gives life to this statement?
3. In what tense is "A Story of War and Change" written? Does this choice weaken or strengthen the *narrative?*

Ideas for Discussion and Writing:

1. Does the original title, "New Year's Eve," or the present title, given by the student newspaper which published Kiarash, best reflect the meanings of this narrative?
2. How do you view the narrator's actions and thoughts: is he a hero, or just a paramedic doing his job? Give reasons.
3. Kiarash, sure that the wounded soldier will die, never gives up trying to save him. Why? Name one ideal or belief of your own which you would uphold against all hope.
4. Many Canadians, like Kiarash, have come from countries at war. If this is your story, *narrate* a crucial chapter of it to the class.

5. Can *narrating* a hard experience help the writer? Do you think it helped Kiarash? How? Can it also help the reader? How?

6. Kiarash's life as a paramedic in war made him wish to study medicine (see the introduction). What experience or situation helped you see your own future goals? Tell about it.

7. **PROCESS IN WRITING:** *Change is said to be the most interesting thing in life. Think of an event that changed you, as Reza Kiarash's life at war changed him. Choose the key part of this story, and* narrate *it in a fast discovery draft, not stopping now to edit or polish. The next day look it over. Does it begin and end at just the right places?* Do *sense images (like the "salty blood" of Kiarash's narrative) help readers "see" or "hear" or "feel" or "smell" or "taste"?* Do *transitions like "now," "then" and "suddenly" speed the action? Have you, like Kiarash, tried the* present tense? *If not, should you? After you revise, edit for things like grammar and spelling as you produce your final draft. Finally, read it aloud to the class, with feeling.*

Note: See also the Topics for Writing at the end of this chapter.

Gary Lautens

Man, You're a Great Player!

*"An old English teacher of mine," wrote Gary Lautens, "once said she'd drop
dead if I ever made a living as a writer. Now, if she's a good sport, she'll keep her
end of the bargain." Lautens not only went on to make a living by writing, but
became the nation's best-loved humour columnist, syndicated across Canada.
Born in 1928 in Fort William, Ontario, he graduated from McMaster in 1950
with a B.A. in history — then went to work at* The Hamilton Spectator *as a
sports columnist. Moving to* The Toronto Star *in 1962, he began the column
of zany humour which brought him to prominence, and which overshadowed
even the two years he later spent as executive managing editor of* The Star. *These
columns twice won the Leacock Medal for Humour, and were published in
several collections:* Laughing with Lautens *(1964),* Take My Family —
Please! *(1980), and* No Sex Please. . .We're Married *(1983). Readers were
so saddened at Lautens' untimely death in 1992 that* The Star *began reprint-
ing earlier columns for those who, as his widow said, "miss their daily walk with
Gary." She, as well, collected more columns in a posthumous collection entitled*
Peace, Mrs. Packard and the Meaning of Life. *Our selection is from*
Laughing with Lautens. *It reflects the author's experience both as sports writer
and humorist, and the friendly common sense behind his humour.*

1   Occasionally I run into sports figures at cocktail parties, on the
street, or on their way to the bank.

2   "Nice game the other night," I said to an old hockey-player pal.

3   "Think so?" he replied.

4   "You've come a long way since I knew you as a junior."

5   "How's that?"

6   "Well, you high-stick better for one thing — and I think the way you
clutch sweaters is really superb. You may be the best in the league."

7   He blushed modestly. "For a time," I confessed, "I never thought you'd
get the hang of it."

8   "It wasn't easy," he confided. "It took practice and encouragement.
You know something like spearing doesn't come naturally. It has to be
developed."

44

"I'm not inclined to flattery but, in my book, you've got it made.   9
You're a dirty player."

"Stop kidding."   10

"No, no," I insisted. "I'm not trying to butter you up. I mean it. When   11
you broke in there were flashes of dirty play — but you weren't consistent.
That's the difference between a dirty player and merely a colourful
one."

"I wish my father were alive to hear you say that," he said quietly. "He   12
would have been proud."

"Well, it's true. There isn't a player in the league who knows as many   13
obscene gestures."

"I admit I have been given a few increases in pay in recent years.   14
Management seems to be treating me with new respect."

"You're selling tickets," I said. "You're a gate attraction now — not   15
some bum who only can skate and shoot and the rest of it. Your profanity
is beautiful."

"C'mon."   16

"No, I'm serious. I don't think anyone in the league can incite a riot   17
the way you can."

"I've had a lot of help along the way. You can't make it alone," he   18
stated generously.

"No one does," I said.   19

"Take that play where I skate up to the referee and stand nose-to-   20
nose with my face turning red. It was my old junior coach who taught
me that. He was the one who used to toss all the sticks on the ice and
throw his hat into the stands and pound his fist on the boards."

"You were lucky to get that sort of training. A lot of players never   21
learn the fundamentals."

"I think there are a few boys in the league who can spit better than   22
me."

"Farther, perhaps, but not more accurately," I corrected.   23

"Well, thanks anyway. I've always considered it one of my weaknesses."   24

"That last brawl of yours was perfectly executed. Your sweater was   25
torn off, you taunted the crowd, you smashed your stick across the
goalposts. Really a picture Donnybrook."

"The papers gave me a break. The coverage was outstanding."   26

"Do you ever look back to the days when you couldn't cut a forehead   27
or puff a lip or insult an official?"

"Everyone gets nostalgic," he confessed. "It's a good thing I got away   28
from home by the time I was fifteen. I might never have been any more
than a ham-and-egger, you know, a twenty-goal man who drifts through
life unnoticed."

"What was the turning point?"   29

"I had heard prominent sportsmen say that nice guys finish last, and   30 that you have to beat them in the alley if you hope to beat them in the rink. But it didn't sink in."

31 "Nobody learns overnight."

32 "I wasted a few years learning to play my wing and to check without using the butt of the stick. But I noticed I was being passed by. I skated summers to keep in shape, exercised, kept curfew."

33 "Don't tell me. They said you were dull."

34 "Worse than that. They said I was clean. It's tough to live down that sort of reputation."

35 I nodded.

36 "Anyway, during a game in the sticks, I was skating off the ice — we had won five-one and I had scored three goals. The home crowd was pretty listless and there was some booing. Then it happened."

37 "What?"

38 "My big break. My mother was in the stands and she shouted to me. I turned to wave at her with my hockey stick and I accidentally caught the referee across the face. He bled a lot — took ten stitches later."

39 "Is that all?"

40 "Well someone pushed me and I lost my balance and fell on the poor man. A real brawl started. Luckily, I got credit for the whole thing — went to jail overnight, got a suspension. And, talk about fate! A big league scout was in the arena. He offered me a contract right away."

41 "It's quite a success story," I said.

42 "You've got to get the breaks," he replied, humbly.

△△△

Further Reading:

Gary Lautens
　　Laughing With Lautens
　　Mrs. Packard and the Meaning of Life
Ken Dryden, *The Game*
Peter Gzowski, *The Game of Our Lives*

Structure:

1. How much of this piece is DIALOGUE? What do the parts do that are not dialogue?
2. This *narrative* has two parts. Where do they join, and how do they differ? In what order is each organized?
3. Should this selection be labelled ESSAY or FICTION? In what sense might it be both?

Style:

1. Why are there so many short paragraphs?
2. In paragraph 9 our narrator tells the friend, "I'm not inclined to flattery but, in my book, you've got it made. You're a dirty player." How important are such ironies to Lautens' humour and overall message? Point out all the IRONIES you see in the title and in paragraphs 1, 8, 12, 15, 20, 21, 34 and 40.
3. Has Lautens' humour strengthened the message? Would a conventional serious approach work better?
4. Find five COLLOQUIAL or SLANG terms that seem more at home here than they would in a conventional essay.

Ideas for Discussion and Writing:

1. As the saying puts it, "I went to the fights and a hockey game broke out."Do we watch hockey to see skating and shooting, or to see brawls? Is violence needed to attract fans? What could produce more interesting hockey even without fights?
2. In his look at violence in hockey, where does Lautens blame parents? Fans? Coaches? Management? Sportswriters?
3. It is said that soccer originated in warfare: villagers would kick the severed head of an enemy, like a ball, from one end of the village to the other. Think of the sports you play. What resemblances do you see between competition on the playing field and competition on the battlefield?
4. Must a sport be based on conflict, as in teams moving a puck or ball in the opposite direction? Think up a sport free of conflict. Can such a sport be interesting?
5. **PROCESS IN WRITING:** Narrate *a violent incident that you witnessed at a sports event, either in person or on television. First freewrite, then channel your momentum into a quick first draft. The next day look it over. Does the action begin and end at the right moments, so as to waste no words? Do time signals such as "next," "then" and "immediately" speed the action? Do SENSE IMAGES help the audience "see" and "hear"? Is the TONE consistent (comic, earnest, ironic or tragic all the way through)? If you use dialogue, are all quotation marks there, and does a change of paragraph signal each change of speaker? Finally, have you read aloud, to fine-tune your style?*

Note: See also the Topics for Writing at the end of this chapter.

Topics for Writing

Chapter 1: Narration

WRITING ABOUT MYSELF

Choose one of these topics as the basis of a narrative about yourself. Tell a good story: give colourful details and all the facts needed to help your reader understand and appreciate the event. (See also the guidelines that follow.)

1. My earliest memory
2. My escape from another country
3. The day I learned to love (or hate) school
4. My moment as a sports hero
5. The day I was a victim of crime
6. The day I was a victim of sexism
7. An event that changed my life
8. My encounter with a dangerous animal
9. My encounter with bureaucracy
10. The time I went hungry
11. My brush with the law
12. My car accident
13. The day I realized I was an adult
14. The day I conquered a fear
15. The day I was right and my friends were wrong

WRITING ABOUT OTHERS

From this list of events, choose one that you witnessed in person. Narrate it, giving colourful details and all the facts needed to help your reader understand and appreciate the event. (See also the guidelines that follow.)

16. A violent incident at a school
17. An incident on public transit
18. A rescue
19. A practical joke that backfired
20. An example of courage in action
21. A major failure of communication
22. A brush with death
23. A tornado or flood
24. A demonstration
25. A riot
26. An incident caused by alcohol or drugs
27. An incident at the prom
28. A case of police brutality
29. A disastrous fire or explosion
30. A transaction in the underground economy

Note also the Process in Writing topic after each selection in this chapter.

Process in Writing: Guidelines

Follow at least some of these steps in the act of writing your narrative (your teacher may suggest which ones).

1. *Search your memory, or search any diary or journal that you keep, for an incident that could develop one of our topics.*

2. *When you have chosen an incident, freewrite on it nonstop for at least five minutes. The results will show whether your choice is good. If it is, use the best parts in your first draft. If it is not, try another topic.*

3. *Write your first draft rapidly, letting the story just flow out onto the paper. Double-space, leaving room for revision. Do not stop now to fix things like spelling and grammar, for you will lose momentum. Consider narrating in the* present tense, *making the action seem to happen* now.

4. *Look over this draft: Does it begin and end at just the right places, narrating the event itself but omitting parts that don't matter? If you see deadwood, chop it out.*

5. *In your second draft, add more* SENSE IMAGES *to heighten the realism. Add more time signals, such as "first," "next," "then," "suddenly" and "at last," to speed the action.*

6. *Read a draft to family members, friends or classmates. Does it sound good? Revise awkward passages. Does it communicate with your audience? Revise any part that does not.*

7. *Finally, edit for spelling, grammar and other aspects of "correctness" before writing and proofreading the final copy. (If you use a computer, save this version on disk in case your teacher suggests further revision.)*

John Moore/Canapress Photo Service

"When enough people absorb the idea that all children have fundamental rights, we lucky ones in the West will begin to accept responsibility."

— Michele Landsberg, "West Must Confront Anonymous Misery of the World's Children"

CHAPTER

2

EXAMPLE

For example. . . .

Many an audience, after struggling to grasp a speaker's message, has been saved from boredom or even sleep by the powerful words *"for example. . . ."* Heads lift up, eyes return to the front, bodies shift in their chairs, and suddenly the message is clear to all.

Writers, like speakers, use examples. Do you enjoy reading pages of abstract reasoning, generalizations, theory without application? You have heard the Chinese proverb "A picture is worth a thousand words." When the writer's words never form "pictures," how can you "see the point"? Of course generalizations have their place. For example your thesis statement is one, and so are subpoints, summaries and conclusions. These and others are needed, but they cannot do the job alone. If you do not "show" as well as "tell," your reader will be like the people in the audience sinking into their seats — until you, like the speaker, say "for example. . . ."

Why not try for at least 50 percent example content in every essay, to avoid the hot-air approach to writing? The only trouble with using more examples is that you have to know the subject. Two suggestions:

■ If you cannot think of examples, then you have probably chosen the wrong topic. Try another. The best essays are like icebergs: only a tenth of what you know shows above the surface, but it is supported by the other nine-tenths.

■ If you cannot think of examples, go to the library and find them. Read. Use the on-line catalog and periodical indexes. In other words, do some *work.*

Examples take many forms:

Personal experience: To illustrate your point, narrate an incident you have experienced. Did an earthquake or tornado or flood show you the power of nature? Did an accident illustrate the danger of drinking and driving, or a fire the danger of smoking in bed? Did a major success or failure demonstrate the importance of work or planning or persistence?

The experience of others: To illustrate your point, narrate an incident you saw in person or heard about from others. Did your neighbour's unloved child run away from home or rob a milk store or get married at age 16? Did your cousin lose her job because of automation or recession or free trade? Did a famous person succeed despite a physical handicap or a deprived childhood?

Hypothetical examples: In a future-oriented society like ours, many arguments speculate about what might happen *if.* . . . Since the event or situation has not yet come to pass, use your best judgement to imagine the results. What would happen if children had the vote? If street drugs were legalized? If the rain forests were all cut? If the national debt were paid off? If gasoline were five dollars a litre? If a world government were adopted?

Quotations: If the words of a poet, politician, scientist or other prominent person illustrate your point clearly and authoritatively, quote them and of course state who said them. What did Aristotle, Shakespeare, Machiavelli, Freud, Marx, Jane Jacobs, Lester Pearson or Margaret Atwood say about love or power or sex or money or old age or war? Start with the index of *Bartlett's Familiar Quotations* or *Colombo's Canadian Quotations* to find an apt statement on almost any important topic.

Statistics: These numerical examples lend a scientific, objective quality to your argument. Tell what percentage of marriages will end in divorce or how many minutes each cigarette takes off your life or how much energy a person consumes travelling by car as opposed to train, bus or airplane. Five good sources of statistics are *Information Please Almanac, The World Almanac and Book of Facts, The Corpus Almanac of Canada, Canada Year Book* and any good atlas. Be scrupulously honest, because everyone knows how statistics can lie. (Remember the statistician who drowned in the river that averaged two feet deep!)

Other devices: Later chapters in this book discuss cause and effect, comparison and contrast, and analogy. These devices may be used not

EXAMPLE   **53**

only to plan the structure of an entire essay, but also to construct short and vivid examples within the essay.

Almost all good writing has examples, but some writing has so many that they become a means of organizing as well as illustrating. Ray Guy's essay "Outharbor Menu" has a brief introduction, a one-sentence closing, and a body made of nothing but examples. Such a collection could be a mere list of trivia, but Ray Guy — like anyone who writes well — has chosen his examples well for their colour and for the support they give his point.

Like Ray Guy, Amy Willard Cross and Michele Landsberg in this chapter have gone far beyond the suggested 50 percent example content for good essays. Though we could still disagree with their views, it would be astonishing if we did not at least *understand* them after "seeing" them so clearly in action.

Another way to use examples is to let one long one, for example a narrative, make the point. On page 136 of another chapter, Alison Acker shows us the life of only one small boy, Tito, in one small country, Honduras. But through this detailed example she helps us "see" poverty throughout the Third World: its causes and its effects on millions. Of course one example — or a hundred — will prove nothing. Statistics come close to proof, especially when based on a large and carefully designed study. But in general an example is not proof; it is a device of illustration and therefore an aid to both understanding and enjoyment.

Note: Authors in other chapters also use many examples, as well as other ways to develop their point. See especially these selections:

Margaret Laurence, "Where the World Began," p. 86
David Suzuki, "Hidden Lessons," p. 114
Doris Anderson, "The 51-Per-Cent Minority," p.156
Phil Edmonston, "Dealer Tricks," p.219
Judy Stoffman, "The Way of All Flesh," p. 250
June Callwood, "Making a Difference," p. 265
Margaret Atwood, "Canadians: What Do They Want?" p. 306

Ray Guy

Outharbor Menu

Ray Guy's authentic and direct voice of the Newfoundland outports is witness that, despite globalization and standardization, today's Canada still includes peoples rooted in other ways, other views. Guy was born in 1939 at Arnold's Cove, an isolated fishing village on Placentia Bay. As a child he learned the self-reliance of a life little changed in centuries. Then after attending Memorial University for two years he went to Toronto, where in 1963 he earned a diploma in journalism at Ryerson. Back in Newfoundland he began reporting for the St. John's Evening Telegram, *but found that reporting was not enough. His distaste for the Liberal government of Joey Smallwood, and especially its policy of closing down the outports where for centuries Newfoundlanders had lived by fishing, led Guy to become a political columnist. His satirical attacks on Smallwood were so devastating that many credit him with the Liberals' defeat in the provincial election of 1971. Leaving the* Telegram *when the Thomson chain bought it, Guy went freelance, continuing to pour satire on his targets. Guy's newest departure is writing plays, whose salty humour is much like that of his columns. His best writings are collected in* You May Know Them as Sea Urchins, Ma'am *(1975);* That Far Greater Bay *(1976), which won the Leacock Medal for Humour; and* Ray Guy's Best *(1987). Our selection comes from* That Far Greater Bay.

1   What feeds we used to have. Not way back in the pod auger days,° mind you. That was before my time. I mean not long ago, just before the tinned stuff and the packages and the baker's bread started to trickle into the outports.

2   Out where I come from the trickle started when I was about six or seven years old. One day I went next door to Aunt Winnie's (that's Uncle John's Aunt Winnie) and she had a package of puffed rice someone sent down from Canada.°

° the pod auger days: a common Newfoundland expression meaning "the old days." A pod auger is an auger with a lengthwise groove.
° from Canada: Newfoundland did not join Confederation until 1949, after the time Ray Guy describes.

She gave us youngsters a small handful each. We spent a long time admiring this new exotic stuff and remarking on how much it looked like emmets' eggs. We ate it one grain at a time as if it were candy, and because of the novelty didn't notice the remarkable lack of taste. 3

"Now here's a five cent piece and don't spend it all in sweets, mind." You never got a nickel without this caution attached. 4

Peppermint knobs. White capsules ringed around with flannelette pink stripes. Strong! You'd think you were breathing icewater. They're not near as strong today. 5

Chocolate mice shaped like a crouching rat, chocolate on the outside and tough pink sponge inside. Goodbye teeth. Bullseyes made from molasses. And union squares — pastel blocks of marshmallow. 6

Those mysterious black balls that were harder than forged steel, had about 2,537 different layers of color and a funny tasting seed at the centre of the mini-universe. 7

Soft drinks came packed in barrels of straw in bottles of different sizes and shapes and no labels. Birch beer, root beer, chocolate, lemonade, and orange. 8

Spruce beer, which I could never stomach, but the twigs boiling on the stove smelled good. Home brew made from "Blue Ribbon" malt and which always exploded like hand grenades in the bottles behind the stove. 9

Rum puncheons. Empty barrels purchased from the liquor control in St. John's. You poured in a few gallons of water, rolled the barrel around, and the result was a stronger product than you put down $7.50 a bottle for today. 10

Ice cream made in a hand-cranked freezer, the milk and sugar and vanilla in the can in the middle surrounded by ice and coarse salt. I won't say it was better than the store-bought stuff today but it tasted different and I like the difference. 11

Rounders (dried tom cods) for Sunday breakfast without fail. Cods heads, boiled sometimes, but mostly stewed with onions and bits of salt pork. 12

Fried cod tongues with pork scruncheons.° Outport soul food. Salt codfish, fish cakes, boiled codfish and drawn butter, baked cod with savoury stuffing, stewed cod, fried cod. 13

Lobsters. We always got the bodies and the thumbs from the canning factories. When eating lobster bodies you must be careful to stay away from the "old woman," a lump of bitter black stuff up near the head which is said to be poisonous. 14

I was always partial to that bit of red stuff in lobster bodies but never went much on the pea green stuff although some did. 15

° pork scruncheons: crisp slices of fried pork fat.

16   We ate turrs° (impaled on a sharpened broomstick and held over the damper hole to singe off the fuzz), some people ate tickleaces° and gulls but I never saw it done.

17   We ate "a meal of trouts," seal, rabbits that were skinned out like a sock, puffin' pig (a sort of porpoise that had black meat), mussels and cocks and hens, otherwise known as clams, that squirt at you through air holes in the mud flats.

18   Potatoes and turnips were the most commonly grown vegetables although there was some cabbage and carrot. The potatoes were kept in cellars made of mounds of earth lined with sawdust or goosegrass. With the hay growing on them they looked like hairy green igloos.

19   A lot was got from a cow. Milk, certainly, and cream and butter made into pats and stamped with a wooden print of a cow or a clover leaf, and buttermilk, cream cheese. And I seem to remember a sort of jellied sour milk. I forget the name but perhaps the stuff was equivalent to yogurt.

20   There was no fresh meat in summer because it wouldn't keep. If you asked for a piece of meat at the store you got salt beef. If you wanted fresh beef you had to ask for "fresh meat."

21   Biscuits came packed in three-foot long wooden boxes and were weighed out by the pound in paper bags. Sultanas, Dad's cookies, jam jams, lemon creams with caraway seeds, and soda biscuits.

22   Molasses was a big thing. It was used to sweeten tea, in gingerbread, on rolled oats porridge, with sulphur in the spring to clean the blood (eeeccchhhh), in bread, in baked beans, in 'lassie bread.

23   It came in barrels and when the molasses was gone, there was a layer of molasses sugar at the bottom.

24   Glasses of lemon crystals or strawberry syrup or limejuice. Rolled oats, farina, Indian meal. Home-made bread, pork buns, figgy duff,° partridgeberry tarts, blanc mange, ginger wine, damper cakes.°

25   Cold mutton, salt beef, peas pudding, boiled cabbage, tinned bully beef for lunch on Sunday, tinned peaches, brown eggs, corned caplin.°

26   And thank God I was twelve years old before ever a slice of baker's bread passed my lips.

∆∆∆

° turr: the murre, an edible seabird.
° tickleace: the kittiwake, a kind of gull.
° figgy duff: boiled raisin pudding.
° damper cakes: a kind of bannock made on the damper (upper surface) of a cookstove.
° caplin: a small and edible ocean fish often used by cod fishermen as bait.

Further Reading:

Ray Guy,
>*That Far Greater Bay*
>*Ray Guy's Best*

David Macfarlane, *The Danger Tree*
Farley Mowat, *This Rock Within the Sea: A Heritage Lost*
Al Pittman, *Once When I Was Drowning: Poems*

Structure:

1. Identify every fact which the opening sentence states or implies about the essay that will follow.
2. At the end Ray Guy exclaims, "And thank God I was twelve years old before ever a slice of baker's bread passed my lips." What does this final sentence do that qualifies it to close the essay?
3. Roughly what percentage of this essay consists of *examples?* Are there enough to make the point? Are there too many?
4. Why does Guy tell the incident of the puffed rice (pars. 2 and 3)?

Style:

1. Do you find Ray Guy's vocabulary difficult? For what audience is he writing? If he had known people outside Newfoundland would read this essay, what might he have done differently?
2. Does Guy waste words or save them? Give *examples.*
3. Find five sentence fragments. Are they errors? Why does Guy use them?
4. Point out expressions that make the essay folksy and COLLOQUIAL. Does Guy's TONE fit his topic?
5. In paragraph 18 Guy describes root cellars: "With the hay growing on them they looked like hairy green igloos." Where else does he use SIMILES?

Ideas for Discussion and Writing:

1. Through newspaper columns Guy fought the government's forcing people from Newfoundland's outports — such as the one described in this essay — to central locations where they would do factory work instead of fish. Should traditional cultures be preserved? Are governments ever right in forcing them to change? Defend your answer with *examples.*
2. Fast-food chains have been Americanizing the eating habits not only of Canada but also of many other countries. In this process what have we gained? What have we lost?

3. **PROCESS IN WRITING:** *Guy refers to "outport soul food" (par. 13). In an essay, describe the "soul food" of your own childhood. Take notes over several days, letting one memory lead to the next. Then fill a draft with large numbers of* examples. *In further drafts add more SENSE IMAGES and FIGURES OF SPEECH, to bring this cuisine alive for readers who grew up elsewhere. Finally, read aloud to detect repetition or other weak style, before writing the good draft.*

Note: See also the Topics for Writing at the end of this chapter.

Amy Willard Cross

Safety First, Fun a Distant Second

"Write about things that impassion you," advises Amy Willard Cross. She also advises not to write for a living as she does; only rarely, she says, does the freelance writer get to work on topics of personal interest. Cross holds a B.A. in French literature from Wellesley, and has studied in Paris. Since then she has worked as a magazine editor in Los Angeles and Toronto, has broadcast radio essays on the CBC, and has contributed many articles to The Globe and Mail, The Toronto Star, Toronto Life Fashion, Ms, Glamour, Self *and* Working Woman. *Several of these writings have been anthologized. She has also published books, such as* The Summer House: A Tradition of Leisure *(1992). Our selection appeared on January 8, 1991 in* The Globe and Mail. *Though Cross does not consider herself a humorist, here she deftly reduces to absurdity a growing trend in Canada.*

My sister used to be fearless. She lived by herself in neighbourhoods where people held riots on their days off. She hitch-hiked. Snorkled in shark-infested waters. Dared. 1

Then she had a child. Her first Christmas as a mother, she met me at the airport in a new car: a big, silver car of European extraction with heavy metal exterior, buttery leather interior. 2

"Nice car, eh?" she said, "We got it for the baby. It's got great crash stats. If I collide with a small import, my hood might crunch, but I could probably hop out and play tennis." 3

"Would you really feel like tennis after trash-compacting somebody — even if he did drive a Japanese car?" 4

"Buckle your seat belt," she said. Despite the one-in-a-something chance of having an accident within a five-mile radius from her house, we arrived unscathed. 5

Once home, it was clear she had redecorated: the look was late 20th-Century Safety. Knee-high plastic gates closed off areas unsupervised by adults. Smoke alarms stood guard in every room, shrieking warnings at exuberant smokers or burnt toast. What really stood out was the TV. It 6 had been moved some 15 feet away from the sofa, so you would need binoculars to see the weather map. I moved closer, turned it on.

7   "Get back," my sister cried, "you're in the electromagnetic field." Apparently, those friendly watts and volts that had once powered our nightlight when we were kids and chilled our Jell-O had mutated into agents of danger that threatened cancer and other bad luck. To contain this malevolent force, plastic covers blocked each plug — staving off electrocution and keeping electromagnetic fields where they belonged.

8   Like others who have managed to reproduce themselves genetically, my sister sees potential danger in any situation — call it Dangervision. As the gift of prophecy yields glimpses of the future, Dangervision reveals a parallel reality of worst-case scenarios: freak accidents, falls, fires, or drowning in bath water.

9   Dangervision probably has an evolutionary role. But even those without this second sight get help protecting themselves against themselves. Well-meaning safety campaigns warn against things most of us avoid instinctively, slowly undoing the undemocratic notion that only the fittest survive. Nowadays, anybody can survive — just follow the safety tips inside every package. In fact, during the past decade accidental deaths have plummeted. Fewer and fewer people go with a bang, splat or gurgle; most of us die slowly, remaining eligible for an open casket. The Heimlich manoeuvre, pool covers, home fire extinguishers, child-proof caps, guard rails, seat belts, smoke-free dining rooms and life vests certainly played a part. Finally, we know that plastic dry-cleaning bags are *not* toys. And lots of guardian angels are out of work.

10   Sure we're living longer, but it seems longer, too. It's hard to have fun when you're being careful. You can't drink champagne on afternoon canoe rides any more — it's the law. Heaven knows, you could pass out, fall into the lake and drown. You can't feel crispness of wind in your hair while galloping through the meadows, or racing country roads on a 10-speed, because helmets trap a steamy, sweaty halo of dead air around your head. God forbid, the horse could shy, your tire could blow, and your brains could split open.

11   Children suffer from safety even more. Their fearlessness is very quickly beaten out of them by adoring parents. Following the advice of kid safety handbooks, new moms and dads crawl around the floor to experience coffee-table-level perils as their toddler would. They bug their kid's room with baby intercoms. Parents won't let kids play in the park without a grown-up around to stop them from climbing trees or swinging upside down. Like Irish crystal, kids get dusted off on important occasions and handled ever so carefully — after all, there's usually only one to the set. You wonder, will children raised in padded environments languish like domesticated animals released into the wild, unable to fend off normal predators?

Besides editing all risk from our lives, Dangervision has robbed us of the pleasure of surviving. Those few sweet moments after a close call felt great: nearly fell off the observation deck, nearly drowned, nearly went over the median! 12

Now people take safe, accident-free lives for granted. If the average life span is 73 years, they figure they've got it coming to them. Fate or God's will or bad luck better not get in the way. And if it does, watch out. Accidents don't just happen, they're someone else's fault. And faults get sued. For a lot of money. Disclaimers are posted everywhere in a vain effort to prevent product liability suits: not responsible for accidental dismemberment with the Brush 'Em automatic tooth-cleaning system. 13

Europeans don't share this need to protect their fellow citizens from themselves. They don't ruin architecture with unsightly metal guard rails, but let any stupid tourist climb up fortifications or Roman amphitheatres. The attitude is probably a form of population control for a very crowded continent. 14

Now that cleaners hide behind childproof cabinets, now that railings protect balconies, now that no one smokes in bed after tousling the sheets, we're finally safe. Strangely, people flirt with danger recreationally. The same people with air bags, life vests and smoke alarms spend their weekends heli-skiing, hang-gliding, parachuting and racing cars. So bridled in normal life, people travel miles to dare the latest craze: bungy-jumping. They pay piles of money to jump off bridges attached to nothing but a giant rubber band from which they bounce — narrowly escaping the water's surface. Apparently, it's an exhilarating nearly. 15

By the time the nephew makes it to adulthood accident-free, he'll probably fly straight to Australia and jump some bungies. 16

∆ ∆

Further Reading:

Jack Dowie and Paul Lefrere, eds., *Risk and Chance: Selected Readings*
Aldous Huxley, *Brave New World*
George Orwell, *1984*

Structure:

1. Rate the opening ANECDOTE: Does it draw our interest? Does it lead into Cross's subject?
2. Show how the device of *contrast* powers both the opening and closing *examples*.
3. Cross's THESIS does not appear in the opening. Where is it?
4. How much room in this essay does Cross give to *examples*? Take out

your own latest essay and estimate its example content. Do you need to go higher? How much higher?

Style:

1. Analyze Cross's TONE: does she just amuse us with scenes of ridiculous behaviour, or behind the laughs is there a serious message? Identify one *example* that seems exaggerated or even made up; identify another that seems serious.
2. Cross states that "fewer and fewer people go with a bang, splat or gurgle" (paragraph 9). What kind of death does each of these SENSE IMAGES imply? Without the images, how many more words might Cross have needed here?
3. Paragraph 1 ends with sentence fragments. Why? How does the essayist distinguish between fragments as errors and as devices of style?
4. What device powers Cross's observation that "the same people with air bags, life vests and smoke alarms spend their weekends heli-skiing, hang-gliding, parachuting and racing cars"?

Ideas for Discussion and Writing:

1. Has "Dangervision," either your own or other people's, reduced your fun? Give *examples.*
2. Cross states that children's fearlessness "is quickly beaten out of them by adoring parents" (par. 11). Do you agree? If you have children, will you favour their physical safety or their learning to manage risk? In today's society is the latter skill still important?
3. If our society shuns danger, then why do we flock to rides at midways and amusement parks, watch horror and disaster films, and read tabloids that glory in axe murders?
4. If we are "finally safe" from the old dangers Cross describes, have new ones in the world taken their place? Give *examples.* Is there any way to be safe from these as well?
5. **PROCESS IN WRITING:** *Do you believe that taking risks is an essential and desirable part of living, or do you prefer safety? Take a side in your* THESIS. *Now brainstorm a page full of* examples, *either of dangers that need to be contained, or of legitimate activities that have been unjustly limited (for example is it good that diving boards are being removed from public pools?). Arrange your examples so the best come last, then write them into a fast discovery draft. When this has "cooled off," look it over. Have you reached an* example content of 70 to 80 percent? *If not, cross out any generalizing that is vague or repetitious, and in its place add more good examples. Do* SENSE IMAGES *spark your examples? If not, add. Do* TRANSITIONS *link your examples? If not, add. Finally, read aloud as you fine-tune the argument into a final version.*

Note: See also the Topics for Writing at the end of this chapter.

Michele Landsberg

West Must Confront Anonymous Misery of the World's Children

Michele Landsberg is one of the nation's most liked and trusted journalists, a voice of compassion and common sense. Her career could be summed up in the words Women & Children First, *the title of her 1982 book. In it she collects some of her best newspaper columns on abuses such as rape and domestic violence, but also on the joys of family life such as birth, holiday rituals, graduation and marriage. This split focus illustrates Landsberg's position as feminist: though she fights inequalities suffered by women, she strongly believes in marriage and family life. Her attempts to reconcile these sometimes opposing values lend an often dramatic power to her essays. Landsberg was born in 1939 in Toronto, and studied at the University of Toronto. Since then she has written for the* Toronto Globe and Mail, Chatelaine *and* The Toronto Star, *winning National Newspaper Awards for both her columns and feature articles. In 1986 her family interests led to* Michele Landsberg's Guide to Children's Books. *Then living in New York City as wife of Canada's ambassador to the United Nations, Stephen Lewis, Landsberg produced a series of columns for the Toronto* Globe and Mail *about New York and about international issues at the U.N., which has its headquarters there. One of these articles is our selection, from November 7, 1987. (Its point was in fact realised when in September 1990, 20 countries ratified the United Nations Convention on the Rights of the Child.) To round off her American experiences, in 1989 Landsberg published* "This is New York, Honey!" A Homage to Manhattan with Love & Rage.

International Declarations come in for a lot of derision. Any hostile   1
observer at the United Nations Commission on Human Rights in Geneva, for example, might well snicker as delegates lengthily debate each parenthesis, comma, word, in the draft Convention on the Rights of the Child.

The process has gone on for years, and will not come to fruition   2
for several more. Can the verbiage really make that much difference

to the millions of the world's children who suffer and die in anonymous misery?

3   Yes. Ten years ago, the mere phrase "children's rights" was, to most people, a joke, a ludicrous extension of the "rights" frenzy of the '70s. Today it has entered our consciousness as a legitimate and forceful claim. The Declaration process itself (now pressing forward more rapidly under the leadership of Poland and Canada), involving hundreds of volunteer organizations and government officials, has turned many governments' attention, some for the first time, to the agony of their children.

4   An essential part of social change is the forcing of this attention. What newspaper, a decade ago, wrote about child labor in the Third World? Now, in recent weeks and months, well-researched documents — from the Christian Science Monitor, the Cox Newspaper Service, the International Defence and Aid Fund, the United Nations sub-commission on the prevention of discrimination against minorities — have heaped up on my desk.

5   They catalogue a horror that has been invisible to most of us.

6   They tell of Gypsy children who are kidnapped or sold from Yugoslavia to criminal gangs in Italy, where they are beaten into performing as thieves and beggars.

7   Thirteen- and 14-year-old girls work 17-hour days at their sewing machines in Manila sweatshops. The pay: 13 cents an hour.

8   That's better than the one cent a day earned by 5-year-olds who weed the tea plantations in Sri Lanka.

9   In the Ashanti Goldfields (jointly owned by the Government of Ghana and a company called Lonrho International), 11-year-old boys labor naked in pools of cyanide to extract gold from rock.

10   Girls as young as 4 are virtual slaves in Moroccan carpet factories, crouched on their benches for 12-hour days, sleeping on the floor next to their looms at night, breathing air thick with fluff and fibre.

11   They compete with Indian carpet-makers for the North American market. In New York department stores like Bloomingdale's, the luscious glowing colors of the carpets fetch prices in the thousands. But the small Indian and Moroccan weavers themselves earn a pittance of pennies an hour.

12   World Health Organization officials are researching the trauma of children as young as 7, in countries like Kenya, who drudge through 15-hour days as household servants. They weep at night, refuse to speak, wet their beds. They mind the babies, scrub dishes, floors and laundry, live like little household animals.

13   Brazil has 30 million street children; many more are actually sold for forced labor. On rice plantations, children of 6 or 7 are primed with alcohol in the pre-dawn to get ready for work. Their beds are the bare

ground, their wages a plate of rice; little girls are used as prostitutes by their overseers. On Brazil's tea plantations, 10,000 children ages 5 to 13 wade through pesticide muck. They get 15 cents for every 52-pound sack of tea they pick and carry.

You'll switch to cocoa? Thousands of Nigerian children are kidnapped — some as young as 5 or 6 — to slave in cocoa plantations.   14

In Mozambique and Angola, 375 of every 1,000 infants die — the highest infant mortality rate in the world — because of devastation caused by South African armed aggression.   15

Thailand has at least 30,000 child prostitutes. In one Bangkok house, owned by a prominent man active in charity, the little girls crawl through a hole in the wall at the sound of the madame's whistle, and sit on benches wearing numbered shirts, to be picked by customers. Their faces, in Cox News photographs, are ravishingly lovely, shatteringly sad.   16

In most of these countries, governments are struggling to overcome the kind of poverty that makes child labor a condition of life. Much of the poverty is caused by debt. Third World countries are economically strangled by the high interest rates on the money they owe to us First Worlders.   17

In some countries, however, it is the government that orchestrates the horror. South African news censorship means that we no longer see the sudden, irrational descent of gun-wielding police from their armored cars to shoot at random as black children scatter, terrified, in the dusty township streets. But volunteer organizations doggedly collect the evidence. They tell us that last year, 59,000 children were detained by South African police.   18

Children as young as 7 and 8 are cross-questioned for hours in court, denied lawyers or visits from parents. They are so small that all we can see of them over the edge of the dock are their troubled, panicky eyes.   19

Fathers tell of finding their broken, tortured children lying on concrete floors of police stations, trembling and speechless and sometimes dying. Children in jail are routinely beaten and whipped; many have been tear-gassed, scarred with boiling water, hosed, electric-shocked, raped, beaten into permanent brain damage or death.   20

Can a United Nations Convention on children's rights make a difference? The people at work in the field say yes. When enough people absorb the idea that all children have fundamental rights, we lucky ones in the West will begin to accept responsibility. We buy the carpets, the cocoa, the rice, the cheap shirts, the pornography, the South African gold. One day we'll buy the idea that we can, through our foreign policy, help the children.   21

△ △

Further Reading:

Michele Landsberg, *Women & Children First*
Alison Acker, *Children of the Volcano*
Rigoberta Menchu, *I, Rigoberta Menchu: an Indian Woman in Guatemala*

Structure:

1. Landsberg opens her argument with a question (in par. 2) and closes it with another (in par. 21). Both have the same answer. Analyze the effects of these parallels.
2. What share of this essay is *examples*? Are there enough? Too many? Compare "Outport Menu," this chapter's first essay. Do you prefer Ray Guy's almost exclusive use of examples, or Landsberg's more mixed use of examples and generalizations? Why?
3. In what ways do Landsberg's many statistics function as *examples*? How important are they to her argument?
4. Explore the parallelism of the words "we buy" in Landsberg's final two sentences: How does it help engineer her closing?
5. What rhetorical principle has Landsberg used in placing "children" as the very last word of her argument?

Style:

1. Analyze how Landsberg uses IRONY in each of these *examples*: the wages of carpet makers compared to the price of their carpets (par. 10–11), our use of tea vs. our use of cocoa (par. 13–14), and the case of the man active in charity who owns a house of child prostitution (par. 16).
2. Has Landsberg achieved a good ratio of content to length? Has her proliferation of *examples* just led to wordiness, or has it fostered CONCISENESS? Explain.

Ideas for Discussion and Writing:

1. Why does Landsberg not include examples from our own country? Is the First World free of the problems she cites in the Third World?
2. When Landsberg wrote this column her husband Stephen Lewis was Canada's ambassador to the United Nations. Does this give special value to her argument, or should we judge it strictly on its own worth?
3. In closing, Landsberg links our shopping habits to the fate of Third-World children. Add to her suggestions: What more can we do in Canada, besides selective shopping, to reduce misery among the world's young? In particular, how might we apply Landsberg's idea of using our foreign policy to help the children?

4. **PROCESS IN WRITING:** *For one week read the international section of a daily newspaper, collecting, as Landsberg did, reports with implications for Third-World children. Highlight key examples, then choose an event or situation that makes you react. Freewrite to focus your argument. Now draft a letter to the editor of the same newspaper, stating your* THESIS *clearly, then, like Landsberg, letting examples from your reading do most of the arguing. Keep in mind that now you have a real* AUDIENCE; *are your vocabulary and whole approach suitable to the kind of person who reads this newspaper? If not, revise. Also cut every scrap of deadwood, because editors like letters short. Finally, show your teacher a draft before writing and mailing the final version. Continue reading the newspaper for a week or two; if you see your letter, bring it to class to share.*

Note: See also the Topics for Writing at the end of this chapter.

Robert Fulford

Where, Exactly, Are This Book's Readers?

A high school dropout and former copy boy at the Toronto Globe and Mail, *Robert Fulford rose to become the nation's most respected journalist writing in English. He has reported, edited and been columnist for several newspapers, including* The Globe and Mail, The Toronto Star *and* The Financial Times, *and has hosted many radio broadcasts for the CBC and television broadcasts for TVOntario. Fulford's greatest contribution to public life, though, began in 1968 when he was named editor in chief of the nation's oldest magazine. For 19 years his editorial abilities and his penetrating and well-written columns made* Saturday Night *English Canada's most important magazine of culture and public affairs. However, when financier Conrad Black acquired the venerable publication in its centennial year, Fulford quit rather than accept restrictions on editorial freedom. Continuing to write, he also taught journalism and broadcasting ethics from 1989 to 1993 at Ryerson Polytechnic University. Through the years Fulford has collected the best of his columns and articles into books, such as* Crisis at the Victory Burlesk: Culture, Politics & Other Diversions *(1968), from which our selection comes. After leaving* Saturday Night *he told his story in his 1988 autobiography* Best Seat in the House: Memoirs of a Lucky Man.

1   There's always the possibility, of course, that the world already has enough books; may, in fact, have *too many* books. This thought has never occurred to a publisher; it has probably occurred to only a minority of authors; but certainly it has occurred at one time or another to every book reviewer in the world.

2   For the fact is that book reviewers spend their lives surrounded by piles of books they will never read and they can't imagine anyone else reading. Every morning a young man comes into my office with a pile of half a dozen books, and on the average three of them fall into this category.

3   Take one that turned up yesterday: *They Gave Royal Assent,* subtitled *The Lieutenant-Governors of British Columbia.* Imagine it. Not just a book on lieutenant-governors — a subject with truly monumental possibilities

for producing boredom — but a book on *British Columbia* lieutenant-governors.

Now the thing about lieutenant-governors is that, in general, they don't do anything. They just sort of *preside*. Their lives lack, not to put too fine a point on it, drama. So who will read this book? If you were lieutenant-governor of British Columbia you might well want to read it, and if you aspired to that office you would almost certainly be anxious to obtain a copy. But surely that makes a limited market. In addition there are descendants and other connections of lieutenant-governors; but this, too, must be a comparatively small group. Will the author, D. A. McGregor ('veteran journalist, editor and history-researcher,' the jacket says) meet friends who have read his book and who will congratulate him on it? 'Nice job on the lieutenant-governors, old man,' one imagines them saying. But who would they be?

The publishers, Mitchell Press of Vancouver, have dutifully sent out review copies. Why? Because publishers do this — they operate automatically on the I-shot-an-arrow-into-the-air theory of publicity. They just send out books at random, whether anybody wants them or not. It gives them some queer sense of satisfaction. They feel they are playing their part.

So here are all these books floating around in the mails and then ending up on the desks of people who view them with apathy if not distaste. Any book reviewer can at any moment, and to his horror, look around his office and instantly spot three books on the Quebec crisis, four histories of Ontario counties, five books on how to diet, two authorized biographies of Teilhard de Chardin, and one book by a man who lived six months with a colony of apes and didn't find out anything.

Right now I have here, in front of me: *The Bahamas Handbook* (547 pages, would you believe it?); *One of Our Brains is Draining*, a novel by someone named Max Wilk; *The Nation Keepers*, a book of essays by the likes of Wallace McCutcheon and John Robarts; *Brant County, A History, 1784–1945; Success at the Harness Races*, by Barry Meadow, 'a practical guide for handicapping winners'; *Churchill, His Paintings*, a gift book priced at only $12.50 and worth, anyway, a nickel; *Vigor for Men Over 30*, as depressing a title as any I've encountered this season, by Warren Guild, M.D., Stuart D. Cowan, and Samm Sinclair Baker (a slim book, but it took three men to write it); *A History of Peel County, 1867–1967; Nineteenth Century Pottery and Porcelain in Canada*; and *Great True Hunts*, a $17.95 picture book all about how various famous men — such as the Shah of Iran, Tito, and Roy Rogers — go out and kill beautiful animals for fun.

I can't get a copy of the new John O'Hara novel, no matter how hard I try, but I have all these other books around me, and they're piling up, piling up. A man came to my office yesterday and claimed he couldn't find me. I was there all the time, but hidden. The situation, as it often does in December, is reaching a critical phase.

9   But what about those Vancouver publishers? What exactly did they have in mind when they sent out those review copies of their lieutenant-governor book? Did they think people would *read* it, and then *write* something about it? Did they anticipate that soon they would begin receiving clippings, full of praise for their courage, imagination, and resourcefulness in publishing this significant volume? One can imagine the quotes:

10   'A stimulating and indeed an engrossing account of . . . in places thrilling, in others richly analytical . . . abrasive, tough, probing . . . profound and moving in its depiction of . . . . a very badly needed contribution to the history of . . . full of those insights we have come to expect from. . .'

11   Or did they, retaining some grasp on reality, know all the time what would happen — that one book editor after another across the country would silently pass the book along to his paper's library, hoping that someday someone on the staff — for some unthinkable reason — would want to know something about the lieutenant-governors of British Columbia?

12   The notion that perhaps there may be too many books in the world, that perhaps it is more creative *not* to write a book than to write one, occurred to me when I returned the other day from two weeks of leave and began wading through a pile of books on Christian revival, books on space exploration, and books on nineteenth-century Canada. . . . But I immediately set that whole subversive idea aside. Because after all I'd just spent the previous two weeks, uh, writing a book.

△△△

Further Reading:

Robert Fulford,
>   *Best Seat in the House: Memoirs of a Lucky Man*
>   *An Introduction to the Arts in Canada*

Structure:

1. Identify Fulford's THESIS STATEMENT.
2. Why does Fulford devote a full six paragraphs to *They Gave Royal Assent: The Lieutenant-Governors of British Columbia*, but only a few words to each of the many other books he names?
3. How convincing are Fulford's *examples*? Would you want to read any of the books he pokes fun at?
4. What technique does Fulford exploit in the very last sentence when he confesses to having just written a book, himself?

Style:

1. Where did you first detect the light TONE of this essay?
2. "Uh" is said, rarely written. Why does Fulford write it in his last sentence? Point out other examples of COLLOQUIAL language and its effects.
3. Fulford notes that *Vigor for Men Over 30* is "a slim book, but it took three men to write it" (par. 7). Point out more IRONIES in this essay.
4. Why is paragraph 7 given as one huge sentence?
5. What do the imagined book review quotations in paragraph 10 make fun of?

Ideas for Discussion and Writing:

1. Fulford begins by stating, "There's always the possibility, of course, that the world already has enough books; may, in fact, have *too many* books." Is he right? How do you feel surrounded by all the books of a library? Yet why might libraries collect the titles Fulford criticizes?
2. What kinds of books do you own? Name favourites. How do you choose one to buy?
3. Give reasons why people write books. Are all the reasons admirable?
4. **PROCESS IN WRITING:** *Review a book you have recently read, arguing with many well-chosen examples (but not with long plot summary, which bores readers). First freewrite to awaken your thoughts. Seeing what you have produced, now choose your THESIS, AUDIENCE and TONE. Do a discovery draft, then look it over. Is your point of view clear? Are there enough examples, and does each support the thesis? Whatever your tone, is it consistent? In further drafts, revise till these goals are met.*

Note: See also the Topics for Writing at the end of this chapter.

Topics for Writing

Chapter 2: Example

Search this list for the topic on which you have the most to say. Develop it in an essay that supports your point either through many short examples, or through one or more long examples. (Review the kinds *of examples listed in our chapter introduction. Also see the guidelines that follow these topics.)*

1. The way to become popular is _____.
2. One kind of music I really detest is _____.
3. _____ is my favourite holiday spot.
4. _____ is the best software for word processing.
5. My way of keeping fit is _____.
6. What I most (like/dislike) about having brothers and sisters is _____.
7. My favourite sports team is _____.
8. _____ is the sport I most like to play.
9. The most important thing I learned from my parents is _____.
10. _____ is my favourite cuisine.
11. The radio station I prefer is _____.
12. _____ is my favourite city.
13. My favourite Canadian musician is _____.
14. If I have children, the most important thing I hope to teach them is _____.
15. _____ is the world's most serious environmental problem.
16. The newspaper or magazine I like best is _____.
17. _____ is the most important social issue in Canada.
18. My favourite pastime is _____.
19. My preferred style in clothing is _____.
20. _____ is my favourite language.
21. The best way to gain self-confidence is _____.
22. The worst job I have ever had was _____.
23. My favourite type of movie is _____.
24. _____ is the most practical type of computer for my needs.
25. _____ is the best teacher I've ever had.
26. The (best/worst) program on television is _____.
27. _____ is the key to a happy marriage.
28. The (best/worst) spectator sport of all is _____.
29. _____ is the (best/worst) restaurant I've ever tried.
30. My greatest fear about the future is _____.

EXAMPLE **73**

Process in Writing: Guidelines

Follow at least some of these steps in developing your essay through examples (your teacher may suggest which ones).

1. *Take time choosing your topic, then try it out through brainstorming or freewriting. Do you have something to say? Can you supply examples? If not, try another topic.*

2. *Visualize your audience: What level of language, what* TONE, *what examples, will communicate with this person or persons? (Remember the kinds of examples listed in our chapter introduction.)*

3. *Do a rapid "discovery draft," double-spaced. Do not stop now to fix things like spelling and grammar; just get the material safely out on paper.*

4. *The next day, look this draft over. Are there enough examples? Or: Is your one long example explained in enough depth? If not, add. Does every example support your main point? If not, revise. Are examples in order of increasing importance? If not, consider rearranging to build a climax.*

5. *Check your second draft for* TRANSITIONS, *and if necessary add. Test your prose by reading aloud, then revise awkward or unclear passages. Now use the dictionary and grammar book if you need them.*

6. *Proofread your final copy slowly, word by word (if your eyes move too fast, they will "see" what* should *be there, not necessarily what* is *there).*

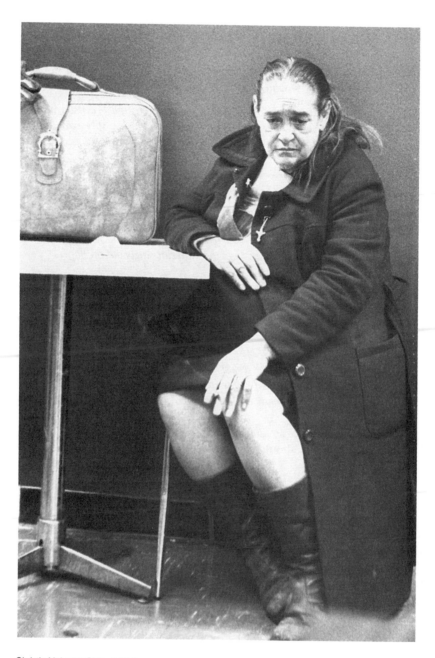

Christie McLaren/Globe & Mail

"'I bum on the street. I don't like it, but I have to. I have to survive. The only pleasure I got is my cigaret. . . . It's not a life.'"

—*Christie McLaren, "Suitcase Lady"*

DESCRIPTION

It's large and yellow and . . .

Consider the writer's tools: words in rows on a page. The writer cannot use gestures, facial expression or voice, as the public speaker does. The writer cannot use colour, shape, motion or sound, as the film-maker does. Yet words on a page can be powerful. We have all seen readers so involved in the words of a book that they forget where they are; they will fail to hear their own name called or will pass their own stop on the bus. These readers have passed into another world, living at second hand what the writer has lived or at least imagined at first hand. How does writing convey experience so vividly? In many ways. One of the most effective is description.

In simulating direct experience, description makes frequent appeals to our senses:

sight

hearing

touch

smell

taste

Emily Carr appeals to our senses of smell and sight together when in "D'Sonoqua" she writes, "Smell and blurred light oozed thickly out of the engine room, and except for one lantern on the wharf everything else was dark." Then in the next paragraph she moves on to hearing and touch: "Every gasp of the engine shook us like a great sob."

Throughout his selection "In the Trenches," Charles Yale Harrison masterfully conveys how a shelling attack looked, sounded, felt, smelled and even tasted (a piece of mud flies into the narrator's mouth. "It is cool and refreshing. It tastes earthy.") We readers were not in the front lines of World War I as Harrison was, but by the time we finish reading his description we have all too good an idea what it was like. Of course that is his purpose; in showing us the horrors he witnessed, he is telling us between the lines that war is a tragedy.

Similarly, behind every descriptive choice you make, behind every image you supply to your reader, should be your own overall purpose. In a warmup exercise such as freewriting, or even as you begin a "discovery draft," you may not yet know that purpose. But the act of writing should soon make it clear: Is your subject scary, inspiring, pitiful, exasperating, ugly, beautiful, calm or violent? Once you know, help your audience to know as well.

Sometimes a piece of descriptive writing has no thesis, because it is presented as a sketch or narrative, not as an essay. Even then it usually does have an overall purpose, like the value judgement Harrison implies about war. As you produce description, whether in an essay or not, keep that purpose in mind as you choose each detail, each image, each word. Apply it again as you revise. By the time you finish, your description, whether or not it has a thesis, will convey a message.

Figures of speech — such as the similes and metaphors discussed in Chapter 6 — are powerful tools of description. When Emily Carr writes that a person's face is "greeny-brown and wrinkled like a baked apple," or when Thierry Mallet writes that a woman's throat, "thin and bare as a vulture's neck, showed the muscles like cords," the idea of old age is swiftly and powerfully conveyed. Onomatopoetic language — words like "scuttled," "slithered," "grated" and "ooze" — describes by sounding like what it means. Emily Carr enriches her writing with these and many others. (See FIGURES OF SPEECH in the glossary of this book.)

In a description not all words are equal. Use short and strong ones from everyday life, not the long and flabby ones that some writers imagine are eloquent. Do we really "perspire" or do we "sweat"? "Ambulate" or "walk"? "Altercate" or "argue"? "Masticate" or "chew"? "Expectorate" or "spit"? It is obvious that the second term in each case is stronger, more vivid, more descriptive. Why, then, would we use the first?

Choose words that convey the right feeling as well as the right dictionary meaning. One student closed a pretty description of the ocean by saying "the water was as still as a pan full of oil." The image of water as oil may imply stillness, but this water is not exactly something we would want to dive into or even watch at sunset — we'd be too busy thinking of pollution! Another person described forest trees in autumn as being the colour of a fire engine. The colour may be right, but will the image of a large truck perched in the tree branches really give us that autumn feeling?

Spend the time, then, to "feel" as well as "think" your words. Search drafts for weak or inexact or inappropriate terms, and replace them. If the right word doesn't come, find it in a dictionary or thesaurus. If you are computerized, your electronic thesaurus is so fast that now you can afford to check out dozens of words, making sure your overall idea or feeling, whatever it is, comes through clearly.

Note: Many authors in other chapters use description to help make their point. See especially these examples:

Sylvia Fraser, "My Other Self," p. 27
Ray Guy, "Outharbor Menu," p. 54
Catherine Pigott, "Chicken-Hips," p. 160
Joy Kogawa, "Grinning and Happy," p. 312
Wendy Dennis, "A Tongue-Lashing for Deaf Ears," p. 332

Thierry Mallet

The Firewood Gatherers*

Thierry Mallet joined the French fur company Revillon Frères as an apprentice trader, and went on to establish and oversee a large group of trading posts in the Barrens of the Canadian arctic. Through each of the 20 years before our selection was published, Mallet had travelled through the region, sometimes at great risk, inspecting those posts. His intimate knowledge of the land and of the people who lived on it led him to write a small book, Plain Tales of the North. *Then in 1930 appeared his second small volume,* Glimpses of the Barren Lands. *Both books were published in New York by Revillon Frères. Mallet's style is spare but powerful, as if to reflect the arctic itself. Our selection comes from* Glimpses *of the Barren Lands.*

1   Our camp had been pitched at the foot of a great, bleak, ragged hill, a few feet from the swirling waters of the Kazan River. The two small green tents, pegged down tight with heavy rocks, shivered and rippled under the faint touch of the northern breeze. A thin wisp of smoke rose from the embers of the fire.

2   Eleven o'clock, and the sun had just set under a threatening bank of clouds far away to the northwest. It was the last day of June and daylight still. But the whole country seemed bathed in gray, boulders, moss, sand, even the few willow shrubs scattered far apart in the hollows of the hills. Half a mile away, upstream, the caribou-skin topeks of an Eskimo settlement, fading away amid the background, were hardly visible to the eye.

3   Three small gray specks could be seen moving slowly above our camp. Human shapes, but so puny, so insignificant-looking against the wild rocky side of that immense hill! Bending down, then straightening up, they seemed to totter aimlessly through the chaos of stone, searching for some hidden treasure.

4   Curiosity, or perhaps a touch of loneliness, suddenly moved me to leave camp and join those three forlorn figures so far away above me near the sky line.

*Editor's title.

Slowly I made my way along the steep incline, following at first the bed of a dried-up stream. Little by little the river sank beneath me, while the breeze, increasing in strength, whistled past, lashing and stinging my face and hands. I had lost sight momentarily of the three diminutive figures which had lured me on to these heights. After a while a reindeer trail enabled me to leave the coulee and led me again in the right direction, through a gigantic mass of granite which the frost of thousands of years had plucked from the summit of the hill and hurled hundreds of feet below.

At last I was able to reach the other side of the avalanche of rocks and suddenly emerged comparatively in the open, on the brim of a slight depression at the bottom of which a few dead willow bushes showed their bleached branches above the stones and the gray moss. There I found the three silent figures huddled close together, gathering, one by one, the twigs of the precious wood. Two little girls, nine or ten years old, so small, so helpless, and an aged woman, so old, so frail, that my first thought was to marvel at the idea of their being able to climb so far from their camp to that lonely spot.

An Eskimo great-grandmother and her two great-granddaughters, all three contributing their share to the support of the tribe. Intent on their work, or most probably too shy to look up at the strange white man whom, until then, they had only seen at a distance, they gave me full opportunity to watch them.

All were dressed alike, in boots, trousers, and coats of caribou skin. The children wore little round leather caps reaching far over their ears, the crown decorated with beadwork designs. One of them carried on the wrist, as a bracelet, a narrow strip of bright red flannel. Their faces were round and healthy, the skin sunburned to a dark copper color, but their cheeks showed a tinge of blood which gave them, under the tan, a peculiar complexion like the color of a ripe plum. Their little hands were bare and black, the scratches caused by the dead twigs showing plainly in white, while their fingers seemed cramped with the cold.

The old woman was bareheaded, quite bald at the top of the head, with long wisps of gray hair waving in the wind. The skin of her neck and face had turned black, dried up like an old piece of parchment. Her cheeks were sunken and her cheek bones protruded horribly. Her open mouth showed bare gums, for her teeth were all gone, and her throat, thin and bare as a vulture's neck, showed the muscles like cords. Her hands were as thin as the hands of a skeleton, the tip of each finger curved in like a claw. Her eyes, once black, now light grey, remained half closed, deep down in their sockets.

She was stone blind.

Squatting on her heels, she held, spread in front of her, a small reindeer skin. As soon as the children dropped a branch beside her, she felt for it gropingly; then, her hands closing on it greedily, like talons, she would break it into small pieces, a few inches long, which she carefully placed on the mat at her feet.

12   Both little girls, while searching diligently through the clumps of dead willows for what they could break off and carry away, kept absolutely silent. Not only did they never call to one another when one of them needed help, but they seemed to watch each other intently whenever they could. Now and then, one of them would hit the ground two or three times with the flat of her hand. If the other had her head turned away at the time, she appeared to be startled and always wheeled round to look. Then both children would make funny little motions with their hands at one another.

13   The little girls were deaf and dumb.

14   After a while they had gathered all the wood the reindeer skin could contain. Then the children went up to the old woman and conveyed to her the idea that it was time to go home. One of them took her hands in hers and guided them to two corners of the mat, while the other tapped her gently on the shoulder.

15   The old, old woman understood. Slowly and carefully she tied up the four corners of the caribou skin over the twigs, silently watched by the little girls. Groaning, she rose to her feet, tottering with weakness and old age, and with a great effort swung the small bundle over her back. Then one little girl took her by the hand, while the other, standing behind, grasped the tail of her caribou coat. Slowly, very slowly, step by step they went their way, following a reindeer trail around rocks, over stones, down, down the hill, straight toward their camp, the old woman carrying painfully for the young, the deaf and dumb leading and steering safely the blind.

△ △

Further Reading:

Maurice Metayer, ed. and trans., *I, Nuligak* (autobiography)
Dorothy Eber, ed., *Pitseolak: Pictures out of My Life*
Penny Petrone, ed., *Northern Voices: Inuit Writing in English*
Farley Mowat, *People of the Deer*
Yves Thériault, *Agaguk* (novel)

Structure:

1. "The Firewood Gatherers" is *narrated* in chronological order. Find at least 15 words or phrases that signal the flow of time.
2. Which paragraphs suspend the narration to *describe?*
3. To what extent is "The Firewood Gatherers" based on *comparison and contrast?*
4. What gives the final sentence its power?

Style:

1. How CONCRETE or ABSTRACT is the language of this selection? Point out passages that illustrate your answer.
2. How economical or wasteful is Mallet's writing? Does all the description make this passage wordy? Why or why not?
3. Mallet's description of the old woman, in paragraph 9, is clothed in SIMILES (her throat is "thin and bare as a vulture's neck.") Point out others in this paragraph.
4. In paragraph 5 Mallet tells of "a gigantic mass of granite which the frost of thousands of years had plucked from the summit of the hill and hurled hundreds of feet below." Where else does he use PERSONIFICATION?

Ideas for Discussion and Writing:

1. How do this traditional society and our own differ in their views of the old and the disadvantaged? What would the blind great-grandmother and her handicapped descendants be doing today in your town or city?
2. If you live with your parents and grandparents, analyze the benefits and drawbacks for all three generations. Now imagine yourself retired. Would you rather live alone, or with your descendants, or in an institution for others your age? Why? And what things could you now do to feel useful?
3. If you have read "Suitcase Lady" by Christie McLaren, compare the two women. If you had to choose, would you be the Inuit great-grandmother of the Barrens or the homeless "suitcase lady" of Toronto? Why?
4. **PROCESS IN WRITING:** *Go to see the oldest or youngest person you know. Take notes. At home or in class, draft a vivid description. Then in further drafts sharpen word choice, IMAGES and FIGURES OF SPEECH, to present your subject strongly. Test the prose aloud before doing your final version.*

Note: See also the Topics for Writing at the end of this chapter.

Christie McLaren

Suitcase Lady*

When Christie McLaren wrote "Suitcase Lady" she was a student at the University of Waterloo, reporting for the Toronto Globe and Mail as a part of her English co-op work experience. After graduation she spent a year and a half at the Winnipeg Free Press, then returned to the Globe, where she continued to report on a variety of issues. An avid hiker, skier and canoeist, McLaren channelled her love of the outdoors into several years of reporting on forestry, energy and other environmental issues. Another of McLaren's interests is photography (she took the portrait used at the beginning of this chapter). Though a professional journalist, she says that "writing is nothing but pain while you're doing it and nothing but relief when it's done. Any joy or satisfaction, I think, is a bit of fleeting luck." McLaren spent several nights with "the Vicomtesse" before hearing the story she reports in this selection. The article and photograph first appeared in 1981 in the Globe.

1   Night after night, the woman with the red hair and the purple dress sits in the harsh light of a 24-hour doughnut shop on Queen Street West.

2   Somewhere in her bleary eyes and in the deep lines of her face is a story that probably no one will ever really know. She is taking pains to write something on a notepad and crying steadily.

3   She calls herself Vicomtesse Antonia The Linds'ays. She's the suitcase lady of Queen Street.

4   No one knows how many women there are like her in Toronto. They carry their belongings in shopping bags and spend their days and nights scrounging for food. They have no one and nowhere to go.

5   This night, in a warm corner with a pot of tea and a pack of Player's, the Vicomtesse is in a mood to talk.

6   Out of her past come a few scraps: a mother named Savaria; the child of a poor family in Montreal; a brief marriage when she was 20; a son in

---

*Editor's title.

Toronto who is now 40. "We never got along well because I didn't bring him up. I was too poor. He never call me mama."

She looks out the window. She's 60 years old. 7

With her words she spins herself a cocoon. She talks about drapes 8
and carpets, castles and kings. She often lapses into French. She lets her tea get cold. Her hands are big, rough, farmer's hands. How she ended up in the doughnut shop remains a mystery, maybe even to her.

"Before, I had a kitchen and a room and my own furniture. I had to 9
leave everything and go."

It's two years that she's been on the go, since the rooming houses 10
stopped taking her. "I don't have no place to stay."

So she walks. A sturdy coat covers her dress and worn leather boots 11
are on her feet. But her big legs are bare and chapped and she has a ragged cough.

Yes, she says, her legs get tired. She has swollen ankles and, with no 12
socks in her boots, she has blisters. She says she has socks — in the suitcase — but they make her feet itch.

As for money, "I bum on the street. I don't like it, but I have to. I 13
have to survive. The only pleasure I got is my cigaret." She lights another one. "It's not a life."

She recalls the Saturday, a long time ago, when she made $27, and 14
laughs when she tells about how she had to make the money last through Sunday, too. Now she gets "maybe $7 or $8," and eats "very poor."

When she is asked how people treat her, the answer is very matter-of- 15
fact: "Some give money. Some are very polite and some are rude."

In warm weather, she passes her time at the big square in front of City 16
Hall. When it's cold she takes her suitcase west to the doughnut shop.

The waitresses who bring food to the woman look upon her with 17
compassion. They persuaded their boss that her sitting does no harm.

Where does she sleep? "Any place I can find a place to sleep. In the 18
park, in stores — like here I stay and sit, on Yonge Street." She shrugs. Sometimes she goes into an underground parking garage.

She doesn't look like she knows what sleep is. "This week I sleep 19
three hours in four days. I feel tired but I wash my face with cold water and I feel okay." Some questions make her eyes turn from the window and stare hard. Then they well over with tears. Like the one about loneliness. "I don't talk much to people," she answers. "Just the elderly, sometimes, in the park."

Her suitcase is full of dreams. 20

Carefully, she unzips it and pulls out a sheaf of papers — "my 21
concertos."

Each page is crammed with neatly written musical notes — the careful 22
writing she does on the doughnut shop table — but the bar lines are missing. Questions about missing bar lines she tosses aside. Each

"concerto" has a French name — Tresor, La Tempete, Le Retour — and each one bears the signature of the Vicomtesse. She smiles and points to one. "A very lovely piece of music. I like it."

23   She digs in her suitcase again, almost shyly, and produces a round plastic box. Out of it emerges a tiara. Like a little girl, she smooths back her dirty hair and proudly puts it on. No one in the doughnut shop seems to notice.

24   She cares passionately about the young, the old and the ones who suffer. So who takes care of the suitcase lady?

25   "God takes care of me, that's for sure," she says, nodding thoughtfully. "But I'm not what you call crazy about religion. I believe always try to do the best to help people — the elderly, and kids, and my country, and my city of Toronto, Ontario."

△△△

Further Reading:

Ian Adams, *The Poverty Wall*
George Orwell, *Down and Out in Paris and London*
Things I Cannot Change (NFB documentary, 55 minutes)

Structure:

1. "Suitcase Lady" was a feature article in the Toronto *Globe and Mail.* As newspaper journalism, how does it differ from a typical ESSAY?
2. What does the opening description achieve?
3. What do the many quotations do for the *description?*
4. McLaren's own photograph of "the Vicomtesse" appeared with the article in *The Globe.* What does her photograph do that the descriptive article cannot do? What does the article do that the photograph cannot do?
5. Explain the IRONY of the closing.

Style:

1. Why is the vocabulary of "Suitcase Lady" so easy?
2. "With her words she spins herself a cocoon," states McLaren in paragraph 8. How appropriate is this METAPHOR?
3. Which of the many concrete details most strongly convey the flavour of this suitcase lady's life?

Ideas for Discussion and Writing:

1. If you have read "The Firewood Gatherers," by Thierry Mallet, compare the worlds of the aboriginal great-grandmother in the arctic

and of the suitcase lady in the big city. In what ways is each person better off? In what ways is each worse off? If you had to choose, which person would you be, and why?

2. "It's not a life," says "the Vicomtesse" in paragraph 13. What is our nation doing to help make it "a life" for the homeless? What prevents further action?

3. How do you react to people who, like the suitcase lady, "bum on the street"? When do you give and when do you not give? How do your choices make you feel, and why?

4. In paragraph 6 the suitcase lady speaks of her son in Toronto: "We never got along well because I didn't bring him up. I was too poor. He never call me mama." In the area where you live, how much money does a family need to stay together? To avoid quarrels over money? To feel hopeful about the future?

5. **PROCESS IN WRITING:** *Tape an interview with someone who in economic status, age, values or some other respect is your opposite. Then write a profile. Like McLaren, portray your subject through his or her best comments. Now add many* IMAGES *of physical appearance. Edit for conciseness and finally correctness. Then read your final draft, with feeling, to the class.*

Note: See also the Topics for Writing at the end of this chapter.

Margaret Laurence

Where the World Began

Margaret Laurence's untimely death in 1987 was mourned across the nation by readers who had seen their own humanity reflected in her novels, and by many writers who had lost a generous friend. Born in 1926 in the prairie town of Neepawa, Manitoba and educated in Winnipeg, Laurence spent 1950 to 1957 in Somalia and Ghana with her engineer husband. There she began to write some of the best fiction yet produced by a Canadian about the Third World. Laurence later separated from her husband, and in 1962 moved with the children to England. In her writing, though, she returned to western Canada. Renaming her hometown "Manawaka" and recasting it in fiction, she completed what is probably our best-loved Canadian novel, The Stone Angel *(1964). It is the story of proud and stubborn Hagar Shipley, one of many strong women who would be central to Laurence's fiction. More novels followed:* A Jest of God *(1966),* The Fire-Dwellers *(1969), and* The Diviners *(1974; adapted as a CBC television special in 1992). These, along with her book of collected short stories* A Bird in the House *(1970), made of "Manawaka" and its people a celebrated microcosm of the larger world. By the early seventies Laurence had returned to Canada, settling in Lakefield, Ontario. But* The Diviners *was to be her last novel. She now turned to activism as a feminist, as a human rights advocate, and as a foe of the nuclear arms race. "It is my feeling," she wrote, "that as we grow older we should become not less radical but more so." In her last years she worked tirelessly to save the planet that she had first known "where the world began." Our selection is from Laurence's 1976 book of essays,* Heart of a Stranger. *(See also p. 193 of this book for another selection by Laurence.)*

1   A strange place it was, that place where the world began. A place of incredible happenings, splendours and revelations, despairs like multitudinous pits of isolated hells. A place of shadow-spookiness, inhabited by the unknowable dead. A place of jubilation and of mourning, horrible and beautiful.

2   It was, in fact, a small prairie town.

3   Because that settlement and that land were my first and for many years my only real knowledge of this planet, in some profound way they remain my world, my way of viewing. My eyes were formed there. Towns

86

like ours, set in a sea of land, have been described thousands of times as dull, bleak, flat, uninteresting. I have had it said to me that the railway trip across Canada is spectacular, except for the prairies, when it would be desirable to go to sleep for several days, until the ordeal is over. I am always unable to argue this point effectively. All I can say is — well, you really have to live there to know that country. The town of my childhood could be called bizarre, agonizingly repressive or cruel at times, and the land in which it grew could be called harsh in the violence of its seasonal changes. But never merely flat or uninteresting. Never dull.

In winter, we used to hitch rides on the back of the milk sleigh, our   4 moccasins squeaking and slithering on the hard rutted snow of the roads, our hands in ice-bubbled mitts hanging onto the box edge of the sleigh for dear life, while Bert grinned at us through his great frosted moustache and shouted the horse into speed, daring us to stay put. Those mornings, rising, there would be the perpetual fascination of the frost feathers on windows, the ferns and flowers and eerie faces traced there during the night by unseen artists of the wind. Evenings, coming back from skating, the sky would be black but not dark, for you could see a cold glitter of stars from one side of the earth's rim to the other. And then the sometime astonishment when you saw the Northern Lights flaring across the sky, like the scrawled signature of God. After a blizzard, when the snowploughs hadn't yet got through, school would be closed for the day, the assumption being that the town's young could not possibly flounder through five feet of snow in the pursuit of education. We would then gaily don snowshoes and flounder for miles out into the white dazzling deserts, in pursuit of a different kind of knowing. If you came back too close to night, through the woods at the foot of the town hill, the thin black branches of poplar and chokecherry now meringued with frost, sometimes you heard coyotes. Or maybe the banshee wolf-voices were really only inside your head.

Summers were scorching, and when no rain came and the wheat   5 became bleached and dried before it headed, the faces of farmers and townsfolk would not smile much, and you took for granted, because it never seemed to have been any different, the frequent knocking at the back door and the young men standing there, mumbling or thrusting defiantly their requests for a drink of water and a sandwich if you could spare it. They were riding the freights, and you never knew where they had come from, or where they might end up, if anywhere. The Drought and Depression were like evil deities which had been there always. You understood and did not understand.

Yet the outside world had its continuing marvels. The poplar bluffs   6 and the small river were filled and surrounded with a zillion different grasses, stones, and weed flowers. The meadowlarks sang undaunted from the twanging telephone wires along the gravel highway. Once we found an old flat-bottomed scow, and launched her, poling along the shallow brown waters, mending her with wodges of hastily chewed Spearmint, grounding her among the tangles of yellow marsh marigolds that grew succulently along the banks of the shrunken river, while the sun made our skins smell dusty-warm.

7   My best friend lived in an apartment above some stores on Main Street (its real name was Mountain Avenue, goodness knows why), an elegant apartment with royal-blue velvet curtains. The back roof, scarcely sloping at all, was corrugated tin, of a furnace-like warmth on a July afternoon, and we would sit there drinking lemonade and looking across the back lane at the Fire Hall. Sometimes our vigil would be rewarded. Oh joy! Somebody's house burning down! We had an almost-perfect callousness in some ways. Then the wooden tower's bronze bell would clonk and toll like a thousand speeded funerals in a time of plague, and in a few minutes the team of giant black horses would cannon forth, pulling the fire wagon like some scarlet chariot of the Goths, while the firemen clung with one hand, adjusting their helmets as they went.

8   The oddities of the place were endless. An elderly lady used to serve, as her afternoon tea offering to other ladies, soda biscuits spread with peanut butter and topped with a whole marshmallow. Some considered this slightly eccentric, when compared with chopped egg sandwiches, and admittedly talked about her behind her back, but no one ever refused these delicacies or indicated to her that they thought she had slipped a cog. Another lady dyed her hair a bright and cheery orange, by strangers often mistaken at twenty paces for a feather hat. My own beloved stepmother wore a silver fox neckpiece, a whole pelt, *with the embalmed (?) head still on.* My Ontario Irish grandfather said, "sparrow grass," a more interesting term than asparagus. The town dump was known as "the nuisance grounds," a phrase fraught with weird connotations, as though the effluvia of our lives was beneath contempt but at the same time was subtly threatening to the determined and sometimes hysterical propriety of our ways.

9   Some oddities were, as idiom had it, "funny ha ha"; others were "funny peculiar." Some were not so very funny at all. An old man lived, deranged, in a shack in the valley. Perhaps he wasn't even all that old, but to us he seemed a wild Methuselah figure, shambling among the underbrush and the tall couchgrass, muttering indecipherable curses or blessings, a prophet who had forgotten his prophesies. Everyone in town knew him, but no one knew him. He lived among us as though only occasionally and momentarily visible. The kids called him Andy Gump, and feared him. Some sought to prove their bravery by tormenting him. They were the mediaeval bear baiters, and he the lumbering bewildered bear, half blind, only rarely turning to snarl.

Everything is to be found in a town like mine. Belsen,° writ small but with the same ink.

All of us cast stones in one shape or another. In grade school, among   10 the vulnerable and violet girls we were, the feared and despised were those few older girls from what was charmingly termed "the wrong side of the tracks." Tough in talk and tougher in muscle, they were said to be whores already. And may have been, that being about the only profession readily available to them.

The dead lived in that place, too. Not only the grandparents who   11 had, in local parlance, "passed on" and who gloomed, bearded or bonneted, from the sepia photographs in old albums, but also the uncles, forever eighteen or nineteen, whose names were carved on the granite family stones in the cemetery, but whose bones lay in France. My own young mother lay in that graveyard, beside other dead of our kin, and when I was ten, my father, too, only forty, left the living town for the dead dwelling on the hill.

When I was eighteen, I couldn't wait to get out of that town, away   12 from the prairies. I did not know then that I would carry the land and town all my life within my skull, that they would form the mainspring and source of the writing I was to do, wherever and however far away I might live.

This was my territory in the time of my youth, and in a sense my life   13 since then has been an attempt to look at it, to come to terms with it. Stultifying to the mind it certainly could be, and sometimes was, but not to the imagination. It was many things, but it was never dull.

The same, I now see, could be said for Canada in general. Why on   14 earth did generations of Canadians pretend to believe this country dull? We knew perfectly well it wasn't. Yet for so long we did not proclaim what we knew. If our upsurge of so-called nationalism seems odd or irrelevant to outsiders, and even to some of our own people (*what's all the fuss about?*), they might try to understand that for many years we valued ourselves insufficiently, living as we did under the huge shadows of those two dominating figures, Uncle Sam and Britannia. We have only just begun to value ourselves, our land, our abilities. We have only just begun to recognize our legends and to give shape to our myths.

There are, God knows, enough aspects to deplore about this country.   15 When I see the killing of our lakes and rivers with industrial wastes, I feel rage and despair. When I see our industries and natural resources increasingly taken over by America, I feel an overwhelming discouragement, especially as I cannot simply say "damn Yankees." It should never be forgotten that it is we ourselves who have sold such a large amount

---

°Belsen: a notorious Nazi death camp.

of our birthright for a mess of plastic Progress.° When I saw the War Measures Act being invoked in 1970, I lost forever the vestigial remains of the naive wish-belief that repression could not happen here, or would not. And yet, of course, I had known all along in the deepest and often hidden caves of the heart that anything can happen anywhere, for the seeds of both man's freedom and his captivity are found everywhere, even in the microcosm of a prairie town. But in raging against our injustices, our stupidities, I do so *as family*, as I did, and still do in writing, about those aspects of my town which I hated and which are always in some ways aspects of myself.

16   The land still draws me more than other lands. I have lived in Africa and in England, but splendid as both can be, they do not have the power to move me in the same way as, for example, that part of southern Ontario where I spent four months last summer in a cedar cabin beside a river. "Scratch a Canadian, and you find a phony pioneer," I used to say to myself in warning. But all the same it is true, I think, that we are not yet totally alienated from physical earth, and let us only pray we do not become so. I once thought that my lifelong fear and mistrust of cities made me a kind of old-fashioned freak; now I see it differently.

17   The cabin has a long window across its front western wall, and sitting at the oak table there in the mornings, I used to look out at the river and at the tall trees beyond, green-gold in the early light. The river was bronze; the sun caught it strangely, reflecting upon its surface the near-shore sand ripples underneath. Suddenly, the crescenting of a fish, gone before the eye could clearly give image to it. The old man next door said these leaping fish were carp. Himself, he preferred muskie, for he was a real fisherman and the muskie gave him a fight. The wind most often blew from the south, and the river flowed toward the south, so when the water was wind-riffled, and the current was strong, the river seemed to be flowing both ways. I liked this, and interpreted it as an omen, a natural symbol.

18   A few years ago, when I was back in Winnipeg, I gave a talk at my old college. It was open to the public, and afterward a very old man came up to me and asked me if my maiden name had been Wemyss. I said yes, thinking he might have known my father or my grandfather. But no. "When I was a young lad," he said, "I once worked for your great-grandfather, Robert Wemyss, when he had the sheep ranch at Raeburn." I think that was a moment when I realized all over again something of great importance to me. My long-ago families came from Scotland and Ireland, but in a sense that no longer mattered so much. My true roots were here.

°for a mess of plastic Progress: allusion to Genesis 25, in which the hunter Esau sells his birthright to his brother Jacob for a mess of "pottage."

I am not very patriotic, in the usual meaning of that word. I cannot 19
say "My country right or wrong" in any political, social or literary context. But one thing is inalterable, for better or worse, for life.

This is where my world began. A world which includes the ancestors 20
— both my own and other people's ancestors who become mine. A
world which formed me, and continues to do so, even while I fought it
in some of its aspects, and continue to do so. A world which gave me
my own lifework to do, because it was here that I learned the sight of
my own particular eyes.

∆ ∆

Further Reading:

Margaret Laurence,
> *The Stone Angel*
> *The Diviners*
> *A Bird in the House*
> *Dance on the Earth* (memoir)

Clara Thomas, *The Manawaka World of Margaret Laurence*
Alice Munro, *Lives of Girls and Women* (novel)
Sinclair Ross, *As for Me and My House* (novel)

Structure:

1. What organizational goals does Laurence achieve by repeating her title phrase in both the opening and closing?
2. Early in the essay, Laurence puts her main point into a THESIS STATE-MENT. Identify it.
3. Does Laurence mostly *compare* or *contrast* her prairie town to the nation as a whole?
4. Point out three qualities of her home town that Laurence later sees in her nation — or even in the world as a whole. Cite a passage to illustrate each *comparison.*
5. What key role do paragraphs 12-14 play in organizing the argument?
6. Point out three paragraphs that develop this essay mainly through *description.* Which one seems to convey most strongly the flavour of Laurence's prairie childhood? Point out its best IMAGES and tell what each contributes.
7. Why does Laurence end with the word "eyes"?

Style:

1. Why does Laurence begin with pairs of opposites ("A place of jubila-tion and of mourning, horrible and beautiful"—par. 1)?
2. Like Emily Carr in "D'Sonoqua," Laurence plays with words. Discuss

the effects of these terms: "zillion" (par. 6), "wodges" (par. 6), "clonk" (par. 7), "cannon forth" (par. 7) and "gloomed" (par. 11).

3. To *describe* winter on the prairie, paragraph 4 gives a profusion of SENSE IMAGES. While one person reads this passage aloud, other class members can raise their hand every time they detect an appeal to their sense of sight, hearing or touch. What is the total effect of these images?

4. In paragraph 3 the prairie is "a sea of land," and in paragraph 4 it becomes "white dazzling deserts." Locate at least five other FIGURES OF SPEECH in this descriptive essay, and analyze the impact of each.

Ideas for Discussion and Writing:

1. "Why on earth did generations of Canadians pretend to believe this country dull?" Laurence asks in paragraph 14. What is your answer? How dull or exciting do you consider your corner of Canada? Defend your view with examples.

2. "Everything is to be found in a town like mine. Belsen, writ small but with the same ink," Laurence writes in paragraph 9. Give one image of "Belsen, writ small" that you saw in your own childhood neighbourhood. Name one time and place in Canada where "Belsen" has been "writ large."

3. In paragraph 15 Laurence calls her home town a "microcosm" (literally "small world"). As you think of the town or the city neighbourhood of your own childhood (whether in Canada or abroad), does it also seem a microcosm of the world? Does it illustrate Laurence's idea that "anything can happen anywhere" (par. 15)? And as you imagine other "microcosms" around the world, do you see mostly differences or mostly similarities to the people in your own?

4. **PROCESS IN WRITING:** Describe *your own home town or neighbourhood, in an essay entitled "Where My World Began." First close your eyes for a long time, and remember. Now fill a page with brainstorming or freewriting. Look it over. Have you put the physical appearance of the houses, the streets and the people into words? Have you shown also how things sounded, felt, smelled and tasted? If not, take more notes. Now choose a* THESIS *that represents the overall impression, the overall meaning, of your memories. Write a fast discovery draft, drawing on both your notes and thesis. A day later look the draft over. Can your audience "see" the point yet? If not, add still more* SENSE IMAGES. *Finally, edit for style and correctness before doing the final draft. Read aloud, with feeling, to the class.*

Note: See also the Topics for Writing at the end of this chapter.

Charles Yale Harrison

In the Trenches

Charles Yale Harrison (1898–1954) was born in Philadelphia and grew up in Montreal. His independent spirit revealed itself early: in grade four he condemned Shakespeare's The Merchant of Venice *as anti-Semitic, and when his teacher beat him he quit school. At 16 he went to work for the* Montreal Star *and at 18 joined the Canadian army. As a machine gunner in France and Belgium during 1917 and 1918, Harrison witnessed the gruesome front-line scenes he was later to describe in fiction. He was wounded at Amiens and decorated for bravery in action. After the war Harrison returned to Montreal but soon left for New York, where he began a career in public relations for the labour movement and for numerous humanitarian causes. He also wrote several books, both non-fiction and fiction. By far the best is* Generals Die in Bed, *an account of trench warfare that shocked the public and became the best seller of 1930. Spare in style, biting and vivid, this autobiographical novel was described by the* New York Evening Post *as "the best of the war books." From it comes our selection.*

We leave the piles of rubble that was once a little Flemish peasant town and wind our way, in Indian file, up through the muddy communication trench. In the dark we stumble against the sides of the trench and tear our hands and clothing on the bits of embedded barbed wire that runs through the earth here as though it were a geological deposit. 1

Fry, who is suffering with his feet, keeps slipping into holes and crawling out, all the way up. I can hear him coughing and panting behind me. 2

I hear him slither into a water-filled hole. It has a green scum on it. Brown and I fish him out. 3

"I can't go any farther," he wheezes. "Let me lie here, I'll come on later." 4

We block the narrow trench and the oncoming men stumble on us, banging their equipment and mess tins on the sides of the ditch. Some trip over us. They curse under their breaths. 5

Our captain, Clark, pushes his way through the mess. He is an Imperial, an Englishman, and glories in his authority. 6

7   "So it's you again," he shouts. "Come on, get up. Cold feet, eh, getting near the line?"

8   Fry mumbles something indistinctly. I, too, offer an explanation. Clark ignores me.

9   "Get up, you're holding up the line," he says to Fry.

10   Fry does not move.

11   "No wonder we're losing the bloody war," Clark says loudly. The men standing near-by laugh. Encouraged by his success, the captain continues:

12   "Here, sergeant, stick a bayonet up his behind — that'll make him move." A few of us help Fry to his feet, and somehow we manage to keep him going.

13   We proceed cautiously, heeding the warnings of those ahead of us. At last we reach our positions.

Δ Δ Δ

14   It is midnight when we arrive at our positions. The men we are relieving give us a few instructions and leave quickly, glad to get out.

15   It is September and the night is warm. Not a sound disturbs the quiet. Somewhere away far to our right we hear the faint sound of continuous thunder. The exertion of the trip up the line has made us sweaty and tired. We slip most of our accouterments off and lean against the parados. We have been warned that the enemy is but a few hundred yards off, so we speak in whispers. It is perfectly still. I remember nights like this in the Laurentians. The harvest moon rides overhead.

16   Our sergeant, Johnson, appears around the corner of the bay, stealthily like a ghost. He gives us instructions:

17   "One man up on sentry duty! Keep your gun covered with the rubber sheet! No smoking!"

18   He hurries on to the next bay. Fry mounts the step and peers into No Man's Land. He is rested now and says that if he can only get a good pair of boots he will be happy. He has taken his boots off and stands in his stockinged feet. He shows us where his heel is cut. His boots do not fit. The sock is wet with blood. He wants to take his turn at sentry duty first so that he can rest later on. We agree.

19   Cleary and I sit on the firing-step and talk quietly.

20   "So this is war."

21   "Quiet."

22   "Yes, just like the country back home, eh?"

23   We talk of the trench; how we can make it more comfortable.

24   We light cigarettes against orders and cup our hands around them to hide the glow. We sit thinking. Fry stands motionless with his steel helmet shoved down almost over his eyes. He leans against the parapet motionless. There is a quiet dignity about his posture. I remember what

we were told at the base about falling asleep on sentry duty. I nudge his leg. He grunts.

"Asleep?" I whisper. 25

"No," he answers, "I'm all right." 26

"What do you see?" 27

"Nothing. Wire and posts." 28

"Tired?" 29

"I'm all right." 30

The sergeant reappears after a while. We squinch our cigarettes. 31

"Everything O.K. here?" 32

I nod. 33

"Look out over there. They got the range on us. Watch out." 34

We light another cigarette. We continue our aimless talk. 35

"I wonder what St. Catherine Street looks like —" 36

"Same old thing, I suppose — stores, whores, theaters —" 37

"Like to be there just the same —" 38

"Me too." 39

We sit and puff our fags for half a minute or so. 40

I try to imagine what Montreal looks like. The images are murky. All 41
that is unreality. The trench, Cleary, Fry, the moon overhead — this is real.

In his corner of the bay Fry is beginning to move from one foot to 42
another. It is time to relieve him. He steps down and I take his place. I
look into the wilderness of posts and wire in front of me.

After a while my eyes begin to water. I see the whole army of wire 43
posts begin to move like a silent host towards me.

I blink my eyes and they halt. 44

I doze a little and come to with a jerk. 45

So this is war, I say to myself again for the hundredth time. Down on 46
the firing-step the boys are sitting like dead men. The thunder to the
right has died down. There is absolutely no sound.

I try to imagine how an action would start. I try to fancy the preliminary 47
bombardment. I remember all the precautions one has to take to protect
one's life. Fall flat on your belly, we had been told time and time again.
The shriek of the shell, the instructor in trench warfare said, was no
warning because the shell traveled faster than its sound. First, he had
said, came the explosion of the shell — then came the shriek and then
you hear the firing of the gun . . . .

From the stories I heard from veterans and from newspaper reports I 48
conjure up a picture of an imaginary action. I see myself getting the
Lewis gun in position. I see it spurting darts of flame into the night. I
hear the roar of battle. I feel elated. Then I try to fancy the horrors of
the battle. I see Cleary, Fry and Brown stretched out on the firing-step.
They are stiff and their faces are white and set in the stillness of death.
Only I remain alive.

49   An inaudible movement in front of me pulls me out of the dream. I look down and see Fry massaging his feet. All is still. The moon sets slowly and everything becomes dark.

50   The sergeant comes into the bay again and whispers to me:

51   "Keep your eyes open now — they might come over on a raid now that it's dark. The wire's cut over there — " He points a little to my right.

52   I stand staring into the darkness. Everything moves rapidly again as I stare. I look away for a moment and the illusion ceases.

53   Something leaps towards my face.

54   I jerk back, afraid.

55   Instinctively I feel for my rifle in the corner of the bay.

56   It is a rat.

57   It is as large as a tom-cat. It is three feet away from my face and it looks steadily at me with its two staring, beady eyes. It is fat. Its long tapering tail curves away from its padded hindquarters. There is still a little light from the stars and this light shines faintly on its sleek skin. With a darting movement it disappears. I remember with a cold feeling that it was fat, and why.

58   Cleary taps my shoulder. It is time to be relieved.

Δ Δ Δ

59   Over in the German lines I hear quick, sharp reports. Then the red-tailed comets of the *minenwerfer*° sail high in the air, making parabolas of red light as they come towards us. They look pretty, like the fireworks when we left Montreal. The sergeant rushes into the bay of the trench, breathless. "Minnies," he shouts, and dashes on.

60   In that instant there is a terrific roar directly behind us.

61   The night whistles and flashes red.

62   The trench rocks and sways.

63   Mud and earth leap into the air, come down upon us in heaps.

64   We throw ourselves upon our faces, clawing our nails into the soft earth in the bottom of the trench.

65   Another!

66   This one crashes to splinters about twenty feet in front of the bay.

67   Part of the parapet caves in.

68   We try to burrow into the ground like frightened rats.

69   The shattering explosions splinter the air in a million fragments. I taste salty liquid on my lips. My nose is bleeding from the force of the detonations.

70   SOS flares go up along our front calling for help from our artillery.

°*minenwerfer*: mine-throwing trench mortars.

The signals sail into the air and explode, giving forth showers of red, white and blue lights held aloft by a silken parachute.

The sky is lit by hundreds of fancy fireworks like a night carnival. 71

The air shrieks and cat-calls. 72

Still they come. 73

I am terrified. I hug the earth, digging my fingers into every crevice, every hole. 74

A blinding flash and an exploding howl a few feet in front of the trench. 75

My bowels liquefy. 76

Acrid smoke bites the throat, parches the mouth. I am beyond mere fright. I am frozen with an insane fear that keeps me cowering in the bottom of the trench. I lie flat on my belly, waiting. . . . 77

Suddenly it stops. 78

The fire lifts and passes over us to the trenches in the rear. 79

We lie still, unable to move. Fear has robbed us of the power to act. I hear Fry whimpering near me. I crawl over to him with great effort. He is half covered with earth and débris. We begin to dig him out. 80

To our right they have started to shell the front lines. It is about half a mile away. We do not care. *We* are safe. 81

Without warning it starts again. 82

The air screams and howls like an insane woman. 83

We are getting it in earnest now. Again we throw ourselves face downward on the bottom of the trench and grovel like savages before this demoniac frenzy. 84

The concussion of the explosions batters against us. 85

I am knocked breathless. 86

I recover and hear the roar of the bombardment. 87

It screams and rages and boils like an angry sea. I feel a prickly sensation behind my eyeballs. 88

A shell lands with a monster shriek in the next bay. The concussion rolls me over on my back. I see the stars shining serenely above us. Another lands in the same place. Suddenly the stars revolve. I land on my shoulder. I have been tossed into the air. 89

I begin to pray. 90

"God — God — please . . ." 91

I remember that I do not believe in God. Insane thoughts race through my brain. I want to catch hold of something, something that will explain this mad fury, this maniacal congealed hatred that pours down on our heads. I can find nothing to console me, nothing to appease my terror. I know that hundreds of men are standing a mile or two from me pulling gun-lanyards, blowing us to smithereens. I know that and nothing else. 92

I begin to cough. The smoke is thick. It rolls in heavy clouds over the trench, blurring the stabbing lights of the explosions. 93

94   A shell bursts near the parapet.

95   Fragments smack the sandbags like a merciless shower of steel hail.

96   A piece of mud flies into my mouth. It is cool and refreshing. It tastes earthy.

97   Suddenly it stops again.

98   I bury my face in the cool, damp earth. I want to weep. But I am too weak and shaken for tears.

99   We lie still, waiting. . . .

∆∆

Further Reading:

Charles Yale Harrison, *Generals Die in Bed*
Erich Maria Remarque, *All Quiet on the Western Front* (novel)
Ernest Hemingway, *A Farewell to Arms* (novel)
Timothy Findley, *The Wars* (novel)
Heather Robertson, ed., *A Terrible Beauty: The Art of Canada at War*

Structure:

1. In *narrating* his description of trench warfare, does Harrison ever deviate from straight chronological order? If so, where and how?

2. Harrison uses SENSE IMAGES so often that throughout this passage *description* carries the main weight of development. Find one example each of a strong appeal to our senses of sight, hearing, touch, taste and smell.

3. Many of the paragraphs are small, some only a word or two long. Examine paragraphs 25–30, 53–56, and 60–68, determining in each passage why the paragraphs are so short.

4. This account of an artillery attack ends with the words "We lie still, waiting. . . ." Is the ending effective, and if so, how?

Style:

1. What degree of CONCISENESS has Harrison achieved in this selection?

2. Harrison tells of the rat: "I remember with a cold feeling that it was fat, and why" (par. 57). How does he convey so much horror in so few words?

3. Analyze the power of the deceptively simple events of paragraph 89: "A shell lands with a monster shriek in the next bay. The concussion rolls me over on my back. I see the stars shining serenely above us. Another lands in the same place. Suddenly the stars revolve. I land on my shoulder. I have been tossed into the air."

4. In describing, Harrison exploits FIGURES OF SPEECH. Point out at least one good SIMILE and one good METAPHOR.

5. Why is "In the Trenches" told in the present tense, even though the book in which it appeared was published years after the war?

Ideas for Discussion and Writing:

1. Our narrator relates his first experience of war. What has it taught him?
2. Have you read books or seen films that show war in a positive light? Name them. In what ways does "In the Trenches" differ from those accounts?
3. "In the Trenches" is part of a book entitled *Generals Die in Bed*. Discuss the implications of this title.
4. If you have read "Coming of Age in Putnok," compare the conflict described by George Gabori with that described by Harrison. Does hostility between individuals contribute to hostility between nations?
5. **PROCESS IN WRITING**: *Have you lived through a violent or even life-threatening experience, as Harrison did? Close your eyes and remember it. Then in a rapid first draft,* describe *to your audience what it was really like. How did things look, sound, feel, smell or even taste? Use* SENSE IMAGES, *as Harrison does, to help your reader know too. The next day look your description over. Does it begin and end at the right spots, to emphasize the important things? If not, chop or add. Are there unimportant details? If so, chop. Are some parts "thin"? If so, add. Are paragraphs longer in the slower parts and shorter in the tenser parts, like Harrison's? If not, adjust them. Finally, edit for correctness and style before producing your final version.*

Note: See also the Topics for Writing at the end of this chapter.

Emily Carr

D'Sonoqua

Although Emily Carr (1871–1945) was born to a conservative family in the restrictive atmosphere of 19th-century Victoria, British Columbia, she emerged as one of the nation's most original painters and writers. Strong-willed and independent, she turned down several offers of marriage because she believed men "demanded worship" and would only hold her back. Instead she pursued her goal to San Francisco, London and Paris, where she studied art. Home again, with a new way of seeing inspired by post-impressionist artists in France, she embarked alone on expeditions to remote Indian villages along the mainland coast and in the Queen Charlotte Islands, where she expressed on canvas the power she felt in the ruins of ancient cultures. Our selection describes three such trips. The public laughed at her bold and free art, but she kept on. Around 1929 Carr shifted focus to the paintings for which she is now best known, her looming, energetic and explosive visions of the coastal rain forest itself. Emily Carr spent most of her life in poverty, for recognition was late in coming. She managed a rooming house for many years, and would sometimes paint on cardboard because canvas cost too much. In her last years, plagued by ill health, she abandoned painting for writing. Our selection comes from her first and best book, published in 1941, Klee Wyck *(the title is her name, "Laughing One," given her by the Nootka Indians).* Klee Wyck *is an extension of her painting: a collection of word sketches in which language is at once rich and suggestive, yet pared down to the bone. During her lifetime she published two more books,* The Book of Small *(1942) and* The House of All Sorts *(1944). Others did not appear till after her death:* Growing Pains *(autobiography, 1946),* The Heart of a Peacock *(1953),* Pause: A Sketch Book *(1953), and finally her journals, published as* Hundreds and Thousands *(1966).*

1   I was sketching in a remote Indian village when I first saw her. The village was one of those that the Indians use only for a few months in each year; the rest of the year it stands empty and desolate. I went there in one of its empty times, in a drizzling dusk.

2   When the Indian agent dumped me on the beach in front of the village, he said "There is not a soul here. I will come back for you in two days." Then he went away.

I had a small Griffon dog with me, and also a little Indian girl, who,   3
when she saw the boat go away, clung to my sleeve and wailed, "I'm 'fraid."

We went up to the old deserted Mission House. At the sound of the   4
key in the rusty lock, rats scuttled away. The stove was broken, the wood
wet. I had forgotten to bring candles. We spread our blankets on the
floor, and spent a poor night. Perhaps my lack of sleep played its part
in the shock that I got, when I saw her for the first time.

Water was in the air, half mist, half rain. The stinging nettles, higher   5
than my head, left their nervy smart on my ears and forehead, as I beat
my way through them, trying all the while to keep my feet on the plank
walk which they hid. Big yellow slugs crawled on the walk and slimed it.
My feet slipped, and I shot headlong to her very base, for she had no
feet. The nettles that were above my head reached only to her knee.

It was not the fall alone that jerked the "Oh's" out of me, for the   6
great wooden image towering above me was indeed terrifying.

The nettle-bed ended a few yards beyond her, and then a rocky bluff   7
jutted out, with waves battering it below. I scrambled up and went out
on the bluff, so that I could see the creature above the nettles. The
forest was behind her, the sea in front.

Her head and trunk were carved out of, or rather into, the bole of a   8
great red cedar. She seemed to be part of the tree itself, as if she had
grown there at its heart, and the carver had only chipped away the
outer wood so that you could see her. Her arms were spliced and
socketed to the trunk, and were flung wide in a circling, compelling
movement. Her breasts were two eagle heads, fiercely carved. That much,
and the column of her great neck, and her strong chin, I had seen
when I slithered to the ground beneath her. Now I saw her face.

The eyes were two rounds of black, set in wider rounds of white, and   9
placed in deep sockets under wide, black eyebrows. Their fixed stare
bored into me as if the very life of the old cedar looked out, and it
seemed that the voice of the tree itself might have burst from that great
round cavity, with projecting lips, that was her mouth. Her ears were
round, and stuck out to catch all sounds. The salt air had not dimmed
the heavy red of her trunk and arms and thighs. Her hands were black,
with blunt finger-tips painted a dazzling white. I stood looking at her
for a long, long time.

The rain stopped, and white mist came up from the sea, gradually   10
paling her back into the forest. It was as if she belonged there, and the
mist were carrying her home. Presently the mist took the forest too,
and, wrapping them both together, hid them away.

"Who is that image?" I asked the little Indian girl, when I got back to   11
the house.

She knew which one I meant, but to gain time, she said, "What image?"   12

"The terrible one, out there on the bluff." The girl had been to   13

Mission School, and fear of the old, fear of the new, struggled in her eyes. "I dunno," she lied.

14   I never went to that village again, but the fierce wooden image often came to me, both in my waking and in my sleeping.

15   Several years passed, and I was once more sketching in an Indian village. There were Indians in this village and in a mild backward way it was "going modern." That is, the Indians had pushed the forest back a little to let the sun touch the new buildings that were replacing the old community houses. Small houses, primitive enough to a white man's thinking, pushed here and there between the old. Where some of the big community houses had been torn down, for the sake of the lumber, the great corner posts and massive roof-beams of the old structure were often left, standing naked against the sky, and the new little house was built inside, on the spot where the old one had been.

16   It was in one of these empty skeletons that I found her again. She had once been a supporting post for the great centre beam. Her pole-mate, representing the Raven, stood opposite her, but the beam that had rested on their heads was gone. The two poles faced in, and one judged the great size of the house by the distance between them. The corner posts were still in place, and the earth floor, once beaten to the hardness of rock by naked feet, was carpeted now with rich lush grass.

17   I knew her by the stuck-out ears, shouting mouth, and deep eye-sockets. These sockets had no eye-balls, but were empty holes, filled with stare. The stare, though not so fierce as that of the former image, was more intense. The whole figure expressed power, weight, domination, rather than ferocity. Her feet were planted heavily on the head of the squatting bear, carved beneath them. A man could have sat on either huge shoulder. She was unpainted, weather-worn, sun-cracked, and the arms and hands seemed to hang loosely. The fingers were thrust into the carven mouths of two human heads, held crowns down. From behind, the sun made unfathomable shadows in eye, cheek and mouth. Horror tumbled out of them.

18   I saw Indian Tom on the beach, and went to him.

19   "Who is she?"

20   The Indian's eyes, coming slowly from across the sea, followed my pointing finger. Resentment showed in his face, greeny-brown and wrinkled like a baked apple, — resentment that white folks should pry into matters wholly Indian.

21   "Who is that big carved woman?" I repeated.

22   "D'Sonoqua." No white tongue could have fondled the name as he did.

23   "Who is D'Sonoqua?"

24   "She is the wild woman of the woods."

25   "What does she do?"

"She steals children."   26

"To eat them?"   27

"No, she carries them to her caves; that," pointing to a purple scar   28
on the mountain across the bay, "is one of her caves. When she cries
'OO-oo-oo-oeo', Indian mothers are too frightened to move. They stand
like trees, and the children go with D'Sonoqua."

"Then she is bad?"   29

"Sometimes bad . . . sometimes good," Tom replied, glancing furtively   30
at those stuck-out ears. Then he got up and walked away.

I went back, and, sitting in front of the image, gave stare for stare.   31
But her stare so over-powered mine, that I could scarcely wrench my
eyes away from the clutch of those empty sockets. The power that I felt
was not in the thing itself, but in some tremendous force behind it, that
the carver had believed in.

A shadow passed across her hands and their gruesome holdings. A   32
little bird, with its beak full of nesting material, flew into the cavity of
her mouth, right in the pathway of that terrible OO-oo-oo-oeo. Then
my eye caught something that I had missed — a tabby cat asleep between
her feet.

This was D'Sonoqua, and she was a supernatural being, who belonged   33
to these Indians.

"Of course," I said to myself, "I do not believe in supernatural beings.   34
Still — who understands the mysteries behind the forest? What would
one do if one did meet a supernatural being?" Half of me wished that I
could meet her, and half of me hoped I would not.

Chug — chug — the little boat had come into the bay to take me to   35
another village, more lonely and deserted than this. Who knew what I
should see there? But soon supernatural beings went clean out of my
mind, because I was wholly absorbed in being naturally seasick.

When you have been tossed and wracked and chilled, any wharf   36
looks good, even a rickety one, with its crooked legs stockinged in
barnacles. Our boat nosed under its clammy darkness, and I crawled up
the straight slimy ladder, wondering which was worse, natural seasickness,
or supernatural "creeps." The trees crowded to the very edge of the
water, and the outer ones, hanging over it, shadowed the shoreline into
a velvet smudge. D'Sonoqua might walk in places like this. I sat for a
long time on the damp, dusky beach, waiting for the stage. One by one
dots of light popped from the scattered cabins, and made the dark
seem darker. Finally the stage came.

We drove through the forest over a long straight road, with black   37
pine trees marching on both sides. When we came to the wharf the
little gas mail-boat was waiting for us. Smell and blurred light oozed
thickly out of the engine room, and except for one lantern on the

wharf everything else was dark. Clutching my little dog, I sat on the mail sacks which had been tossed on to the deck.

38   The ropes were loosed, and we slid out into the oily black water. The moon that had gone with us through the forest was away now. Black pine-covered mountains jagged up on both sides of the inlet like teeth. Every gasp of the engine shook us like a great sob. There was no rail round the deck, and the edge of the boat lay level with the black slithering horror below. It was like being swallowed again and again by some terrible monster, but never going down. As we slid through the water, hour after hour, I found myself listening for the OO-oo-oo-oeo.

39   Midnight brought us to a knob of land, lapped by the water on three sides, with the forest threatening to gobble it up on the fourth. There was a rude landing, a rooming-house, an eating-place, and a store, all for the convenience of fishermen and loggers. I was given a room, but after I had blown out my candle, the stillness and the darkness would not let me sleep.

40   In the brilliant sparkle of the morning when everything that was not superlatively blue was superlatively green, I dickered with a man who was taking a party up the inlet that he should drop me off at the village I was headed for.

41   "But," he protested, "there is nobody there."

42   To myself I said, "There is D'Sonoqua."

43   From the shore, as we rowed to it, came a thin feminine cry — the mewing of a cat. The keel of the boat had barely grated in the pebbles, when the cat sprang aboard, passed the man shipping his oars, and crouched for a spring into my lap. Leaning forward, the man seized the creature roughly, and with a cry of "Dirty Indian vermin!" flung her out into the sea.

44   I jumped ashore, refusing his help, and with a curt "Call for me at sundown," strode up the beach; the cat followed me.

45   When we had crossed the beach and come to a steep bank, the cat ran ahead. Then I saw that she was no lean, ill-favoured Indian cat, but a sleek aristocratic Persian. My snobbish little Griffon dog, who usually refused to let an Indian cat come near me, surprised me by trudging beside her in comradely fashion.

46   The village was typical of the villages of these Indians. It had only one street, and that had only one side, because all the houses faced the beach. The two community houses were very old, dilapidated and bleached, and the handful of other shanties seemed never to have been young; they had grown so old before they were finished, that it was then not worth while finishing them.

47   Rusty padlocks carefully protected the gaping walls. There was the usual broad plank in front of the houses, the general sitting and sun-

ning place for Indians. Little streams ran under it, and weeds poked up through every crack, half hiding the companies of tins, kettles, and rags, which patiently waited for the next gale and their next move.

In front of the Chief's house was a high, carved totem pole, sur- 48
mounted by a large wooden eagle. Storms had robbed him of both wings, and his head had a resentful twist, as if he blamed somebody. The heavy wooden heads of two squatting bears peered over the nettle-tops. The windows were too high for peeping in or out. "But, save D'Sonoqua, who is there to peep?" I said aloud, just to break the silence. A fierce sun burned down as if it wanted to expose every ugliness and forlornness. It drew the noxious smell out of the skunk cabbages, grow-ing in the rich black ooze of the stream, scummed the water-barrels with green slime, and branded the desolation into my very soul.

The cat kept very close, rubbing and bumping itself and purring 49
ecstatically; and although I had not seen them come, two more cats had joined us. When I sat down they curled into my lap, and then the strangeness of the place did not bite into me so deeply. I got up, determined to look behind the houses.

Nettles grew in the narrow spaces between the houses. I beat them 50
down, and made my way over the bruised dank-smelling mass into a space of low jungle.

Long ago the trees had been felled and left lying. Young forest had 51
burst through the slash, making an impregnable barrier, and sealing up the secrets which lay behind it. An eagle flew out of the forest, circled the village, and flew back again.

Once again I broke silence, calling after him, "Tell D'Sonoqua —" 52
and turning, saw her close, towering above me in the jungle.

Like the D'Sonoqua of the other villages she was carved into the bole 53
of a red cedar tree. Sun and storm had bleached the wood, moss here and there softened the crudeness of the modelling; sincerity underlay every stroke.

She appeared to be neither wooden nor stationary, but a singing 54
spirit, young and fresh, passing through the jungle. No violence coars-ened her; no power domineered to wither her. She was graciously femi-nine. Across her forehead her creator had fashioned the Sistheutl, or mythical two-headed sea serpent. One of its heads fell to either shoulder, hiding the stuck-out ears, and framing her face from a central parting on her forehead which seemed to increase its womanliness.

She caught your breath, this D'Sonoqua, alive in the dead bole of the 55
cedar. She summed up the depth and charm of the whole forest, driving away its menace.

I sat down to sketch. What was this noise of purring and rubbing 56
going on about my feet? Cats. I rubbed my eyes to make sure I was

seeing right, and counted a dozen of them. They jumped into my lap and sprang to my shoulders. They were real — and very feminine.

57   There we were — D'Sonoqua, the cats and I — the woman who only a few moments ago had forced herself to come behind the houses in trembling fear of the "wild woman of the woods" — wild in the sense that forest-creatures are wild — shy, untouchable.

△ △

Further Reading:

Emily Carr,
  Klee Wyck
  The Book of Small
Maria Tippett, *Emily Carr: A Biography*
Doris Shadbolt, *The Art of Emily Carr*
Paula Blanchard, *The Life of Emily Carr*
Germaine Greer, *The Obstacle Race*

Structure:

1. Carr's opening words are, "I was sketching in a remote Indian village when I first saw her." Why are we not shown "her" identity till paragraph 6?
2. Where do the three parts of this selection each begin and end? How do the three images of D'Sonoqua form a progression?
3. A voyage by water precedes Carr's visit to each image. Beyond its structural function, does it have a symbolic role? Consider this passage from paragraph 38:

   > There was no rail round the deck, and the edge of the boat lay level with the black slithering horror below. It was like being swallowed again and again by some terrible monster, but never going down. As we slid through the water, hour after hour, I found myself listening for the OO-oo-oo-oeo.

Style:

1. Although Carr is esteemed as a writer, she is better known as a painter. What aspects of her prose remind you of the visual arts? Point out passages that illustrate your answers.
2. What does Carr gain by words such as "scuttled" (par. 4), "slithered" (par. 8), "grated" (par. 43) and "ooze" (par. 48)?
3. Carr plays with words. Rather than describe the walk as "slimy," she writes that slugs "slimed" the walk. Find other words she uses in new ways.
4. What FIGURE OF SPEECH depicts the wharf's "crooked legs stockinged

in barnacles" (par. 36)? Where else does it occur? How does it further the *description?*

5. The term "Indian," current when Carr published *Klee Wyck* in 1941, is going out of use. Why? Name all the reasons why the original Canadians now prefer the term "First Nations People."

Ideas for Discussion and Writing:

1. In paragraph 31 Carr states of the second D'Sonoqua, "The power that I felt was not in the thing itself, but in some tremendous force behind it, that the carver had believed in." Is skill itself enough to create art, or must the artist believe in some "tremendous force"?
2. What is art for? Think of these:
   — Monumental architecture, as in banks, cathedrals and airports
   — Pretty paintings and photographs on living room walls
   — Bronzes of generals or politicians mounted on horses
   — Nonrepresentational art in its many forms: impressionism, cubism, surrealism, expressionism, etc.
   — The images of D'Sonoqua described by Carr
3. The narrator and others fear D'Sonoqua. Why have humans always imagined monsters such as the Minotaur, Grendel, Dracula, Frankenstein, King Kong and Godzilla, not to mention the traditional witches and ghosts?
4. In what ways might "D'Sonoqua" be considered a feminist essay?
5. **PROCESS IN WRITING:** *Describe a work of art that you see every day (an unusual building, a public sculpture, a favourite poster on your wall, etc.). First brainstorm to generate material, then examine these notes to find your overall effect. After a quick "discovery draft," add more sense images and figures of speech. Then, like Carr, trim every single word that does not in some way further your main effect.*

Note: See also the Topics for Writing at the end of this chapter.

Topics for Writing

Chapter 3: Description

Applying techniques from our chapter introduction, describe one of the following as vividly as you can. (See also the guidelines that follow.)

1. Your room
2. The subway platform during rush hour
3. A New Year's celebration
4. The oldest person you know
5. An assembly line
6. A food store of a culture not your own
7. Your city or town seen from its tallest building
8. Your fitness club or gym on a busy day
9. A junkyard or a dump
10. The interior of a bus, subway car or streetcar in rush hour
11. A club on a Saturday night
12. Your attic or storeroom
13. A polluted river or lake
14. A retirement home or nursing home
15. Your street on the coldest or hottest day of the year
16. The interior of a police station or courtroom
17. A pool hall
18. A cathedral, palace or castle that you have seen
19. A popular beach on a hot weekend
20. A construction site
21. Your school cafeteria
22. Your favourite spot in the neighbourhood
23. A body shop or garage in operation
24. A market you have seen in another country
25. A piece of public art in your town or city
26. The hottest or coldest day you have lived through
27. A swamp, a meadow, the deep woods or the seashore
28. The oldest building in your city or town
29. A video arcade
30. A thunderstorm, blizzard, tornado, hurricane, flood or earthquake

Process in Writing: Guidelines

Follow at least some of these steps in the act of writing your description (your teacher may suggest which ones).

1. *If you can, take eyewitness notes for your description. If you cannot, choose a topic you know so well that you can make exact notes from memory.*

2. *Look these notes over. What is your dominant impression, main feeling or idea of the subject? Put it into a sentence (this will be your* THESIS, *whether or not you will actually state it in the description).*

3. *With your notes and thesis before you, write a rapid first draft, double-spaced. Get your subject clearly down on paper, rather than stopping now to revise.*

4. *When your first draft has "cooled off," look it over. Does every line of your description contribute to the main overall effect? If not, revise. Does each word "feel" right? When one does not, consult your thesaurus for another.*

5. *In the next draft add more* SENSE IMAGES — *appeals to sight, hearing, touch, smell and maybe even taste. Add more* TRANSITIONS. *Read aloud to* hear *defects you did not see. Then revise.*

6. *Finally, look over the spelling and grammar before writing your good copy. Afterward, proofread word by word. If you have used a computer, save the essay on disk in case your teacher suggests further revision.*

P. Obendrauf/Canapress Photo Service

"As we walk home on this bright autumn morning, my mother clutches her piece of paper. Citizenship. She says she will go up to the cemetery and talk to my father this afternoon. She has something to tell him."

—Garry Engkent, *"Why My Mother Can't Speak English"*

CHAPTER

◇ 4 ◇

CAUSE AND EFFECT

Here's why. . . .

O ne of our most human traits is a desire to make sense of things by
asking *"why?"* If something good happens, we naturally want to
know *why* so we can repeat it. If something bad happens, we want to
know *why* so in future we can avoid it. On news reports of earthquakes,
hurricanes, fires, accidents and crimes, victims are always shaking their
heads and asking *"why?"*

In the financial world investors bite their nails guessing what makes
stocks go up or down. Will a growing economy push stocks up? Or will
it cause inflation, which will cause us to stop buying things, which in
turn will cause stocks to fall? Will a controversial election send stocks
crashing? Or will it just clear the air of uncertainty, making stocks soar?
Will a devastating earthquake harm the economy and the stock market?
Or will the cleanup just create employment, sending stocks up? Using
the same data, hundreds of experts reason that stocks will rise, while
hundreds of others reason that they will fall. Do these experts, or do
we, think cause and effect logic is easy?

Yet it is important. We use it in everyday life, and many of our essays
are based on it. So when you investigate causes and effects, think hard
to get them right.

Some time ago a church in Florida began a campaign to burn records

111

by Elton John and other rock stars. A survey had reported that 984 out of 1000 teenagers who had become pregnant had "committed fornication while rock music was played." The assumption was automatic: rock music causes pregnancy. Before they lit the first match, though, the church members might have asked what *other* causes contributed to the effect. How many of the music lovers had also taken alcohol or drugs? How many had not thought of birth control? Was the music played because such encounters often take place inside a building, where sound systems also happen to be? The church might also have investigated causes further in the past: What life circumstances or influences of society encouraged these teens to enter the situation in the first place? Finally, the church might have asked how often people this age listen to Elton John and other musicians while *not* fornicating. Rock music may still be a factor — but who knows without a more objective and thorough search of causes? When you trace causes and effects, consider these principles:

Just because one event follows another, don't assume the first causes the second. If a black cat crosses the road just before your car blows up, put the blame where it belongs: not on the cat but on the mechanic who forgot to replace your crankcase oil.

Control your prejudices. If the bank manager refuses to give you a loan, is it because bankers are capitalist exploiters who like to keep the rest of us down? Or is it because this one had to call the collection agency the last time you took out a loan?

Explore causes behind causes. Your employer fired you because you didn't work hard enough. But *why* didn't you work hard enough? Because the job was a bore and the employer a jerk? Or because you have two other jobs as well, and sleep only three hours a night? And if so, do you work these hours because the car you bought consumes every cent you earn? Finally, the real question may be *why did you buy the car?*

Many events have multiple causes and multiple effects:

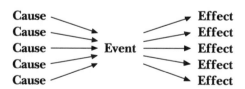

In addition, each cause may have one or more causes behind it, and each effect may produce further effects, leading to an infinite chain of causality receding into the past and reaching into the future.

Where, then, do you draw the boundaries as you plan an essay of cause and effect? The answer lies in your own common sense: include enough to make the point clearly and fairly, then stop. If your parents are workaholics, a description of their behaviour may help a reader understand your own. But do we need to hear about your grandparents as well? If we do, would a quick summary be enough, since we've already heard the details in your parents' case?

All the essays in this chapter show at least one clear-cut cause and at least one clear-cut effect. But while some pay equal attention to both, others focus down to emphasize *mostly* cause or *mostly* effect. And while some show only one major cause or one major effect, others show a great number of causes or a great number of effects. As you choose your own approach to the organization of a cause-and-effect essay, remember above all your purpose: What arrangement will most strongly explain and support your main point? Once you know, use it.

Note: Many essays in other chapters use cause and effect to help make their point. See especially these:

Catharine Parr Traill, "Remarks of Security of Person and Property in Canada," p. 169
Judy Stoffman, "The Way of All Flesh," p. 250
Margaret Atwood, "Canadians: What Do They Want?" p. 306
Nathalie Petrowski, "The Seven-Minute Life of Marc Lépine," p. 322
Wendy Dennis, "A Tongue-Lashing for Deaf Ears," p. 332

David Suzuki

Hidden Lessons*

David Suzuki is a scientist who, as host of the CBC's popular and long-lived television series The Nature of Things, *has become one of Canada's best-known public figures. Born in Vancouver in 1936, he earned a Ph.D. at the University of Chicago in 1961, specializing in genetics, then quickly gained an international reputation for his genetic research on fruit flies. In 1969 he won a prize as "outstanding research scientist in Canada," and since then has received many other awards, grants and honourary degrees. He lectures internationally, writes a syndicated newspaper column, and in addition to scholarly publications has written many books for a larger audience, among them* Metamorphosis *(autobiography, 1987),* Inventing the Future: Reflections on Science, Technology and Nature *(1989), and many books explaining nature to children. Suzuki rejects the narrowness that sometimes underlies the specialized vision of the research scientist, and instead has for years used his broadcasts and newspaper columns as platforms from which to educate the larger public about both the promise and dangers of science: the application of little-understood technologies; unchecked economic and industrial expansion; and the consequent devastation of other plant and animal species through our consumption of their habitat. The essay that follows, from the February 7, 1987 Toronto* Globe and Mail, *makes the point in an especially concrete way.*

1   In spite of the vast expanse of wilderness in this country, most Canadian children grow up in urban settings. In other words, they live in a world conceived, shaped and dominated by people. Even the farms located around cities and towns are carefully groomed and landscaped for human convenience. There's nothing wrong with that, of course, but in such an environment, it's very easy to lose any sense of connection with nature.

2   In city apartments and dwellings, the presence of cockroaches, fleas, ants, mosquitoes or houseflies is guaranteed to elicit the spraying of insecticides. Mice and rats are poisoned or trapped, while the gardener wages a never-ending struggle with ragweed, dandelions, slugs and root-

---

*Editor's title.

rot. We have a modern arsenal of chemical weapons to fight off these invaders and we use them lavishly.

We worry when kids roll in the mud or wade through a puddle   3
because they'll get "dirty." Children learn attitudes and values very quickly and the lesson in cities is very clear — nature is an enemy, it's dirty, dangerous or a nuisance. So youngsters learn to distance themselves from nature and to try to control it. I am astonished at the number of adults who loathe or are terrified by snakes, spiders, butterflies, worms, birds — the list seems endless.

If you reflect on the history of humankind, you realize that for 99 per   4
cent of our species' existence on the planet, we were deeply embedded in and dependent on nature. When plants and animals were plentiful, we flourished. When famine and drought struck, our numbers fell accordingly. We remain every bit as dependent upon nature today — we need plants to fix photons of energy into sugar molecules and to cleanse the air and replenish the oxygen. It is folly to forget our dependence on an intact ecosystem. But we do whenever we teach our offspring to fear or detest the natural world. The urban message kids get runs completely counter to what they are born with, a natural interest in other life forms. Just watch a child in a first encounter with a flower or an ant — there is instant interest and fascination. We condition them out of it.

The result is that when my 7-year-old daughter brings home new   5
friends, they invariably recoil in fear or disgust when she tries to show them her favorite pets — three beautiful salamanders that her grandfather got for her in Vancouver. And when my 3-year-old comes wandering in with her treasures — millipedes, spiders, slugs and sowbugs that she catches under rocks lining the front lawn — children and adults alike usually respond by saying "yuk."

I can't overemphasize the tragedy of that attitude. For, inherent in   6
this view is the assumption that human beings are special and different and that we lie outside nature. Yet it is this belief that is creating many of our environmental problems today.

Does it matter whether we sense our place in nature so long as we   7
have cities and technology? Yes, for many reasons, not the least of which is that virtually all scientists were fascinated with nature as children and retained that curiosity throughout their lives. But a far more important reason is that if we retain a spiritual sense of connection with all other life forms, it can't help but profoundly affect the way we act. Whenever my daughter sees a picture of an animal dead or dying, she asks me fearfully, "Daddy, are there any more?" At 7 years, she already knows about extinction and it frightens her.

The yodel of a loon at sunset, the vast flocks of migrating waterfowl   8
in the fall, the indomitable salmon returning thousands of kilometres

— these images of nature have inspired us to create music, poetry and art. And when we struggle to retain a handful of California condors or whooping cranes, it's clearly not from a fear of ecological collapse, it's because there is something obscene and frightening about the disappearance of another species at our hands.

9   If children grow up understanding that we are animals, they will look at other species with a sense of fellowship and community. If they understand their ecological place — the biosphere — then when children see the great virgin forests of the Queen Charlotte Islands being clearcut, they will feel physical pain, because they will understand that those trees are an extension of themselves.

10   When children who know their place in the ecosystem see factories spewing poison into the air, water and soil, they will feel ill because someone has violated their home. This is not mystical mumbo-jumbo. We have poisoned the life support systems that sustain all organisms because we have lost a sense of ecological place. Those of us who are parents have to realize the unspoken, negative lessons we are conveying to our children. Otherwise, they will continue to desecrate this planet as we have.

11   It's not easy to avoid giving these hidden lessons. I have struggled to cover my dismay and queasiness when Severn and Sarika come running in with a large wolf spider or when we've emerged from a ditch covered with leeches or when they have been stung accidentally by yellowjackets feeding on our leftovers. But that's nature. I believe efforts to teach children to love and respect other life forms are priceless.

△ △

Further Reading:

David Suzuki, *Metamorphosis*
Rachel Carson, *Silent Spring*
Annie Dillard, *Pilgrim at Tinker Creek*
Robert Ornstein and Paul Ehrlich: *New World, New Mind*
Henry David Thoreau, *Walden*

Structure:

1. What device of emphasis sparks the opening sentence, and how does it begin to introduce Suzuki's subject?
2. Does Suzuki explore more fully the *causes* or the *effects* of children's attitudes toward nature? Which paragraphs analyze mostly causes and which mostly effects? Is Suzuki right to place the causes first?
3. How long a chain of cause and effect does Suzuki show us? Point out each link.

4. Suzuki no doubt hopes his argument will spur us to action. Does his closing promote this goal? When he admits in paragraph 11 that "It's not easy to avoid giving these hidden lessons," are you discouraged or challenged?

Style:

1. Describe Suzuki's prose: Is it full of strategies calculated to affect us, or is it a plain and direct message? Which mode do you prefer when you read? When you write? Why?
2. Why is paragraph 6 the shortest one of the essay?

Ideas for Discussion and Writing:

1. Do you dread insects, worms, snakes, mice or weeds? If so, how did you learn to? How close are your attitudes to those of your parents? What actual dangers, if any, may these life forms pose to you?
2. In paragraph 8 Suzuki writes, "there is something obscene and frightening about the disappearance of another species at our hands." Elsewhere he has stated that two species an hour disappear from the earth, mostly because we "develop" natural habitats for our own profit. How important to you is a new paper mill, a logging project in the rain forest, a highway, dam, subdivision, ski resort, oil well or aluminum smelter — compared to the existence of a species? Defend your view.
3. First we learned to shun *racism,* and then *sexism.* Is *speciesism* next? Argue for or against our present belief that we are far more important than other members of our ecosystem.
4. How desirable is economic growth when it is based on exploiting nature? If we could save the rivers, the lakes and the rain forests by consuming less, how would you react? How large a cut in income would you accept to achieve the goal: 10 percent, 25 percent, 50 percent — or none at all? Defend your view.
5. **PROCESS IN WRITING:** *In a current newspaper or newsmagazine, choose an article about an environmental problem. In response, write a short but hard-hitting letter to the editor exposing the effects of this problem. Since editors love conciseness, polish your second draft till every word counts. Cut deadwood. Use a thesaurus to replace vague or weak terms with exact and strong ones. "Show" through examples rather than "telling" through generalizations. Now try out a draft on an audience of three or four classmates; incorporate their best advice before mailing your final copy. Then watch the next issues to see if your message is published. If an editor has cut any part of your letter, analyze why: Was the part wordy? Off topic? General instead of specific?*

Note: See also the Topics for Writing at the end of this chapter.

Naheed Mustafa

My Body Is My Own Business

Born in England, Naheed Mustafa came as an infant to Canada and grew up here. In 1992 she completed an honours degree in political science and philosophy at the University of Toronto, specializing in Third-World development. Then she studied journalism at Ryerson Polytechnic University until moving to Pakistan to be with her husband, who works for the Food and Agricultural Organization of the United Nations. There, Mustafa writes about development issues such as literacy and the environment, for local newspapers and magazines (her articles are in English because, although she speaks Urdu, she does not read or write it). She believes that, however well intentioned the international aid efforts of the First World, many donors pull out their money for disasters like earthquakes and famines, while ignoring basic development work such as education. Mustafa says she is not required by her culture or her muslim faith to wear the hijab *described in her essay (from the June 29, 1993 Toronto Globe and Mail), but feels that her liberating decision to cover herself has roots in both feminism and Islam.*

1 I often wonder whether people see me as a radical, fundamentalist Muslim terrorist packing an AK-47 assault rifle inside my jean jacket. Or maybe they see me as the poster girl for oppressed womanhood everywhere. I'm not sure which it is.

2 I get the whole gamut of strange looks, stares and covert glances. You see, I wear the *hijab,* a scarf that covers my head, neck and throat. I do this because I am a Muslim woman who believes her body is her own private concern.

3 Young Muslim women are reclaiming the *hijab,* reinterpreting it in light of its original purpose — to give back to women ultimate control of their own bodies.

4 The Koran teaches us that men and women are equal, that individuals should not be judged according to gender, beauty, wealth or privilege. The only thing that makes one person better than another is her or his character.

5 Nonetheless, people have a difficult time relating to me. After all,

I'm young, Canadian born and raised, university-educated — why would I do this to myself, they ask.

Strangers speak to me in loud, slow English and often appear to be 6
playing charades. They politely inquire how I like living in Canada and whether or not the cold bothers me. If I'm in the right mood, it can be very amusing.

But why would I, a woman with all the advantages of a North American 7
upbringing, suddenly, at 21, want to cover myself so that with the *hijab* and the other clothes I choose to wear, only my face and hands show?

Because it gives me freedom. 8

Women are taught from early childhood that their worth is propor- 9
tional to their attractiveness. We feel compelled to pursue abstract notions of beauty, half realizing that such a pursuit is futile.

When women reject this form of oppression, they face ridicule and 10
contempt. Whether it's women who refuse to wear makeup or to shave their legs or to expose their bodies, society, both men and women, have trouble dealing with them.

In the Western world, the *hijab* has come to symbolize either forced 11
silence or radical, unconscionable militancy. Actually, it's neither. It is simply a woman's assertion that judgment of her physical person is to play no role whatsoever in social interaction.

Wearing the *hijab* has given me freedom from constant attention to 12
my physical self. Because my appearance is not subjected to public scrutiny, my beauty, or perhaps lack of it, has been removed from the realm of what can legitimately be discussed.

No one knows whether my hair looks as if I just stepped out of a 13
salon, whether or not I can pinch an inch, or even if I have unsightly stretch marks. And because no one knows, no one cares.

Feeling that one has to meet the impossible male standards of beauty 14
is tiring and often humiliating. I should know, I spent my entire teen-age years trying to do it. I was a borderline bulimic and spent a lot of money I didn't have on potions and lotions in hopes of becoming the next Cindy Crawford.

The definition of beauty is ever-changing; waifish is good, waifish is 15
bad, athletic is good — sorry, athletic is bad. Narrow hips? Great. Narrow hips? Too bad.

Women are not going to achieve equality with the right to bare their 16
breasts in public, as some people would like to have you believe. That would only make us party to our own objectification. True equality will be had only when women don't need to display themselves to get attention and won't need to defend their decision to keep their bodies to themselves.

△ △

Further Reading:

Bharati Mukherjee, *Jasmine* (novel)
Salman Rushdie, *Shame* (novel)
Richard Gordon, *Anorexia and Bulimia: Anatomy of a Social Epidemic*
Naomi Wolf, *The Beauty Myth: How Images of Beauty Are Used Against
    Women*

Structure:

1. Why does Mustafa open with two STEREOTYPES? Do they draw your attention? Do they go straight to her topic?
2. In her argument does Mustafa give more attention to *causes* or *effects*? Name the main causes. Name the main effects.
3. Why does Mustafa explore effects *first* and causes *after*, reversing the logical order of the two?
4. Identify the TRANSITION in which Mustafa actually asks "why" and answers with "because. . . .," as she moves from *effects* to *causes*.

Style:

1. Ending on a key word is a powerful device of emphasis. Note the final word in each half of Mustafa's argument; what makes "freedom" and "themselves" good choices for these positions?
2. Language can speak through rhythm as much as through words. Read aloud the first sentence of paragraph 6, then analyze how its sound reinforces its meaning.

Ideas for Discussion and Writing:

1. Mustafa says male standards of beauty for women are "impossible" and that feeling the need to meet them is "humiliating" (paragraph 14). Is she right? Whether you are male or female, give examples of your own to defend or attack her view.
2. Examine the PARADOX of paragraph 8: that the effect of covering oneself with the *hijab* is "freedom." Do non-Muslims have means of shielding themselves, as well, from the unreasonable scrutiny and expectations of others? Name any you have used.
3. Though born in another country, Mustafa was raised in Canada. If your own origins are in another culture, how fully do you plan to retain the clothes, the foods, the religion and language of that culture, while living in Canada? Predict the *effects* of your decision.
4. Mustafa confesses that as a teen she was a "borderline bulimic" (paragraph 14). What do you see as the main *causes* of bulimia and anorexia nervosa? What *causes* women, not men, to be the main victims?

5. At the library look through an illustrated history of art, taking notes on how the ideal of beauty in women has changed through the centuries. Then report your findings to the class, showing illustrations as evidence for your conclusions.

6. Watch your favourite television channel for one hour, taking notes on how women are presented both in programs and commercials. Then report to the class on the attitudes, especially any STEREOTYPES, which you detected. What *effects*, in both male and female viewers, do you think these attitudes will *cause?*

7. **PROCESS IN WRITING:** *Do number 6 above, except as an essay. Look over your notes, then choose a THESIS that expresses the main* effect(s) *on viewers of the examples you observed. Now write a rapid first draft, supporting your thesis with large numbers of these examples. When the draft has "cooled off" look it over. Do the* causes *and* effects *seem reasonable? Have you tried to be objective, rather than interpret according to your own prejudices? Are there causes behind causes, or effects of effects, which might enrich your analysis? Do transitions such as "since," "because" and "therefore" help the audience follow your logic? If not, add. Finally, edit for things like punctuation and spelling before doing the final version. Read it to the class, and be ready to answer questions from other points of view.*

Note: See also the Topics for Writing at the end of this chapter.

Stuart McLean

The Shocking Truth About
Household Dust

Stuart McLean is a broadcaster with a difference. Though he jokes about aiming for the "cutting edge of journalism," it is the odd little details of life — the yo-yo, the popsicle, or our present subject, household dust — that catch his attention and delight his audiences. "He sees what sparkles in the ordinary and he cel-ebrates the common stuff of which most of our lives are made," says The Edmonton Herald. *Born in Montreal in 1948, McLean studied at Sir George Williams. After a time producing CBC Radio's* Sunday Morning, *he began to write a weekly series of quirky and poignant essays for CBC Radio's* Morningside, *where, appearing with host Peter Gzowski, he won a fanatic audience. Novelist Timothy Findley wrote, "For those of us who are Morningside addicts, Stuart McLean is a primal fix." In 1989 he gathered 30 of these radio essays in a book,* The Morningside World of Stuart McLean. *One of these was our selection, which former* Morningside *producer Catherine Pigott (see her own essay on page 160) calls "legendary." McLean also contributed to* The New Morningside Papers *(1987) and* The Latest Morningside Papers *(1989) edited by Gzowski, and in 1992 published his own second book* Travels in Small Town Canada. *He has also written documentaries and a feature film. McLean now combines writing with education; since 1984 he has been Director of Broadcast Journalism at Ryerson Polytechnic University.*

1 So. From time to time I joke about being out on the cutting edge of journalism. If pressed, however, I would be the first to admit that the majority of what I seem to end up writing about lies well off the beaten track. I try hard to follow world events. I do. But it is a struggle. I am easily distracted by those bits in my newspaper about the parrot who has been taught to whistle a Chopin sonata by the out-of-work conductor. And once I have read something like that, I just can't help myself.

2 This can be a problem for somebody like me who counts among his friends a number of this country's distinguished journalists. We go out for lunch together, my friends and I, and they will argue for hours about the implications of their upcoming interview with the minister of

finance, while I push at my salad and silently ponder my profile of the Popsicle, or the history of the Yo-Yo. I leave these lunches determined to do something journalistically credible before I see anyone again.

Such was my mood on an otherwise pleasant Tuesday afternoon several years ago. I would, I seethed, storming through the Yonge Street lunch crowd with my elbows just a little too far from my sides, uncover a real story. In this frame of investigative frenzy I returned to my desk and, unfortunately, fell into a telephone conversation with my friend Robert Krulwich of CBS about . . . dust. Common household dust. As usual, Krulwich had some questions that neither of us could answer. Dust questions.

Like how come the dust on the top of your refrigerator lies there like a layer of velvet, while the stuff under your bed rolls around like tumbleweeds in the interior of British Columbia? And the little specks in the sunbeam, are they floating or falling? And where does dust come from, anyway? How come you can vacuum your heart out one day and the next morning there'll be a dust bunny in the cupboard?

As the afternoon wore on, my need to know the answer to these and other puzzles overtook whatever it was I was supposed to be doing. I should have known better, but I shrugged and reached for the phone. What follows is the weird and shocking truth I discovered that day about household dust. Like all good stories it begins at the beginning.

Ever wonder where dust comes from? How about outer space? There is extraterrestrial dust in your living-room. Probably not a lot of it, but it is there, and I offer that up at the beginning as a kind of warning, because this is going to get a lot weirder before we are finished. Space dust comes from meteorites. When meteorites strike the earth's atmosphere they disintegrate and turn to, you guessed it, dust, increasing the bulk of our planet, incidentally, by 10,000 tons a year. I am told by eminent scientists who study dust that if you were to run your finger along a window ledge somewhere, anywhere, you are almost certain to pick up some dust from outer space.

I learned about space dust from a Dr John Ferguson, who is a dust scientist for Bristol-Myers. They are the folks who produce, among other things, Endust, so he should know. He did assure me that meteorites are not the major cause of the dust in my house.

> **We create an awful lot of dust by our daily living inside the house, the most common thing being, of course, through our cooking and our grooming habits, or the clothes that we wear. Also, there's the normal wearing away of the interior of the house — paint chipping off, bits of paper coming from wallpaper, things like that.**

In fact, the majority of the dust in your house comes from the house itself and everything in it, wearing away. The same thing happens outdoors. There is a lot of concrete dust floating around, for example.

Every time someone drives down the road, tiny bits of road are knocked off, and these microscopic bits float away and become specks of dust on someone's basement window. There is also rubber dust that comes from the tires that are busy wearing away the street, and chances are they will end up on the same basement window.

9   To these normal, everyday happenings you have to add something called "dust events" — things like volcanic eruptions, forest fires and other natural phenomena that spew ash into the atmosphere.

10   But that's not all — a significant amount of the dust in your home is, in fact, made up of little bits and pieces of you. In this way, you are no different from the wallpaper in your bathroom. The outermost layer of your skin is known as the stratum corneum. You shed your stratum corneum every three days, just like a snake. That's about fifty thousand skin cells. Or so says Dr Charles McLeod, a pathologist from Washington, D.C., who recently studied dust for *Discover* magazine.

> **If you brush through your hair in the right light, you can see small flecks of dander or dandruff that flake off your scalp, and this process is continuous on all the skin surfaces of your body. People are constantly shedding little flakes of dead skin. It is a normal process.**

11   Now we come to the good part. Having established where dust comes from, it is time to take a closer look at dust itself. This is the part that upsets people. If you are squeamish about these sorts of things you might consider putting this book away now. There are only a few pages left anyway and you might be better off, happier, more relaxed just not knowing about this next bit.

12   Don't say I didn't warn you. There are, uh, animals that live in the dust in your house. Millions and millions of animals. They are called dust mites. And they may be tiny, but they are the most horrible little creatures you can imagine. They feed on floating bits of skin. They suck in air through their toes. And they look like monsters from outer space. Don't take my word for it. Dr McLeod has actually looked at dust mites, face to face, through a microscope.

> **They have these very large mouth parts that allow them to chew their food. And depending on the stage at which you look at them, they may have up to eight legs. Have you ever seen a lobster? Have you ever seen a cockroach? Well, imagine breeding those two and looking at their offspring, and you have a good idea of what dust mites look like. They're not insects, now, they're mites. Insects only have six legs. Nobody has ever counted, but you could estimate that there are millions of mites per square yard of space. They don't take up a whole lot of room. They don't make any noise, so you'd never know they're there. If you accumulated enough of them and you bunched them together, you could see them with the naked eye. I'd say it would take a couple of dozen to cover the head of a pin, though.**

Dust mites can walk on their hideous eight legs, but for a mite to travel,   13
say, across the room, would be roughly the equivalent of you setting off
from Moose Jaw to walk to Come-by-Chance to pick up the morning
paper. So you can understand why mites don't do a lot of walking.
What they like to do is ride air currents. Every time you take a deep
breath and blow it out, you're helping a bunch of mites get around.

The good news about these little beasts is that they won't touch you,   14
and they won't eat you. Dr Edward Baker is an acarologist in Alabama
(which means that he studies mites, Alabaman or otherwise). He once
took a garbage pail full of mites and taped them, under capsules, to
various parts of his arm. He was prepared to let them nosh away to their
hearts' delight on his stratum corneum, but when he took off the tape,
they were all dead. Apparently, dust mites only go after the bits and
pieces that slough off. That's the good news.

The bad news about dust mites is that they have normal bodily func-   15
tions. Twenty times a day each mite produces a mite pellet. When
people say they are allergic to dust, they really mean they are allergic to
things in the dust. It might be pollen — there is a lot of pollen in dust
— but it could be that they are allergic to mite poop.

There is no getting around dust mites. As long as you keep sloughing   16
off, as long as there is dust, there are going to be mites. If you have a
vacuum cleaner in your closet, there are, right now, in the bag with the
dust, millions of mites, grazing happily. Turn on the vacuum and the
mites go turtle. They pull their hideous lobster legs into their hideous
bodies and wait until you have finished. Then they come out again and
graze. Tonight when you climb into bed, you will be sharing it with about
two million dust mites. So you might as well start thinking about them
as your friends, because there is nothing else you can do about them.

Another thing you can do nothing about is the dust that floats in the   17
sunbeam. I used to wonder if I left the house quietly and let the air get
real still, whether all that dust would settle, and I could sneak back in
and vacuum it up before it started floating again. Dr Ferguson set me
straight.

> **The larger particles are actually falling. But if the particles are small
> enough, the movement of the air is sufficient to keep them suspended.
> A layman's way of looking at that is if you toss a tin can into the air
> and you shoot at it with a bullet, you can keep that can suspended
> indefinitely so long as you can keep hitting it with a bullet. Essentially,
> if you have a particle of dust that is light enough, the movement of the
> air molecules behave just like the bullets from that gun. They will
> keep bouncing into the dust particle and keep it suspended.**

Some dust particles are so light that a simple wave of your hand or even   18
the cat walking across the kitchen will send them swirling up. And there
it stays, unless, of course, the dust was to meet its mortal enemy — rain.

Dust hates rain. It loves safe places where, through friction or electrostatic energy or, best of all, grease, it can cling to other bits of dust and fulfil its *raison d'être* — become a dust ball. Since grease is dust's best friend, dust's favourite place is, of course, the kitchen. And in the kitchen, says Dr Ferguson, the place where dust reigns supreme is . . .

> . . . **usually behind your refrigerator, or in the circulating fan above your stove or range. It accumulates on the fan because it is so close to the stove where the cooking fats and oils are volatilized. The grease sticks to the blades of the fan and the dust sticks to the grease. Your refrigerator works the same way because it's constantly recirculating the air in back of the coils for cooling. That will collect the fats and the oils and serve as a good sticking place for the dust as well.**

19   And that, more or less, is the story of dust. Some of it might have upset you, but there's not much you can do about it. You could dust more, I guess, or dust better, but it won't do much good. Better just to accept it. Come to terms with the dust in your life. Remember that it is someone's home (ugly they may be, malevolent they are not). It contains matter from outer space. And, after all, you put a lot of yourself into making it.

△△

Further Reading:

Stuart McLean, *Travels in Small Town Canada*
Peter Gzowski, ed., *The Latest Morningside Papers*

Structure:

1. "What follows is the weird and shocking truth I discovered that day about household dust," writes McLean in paragraph 5. What does a THESIS STATEMENT do? Is this a good one?
2. McLean's introduction fills paragraphs 1–5. Point out everything this material does to prepare us for his argument.
3. Analyze the role of *contrast* in paragraphs 1–3 of McLean's introduction.
4. Does McLean analyze mostly *causes* or mostly *effects*? Does he focus on *multiple causes of one effect*, on *one cause of multiple effects*, or on *multiple causes and effects both*?
5. Point out the major *cause(s)* of dust, and point out the major *effect(s)* of dust, in this cause and effect argument.

Style:

1. "The Shocking Truth About Household Dust" was first read as a script over CBC Radio. Identify 10 words or phrases, such as "mite

poop" in paragraph 15, which people would say but normally not write in an essay. Despite its very informal TONE, does this selection work as an essay? Why or why not?

2. How many sentence fragments do you see on these pages? Are fragments acceptable in a personal essay? A more formal essay? A research essay?

Ideas for Discussion and Writing:

1. Would you have imagined a whole essay about a topic as lowly as dust? Yet does it strike your interest? Does McLean's advice to "come to terms with the dust in your life" (par. 19) mean any more than just housecleaning? Can something as small as dust be a SYMBOL of larger things? Explain.

2. How does it strike you, that dust is "made up of little bits and pieces of you" (par. 10)? Analyze the power of this statement.

3. When in paragraph 6 dust on our window sills is said to come from outer space, are you interested? If so why? In which chapter of this book are whole essays powered by this device?

4. Astronomers say that an average galaxy has a hundred billion stars, and the universe has around a hundred billion galaxies. McLean writes that your bed probably contains two million dust mites, yet we know that even a mite dwarfs its own molecules and atoms. Do such contrasts of size make you uneasy? Analyze all the reasons why.

5. **PROCESS IN WRITING:** *On a starry night spend a while outside, contemplating the size and age of the universe. Then think of our earth. Do you know the forces that caused it to form? Now go inside to freewrite on this subject, putting on paper what you know. If there are gaps, investigate the next day in the library. Now make a short outline: choose how many links in the chain of cause and effect you wish to include, so as to control this very large topic. Now write a draft. Looking it over, see if you have used enough transition signals to highlight causality. Have you helped your audience by defining any technical terms? Have you, like McLean, used examples to make hard parts clear? Finally edit for style and correctness as you produce your good version.*

Note: See also the Topics for Writing at the end of this chapter.

Garry Engkent

Why My Mother Can't Speak English

Born in 1948 in Mon-Lau, a village on the Pearl River of China, Garry Engkent was a small boy when the communist army invaded and his father had to flee. Later the father led his son and wife to Hong Kong, where border guards let the son and father pass, but not the mother. After a time as refugees, they were all at last reunited in North Bay, Ontario. As Engkent writes, his mother never did learn English, but he himself was quickly acculturated. Though his education includes a Ph.D. in English (1980) from the University of Ottawa, he remembers an earlier "education" — absorbing American culture from countless hours in movie theatres. Engkent can still speak Cantonese, but almost no one in Canada knows his village dialect. He has taught writing and literature at many universities: Ottawa, Alberta, Guelph, Toronto and Ryerson. To "write about what you know" is not enough, he tells his students; add the widest reading possible, to produce writing that "comes out alive." Engkent's own narrative is based mostly on fact, though fictionalized in some details; since he was away at the time, it was a cousin who helped the mother who could not speak English become a citizen of Canada.

1   **M**y mother is seventy years old. Widowed for five years now, she lives alone in her own house except for the occasions when I come home to tidy her household affairs. She has been in *gum san*, the golden mountain, for the past thirty years. She clings to the old-country ways so much so that today she astonishes me with this announcement:

2   "I want to get my citizenship," she says as she slaps down the *Dai Pao*, "before they come and take away my house."

3   "Nobody's going to do that. This is Canada."

4   "So everyone says," she retorts, "but did you read what the *Dai Pao* said? Ah, you can't read Chinese. The government is cutting back on old-age pensions. Anybody who hasn't got citizenship will lose everything. Or worse."

5   "The *Dai Pao* can't even typeset accurately," I tell her. Sometimes I worry about the information Mother receives from the biweekly community newspaper. "Don't worry — the Ministry of Immigration won't send you back to China."

"Little you know," she snaps back. "I am old, helpless, and without citizenship. Reasons enough. Now, get me citizenship. Hurry!" 6

"Mother, getting citizenship papers is not like going to the bank to cash in your pension cheque. First, you have to —" 7

"Excuses, my son, excuses. When your father was alive —" 8

"Oh, Mother, not again! You throw that at me every —" 9

"— made excuses, too." Her jaw tightens. "If you can't do this little thing for your own mother, well, I will just have to go and beg your cousin to. . ." 10

Every time I try to explain about the ways of the *fan gwei*, she thinks I do not want to help her. 11

"I'll do it, I'll do it, okay? Just give me some time." 12

"That's easy for you," Mother snorts. "You're not seventy years old. You're not going to lose your pension. You're not going to lose your house. Now, how much *lai-shi* will this take?" 13

After all these years in *gum san* she cannot understand that you don't give government officials *lai-shi,* the traditional Chinese money gift to persons who do things for you. 14

"That won't be necessary," I tell her. "And you needn't go to my cousin." 15

Mother picks up the *Dai Pao* again and says: "Why should I beg at the door of a village cousin when I have a son who is a university graduate?" 16

I wish my father were alive. Then he would be doing this. But he is not here, and as a dutiful son, I am responsible for the welfare of my widowed mother. So I take her to Citizenship Court. 17

There are several people from the Chinese community waiting there. Mother knows a few of the Chinese women and she chats with them. My cousin is there, too. 18

"I thought your mother already got her citizenship," he says to me."Didn't your father —" 19

"No, he didn't." 20

He shakes his head sadly. "Still, better now than never. That's why I'm getting these people through." 21

"So they've been reading the *Dai Pao.*" 22

He gives me a quizzical look, so I explain to him, and he laughs. 23

"You are the new generation," he says. "You didn't live long enough in *hon san,* the sweet land, to understand the fears of the old. You can't expect the elderly to renounce all attachments to China for the ways of the *fan gwei.* How old is she, seventy now? Much harder." 24

"She woke me up this morning at six, and Citizenship Court doesn't open until ten." 25

The doors of the court finally open, and Mother motions me to hurry. We wait in line for a while. 26

The clerk distributes applications and tells me the requirements. 27

Mother wants to know what the clerk is saying, so half the time I translate for her.

28   The clerk suggests that we see one of the liaison officers.

29   "Your mother has been living in Canada for the past thirty years and she still can't speak English?"

30   "It happens," I tell the liaison officer.

31   "I find it hard to believe that — not one word?"

32   "Well, she understands some restaurant English," I tell her. "You know, French fries, pork chops, soup, and so on. And she can say a few words."

33   "But will she be able to understand the judge's questions? The interview with the judge, as you know, is an important part of the citizenship procedure. Can she read the booklet? What does she know about Canada?"

34   "So you don't think my mother has a chance?"

35   "The requirements are that the candidate must be able to speak either French or English, the two official languages of Canada. The candidate must be able to pass an oral interview with the citizenship judge, and then he or she must be able to recite the oath of allegiance —"

36   "My mother needs to speak English," I conclude for her.

37   "Look, I don't mean to be rude, but why didn't your mother learn English when she first came over?"

38   I have not been translating this conversation, and Mother, annoyed and agitated, asks me what is going on. I tell her there is a slight problem.

39   "What problem?" Mother opens her purse, and I see her taking a small red envelope — *lai-shi* — I quickly cover her hand.

40   "What's going on?" the liaison officer demands.

41   "Nothing," I say hurriedly. "Just a cultural misunderstanding, I assure you."

42   My mother rattles off some indignant words, and I snap back in Chinese: "Put that away! The woman won't understand, and we'll be in a lot of trouble."

43   The officer looks confused, and I realize that an explanation is needed.

44   "My mother was about to give you a money gift as a token of appreciation for what you are doing for us. I was afraid you might misconstrue it as a bribe. We have no intention of doing that."

45   "I'm relieved to hear it."

46   We conclude the interview, and I take Mother home. Still clutching the application, Mother scowls at me.

47   "I didn't get my citizenship papers. Now I will lose my old-age pension. The government will ship me back to China. My old bones will lie there while your father's will be here. What will happen to me?"

48   How can I teach her to speak the language when she is too old to

learn, too old to want to learn? She resists anything that is *fan gwei*. She does everything the Chinese way. Mother spends much time staring blankly at the four walls of her house. She does not cry. She sighs and shakes her head. Sometimes she goes about the house touching her favourite things.

"This is all your dead father's fault," she says quietly. She turns to the photograph of my father on the mantel. Daily, she burns incense, pours fresh cups of fragrant tea, and spreads dishes of his favourite fruits in front of the framed picture as is the custom. In memory of his passing, she treks two miles to the cemetery to place flowers by his headstone, to burn ceremonial paper money, and to talk to him. Regularly, rain or shine, or even snow, she does these things. Such love, such devotion, now such vehemence. Mother curses my father, her husband, in his grave. 49

When my mother and I emigrated from China, she was forty years old, and I, five. My father was already a well-established restaurant owner. He put me in school and Mother in the restaurant kitchen, washing dishes and cooking strange foods like hot dogs, hamburgers, and French fries. She worked seven days a week from six in the morning until eleven at night. This lasted for twenty-five years, almost to the day of my father's death. 50

The years were hard on her. The black-and-white photographs show a robust woman; now I see a withered, frail, white-haired old woman, angry, frustrated with the years, and scared of losing what little material wealth she has to show for the toil in *gum san*. 51

"I begged him," Mother says. "But he would either ignore my pleas or say: 'What do you need to know English for? You're better off here in the kitchen. Here you can talk to the others in our own tongue. English is far too complicated for you. How old are you now? Too old to learn a new language. Let the young speak *fan gwei*. All you need is to understand the orders from the waitresses. Anyway, if you need to know something, the men will translate for you. I am here; I can do your talking for you.'" 52

As a conscientious boss of the young male immigrants, my father would force them out of the kitchen and into the dining room. "The kitchen is no place for you to learn English. All you do is speak Chinese in here. To survive in *gum san*, you have to speak English, and the only way you can do that is to wait on tables and force yourselves to speak English with the customers. How can you get your families over here if you can't talk to the immigration officers in English?" 53

A few of the husbands who had the good fortune to bring their wives over to Canada hired a retired school teacher to teach a bit of English to their wives. Father discouraged Mother from going to those once-a-week sessions. 54

"That old woman will get rich doing nothing. What have these women learned?" *Fan gwei* ways — make-up, lipstick, smelly perfumes, fancy 55 clothes. Once she gets through with them, they won't be Chinese women any more — and they certainly won't be white either."

56   Some of the husbands heeded the words of the boss, for he was older than they, and he had been in the *fan gwei*'s land longer. These wives stayed home and tended the children, or they worked in the restaurant kitchen, washing dishes and cooking *fan gwei* foods, and talking in Chinese about the land and the life they had been forced to leave behind.

57   "He was afraid that I would leave him. I depended on him for everything. I could not go anywhere by myself. He drove me to work and he drove me home. He only taught me how to print my name so that I could sign anything he wanted me to, bank cheques, legal documents. . ."

58   Perhaps I am not Chinese enough any more to understand why my mother would want to take in the sorrow, the pain, and the anguish, and then to recount them every so often.

59   Once, I was presumptuous enough to ask her why she would want to remember in such detail. She said that the memories didn't hurt any more. I did not tell her that her reminiscences cut me to the quick. Her only solace now is to be listened to.

60   When my father died five years ago, she cried and cried. "Don't leave me in this world. Let me die with you."

61   Grief-stricken, she would not eat for days. She was so weak from hunger that I feared she wouldn't be able to attend the funeral. At his grave side, she chanted over and over a dirge, commending his spirit to the next world and begging the goddess of mercy to be kind to him. By custom, she set his picture on the mantel and burned incense in front of it daily. And we would go to the cemetery often. There she would arrange fresh flowers and talk to him in the gentlest way.

62   Often she would warn me: "The world of the golden mountain is so strong, *fan gwei* improprieties, and customs. They will have you abandon your own aged mother to some old-age home to rot away and die unmourned. If you are here long enough, they will turn your head until you don't know who you are — Chinese."

63   My mother would convert the months and the days into the Chinese lunar calendar. She would tell me about the seasons and the harvests and festivals in China. We did not celebrate any *fan gwei* holidays.

64   My mother sits here at the table, fingering the booklet from the Citizenship Court. For thirty-some years, my mother did not learn the English language, not because she was not smart enough, not because she was too old to learn, and not because my father forbade her, but because she feared that learning English would change her Chinese soul. She only learned enough English to survive in the restaurant kitchen.

65   Now, Mother wants *gum san* citizenship.

66   "Is there no hope that I will be given it?" she asks.

67   "There's always a chance," I tell her. "I'll hand in the application."

"I should have given that person the *lai-shi*," Mother says obstinately.   68

"Maybe I should teach you some English," I retort. "You have about six   69
months before the oral interview."

"I am seventy years old," she says. "*Lai-shi* is definitely much easier."   70

My brief glimpse into Mother's heart is over, and it has taken so long   71
to come about. I do not know whether I understand my aged mother
any better now. Despite my mother's constant instruction, there is too
much *fan gwei* in me.

The booklet from the Citizenship Court lies, unmoved, on the table,   72
gathering dust for weeks. She has not mentioned citizenship again with
the urgency of that particular time. Once in a while, she would say: "They
have forgotten me. I told you they don't want old Chinese women as
citizens."

Finally, her interview date is set. I try to teach her some ready-made   73
phrases, but she forgets them.

"You should not sigh so much. It is bad for your health," Mother   74
observes.

On the day of her examination, I accompany her into the judge's   75
chamber. I am more nervous than my mother.

Staring at the judge, my mother remarks: "*Noi yren.*" The judge shows   76
interest in what my mother says, and I translate it: "She says you're a
woman."

The judge smiles, "Yes. Is that strange?"   77

"If she is going to examine me," Mother tells me, "I might as well start   78
packing for China. Sell my house. Dig up your father's bones, and I'll
take them back with me."

Without knowing what my mother said, the judge reassures her. "This   79
is just a formality. Really. We know that you obviously want to be part of
our Canadian society. Why else would you go through all this trouble?
We want to welcome you as a new citizen, no matter what race, national-
ity, religion, or age. And we want you to be proud — as a new Canadian."

Six weeks have passed since the interview with the judge. Mother   80
receives a registered letter telling her to come in three weeks' time to
take part in the oath of allegiance ceremony.

With patient help from the same judge, my mother recites the oath   81
and becomes a Canadian citizen after thirty years in *gum san*.

"How does it feel to be a Canadian?" I ask.   82

"In China, this is the eighth month, the season of harvest." Then she   83
adds: "The *Dai Pao* says that the old-age pension cheques will be increased by nine dollars next month."

As we walk home on this bright autumn morning, my mother clutches   84
her piece of paper. Citizenship. She says she will go up to the cemetery
and talk to my father this afternoon. She has something to tell him.

△ △

Further Reading:

Bennett Lee and Jim Wong-Chu, eds., *Many-Mouthed Birds: Contemporary Writings by Chinese-Canadians*
Sky Lee, *Disappearing Moon Cafe* (novel)
Amy Tan, *The Joy Luck Club* (novel)

Structure:

1. The author says this piece is at least partly fiction. How well has its chronological *narrative* mode served to present the *cause-and-effect* message?
2. Why are there 84 paragraphs? Why are some so short?
3. As he tells why after 30 years his mother does not speak English, the narrator examines several *causes*: the isolation of her work as cook (paragraphs 51–52), obstruction by her conservative husband (54–57), and finally her age. While these all play a part, what is the key reason he finally grasps in 62–64? Does he deplore or admire this motivation for not learning English?
4. Though in this piece Engkent explores mostly *causes*, what *effect* emerges at the end? How strong is it in the life of the mother and the son? How well does it serve as a closing?

Style:

1. Why does Engkent sprinkle his account with Chinese terms: *gum san, Dai Pao, fan gwei, lai-shi, hon san* and *noi yren*? Does he define each? Do they confuse, or do they enrich the argument? Give reasons.
2. In what tense has Engkent written? What are the advantages of this tense for narratives?

Ideas for Discussion and Writing:

1. Why do people immigrate? Give *causes*. Give *effects*.
2. In Vancouver, Toronto and Montreal, many New Canadians can shop, eat, worship, read, listen to radio or see TV and movies, go out, and work — all in their first language. Why learn English or French?
3. To maintain her identity, the narrator's mother spoke only her first language. If you are from another country, what are *your* techniques for retaining your identity here?
4. Americans view their society as a "melting pot" where new arrivals assimilate, but Canadians have viewed theirs as a "mosaic" where immigrants are encouraged, even funded, to keep their language and culture. Which METAPHOR do you prefer? Which philosophy works

best for the individual? For the nation? Defend your view with reasons.

5. Until now most Canadians have cherished the "Two Nations" concept of our history and culture, and the legal fact that French and English are Canada's official languages. Yet now some English Canadians and some Quebec separatists call bilingualism a waste of money, and many New Canadians ask why French takes precedence over their own language now spoken by many in Canada. What is the solution? What are the implications for Quebeckers? For French Canadians living outside Quebec? For English Canadians living in Quebec? For First Nations People? For New Canadians?

6. **PROCESS IN WRITING:** *Go to the library. Through periodical indexes or CD-ROM data bases of periodicals, examine Canada's current immigration policies. Focus on one question — for example are we accepting fewer or more immigrants? Encouraging or discouraging political refugees? Practising racism in our selection criteria? Make notes on the* effects *of the policy you have selected and, looking them over, write a* THESIS. *Now do a rapid discovery draft, tracing these* effects. *When it "cools off," look it over. Do linking words such as "since," "because" and "therefore" emphasize the* cause-and-effect *logic? Do examples help the reader "see" your point? Is all deadwood cut? If not, revise. Finally check for things like spelling and grammar as you produce your good draft. Read it aloud to the class, and be ready to answer questions asked from other points of view.*

Note: See also the Topics for Writing at the end of this chapter.

Alison Acker

Tito

"Live a lot, or you'll have nothing to write about!" says Alison Acker, who follows her own advice. Retired, twice widowed and a grandmother, she is now chief lyricist for the Victoria Raging Grannies, a group of "guerrilla singers" who stage protests for environmental and antiwar causes, dressed in costume and singing outrageous lyrics to satirize their opponents on national news media. In August 1993 Acker was sentenced to three weeks in jail for her part in a protest to save old-growth forest at Clayoquot Sound, British Columbia. Acker began her political journey far away, as a child in wartime London, England, where nightly bombing attacks, the death of her father in a bomb shelter, and photos of Nazi death camps awakened her social conscience. Thrown out of the University of Nottingham at 17 for painting a phone booth communist red, she became a reporter for London newspapers. When she married, Acker and her husband stuck a pin in a map to see where they would emigrate. The destination: Winnipeg. Over the years she followed careers in reporting, teaching literature at Ryerson Polytechnic University, and writing. Acker's best-known book started with her work helping refugees from Latin America. She became fluent in Spanish, then courageously travelled alone for five months through Guatemala, Nicaragua, El Salvador and Honduras, interviewing children to learn the ultimate effects of repression and war — and on the side smuggling medical supplies to anti-government forces. In his Globe and Mail *review, author Ronald Wright called* Children of the Volcano *"horrifying and uplifting. If there is to be one book on Central America, let it be this." Our selection focuses on Tito, a small boy who lives the social inequalities of Honduras.*

1   Unripe bananas give you stomach-ache. Tito should know, because he eats them a lot when there is nothing else to eat, and that happens often. On good days, there are beans and corn tortillas. Some days there are just tortillas. And sometimes there is nothing at all. So kids like Tito grub around for whatever roots or fruit they can find.

2   Yet Tito lives on what we might call a farm. His family has a *milpa*, all two acres of it, with a patch of corn and a goat and a few chickens.

3   "The goat is no good. She has no milk. She's sick," Tito tells me. And eggs? "Mama sells them in the market."

He is a skinny kid, just eight years old. His T-shirt is torn and he has 4
dirty shorts, knobbly knees, and no shoes. It is difficult to see him at all
because he's hidden under an enormous load of firewood carried on
his shoulder. I met him trudging along the highway twenty kilometres
from Progreso, in the heart of the banana lands. Tito has a machete,
too, wrapped in a rag, under the firewood. He uses it to cut the wood
himself. He has to walk "a long way" to get it, and a long way to get
home. His thatched-roof home is indeed a long way — four kilometres
— from the stand of trees. The trees are private property.

In a country where pine forests abound and mahogany, rosewood, 5
Spanish cedar, and balsa are national riches, there is no wood to gather
for a fire. As well, there is no land for Tito's family, in a country with
112,088 square kilometres of land, and only thirty-two people on each
square kilometre. The land belongs to either the sugar plantation owners and the banana company or the cattle ranchers. Families like Tito's
get the leavings. Their two acres are rented. As rent they hand over
most of the corn they grow. During bad years, they often go in debt
because there's not enough corn to pay the rent.

Tito lives in a little village outside Progreso, inland from the north 6
coast of Honduras. This area has long been a centre of rebellion by
peasant groups enraged by the landowners. Up the road, at El Bálsamo,
I saw the four graves of local men who were shot down by one of the
many private police forces when they tried to take possession of land
involved in a legal dispute. That was in the summer of 1983.

What would Tito do if a man with a gun saw him cutting firewood on 7
someone else's land?

"Run away as fast as I can," he answers. "But I always watch out before 8
I start cutting. I'm afraid of the *hacenderos* [the land-owners]."

My romantic notions of rural simplicity are making it difficult for me 9
to comprehend the harshness of life in Tito's village. I keep thinking
the place is picturesque. But no, I would not like to live in a leaky
thatched-roof hut, without windows, and with rats. Yet the illusion of
tropical simplicity remains. The main "street" of Acaya is fringed with
flowering trees. Bright salmon-pink clashes with turquoise blue, so much
that my eyes miss at first the garbage and the ruts in the road, the
stagnant water, and the rusting remains of a truck. The village boasts a
church with a bell tower and a store; there is no electric light, no water,
no bus service, no school, no telephone. Whenever the kids go to school,
which is not often, they have to walk four kilometres to the next village.
The women cook on open wood-fires.

Tito doesn't know anybody who has a truck or car, except the police, 10
the *hacendero,* and the priest who comes every second Sunday. A literacy
teacher comes on foot once a week. He brings his own lantern and
chalkboard. Tito's mother goes to the classes "sometimes" when she is

not busy with the kids. She has nine other children besides Tito. His father is usually away either working for a banana company or cutting cane, depending on what work is available.

11   The banana lands to the north extend further than I can see. Each plant stands eight feet tall, a fierce green row upon row, behind barbed wire. A single line of railroad snakes toward the banana ports, and the train whistle breaks the silence twice a day. Tito's grandfather used to work as a *venenero*, he tells me — the man with the "poison" who sprayed the banana plants. He worked in a gang that lugged the hoses carrying the blue pesticide that dyed their clothes and made them cough up their lungs and become old men at forty.

12   "My dad says the banana bosses are millionaires. But they don't want any workers now," says Tito. It is true that the "yellow gold" is grown less now in Honduras, as banana companies find other more profitable land in South America. The Honduran land is worn out. Sugar plantations offer back-breaking work for a couple of months a year. Cattle ranches need very few workers. So most of the peasants in Acaya have very little work and very little income. They make less than $10 a week, on a year-round average.

13   Tito tells me his mother keeps "a few *lempiras*" [worth roughly fifty cents] for some medicine or if somebody has to go to the nearest town, Progreso, in an emergency.

14   One of his sisters is blind. She was bitten by a *bicho*, an insect. When people are sick, they usually call in the *curandera*, the local healer. She doesn't cost much and she is someone they know and trust. Tito has never been vaccinated against childhood diseases and has never visited a doctor. He's never been to school either.

15   He refuses to take me inside his little house. I call out, but the voices from inside hush quickly and nobody comes to the open doorway, so I do not intrude.

16   Later I talk about Tito to a nun who works for a church rural training and development program, not far away. She has lived there for five years and now identifies completely with her peasant community.

17   "They live like they did two hundred years ago, and they seem so apathetic, right?" she challenges me. "So would you if you suffered from parasites and malnutrition. In the countryside, three out of four people live in extreme poverty. There isn't enough money for food, let alone school books or shoes. This is why the children don't go to school; it is a vicious circle. Without education, they can't climb out of poverty, and without money, they can't get an education.

18   "When the men try to organize to defend themselves, they are called Communists and cut down by the landowners or the police. I have seen twenty different political murders in this area in the last twelve months. The graves you saw at El Bálsamo are those of four ordinary peasants,

who went to help fellow workers on strike at a banana plantation. They had a truck and were driving home when two members of the territorial forces stopped them for a ride. The soldiers shot four of them; the other three ran away. They piled the four bodies into the truck and drove off. Other peasants saw the bodies when the truck passed through a village. They stopped it, and the soldiers ran off. They were never prosecuted, though everybody knows who they are."

She did not want me to use her name. "This quietness you see every- 19 where isn't peace," she says. "It is fear and despair. The children may talk to you because they are not yet aware of the reality."

But even the children in Tito's village are quiet. A very small boy battles 20 a large pig on the end of a string; the pig oinks and scrabbles on the gritty road. The other kids just watch. Most of the day they fetch and carry and look after the little ones, and plant seeds in the bare ground with a digging stick. When the chores are done, they sit listlessly in the dirt.

What sort of games do you play? I ask Tito. But I don't get any 21 answer. Maybe the words are wrong. What do you do when you are not busy doing chores? "I go to sleep," he replies.

The International Labour Organization in Geneva estimates that more 22 than a third of the world's children work, most of them as unpaid family workers. Tito's chores would not even class him as a worker. He is lucky not to be making bricks in forty-degree heat, or working in a carpet factory, or pulling a cart. He has a home, a mother and a father, brothers and sisters. He is not sick or in jail or a victim of war.

Tito is just a typical child of Third World poverty. Nothing special. 23 No emergency. A common case.

△△

Further Reading:

Alison Acker, *Children of the Volcano*
Rigoberta Menchu, *I, Rigoberta Menchu: an Indian Woman of Guatemala*
Oscar Lewis, *Children of Sanchez* (sociology)
Juan Rulfo, *Pedro Páramo* (novel, Mexico)
Carlos Fuentes, *Death of Artemio Cruz* (novel, Mexico)
Gabriel García Márquez, *Chronicle of a Death Foretold* (novella, Colombia)

Structure:

1. Acker puts her THESIS not at the beginning but at the end. Identify it. Does it have more impact or less impact where it is? Would you put a thesis at the end? How does Acker draw us into her argument without a thesis up front?

2. What IRONIES do you see in Acker's conclusion, which is also her thesis? Point out facts we have learned about Tito which lend surprise and other feelings to this closing.

3. How much of Acker's argument would be left if we took out all the *examples?* Can we ever have too many? Does she? Or is it more common to have too few? Which possibility most concerns you in your own writing?

4. Virtually every detail Acker gives of Tito's life centres on poverty. Are he and his family responsible for it? Or if not, who is? Point out every *cause* Acker shows for the *effects* of this poverty. Does she focus more on the *causes* or *effects?* Would either make sense alone?

5. Analyze the chain of *cause and effect* in the "vicious circle" the nun describes in paragraph 17. Imagine a way to break this chain: what *new causes* could produce *new effects?*

Style:

1. Acker often uses the word "I." Does it work here? Would it in all essays? Should she be more OBJECTIVE, or does being SUBJECTIVE help, as when in paragraph 9 she analyzes her own "romantic" feelings as a foreigner?

2. Do Spanish terms such as *milpa, hacenderos, venenero, lempiras* and *curandera* help us experience this subject? Does the fact that Acker defines them imply that they were unnecessary, or do they have some value not measured in fact?

Ideas for Discussion and Writing:

1. Tito plays no games (paragraph 21). Point out all the *causes* of this deceptively simple fact.

2. Why do only the police, the landowner and the priest have vehicles, while the literacy teacher "comes on foot" (par. 10)?

3. Tito cuts firewood from private property (paragraph 4). If he sees the owners he will "run away as fast as I can." How many Canadians, like Tito in Honduras, break laws to survive economically? Name several *causes* of our underground economy.

4. Acker was able to research this selection because she speaks Spanish. Is language study important? As a Canadian will you need French? As a North American will you need Spanish? The American government envisions NAFTA (the North American Free Trade Act) as spreading to include most of Latin America. What is your own strategy for dealing with such a future?

5. **PROCESS IN WRITING:** *A wage-earner is laid off. What are the effects? Write the words "Job Loss" in the middle of a blank page. Now around it jot down results that "job loss" calls to mind, and connect each with a line to its*

origin. Now highlight the best parts of this cluster outline, and from them decide your THESIS. *Write a rapid discovery draft, not revising now, so your thoughts move quickly onto the page. The next day look it over. Are all the effects really* caused *by "job loss"? Do you avoid prejudice, such as open dislike of corporations or governments? (Review the introduction to this chapter for the logic of cause and effect.) Do transitions like "therefore," "as a result," "since" and "because" signal* causality? *If not, add. Finally edit for correctness, then print out your final version.*

Note: See also the Topics for Writing at the end of this chapter.

Mordecai Richler

1944: The Year I Learned to Love a German

Mordecai Richler is a widely read novelist and the liveliest Canadian essayist of his generation. His carefully crafted, ruthlessly satirical prose devastates its targets: hypocrisy, pretension, self-righteousness, prejudice, provincialism and nationalism (he attacks all these in our selection). Born in 1931 to a working-class family in the Jewish quarter of Montreal, Richler left in 1951 for two years in Paris, where he wrote his first novel. He returned to work at the CBC, then from 1954 to 1972 lived and worked in England. Since 1972 he has made his home in Quebec. Over the years Richler has maintained a steady output of novels: The Acrobats *(1954),* Son of a Smaller Hero *(1955),* A Choice of Enemies *(1957),* The Apprenticeship of Duddy Kravitz *(1959),* The Incomparable Atuk *(1963),* Cocksure *(1968),* St. Urbain's Horseman *(1971) and* Joshua Then and Now *(1980). Both* Duddy Kravitz *and* Joshua *were made into films, as well as his children's book* Jacob Two-Two Meets the Hooded Fang *(1975). Many of Richler's essays and articles have been gathered in books:* Hunting Tigers under Glass *(1968),* Shovelling Trouble *(1972),* Notes on an Endangered Species *(1974),* The Great Comic Book Heroes *(1978),* Home Sweet Home: My Canadian Album *(1984) and* Broadsides: Reviews and Opinions *(1990). His 1992 book* Oh Canada! Oh Quebec! *has been his most controversial: Richler's claims of unfair language laws and of past antisemitism in Quebec stirred debate in both the French and English press. Our own selection is from* The New York Times Book Review *of February 2, 1986. It is a revised version of his introduction to the Book-of-the-Month-Club edition of Remarque's novel.*

1   Reading was not one of my boyhood passions. Girls, or rather the absence of girls, drove me to it. When I was 13 years old, short for my age, more than somewhat pimply, I was terrified of girls. They made me feel sadly inadequate. As far as I could make out, they were attracted only to boys who were tall or played for the school basketball team or at least shaved. Unable to qualify on all three counts, I resorted to subterfuge. I set out to call attention to myself by becoming a character.

142

Retreating into high seriousness, I acquired a pipe, which I chewed on ostentatiously, and made it my business to be seen everywhere, even at school basketball games, absorbed by books of daunting significance. Say, H. G. Wells's "Short History of the World" or Paul de Kruif's "Microbe Hunters" or John Gunther inside one continent or another. I rented these thought-provoking books for three cents a day from a neighborhood lending library that was across the street from a bowling alley where I used to spot pins four nights a week.

Oh, my God, I would not be 13 again for anything. The sweetly scented   2
girls of my dreams, wearing lipstick and tight sweaters and nylon stockings, would sail into the bowling alley holding hands with the boys from the basketball team. "Hi," they would call out, giggly, nudging one another, even as I bent over the pins, "how goes the reading?"

The two women who ran the lending library, possibly amused by my   3
pretensions, tried to interest me in fiction.

"I want fact. I can't be bothered with *stories*," I protested, waving my   4
pipe at them, affronted. "I just haven't got the time for such nonsense."

I knew what novels were, of course. I had read "Scaramouche," by   5
Rafael Sabatini, at school, as well as "Treasure Island" and some Ellery Queens and a couple of thumpers by G. A. Henty. Before that there had been Action Comics, Captain Marvel, Batman and — for educational reasons — either Bible Comics or Classic Comics. All these treasures I bought under the counter, as it were. They were passed hand to hand on dark street corners. Contraband. Our samizdat. The reason for this being that in 1943 the dolts who prevailed in Ottawa had adjudged American comic books unessential to the war effort, a drain on the Canadian dollar.

Novels, I knew, were mere romantic make-believe, not as bad as   6
poetry, to be fair, but bad enough. Our high school class master, a dedicated Scot, had been foolish enough to try to interest us in poetry. A veteran of World War I, he told us that during the nightly bombardments on the Somme he would fix a candle to his steel helmet so that he could read poetry in the trenches. A scruffy lot, we were not moved. Instead we exchanged knowing winks behind that admirable man's back. Small wonder, we agreed, that he had ended up no better than a high school teacher.

My aunts consumed historical novels like pastries. My father read   7
Black Mask and True Detective. My mother would read anything on a Jewish subject, preferably by I. J. Singer or Sholem Asch, though she would never forgive the latter for having written "The Nazarene," never mind "Mary" and "The Apostle." My older brother kept a novel, "Topper Takes a Trip," secure under his mattress in the bedroom we shared, assuring me that it was placed at just such an angle on the springs that

if it were moved so much as a millimeter in his absence he would know and bloody well make me pay for it.

8   I fell ill with a childhood disease. I no longer remember which, but obviously I meant it as a rebuke to those girls in tight sweaters who continued to ignore me. Never mind, they would mourn at my funeral, burying me with my pipe. Too late, they would say, "Boy, was he ever an intellectual!"

9   The women from the lending library, concerned, dropped off books for me at our house. The real stuff. Fact-filled. Providing me with the inside dope on Theodor Herzl's childhood and "Brazil Yesterday, Today, and Tomorrow." One day they brought me a novel: "All Quiet on the Western Front" by Erich Maria Remarque. The painting on the jacket that was taped to the book showed a soldier wearing what was unmistakably a German Army helmet. *What was this,* I wondered, *some sort of bad joke?*

10   Nineteen forty-four that was, and I devoutly wished every German left on the face of the earth an excruciating death. The Allied invasion of France had not yet begun, but I cheered every Russian counterattack, each German city bombed, and — with the help of a map tacked to my bedroom wall — followed the progress of the Canadian troops fighting their way up the Italian boot. Boys from our street had already been among the fallen. Izzy Draper's uncle, Harvey Kugelmass's older brother. The boy who was supposed to marry Gita Holtzman.

11   "All Quiet on the Western Front" lay unopened on my bed for two days. A time bomb ticking away, though I hardly suspected it. Rather than read a novel, a novel written by a German, I tuned in to radio soap operas in the afternoons: "Ma Perkins," "Pepper Young's Family." I organized a new baseball league for short players who didn't shave yet, appointing myself commissioner, the first Canadian to be so honored. Sifting through a stack of my father's back issues of Popular Mechanics, I was sufficiently inspired to invent a spaceship and fly to Mars, where I was adored by everybody, especially the girls. Finally, I was driven to picking up "All Quiet on the Western Front" out of boredom. I never expected that a mere novel, a stranger's tale, could actually be dangerous, creating such turbulence in my life, obliging me to question so many received ideas. About Germans. About my own monumental ignorance of the world. About what novels were.

12   At the age of 13 in 1944, happily as yet untainted by English 104, I couldn't tell you whether Remarque's novel was

    a. a slice of life
    b. symbolic
    c. psychological
    d. seminal.

I couldn't even say if it was well or badly written. In fact, as I recall, it 13 didn't seem to be "written" at all. Instead, it just flowed. Now, of course, I understand that writing that doesn't advertise itself is art of a very high order. It doesn't come easily. But at the time I wasn't capable of making such distinctions. I also had no notion of how "All Quiet on the Western Front" rated critically as a war novel. I hadn't read Stendhal or Tolstoy or Crane or Hemingway. I hadn't even heard of them. I didn't know that Thomas Mann, whoever he was, had praised the novel highly. Neither did I know that in 1929 the judges at some outfit called the Book-of-the-Month Club had made it their May selection. But what I did know is that, hating Germans with a passion, I had read only 20, maybe 30, pages before the author had seduced me into identifying with my enemy, 19-year-old Paul Baumer, thrust into the bloody trenches of World War I with his schoolmates: Müller, Kemmerich and the reluctant Joseph Behm, one of the first to fall. As if that weren't sufficiently unsettling in itself, the author, having won my love for Paul, my enormous concern for his survival, then betrayed me in the last dreadful paragraphs of his book:

"He fell in October 1918, on a day that was so quiet and still on the 14 whole front, that the army report confined itself to the single sentence: All quiet on the Western Front.

"He had fallen forward and lay on the earth as though sleeping. 15 Turning him over one saw that he could not have suffered long; his face had an expression of calm, as though almost glad the end had come."

The movies, I knew from experience, never risked letting you down 16 like that. No matter how bloody the battle, how long the odds, Errol Flynn, Robert Taylor, even Humphrey Bogart could be counted on to survive and come home to Ann Sheridan, Lana Turner or — if they were sensitive types — Loretta Young. Only character actors, usually Brooklyn Dodger fans, say George Tobias or William Bendix, were expendable.

Obviously, having waded into the pool of serious fiction by accident, 17 I was not sure I liked or trusted the water. It was too deep. Anything could happen.

There was something else, a minor incident in "All Quiet on the 18 Western Front" that would not have troubled an adult reader but, I'm embarrassed to say, certainly distressed that 13-year-old boy colliding with his first serious novel.

Sent out to guard a village that has been abandoned because it is 19 being shelled too heavily, Katczinsky, the incomparable scrounger, surfaces with suckling pigs and potatoes and carrots for his comrades, a group of eight altogether:

"The suckling pigs are slaughtered. Kat sees to them. We want to 20 make potato-cakes to go with the roast. But we cannot find a grater for the potatoes. However, that difficulty is soon got over. With a nail we punch a lot of holes in a pot lid and there we have a grater. Three fellows put on thick gloves to protect their fingers against the grater, two others peel the potatoes, and the business gets going."

21   The business, I realized, alarmed — no, *affronted* — was the making of potato latkes, a favorite of mine as well as Paul Baumer's, a dish I had always taken to be Jewish, certainly not a German concoction.

22   What did I know? Nothing. Or, looked at another way, my real education, my lifelong addiction to fiction, began with the trifling discovery that the potato latke was not of Jewish origin, but something borrowed from the Germans and now a taste that Jew and German shared in spite of everything.

23   I felt easier about my affection for the German soldier Paul Baumer once I was told by the women from the lending library that when Hitler came to power in 1933 he had burned all of Erich Maria Remarque's books and in 1938 he took away his German citizenship. Obviously Hitler had grasped that novels could be dangerous, something I learned when I was only 13 years old. He burned them. I began to devour them. I started to read at the breakfast table and on streetcars, often missing my stop, and in bed with benefit of a flashlight. It got me into trouble. I grasped, for the first time, that I didn't live in the center of the world but had been born into a working-class family in an unimportant country far from the cities of light: London, Paris, New York. Of course this wasn't my fault, it was my inconsiderate parents who were to blame. But there was, I now realized, a larger world out there beyond St. Urbain Street in Montreal; a world that could be available to me, even though — to my mother's despair — I had been born left-handed, ate with my elbows on the table and had failed once more to lead the class at school.

24   Preparing myself for the *Rive Gauche*,° I bought a blue beret, but I didn't dare wear it outside, or even in the house if anybody else was at home. I looked at but lacked the courage to buy a cigarette holder. But the next time I took Goldie Zimmerman to a downtown movie and then out to Dinty Moore's for toasted tomato sandwiches, I suggested that instead of milkshakes we each order a glass of *vin ordinaire*. "Are you crazy?" she asked.

25   As my parents bickered at the supper table, trapped in concerns now far too mundane for the likes of me — what to do if Dworkin raised the rent again, how to manage my brother's college fees — I sat with but actually apart from them in the kitchen, enthralled, reading for the first time, "All happy families are alike but an unhappy family is unhappy after its own fashion."

°*Rive Gauche*: the "Left Bank" of Paris, traditional quarter of students and intellectuals.

Erich Maria Remarque, born in Westphalia in 1897, went off to war, 26
directly from school, at the age of 18. He was wounded five times. He
lost all his friends. After the war he worked briefly as a schoolteacher, a
stonecutter, a test driver for a tire company and an editor of Sportbild
magazine. His first novel, "Im Westen Nichts Neues," was turned down
by several publishers before it was brought out by the Ullstein Press in
Berlin in 1928. "All Quiet on the Western Front" sold 1,200,000 copies
in Germany and was translated into 29 languages, selling some four
million copies throughout the world. The novel has been filmed three
times; the first time, memorably, by Lewis Milestone in 1930. The Milestone version, with Lew Ayres playing Paul Baumer, won Academy Awards
for best picture and best direction.

Since "All Quiet on the Western Front" once meant so much to me, I 27
picked it up again with a certain anxiety. After all this time I find it
difficult to be objective about the novel. Its pages still evoke for me
a back bedroom with a cracked ceiling and a sizzling radiator on
St. Urbain Street, mice scrabbling in the walls, a window looking out on
sheets frozen stiff on the laundry line, and all the pain of being too
young to shave, an ignorant and bewildered boy of 13.

Over the years the novel has lost something in shock value. The 28
original jacket copy of the 1929 Little, Brown & Company edition of "All
Quiet on the Western Front" warns the reader that it is "at times crude"
and "will shock the supersensitive by its outspokenness." Contemporary
readers, far from being shocked, will be amused by the novel's discretion,
the absence of explicit sex scenes, the unbelievably polite dialogue of
the men in the trenches.

△△△

The novel also has its poignant moments, both in the trenches and 29
when Paul Baumer goes home on leave, an old man of 19, only to find
insufferably pompous schoolmasters still recruiting the young with
mindless prattle about the fatherland and the glory of battle. Strong
characters are deftly sketched. Himmelstoss, the postman who becomes
a crazed drillmaster, Tjaden, the peasant soldier, Kantorek, the school-
master. On the front line the enemy is never the Frogs or the Limeys,
but the insanity of the war itself. It is the war, in fact, and not even Paul
Baumer, that is the novel's true protagonist. In a brief introduction to
the novel Remarque wrote: "This book is to be neither an accusation
nor a confession, and least of all an adventure, for death is not an
adventure to those who stand face to face with it. It will try simply to tell
of a generation of men who, even though they may have escaped its
shells, were destroyed by the war."

Since World War I we have become altogether too familiar with larger 30
horrors. The Holocaust, Hiroshima, the threat of a nuclear winter.

Death by numbers, cities obliterated by decree. At peace, as it were, we live with the daily dread of the missiles in their silos, ours pointed at them, theirs pointed at us. None of this, however, diminishes the power of "All Quiet on the Western Front," a novel that will endure because of its humanity, its honor and its refusal to lapse into sentimentality or strike a false note. It is a work that has earned its place on that small shelf of World War I classics alongside "Goodbye to All That," by Robert Graves, and Ernest Hemingway's "A Farewell to Arms."

△ △

Further Reading:

Mordecai Richler,
>   *The Apprenticeship of Duddy Kravitz*
>   *The Street* (short stories)
Erich Maria Remarque, *All Quiet on the Western Front*
Charles Yale Harrison, *Generals Die in Bed* (novel)
Ernest Hemingway, *A Farewell to Arms* (novel)

Structure:

1. How does the long opening prepare us for Richler's argument? What do paragraphs 1 and 2 achieve? Paragraphs 3–6?
2. Why does Richler devote so little of his argument to the original *causes* of his reading, and so much to the *effects*?
3. Point out every *effect* on young Richler of reading novels, as shown especially in paragraphs 11, 13–17, 18–22, and 23.
4. Richler uses spaces to divide the essay in parts. What advantages does this technique have? Do you use it?
5. What technique does Richler exploit when in the closing paragraph he refers to nuclear weapons?

Style:

1. Richler's overall message is serious. Why, then, does he poke fun at adolescence, at his own and others' reading habits, at high school English, at the movies and at other targets? Do his humour and even SATIRE help or hurt the argument? Defend your answer with reasons.
2. A key technique of both novelists and essayists is to clothe abstractions in concrete IMAGES — to "show, don't tell." Point out how Richler does so in paragraphs 11, 24 and 27.
3. Explain the IRONY of calling Paul Baumer "an old man of 19" (par. 29). Using this example, analyze how irony promotes CONCISENESS.
4. Is the METAPHOR of Remarque's novel as a "time bomb" (par. 11) well chosen for this topic?

Ideas for Discussion and Writing:

1. Almost every writer, like Richler, has read voraciously. Analyze the apparent *cause-and-effect* relationship: Why does reading other people's writing improve our own? Have you read enough? What are the *causes* of your attitude towards reading? What are the *effects?*

2. Richler admits that, as a Jewish boy growing up during the war, he "devoutly wished every German left on the face of the earth an excruciating death" (par. 10). Why *every* German? Do you see a STEREOTYPE behind this passage? Does it apply to those Germans who hid persecuted Jews? To those who fled Hitler's power, or even tried to assassinate him? Does it apply to Erich Maria Remarque? To Paul Baumer? Are other stereotypes more reliable? Those of women, teenagers, old people, Newfoundlanders, Quebeckers, Jews, Russians?

3. After reading 20 to 30 pages of *All Quiet on the Western Front,* Richler is "seduced" by the author into "identifying" with his "enemy," and even feels "betrayed" when, at the end, Paul Baumer dies. Cite another passage where Richler's reading of fiction dispels STEREOTYPES.

4. "I never expected that a mere novel, a stranger's tale, could actually be dangerous," says Richler in paragraph 11. How can a novel be "dangerous"? Why did Hitler burn this one and strip its author of citizenship (par. 23)? Name other books burned or censored. What may such cases reveal about the importance of writers to society?

5. Extend Richler's analysis to other media. List several films you have recently seen or TV serials you have followed. Which were "dangerous," challenging received attitudes? Which were "safe," propping up received attitudes? Argue with examples.

6. **PROCESS IN WRITING:** *Choose either a "dangerous" or a "safe" film or TV series from the previous question. Now in an essay of* cause and effect, *show how the chosen work affected you: Did it just reinforce old opinions, or did it change your mind? First brainstorm: jot down scenes in which the work either reassured or disturbed you. Now turn the best of these notes into a draft. Did the act of writing call up forgotten details? Add them. Did it challenge your view of the work's "danger" or "safety"? If so, change your thesis and adjust the argument. Now strengthen transitions to speed your argument and highlight its causality. Cut deadwood. Finally, test your prose aloud before writing the final version.*

Note: See also the Topics for Writing at the end of this chapter.

Topics for Writing
Chapter 4: Cause and Effect

Analyze the cause(s) and/or effect(s) of one of the following. (See also the guidelines that follow.)

1. Pirating of software
2. Learning more than one language
3. Being a twin
4. Being the oldest, youngest or middle child of a family
5. Being adopted
6. Moving out on your own
7. Marrying as a teenager
8. Cheating in school
9. Violence in a particular sport
10. Getting into debt
11. Private ownership of handguns
12. Eating junk food
13. Moving to a new school
14. Working while being a student
15. The decline in newspaper readership
16. Hitchhiking
17. Homelessness
18. The underground economy
19. Unemployment
20. Pornography
21. High taxes
22. Playing video games
23. Dyslexia
24. Buying lottery tickets
25. Racial discrimination
26. Obesity
27. The high price of car insurance
28. Moving to another country
29. Crime in the schools
30. The growing popularity of Internet

Note also the Process in Writing topic after each selection in this chapter.

Process in Writing: Guidelines

Follow at least some of these steps in writing your essay of cause and effect (your teacher may suggest which ones).

1. *In the middle of a page, write the subject you wish to explore in your essay of cause and effect. Now around it write many other words that it brings to mind. Connect related items with lines, then use this cluster outline to focus your argument.*

2. *Write a first draft rapidly, double-spaced, getting it all down on paper without stopping yet to revise.*

3. *When this version has "cooled off," analyze it, referring to our chapter introduction: Have you begun and ended at the right places in the chain of causality? If not, cut or add. Have you found the real causes and the real effects? If not, revise. Do you also need causes of causes, or effects of effects? If so, add.*

4. *In your next draft sharpen the* TRANSITIONS, *using expressions like "since," "although," "because" and "as a result" to signal each step of your logic.*

5. *Share this draft with a group of classmates. Revise any places where this audience does not follow your logic.*

6. *Now as you produce your good copy, edit for things like spelling and grammar. Proofread slowly, word by word. If you have used a computer, save the essay on disk in case your teacher suggests further revision.*

Mike Constable

"Women workers earn, on an average, only 69 cents for every $1 a man gets— even though on an average, women are better educated than men."

—*Doris Anderson, "The 51-Per-Cent Minority"*

CHAPTER

5

COMPARISON AND CONTRAST

It's just the opposite of. . . .

One of the most dramatic ways to argue is to compare and contrast. See Mike Constable's cartoon on the opposite page. What is happening? All the runners are in starting position, awaiting the same shot from the same referee, and no doubt aiming for the same finish line. These are the *comparisons* (similarities). Yet at the same time there are *contrasts* (differences). Three of the runners are men, but only one is a woman. The referee holding his gun is also a man, unlike the woman contestant. She will run in skirt and high heels, while the men clearly will not. Worst of all, the men will run straight ahead, while she must race uphill to reach their level. Is there any way the woman can win this race?

Though the cartoon has both comparisons and contrasts, clearly it is the contrasts that send the message — men have advantages in the race of life. In the essay that follows, Doris Anderson uses words to send the same message through the same logic. Though of course there are similarities between the lives of women and men, it is the differences, the *contrasts*, that build Anderson's point that women, though a "majority" in numbers, are a "minority" in power.

When using the logic of comparison and contrast in your own essays, you, too, may find both similarities and differences. Though it is possible to explore both, the need to focus means that using one is often better — and the choice is usually the more dramatic and interesting one: *contrast.*

You have experienced contrast if you have ever known culture shock. As you arrive in a new country, the look of the buildings and streets, the smells in the air, the sounds, the language and customs, all seem strange — because you are contrasting them to what you just left. And if you stay a long time, the same happens in reverse when you return: home seems strange because you are contrasting it to the place where you've just been. The cars may seem too big, the food too bland, the pace of life too fast. Travel is one of the great educational experiences: through contrast, one culture puts another in perspective.

In a comparison and contrast essay, it is essential to choose two subjects *of the same general type:* two countries, two sports, two poems, or two solutions to unemployment. For example, in our chapter Russell Baker focusses on two cities, Toronto and New York, systematically comparing their taxis, noise, garbage, dogs, subway, vandalism and other aspects of urban life. Despite his comic tone, and despite any disagreements we might have as to his verdict, by the time Baker gets done we have the impression of having read a logical argument. After all, Toronto and New York are in the same category: big cities.

But suppose that instead of comparing two cities, Baker had compared a city and an anthill. After all, there are similarities: both are crowded, both are highly organized, both have housing with many rooms located off corridors, etc. But no matter how much fun he might have had or what insights he might have got across, he would prove nothing — for the simple reason that people are not insects. His essay would be an analogy, a more imaginative but less logical kind of argument, which we will explore in the next chapter.

Once you have chosen your two subjects of the same general type, you face another choice: how to arrange them. There are two basic ways:

Divide the essay into halves, devoting the first half to Toronto and the second to New York. This system is natural in a very short essay, because your reader remembers everything from the first half while reading the second half. It is also natural when for some reason it seems the items are most clearly discussed as a whole rather than in parts.

Divide the subjects into separate points. First compare taxis in both cities, then noise in both cities, then garbage in both cities, and so on through your whole list of points. This system is most natural in long essays: putting related material together helps the reader to grasp comparisons or contrasts without the strain of recalling every detail from ten pages back.

Baker organizes by "separate points" even in his brief essay, because the approach fits his way of poking fun at New York: in describing how

Toronto controls its garbage, he implies, without even naming his own city, that New York is full of litter. He could not have achieved this degree of conciseness had he isolated the two sides of each topic into their own "halves" of the essay.

Although "halves" are often best for short papers and "separate points" are often best for long papers, be open to the needs of your particular subject, treatment and purpose. As Russell Baker has done, choose the approach that will most strongly deliver your message.

Finally, the very act of comparing or contrasting means you need examples — either a large number of short ones or a small number of long ones. If these do not make up at least half the content of your essay, you are losing power. Add more.

To generate your examples and points, why not draw a line down the middle of a blank page and put the name of your subjects at the top of each column? Now brainstorm a list of points under each heading. Connect related items from left to right with lines, and, seeing relationships, decide your thesis. Is cash better than credit? Is income tax fairer than sales tax? Are motorcycles more dangerous than cars? Whatever you believe is the truth, now write your essay, letting the examples show your reader why.

Note: Many essays in other chapters use comparison and contrast to help make their point. See especially these:

Thierry Mallet, "The Firewood Gatherers," p. 78
Margaret Laurence, "Where the World Began," p. 86
Mavor Moore, "The Roar of the Greasepaint, the Smell of the Caucus," p. 235
Judy Stoffman, "The Way of All Flesh," p. 250
Kildare Dobbs, "The Scar," p. 292
Bonnie Laing, "An Ode to the User-Friendly Pencil," p. 301 (a strong example of comparison and contrast developed through "separate points")

Doris Anderson

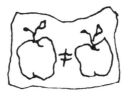

The 51-Per-Cent Minority

Doris Anderson is one of Canada's leading advocates of women's rights. After earning her B.A. at the University of Alberta in 1945, she wrote radio scripts, worked in advertising, then in 1951 joined the staff of Chatelaine. *As editor in chief from 1958 to 1977, Anderson added to the magazine's family emphasis an advocacy of higher social and economic status for women. In 1981, while she was serving as president of the Canadian Advisory Council on the Status of Women, her sudden resignation, in protest against the government's reluctance to guarantee equality of men and women in the new constitution, sparked a campaign by women that did achieve a constitutional guarantee of their rights. From 1982 to 1984 Anderson was president of the National Action Committee on the Status of Women, an umbrella group representing millions of women in numerous organizations. Anderson has published novels,* Two Women *in 1978,* Rough Layout *in 1981 and* Affairs of State *in 1988, in addition to her many editorials and articles. Her latest book is nonfiction,* The Unfinished Revolution, *an inquiry into the status of women in 10 European countries as well as Canada and the United States. Our own selection "The 51-Per-Cent Minority" first appeared in 1980 in* Maclean's. *Anderson has again revised and updated this classic for our present edition.*

1   In any Canadian election the public will probably be hammered numb with talk of the economy, energy and other current issues. But there will always be some far more startling topics that no one will talk about at all.

2   No one is going to say to all new Canadians: "Look, we're going through some tough times. Three out of four of you had better face the fact that you're always going to be poor. At 65 more than likely you'll be living below the poverty level."

3   And no one is going to tell Quebeckers: "You will have to get along on less money than the rest of the country. For every $1 the rest of us earn, you, because you live in Quebec, will earn 69 cents."

4   I doubt very much that any political party is going to level with the Atlantic provinces and say: "We don't consider people living there serious prime workers. Forget about any special measures to make jobs for

you. In fact in future federal-provincial talks we're not even going to discuss your particular employment problems."

And no politician is going to tell all the left-handed people in the country: "Look, we know it looks like discrimination, but we have to save some money somewhere. So, although you will pay into your company pension plan at the same rate as everyone else, you will collect less when you retire."

And no one is going to say to Canadian doctors: "We know you do one of the most important jobs any citizen can perform, but from now on you're going to have to get along without any support systems. All hospital equipment and help will be drastically reduced. We believe a good doctor should instinctively know what to do — or you're in the wrong job. If you're really dedicated you'll get along."

As for blacks: "Because of the color of your skin, you're going to be paid less than the white person next to you who is doing exactly the same job. It's tough but that's the way it is."

As for Catholics: "You're just going to have to understand that you will be beaten up by people with other religious beliefs quite regularly. Even if your assailant threatens to kill you, you can't do anything about it. After all, we all need some escape valves, don't we?"

Does all of the above sound like some nihilistic nightmare where Orwellian forces have taken over? Well, it's not. It's all happening right now, in Canada.

It's not happening to new Canadians, Quebeckers, residents of the Atlantic provinces, left-handed people, doctors, blacks or Indians. If it were, there would be riots in the streets. Civil libertarians would be howling for justice. But all of these discriminatory practices are being inflicted on women today in Canada as a matter of course.

Most women work at two jobs — one inside the home and one outside. Yet three out of four women who become widowed or divorced or have never married live out their old age in poverty. And the situation is going to get worse.

Women workers earn, on an average, only 69 cents for every $1 a man gets — even though on an average, women are better educated than men.

And when companies base pension plans on how long people live, women still pay the same rates as men but often collect less.

What politician could possibly tell doctors to train each other and get along without all their high technology and trained help? Yet a more important job than saving lives is surely creating lives. But mothers get no training, no help in the way of more than a token family allowance, inadequate day-care centres, and almost nonexistent after-school programs.

No politician would dream of telling blacks they must automatically earn less than other people. But women sales clerks, waitresses and hospital orderlies often earn less than males doing the same jobs. It would be called discrimination if a member of a religious group was beaten up, and the assailant would be jailed. But hundreds of wives get beaten by their husbands week in and week out, year after year. Some die, yet society still tolerates the fact that it's happening.

16   Women make up 51 per cent of the population of this country. Think of the kind of clout they could have if they used it at the polls. But to listen to the political parties, the woman voter just doesn't exist. When politicians talk to fishing folk they talk about improved processing plants and new docks. When they talk to wheat farmers they talk of better transportation and higher price supports. When they talk to people in the Atlantic provinces they talk about new federal money for buildings and more incentives for secondary industry. When they talk to ethnic groups they talk about better language training courses. But when they think of women — if they do at all — they assume women will vote exactly as their husbands — so why waste time offering them anything? It's mind-boggling to contemplate, though, how all those discriminatory practices would be swept aside if, instead of women, we were Italian, or black, or lived in Quebec or the Atlantic provinces.

△△△

Further Reading:

Doris Anderson, *The Unfinished Revolution*
Simone de Beauvoir, *The Second Sex*
Germaine Greer, *The Female Eunuch*
Naomi Wolf, *The Beauty Myth: How Images of Beauty Are Used Against Women*
Margaret Atwood, *Bodily Harm* (novel)
    The Handmaid's Tale (novel)

Structure:

1. Is this essay mainly a *comparison* or a *contrast?*
2. Does Anderson argue "point by point" or by "halves"?
3. Point out the passage of transition between Anderson's discussion of minorities and her discussion of women.
4. Why does this feminist essay never mention women until halfway through? How does this tactic help Anderson reach the potentially hostile 49 percent of her audience which is male?
5. If you have read *1984* or *Animal Farm*, tell how the reference to George Orwell in paragraph 9 helps make Anderson's point.
6. Why does the closing offer a series of new examples? Why are they so short?

Style:

1. How important is the title of an essay? What should it do? How effective is this one, and why?
2. Anderson's essay appeared in *Maclean's*, a magazine for the general reader. Name all the ways in which her essay seems designed for that person.

Ideas for Discussion and Writing:

1. Explain the IRONY of Anderson's claim: in what sense are women, 51 percent of the population, a "minority" in Canada?
2. Anderson states in paragraph 11, "Most women work at two jobs — one inside the home and one outside." Suppose that someday you and your spouse both have full-time jobs. If you are a woman, how much of the housework will you expect your husband to do? If you are a man, how much of the housework will you expect your wife to do? Defend your view with reasons.
3. "The 51-Per-Cent Minority" first appeared in 1980. Revising it for this edition 15 years later, Anderson was able to raise from 61 cents to 69 cents the amount that a woman earns for every dol-lar a man earns. At this rate of change, equal pay will not arrive until 2054 A.D., 74 years after the essay was written. Explain why.
4. In paragraph 16 Anderson writes, "Women make up 51 per cent of the population of this country. Think of the kind of clout they could have if they used it at the polls." Do you agree that women have not yet used their votes to best advantage? If so, why not? How could they begin to?
5. In "Canadians: What Do They Want?" Margaret Atwood points out that war and rape are "two activities not widely engaged in by women" (par. 1). Would our world be different if it were run by women? If so, how? If not, why not?
6. **PROCESS IN WRITING:** *Write an essay that* contrasts *the way society trains girls to be women with the way society trains boys to be men. First divide a page into halves, one for each sex, and fill each half with examples. Now from these notes choose contrasting pairs. Decide whether to organize the pairs by "halves" or "point by point," then write a rapid first draft, double-spaced. In your next draft strengthen the transitions, especially signals such as "but," "on the other hand," "however," and "yet," which point out contrast. Share a draft with classmates in small groups to see if all parts work. Revise any that do not. Finally, read your good draft aloud to the whole class, and be ready to answer questions asked from other points of view.*

Note: See also the Topics for Writing at the end of this chapter.

Catherine Pigott

Chicken-Hips*

Seeing a documentary film about eating disorders, The Famine Within, *and interviewing its director Katherine Gilday for a magazine article, Catherine Pigott recalled her time in Africa. It was years earlier, in 1983, while teaching English at a teachers' college, that she had shared the home and culture of a Gambian family. Then returning to Canada, she felt culture shock: through African eyes she now saw North American ideas of eating and bodily appearance to be cruel and misguided. The result was the essay that follows* (The Globe and Mail, 20 March 1991), *a celebration of the natural life she knew in Africa. Not only is its message cross-cultural but also its form: Pigott says "I was aware of speaking as I wrote," as in the oral tradition of African narrative. Now she applies this philosophy daily in her profession. Before the African experience she had been a print journalist at the Kingston* Whig Standard; *upon her return she became editor for CBC Radio News, then producer for the most celebrated of all Canadian radio broadcasts, the CBC's* Morningside, *where she found guests for host Peter Gzowski, and researched and developed a broadcast each day. Currently she is a producer for* Sunday Morning. *Though she still considers herself a writer, her writing is "not for the eye but the ear." It is direct, simple, natural. She recommends the same for student writers.*

1   The women of the household clucked disapprovingly when they saw me. It was the first time I had worn African clothes since my arrival in tiny, dusty Gambia, and evidently they were not impressed. They adjusted my head-tie and pulled my *lappa,* the ankle-length fabric I had wrapped around myself, even tighter. "You're too thin," one of them pronounced. "It's no good." They nicknamed me "Chicken-hips."

2   I marvelled at this accolade, for I had never been called thin in my life. It was something I longed for. I would have been flattered if those ample-bosomed women hadn't looked so distressed. It was obvious I fell far short of their ideal of beauty.

3   I had dressed up for a very special occasion — the baptism of a son. The women heaped rice into tin basins the size of laundry tubs, shaping

---

*Editor's title.

it into mounds with their hands. Five of us sat around one basin, thrusting our fingers into the scalding food. These women ate with such relish, such joy. They pressed the rice into balls in their fists, squeezing until the bright-red palm oil ran down their forearms and dripped off their elbows.

I tried desperately, but I could not eat enough to please them. It was hard for me to explain that I come from a culture in which it is almost unseemly for a woman to eat too heartily. It's considered unattractive. It was even harder to explain that to me thin is beautiful, and in my country we deny ourselves food in our pursuit of perfect slenderness.

That night, everyone danced to welcome the baby. Women swivelled their broad hips and used their hands to emphasize the roundness of their bodies. One needed to be round and wide to make the dance beautiful. There was no place for thinness here. It made people sad. It reminded them of things they wanted to forget, such as poverty, drought and starvation. You never knew when the rice was going to run out.

I began to believe that Africa's image of the perfect female body was far more realistic than the long-legged leanness I had been conditioned to admire. There, it is beautiful — not shameful — to carry weight on the hips and thighs, to have a round stomach and heavy, swinging breasts. Women do not battle the bulge, they celebrate it. A body is not something to be tamed and moulded.

The friends who had christened me Chicken-hips made it their mission to fatten me up. It wasn't long before a diet of rice and rich, oily stew twice a day began to change me. Every month, the women would take a stick and measure my backside, noting with pleasure its gradual expansion. "Oh Catherine, your buttocks are getting nice now!" they would say.

What was extraordinary was that I, too, believed I was becoming more beautiful. There was no sense of panic, no shame, no guilt-ridden resolves to go on the miracle grape-and-water diet. One day, I tied my *lappa* tight across my hips and went to the market to buy beer for a wedding. I carried the crate of bottles home on my head, swinging my hips slowly as I walked. I felt transformed.

In Gambia, people don't use words such as "cheating," "naughty," or "guilty" when they talk about eating. The language of sin is not applied to food. Fat is desirable. It holds beneficial meanings of abundance, fertility and health.

My perception of beauty altered as my body did. The European tourists on the beach began to look strange and skeletal rather than "slim." They had no hips. They seemed devoid of shape and substance. Women I once would have envied appeared fragile and even ugly. The ideal they represented no longer made sense.

After a year, I came home. I preached my new way of seeing to anyone who would listen. I wanted to cling to the liberating belief that losing weight had nothing to do with self-love.

12   Family members kindly suggested that I might look and feel better if I slimmed down a little. They encouraged me to join an exercise club. I wandered around the malls in a dislocated daze. I felt uncomfortable trying on clothes that hung so elegantly on the mannequins. I began hearing old voices inside my head: "Plaid makes you look fat. . . . You're too short for that style. . . . Vertical stripes are more slimming. . . . Wear black."

13   I joined the club. Just a few weeks after I had worn a *lappa* and scooped up rice with my hands, I was climbing into pink leotards and aerobics shoes. The instructor told me that I had to set fitness goals and "weigh in" after my workouts. There were mirrors on the walls and I could see women watching themselves. I sensed that even the loveliest among them felt they were somehow flawed. As the aerobics instructor barked out commands for arm lifts and leg lifts, I pictured Gambian women pounding millet and dancing in a circle with their arms raised high. I do not mean to romanticize their rock-hard lives, but we were hardly to be envied as we ran like fools between two walls to the tiresome beat of synthesized music.

14   We were a roomful of women striving to reshape ourselves into some kind of pubertal ideal. I reverted to my natural state: one of yearning to be slimmer and more fit than I was. My freedom had been temporary. I was home, where fat is feared and despised. It was time to exert control over my body and my life. I dreaded the thought of people saying, "She's let herself go."

15   If I return to Africa, I am sure the women will shake their heads in bewildered dismay. Even now, I sometimes catch my reflection in a window and their voices come back to me. "Yo! Chicken-hips!"

△△△

Further Reading:

Joetta Schlabach, *Extending the Table: A World Community Cookbook*
Richard Gordon, *Anorexia and Bulimia: Anatomy of a Social Epidemic*
Naomi Wolf, *The Beauty Myth: How Images of Beauty Are Used Against Women*
Katherine Gilday, dir., *The Famine Within* (documentary film)

Structure:

1. "Chicken-Hips" is mainly a *contrast* of ideals of beauty in Gambia and Canada. Point out at least two other things, as well, which the essay *compares.*
2. Does Pigott organize her *contrast* mainly "point by point" or by "halves"?

3. How selectively does the author choose details from her year in Africa? In paragraph 1, for example, has she told anything at all that is not vital to her theme?
4. What classic techniques of organization does Pigott exploit in her opening and closing?

Style:

1. The Gambian women nicknamed our author "Chicken-hips" because of her relative thinness. Create five other METAPHORS they could have used to say the same thing.
2. Where do SENSE IMAGES most strongly help us "see" the author's point?
3. Looking at Pigott's vocabulary, what sort of *audience* do you imagine she was aiming at in her essay?

Ideas for Discussion and Writing:

1. How important to you is the appearance of your body? Is there an ideal of shape or size which you attempt to reach? Name all the sources that taught you this ideal.
2. Why is it that in our society it is mostly women who go on diets, and mostly women who incur and even die from *anorexia nervosa?*
3. In paragraph 5 we are told that thinness reminded Gambians of "things they wanted to forget, such as poverty, drought and starvation." How do you see thinness? *Compare* or *contrast* your view, and give reasons.
4. Have you lived in another country, as Pigott did? What did the other culture teach you about life? Now that you are here, are you remembering or forgetting those lessons? Why?
5. Many First-Worlders go abroad, as did Pigott, to "teach" Third-Worlders. Imagine her Gambian friends coming to your school to "teach" you. How easy or difficult would it be to learn their lessons? What might they learn in return?
6. In paragraph 10, watching the "skeletal" Europeans at the beach, Pigott states "My perception of beauty altered. . . ." Examine the illustrations in a book of art history, taking notes on how our current view of human beauty differs from those of past periods. Report these differences to the class.
7. **PROCESS IN WRITING:** *Remember a time when you set out to change your body through a diet, athletics, aerobics, bodybuilding or other means. On a blank piece of paper draw a vertical line. Entitle the left column "before" and the right column "after," then brainstorm to develop the contrast. Now looking at these notes, decide your thesis: In which version of yourself did you actually feel happier, the before or after? Now write a rapid first draft, pro-*

ceeding either by "halves" or "point by point." The next day look it over: Do images help your audience "see" you? If not, add. Is your draft at least 50 percent examples? If not, add. Are any words wasted? If so, cut. Finally, edit for things like grammar and spelling, then produce your good version.

Note: See also the Topics for Writing at the end of this chapter.

Russell Baker

A Nice Place to Visit

Russell Baker is one of America's favourite humorists, author of the "Observer" column in The New York Times. *Since 1993 he has also been host of the PBS television broadcast* Masterpiece Theatre. *It was a month's stay in Toronto that gave Baker the material for our selection, a contrast of cities. Those who have read him already will recognize his distinctive approach: the zany and inventive humour, the satire on human foibles, and the mocking imitations of formal, scholarly or scientific language. Basic to all this is his stance as "observer": he has a keen eye for the telling details that breathe life into writing. Baker was born in 1925 in Virginia. After a degree at Johns Hopkins in 1947, and employment from 1947 to 1954 at the* Baltimore Sun, *he did political reporting for* The New York Times. *A columnist since 1962, he now takes the whole of American life for his subject, but especially his own city, "the Big Apple." Hundreds of Baker's columns have been collected in books, among these* No Cause for Panic *(1964),* Poor Russell's Almanac *(1972) and* The Rescue of Miss Yaskell and Other Pipe Dreams *(1983). His autobiography* Growing Up *won a Pulitzer Prize in 1983. Then in 1993 was published the anthology* Russell Baker's Book of American Humor. *Our own selection appeared first in* The New York Times, *then in Baker's book* So This Is Depravity *(1980).*

Having heard that Toronto was becoming one of the continent's noblest cities, we flew from New York to investigate. New Yorkers jealous of their city's reputation and concerned about challenges to its stature have little to worry about.

After three days in residence, our delegation noted an absence of hysteria that was almost intolerable and took to consuming large portions of black coffee to maintain our normal state of irritability. The local people to whom we complained in hopes of provoking comfortably nasty confrontations declined to become bellicose. They would like to enjoy a gratifying big-city hysteria, they said, but believed it would seem ill-mannered in front of strangers.

Extensive field studies — our stay lasted four weeks — persuaded us that this failure reflects the survival in Toronto of an ancient pattern of social conduct called "courtesy."

4   "Courtesy" manifests itself in many quaint forms appalling to the New York. Thus, for example, Yankee fans may be astonished to learn that at the Toronto baseball park it is considered bad form to heave rolls of toilet paper and beer cans at players on the field.

5   Official literature inside Toronto taxicabs includes a notification of the proper address to which riders may mail the authorities not only complaints but also compliments about the cabbie's behavior.

6   For a city that aspires to urban greatness, Toronto's entire taxi system has far to go. At present, it seems hopelessly bogged down in civilization. One day a member of our delegation listening to a radio conversation between a short-tempered cabbie and the dispatcher distinctly heard the dispatcher say, "As Shakespeare said, if music be the food of love, play on, give me excess of it."

7   This delegate became so unnerved by hearing Shakespeare quoted by a cab dispatcher that he fled immediately back to New York to have his nerves abraded and his spine rearranged in a real big-city taxi.

8   What was particularly distressing as the stay continued was the absence of shrieking police and fire sirens at 3 A.M. — or any other hour, for that matter. We spoke to the city authorities about this. What kind of city was it, we asked, that expected its citizens to sleep all night and rise refreshed in the morning? Where was the incentive to awaken gummy-eyed and exhausted, ready to scream at the first person one saw in the morning? How could Toronto possibly hope to maintain a robust urban divorce rate?

9   Our criticism went unheeded, such is the torpor with which Toronto pursues true urbanity. The fact appears to be that Toronto has very little grasp of what is required of a great city.

10   Consider the garbage picture. It seems never to have occurred to anybody in Toronto that garbage exists to be heaved into the streets. One can drive for miles without seeing so much as a banana peel in the gutter or a discarded newspaper whirling in the wind.

11   Nor has Toronto learned about dogs. A check with the authorities confirmed that, yes, there are indeed dogs resident in Toronto, but one would never realize it by walking the sidewalks. Our delegation was shocked by the presumption of a town's calling itself a city, much less a great city, when it obviously knows nothing of either garbage or dogs.

12   The subway, on which Toronto prides itself, was a laughable imitation of the real thing. The subway cars were not only spotlessly clean, but also fully illuminated. So were the stations. To New Yorkers, it was embarrassing, and we hadn't the heart to tell the subway authorities that they were light-years away from greatness.

13   We did, however, tell them about spray paints and how effectively a few hundred children equipped with spray-paint cans could at least give their subway the big-city look.

It seems doubtful they are ready to take such hints. There is a dis- 14
turbing distaste for vandalism in Toronto which will make it hard for
the city to enter wholeheartedly into the vigor of the late twentieth
century.

A board fence surrounding a huge excavation for a new high- 15
rise building in the downtown district offers depressing evidence of
Toronto's lack of big-city impulse. Embedded in the fence at intervals
of about fifty feet are loudspeakers that play recorded music for passing pedestrians.

Not a single one of these loudspeakers has been mutilated. What's 16
worse, not a single one has been stolen.

It was good to get back to the Big Apple. My coat pocket was bulging 17
with candy wrappers from Toronto and — such is the lingering power
of Toronto — it took me two or three hours back in New York before it
seemed natural again to toss them into the street.

△△△

Further Reading:

Russell Baker,
>   *Poor Russell's Almanac*
>   *Growing Up*

Tom Wolfe, *The Bonfire of the Vanities* (novel)
Michele Landsberg, *"This Is New York, Honey!" A Homage to Manhattan,
    with Love and Rage*

Structure:

1. How vital to this selection are its *examples?* What ratio of space do they
   take up? Point out three or four that work especially well, and tell
   why they do.
2. What considerations do you think led Baker to organize his *contrast*
   not by "halves" but rather "point by point"? Argue for or against his
   method.
3. Baker often omits the New York side of a point. Are these gaps
   accidental or deliberate? Do they hinder or help us as readers?
   Explain.

Style:

1. Baker's title, "A Nice Place to Visit," is unfinished. What is the rest of
   this saying, and why are we left to complete it ourselves?
2. How soon did you detect Baker's heavy IRONY? Where did you first
   realize he means the opposite of what he says?
3. Elsewhere Baker has expressed admiration for Toronto. Does the

irony of this essay weaken or strengthen our understanding of his real opinion?

4. In paragraph 9 Baker writes, "Our criticism went unheeded, such is the torpor with which Toronto pursues true urbanity." Why is the language of this humorous essay so FORMAL? What effect is achieved?

5. Explain the IRONY in each of these passages:
   A. "comfortably nasty confrontations" (par. 2)
   B. "a gratifying big-city hysteria" (par. 2)
   C. "bogged down in civilization" (par. 6)
   D. "a robust urban divorce rate" (par. 8)
   E. "the vigor of the late twentieth century" (par. 14)

6. In his closing Baker calls New York "the Big Apple." Explore the CONNOTATIONS of this METAPHOR.

Ideas for Discussion and Writing:

1. Baker confines his *contrast* of Toronto and New York to the relatively minor topics of taxis, noise, garbage, dogs, the subway and vandalism. Either in class discussion or on paper, extend his contrast to more serious urban problems such as pollution, drugs, poverty and violent crime.

2. Statistics regularly reveal more murders in American cities than in Canadian ones of equal size; the difference sometimes reaches proportions as high as ten to one. Give all the reasons you can think of to explain this *contrast.*

3. **PROCESS IN WRITING:** *During spare moments this week, record in a journal your main impressions of the city or town around you. On other pages, record memories of a city or town elsewhere. Now freewrite on this material several minutes to determine which place you prefer. Next write a discovery draft of an essay that* contrasts *the two, showing through examples why you prefer one of them. Use Baker's* point-by-point *approach. Choose your own* TONE, *humorous or serious, and maintain it. Finally show the piece to a group of other students, then, incorporating the best suggestions, write your final version.*

Note: See also the Topics for Writing at the end of this chapter.

Catharine Parr Traill

Remarks of Security of Person and Property in Canada

Catharine Parr ("Kate") Traill (1802–1899) exemplifies the best of Canadian pioneering life. She spent her early years in England, where she enjoyed the refinements of her father's estate near Southwold and published several books for children. But a reversal of family fortunes and her marriage to a retired half-pay officer meant immigration. In 1832 the Traills joined Catharine's brother Samuel Strickland (who would later write Twenty-Seven Years in Canada West) *near what is now Lakefield, Ontario, and soon they were joined by Catharine's sister Susanna Moodie and her husband. Like her sister, who described pioneering life in* Roughing It in the Bush *and other books, Traill wrote of her own experience in Upper Canada. A collection of letters to her mother appeared in 1836 as* The Backwoods of Canada, *and in 1854 appeared* The Female Emigrant's Guide, *her collection of advice and handbook of techniques. Traill continued to write children's books, and her professionalism as a botanist was widely recognized when in 1868 she published* Canadian Wild Flowers, *and in 1885* Studies of Plant Life in Canada. *All of Kate Traill's writing exemplifies her own life: she was curious, observant, self-reliant — and above all optimistic about the New World. These qualities shine through our selection, which comes from* The Female Emigrant's Guide.

There is one thing which can hardly fail to strike an emigrant from the Old Country, on his arrival in Canada. It is this, — The feeling of complete security which he enjoys, whether in his own dwelling or in his journeys abroad through the land. He sees no fear — he need see none. He is not in a land spoiled and robbed, where every man's hand is against his fellow — where envy and distrust beset him on every side. At first indeed he is surprised at the apparently stupid neglect of the proper means of security that he notices in the dwellings of all classes of people, especially in the lonely country places, where the want of security would really invite rapine and murder. "How is this," he says, "you use neither bolt, nor lock, nor bar. I see no shutter to your windows; nay, you sleep often with your doors open upon the

169

latch, and in summer with open doors and windows. Surely this is fool-hardy and imprudent." "We need no such precautions," will his friend reply smiling; "here they are uncalled for. Our safety lies neither in bars nor bolts, but in our consciousness that we are among people whose necessities are not such as to urge them to violate the laws; neither are our riches such as to tempt the poor man to rob us, for they consist not in glittering jewels, nor silver, nor gold."

2   "But even food and clothes thus carelessly guarded are temptations."

3   "But where others possess these requisites as well as ourselves, they are not likely to steal them from us."

4   And what is the inference that the new comer draws from this statement?

5   That he is in a country where the inhabitants are essentially honest, because they are enabled, by the exertion of their own hands, to obtain in abundance the necessaries of life. Does it not also prove to him that it is the miseries arising from poverty that induce crime. — Men do not often violate the law of honesty, unless driven to do so by necessity. Place the poor Irish peasant in the way of earning his bread in Canada, where he sees his reward before him, in broad lands that he can win by honest toil, and where he can hold up his head and look beyond that grave of a poor man's hope — the parish work house — and see in the far-off vista a home of comfort which his own hands have reared, and can go down to his grave with the thought, that he has left a name and a blessing for his children after him: — men like this do not steal.

6   Robbery is not a crime of common occurrence in Canada. In large towns such acts will occasionally be committed, for it is there that poverty is to be found, but it is not common in country places. There you may sleep with your door unbarred for years. Your confidence is rarely, if ever, abused; your hospitality never violated.

7   When I lived in the backwoods, out of sight of any other habitation, the door has often been opened at midnight, a stranger has entered and lain down before the kitchen fire, and departed in the morning unquestioned. In the early state of the settlement in Douro, now twenty years ago, it was no uncommon occurrence for a party of Indians to enter the house, (they never knock at any man's door,) leave their hunting weapons outside, spread their blankets on the floor, and pass the night with or without leave, arise by the first dawn of day, gather their garments about them, resume their weapons, and silently and noiselessly depart. Sometimes a leash of wild ducks hung to the door-latch, or a haunch of venison left in the kitchen, would be found as a token of gratitude for the warmth and shelter afforded them.

8   Many strangers, both male and female, have found shelter under our roof, and never were we led to regret that we had not turned the houseless wanderer from our door.

It is delightful this consciousness of perfect security: your hand is ⁹
against no man, and no man's hand is against you. We dwell in peace
among our own people. What a contrast to my home, in England,
where by sunset every door was secured with locks and heavy bars and
bolts; every window carefully barricaded, and every room and corner in
and around the dwelling duly searched, before we ventured to lie down
to rest, lest our sleep should be broken in upon by the midnight thief.
As night drew on, an atmosphere of doubt and dread seemed to en-
compass one. The approach of a stranger we beheld with suspicion;
and however great his need, we dared not afford him the shelter of our
roof, lest our so doing should open the door to robber or murderer. At
first I could hardly understand why it happened that I never felt the
same sensation of fear in Canada as I had done in England. My mind
seemed lightened of a heavy burden; and I, who had been so timid,
grew brave and fearless amid the gloomy forests of Canada. Now, I
know how to value this great blessing. Let the traveller seek shelter in
the poorest shanty, among the lowest Irish settlers, and he need fear no
evil, for never have I heard of the rites of hospitality being violated, or
the country disgraced by such acts of cold-blooded atrocity as are recorded by the public papers in the Old Country.

Here we have no bush-rangers, no convicts to disturb the peace of ¹⁰
the inhabitants of the land, as in Australia. No savage hordes of Caffres
to invade and carry off our cattle and stores of grain as at the Cape; but
peace and industry are on every side. "The land is at rest and breaks
forth into singing." Surely we ought to be a happy and a contented
people, full of gratitude to that Almighty God who has given us this fair
and fruitful land to dwell in.

△ △

Further Reading:

Catharine Parr Traill,
   The Female Emigrant's Guide
   The Backwoods of Canada
Susanna Moodie, *Roughing It in the Bush*
Margaret Atwood, *The Journals of Susanna Moodie* (poems)
Marian Fowler, *The Embroidered Tent: Five Gentlewomen in Early Canada*

Structure:

1. The long first paragraph states all the main ideas of this selection.
   What, then, does the rest do?
2. In this *contrast* between the dangers of life in England and the security of life in Canada, why does the latter get most of the attention?

3. Traill develops her main contrast, between England and Canada, in paragraphs 7–9. Why does she then add brief contrasts to Australia and the Cape in the closing?

Style:

1. Catharine Parr Traill published *The Female Emigrant's Guide* in 1854. How does her style in this selection differ from that of today's writers? Analyze the following:
   A. Word choice
   B. Sentences
   C. Paragraphs
   D. TONE
2. Explain the meaning of "want" in the phrase "want of security" (par. 1). Point out other words whose meanings have changed since 1854.
3. In paragraph 7 Traill writes that native persons "never knock at any man's door." In paragraph 9 she states that "your hand is against no man, and no man's hand is against you." In fact she mentions men so often that only once does she refer to women — yet she entitled her book *The Female Emigrant's Guide*. Why do so few people write this way today? Is the generic "he" still accepted at all? As an exercise, put paragraphs 4 and 5 into gender-neutral language, then point out the techniques you used to do so.

Ideas for Discussion and Writing:

1. Does modern Canada resemble more the land to which Traill came or the land she left? Explain.
2. If like Traill you immigrated to Canada, which benefits that she describes have you experienced?
3. Traill states, "it is the miseries arising from poverty that induce crime" (par. 5). Do you agree? Or does crime have other causes too?
4. Traill states, "I, who had been so timid, grew brave and fearless amid the gloomy forests of Canada" (par. 9). In our crowded world, what frontiers remain where we can make a new start?
5. **PROCESS IN WRITING:** *Write an essay that compares and/or contrasts life in two countries, provinces, cities, towns or neighbourhoods. First divide a page in half with a vertical line; jot down facts about item A on the left and item B on the right. Looking over these notes, decide now on your* THESIS STATEMENT *and choose either the "halves" or the "point by point" method of organizing. After a rapid first draft, fine-tune your organization and add more details. Now read the paper aloud, to fix repetition and other flaws of style, before doing your final version.*

Note: See also the Topics for Writing at the end of this chapter.

Ann Ireland

Never a Cowgirl

*"The real story is the rewriting," says Ann Ireland. She followed her own advice
in producing her first novel; as she explains in the essay below, she took* A Certain Mr. Takahashi *through at least nine drafts. Then it was published, won
the Seal First Novel Award for 1985, and was made into a feature-length film,*
The Pianist, *co-produced by Japan and Canada. Ireland is a graduate of the
University of British Columbia's Creative Writing Department, where she studied
under George McWhirter and Audrey Thomas. Since then she has been writer in
residence at public libraries, has written many essays for CBC radio, has spoken
extensively in high schools, and teaches creative writing at Ryerson Polytechnic
University. Though she spends a great deal of time in Mexico, her home these
days is Toronto. "Write about what matters to you," says Ireland. "My opinions
on things are not unique, but if I can turn the idea into a story with some kind
of personal resonance, that's usually closer to what I want to say." In creating
her autobiographical "Never a Cowgirl" for the anthology* Language in Her Eye
*(1990), Ireland again took her own advice, responding to the editors' questions
about what it meant to be both a feminist and a writer.*

1   I'm sitting well to the back of the classroom, in this way hoping not to
be noticed. It is grade seven, I am eleven years old and we have a
teacher, Mr. Hudson, who is handsome, flirtatious, and surrounded by
a buzz of tantalizing rumour.

2   The latest is he broke into Margo M.'s locker, filched her bra then
tossed it down the staircase.

3   Did he saw open the padlock, I wonder. And why Margo? I watch her
out of the corner of my eye and see only the neat plaid jumper and
mass of blonde curls.

4   I've known since day one at this new school that I'm in way over my
head. These girls know something I don't. They slink around in low
heeled 'pumps' or desert boots and have a way of talking and laughing
which I strain to imitate but fail, miserably. They dance skittishly around
boys, congregate around a certain 'Greg' at recess, talk in whispers or

shrieks. I approach their circle, flashing an uneasy smile, and receive only quick stares of contempt. My skirt sags, my shoes are thick and heavy, my blouse is some pukey colour. I know all this but not how to fix it.

5   Until I came here I didn't realize I was different from boys, at least not in any unsettling way. I didn't know enough to be frightened.

6   'Hey Ireland, you in the army or what?'

7   Eyes swing down to my shoes, stern black regimental oxfords. That evening I throw them to the back of the closet and demand desert boots. Now they'll like me.

8   'Hey Ireland, new shoes eh? Pretty *cool.*'

9   Just tell me what to do, how to behave.

10   Mr. Hudson is handing back our history projects. I am proud of mine — full of careful tracings of agricultural tools used in pioneer days. My desire is simple — I want a good mark.

11   The pretty girls scurry to the front of the class and one by one Mr. Hudson makes them sit on his lap before returning their neatly bound essays on 'Pioneer Life in Upper Canada.' I know he won't do this with me. Which is both a great relief and a disappointment.

12   At last he fingers the familiar blue folder. My name is spoken. But the slow way he articulates 'Ann Ireland' makes it sound ridiculous, full of vowels, marbly. Not a girl's name but a piece of geography, a dot on the world map which covers the wall below the clock.

13   I start to rise. But he isn't finished. A smile creeps over his face. The broad lips tighten and curl. I sink back into my seat.

14   'Ann,' he tells the eager class, 'has used black tape to bind her project.'

15   This is true. But I was very neat and clipped the stray threads with scissors.

16   'Black *hockey* tape.' He's holding up the folder so the boys at the back of the class can see.

17   There is noisy snickering.

18   I start to get an uncomfortable buzzing sensation in my ears.

19   'Perhaps,' Mr. Hudson goes on, 'she had just finished taping her *stick* and had some left over.'

20   Howls of laughter.

21   I grin weakly, cheeks flaming. The thing is, he's absolutely right. Mr. Hudson has found me out, exposed the secret life I didn't know I had.

22   Sure I played hockey. We had a rink in the backyard and I sped around day and night with my brothers and practised slapshots and breakaways and skating backwards, even body checks. The self I imagined — always — was some version of Mahovlich, Keon, racing up the ice, deking out the goalie as the announcer shouts, 'He shoots! He scores!' The 'he'

was crucial. Only boys played hockey. Whoever heard of a female in the NHL? It never occurred to me that this inner life was my first fundamental fiction. An invented character. Inside I was a boy; the character I projected in daydreams was always male. Because as far as I could see only boys were hockey players, doctors in African jungles, climbers of Himalayan peaks, cowboys . . .

'Hey, Mahavlich, yer offside!' follows me back to my eat. Something is dreadfully wrong. There is a shudder as my inner life is sucked out, leaving me breathless. The heroic self gone forever. The fictions which have followed me around from the beginning of consciousness high-tail it, glad to be rid of me.   23

Writing life to that point had been consistent. I composed little dramas populated by daring children, androgynous Toms or Sallys who explored tunnels and caves, were stranded on desert islands. My heroines never had to obey any rules of the feminine; my imagination was unfettered by scorecards checking off crossed legs, hem-length, tonality of laughter.   24

'Hey Ireland, you a girl or what?'   25

What indeed?   26

I tried. Beginning with the outside clues: clothes, hair, gestures . . . there were lots of rules to this feminine life but I'd learn! Just give me a little time. The way I saw it, I wasn't *born* female; it was something I had to become, like learning to play the violin, with an audience wincing at each wrong note and pratfall. Then there was the inner life to consider. I began, deliberately, to exorcise all wrong-headed versions from my mind and replace them with appropriate 'female' daydreams. I read *16 Magazine* cover to cover, experimented with makeup, followed boys home. Writing became part of the despised past, an object of scorn. All that mattered now was to 'pass.' Without my heroic (male) self there was virtually no fantasy life. How could I dream of being a cow-*girl?* How can fantasy be populated by underachievers?   27

I think I became a writer out of nostalgia, an attempt to reclaim the inner life that guided childhood. It's a sentimental desire to create adventures, live lives I don't have time for myself. Or courage. I even can, and do, pretend to be male if I feel like it. But it's different now; I know I'm pretending. It's a kind of game.   28

Was there a distinct moment, an audible hiss as the inner self slid back into place? Was there an instant from which I began writing in my own voice?   29

Nothing that clean.   30

31   Fatigue wore me down. Guarding the fences of fantasy life became too much effort. I wrote my way out like some dog burrowing after a bone she knows she buried . . . somewhere. It took five years to write *A Certain Mr. Takahashi* because I kept pushing the characters around, telling them how to speak and feel. I knew something was wrong, but not how to fix it. It didn't occur to me I was mimicking my own experience, sucking away *their* inner lives, as if in revenge. Weariness came to the rescue. By the ninth draft it got so I could see only the page, the characters, and landscape. And then I finally started listening to my own heart because it was the only sound left in the room.

32   I wish I could say I'm comfortable now, meshed into a self-defined role of what is 'female.' That I've cracked the code and spend my days rewriting it. That inner and outer life are twinned, striding together towards an uncertain but exciting future.

33   Not so. There are flashes of the old awkwardness, traces of bulky shoes, the sagging hemline.

34   It's late afternoon and I am at an upscale book launching lured by the free drinks and hot hors d'oeuvres. Slightly tipsy after an hour of cocktail chatter I traipse off to the 'Ladies' Room' (the name should have alerted me) to do what I have to do, then emerge from the cubicle and face the line of half a dozen women bent over the sinks. They press as close as they can to the mirror, mouths pursed, fixing makeup. I don't know where to look. Suddenly I am again the 'other,' the beginner, the impaired one. I would never dare work in public as these women do, so confidently. They don't worry for an instant that their hands will twitch and jab their eyeballs with the mascara wand or smudge an upper lip with a stroke of Guava Stain.

35   I wash my hands quickly, aware I've entered one of those 'third sex' moments. Somehow I've stepped into the wrong washroom and someone's going to discover this any minute. 'Get out of here!' she'll shriek, lifting a silk-covered arm.

36   'I'm leaving,' I mumble before she gets a chance.

△△

Further Reading:

Ann Ireland, *A Certain Mr. Takahashi*
Margaret Atwood, *Cat's Eye*
Alice Munro, *Lives of Girls and Women*

Structure:

1. Ireland opens and closes her essay with traditional gender roles. Tell all the *contrasts* you see in the behaviour of Mr. Hudson and of

the women in the "Ladies' Room." Now tell what you see of *comparison*.

2. In paragraphs 22 and 27, what further *contrasts* does Ireland make between the traditional gender roles?

3. About what percentage of her argument does Ireland devote to examples? What proportion of examples do you aim for in your essays?

4. Why does Ireland indent some paragraphs but not others?

Style:

1. Ireland uses the present tense, even though these events happened years ago. Why?

2. In paragraph 31 Ireland tells how her novel *A Certain Mr. Takahashi* took five years and at least nine drafts to write. How many drafts do you think "Never a Cowgirl" went through? Support your answer with examples. How many drafts do your own essays take to reach their potential?

Ideas for Discussion and Writing:

1. In paragraph 27 Ireland sums up her attempts to learn the "rules" of "feminine life" by saying "All that mattered now was to 'pass.'" Today in the place where you live, what are the rules that males and females learn in order to "pass"? Who awards the grades? What are the benefits and dangers both of "passing" and of "failing"?

2. Ireland's novel *A Certain Mr. Takahashi* depicts the infatuation of two teenage sisters with an older man, a concert pianist. They romanticize him, imitate him, centre their lives around him. How might these actions be related to "lessons" taught by the society which Ireland describes in "Never a Cowgirl"?

3. When a classmate calls the new desert boots "Pretty *cool*," young Ireland thinks, "Just tell me what to do, how to behave" (paragraphs 8 and 9). Look at what you are wearing right now. Tell the class which items you bought to be "cool," and which you chose for their comfort, economy or usefulness.

4. In paragraph 22 Ireland describes her dream of playing in the NHL as "my first fundamental fiction." Does literature come from personal "fictions" like this? How do the rest of us, who are not novelists, develop our own "fictions"?

5. **PROCESS IN WRITING:** *In paragraph 22 Ireland says, ". . . only boys were hockey players, doctors in African jungles, climbers of Himalayan peaks, cowboys . . ." Examine two issues of* Maclean's, *one from this year and one published before you were born (look in a library, either on microfilm or in bound reference copies). To what extent does the older issue bear out Ireland's*

statement about gender? Compare or contrast the newer issue: have things changed? Take notes on two pages, one for each issue. Now looking at your materials, write a thesis and a short outline, organized either by "halves" or "point by point." Do a rapid discovery draft. The next day look it over. Are there enough examples? If not, consult your notes or magazines again, and add. Have you signalled contrasts with terms like "but," "on the other hand," "by contrast" and "however"? If not, add. Finally, edit for correctness before producing the good copy. Read it to the class.

Note: See also the Topics for Writing at the end of this chapter.

John McMurtry

Education for Sale

"I had several more lives to live," said American philosopher Henry David Thoreau as he left his two years of contemplation in the woods. John McMurtry, a Canadian philosopher, has already lived several lives. On his way to being professor of philosophy at the University of Guelph, he has been a professional football player, newspaper reporter, social militant and more. Born in 1939, McMurtry earned a number of undergraduate degrees, played a season with the Calgary Stampeders, then in 1974 completed a Ph.D. in philosophy at the University of London. In the meantime he had worked as scriptwriter for the CBC, columnist for the Toronto Telegram, *a high school English teacher, a lecturer at Chelsea College of Art, and had authored a textbook,* Dimensions of English *(1970). He also took, and still takes, long periods of time to be a "world traveller." From 1970 his academic work grew, as he joined the faculty at Guelph and began to publish what are now more than a hundred chapters and articles in international books and journals. Then in 1978 Princeton University Press published his book* The Structure of Marx's World-View. *(Thought controversial by some, it has been banned and burned in a number of countries.) McMurtry exercises his social conscience in activities ranging from his hundreds of letters to the editor, to chairing jurists of the War Crimes Tribunal at Toronto's Alternate World Summit of 1989, to working for human rights in El Salvador and East Timor, to saving historic buildings in his own city of Guelph. Our selection, a strong example of McMurtry's logic and social commitment, appeared in the November 1989 issue of a newsletter for professors, the* OCUFA Forum. *"Writing," says the author, "is like a cosmic conversation. It includes the living, the dead and the about-to-be born, and the voice that comes through you to speak."*

You don't have to be a Platonist° to know that the free market and education do not have the same methods — or goals. In the free market, you aim to maximize money profit. You do so by providing or producing whatever people want, at whatever price you can get, from 1

°Platonist: a follower of the Greek philosopher Plato, who held that ideas, not things, are the ultimate reality.

whomever has the money to buy it. Education doesn't do any of these things. If it's any good, it challenges all of them. It opposes the sharing of knowledge to private profit, the development of understanding to the gratification of wants, the disinterested instruction to the sales pitch.

2   Yet, the free market, we are told, is the way of the world, and the necessity of the future for all.

3   So it should come as no surprise that education too is being brought into team-spirited dedication to the new Categorical Imperative of Life on Earth: "learning to compete in the tough new international marketplace."

4   Even University and faculty presidents now advocate the value of higher education itself on the grounds that it's . . . "required to compete in the international marketplace."

5   The response of the universities to the advent of the new reality has, from the top down, been acquiescent. By and large they have run for cover. Remaining independent of the demands of commerce and the Furies° of private profit was once a cherished duty and vocation. But now the universities and their researchers are climbing down. They're "establishing links with the business community," and jumping into the new game as players for sale.

6   We of the modern world have long thought of the base-value of everything as its "capital," and of freedom as an "open marketplace" where, in the famous formula of Friedrich Hayek, "all are free to sell and buy at any price at which they can find a partner to the transaction . . . free to produce, buy and sell anything that can be produced or sold at all." In recent years, the language has become more explicitly corporate. It's "the bottom line" and being "internationally competitive" which rule. It's crept up on us. Now it's so deep in the mind-set that even the once critical "pointy-head intellectuals" in the University presuppose the laws of international commodification as the ultimate framework of reality. They can't talk about what used to interrogate the status quo, higher learning, without translating it first into the going jargon of the corporate culture to ensure it makes sense to the Big Buyer out there. "Resource units" for what used to be subject disciplines and their professors. "Clients" and "consumers" for what used to be students. "Uniform standards" for what used to be the search for quality, depth, originality. "Program packages" for what used to be education. "Products" for what used to be graduates. Corporate foundations, grants, and prizes tradenaming every academic recognition that's left. "Credibility" for what used to be "truth."

7   [The] country's leading religious philosopher is crowned a "Molson's Scholar." Universities in the country's largest province have negotiated

---

°Furies: in Greek mythology the three goddesses Alecto, Megaera and Tisiphone, avengers of unpunished crimes.

to sell their library holdings to private corporations. Classroom textbooks have passed under the control of multinational conglomerates. Business schools and programs swagger into ever larger numbers and facilities. And university administrators tub-thump new corporate "links" as higher education's salvation.

And so higher education too has adapted to the "new reality." University administrators, grant-benefactors and multinational text-producers anxious to gear their "services," "packages," and "products" to the new academic program of being competitively for sale in the multinational market.   8

It is an ecumenical mission.   9

But a point needs to be made about education before its absorption into the system of world product mandate is complete.   10

No-one, it seems, has dared to notice yet, in public, that the logic of education and of the corporate market are in fundamental contradiction. An education, unlike a commodity in the free market, cannot be bought or sold (despite the best-selling sycophancy of Alan Bloom in his aptly titled *The Closing of the American Mind* which approves of higher education only if it's for the rich). Education has an opposite logic to the free market. It is earned, not purchased; studied for by oneself, not produced by others; an internal development, not an external product; and a value in itself, not a medium for profit.   11

An education can never come, as every corporate commodity claims to, "problem free." The better it is, the deeper and tougher the problems it poses to the one who has it. Unlike any commercial product, an education cannot be "instant" or "ready-made" for its users. Nor can it be "guaranteed replacement" or "repaired cost-free." It cannot, in truth, be "produced" for, or "delivered to" or "reliably serviced" by another at all. As in learning how to think and write, it can only be achieved by one's own work, and it does not keep past the continuous demands it puts on its bearer. To say that it is consumed is a contradiction in terms, and if it is "sold on the open market," it's a fraud.   12

As for the principles of freedom governing education and the market, what is the best policy for selling a product — to offend no-one and no vested interest — is, as every definition of academic freedom recognizes, the worst policy for an institution seeking to advance and disseminate learning and truth.   13

The great irony of this greatest corporate takeover of all is that its imposition everywhere is sold as "*anti*-totalitarian," as "*freedom*" for all. The deepest signal of its success in stilling our capacity to think past it, is that we have come to assume this logic of the World Corporation Empire as an organizing principle of mind.   14

△ △

Further Reading:

John McMurtry, *The Structure of Marx's World-View*
Alan Bloom, *The Closing of the American Mind*
Charles Sykes, *ProfScam*
Page Smith, *Killing the Spirit*

Structure:

1. Identify McMurtry's THESIS STATEMENT.
2. Why do McMurtry's *comparisons* of education and commerce come first, and most of his *contrasts* after? How does this order help build his argument?
3. Is this *comparison and contrast* arranged by "halves" or "point by point"?
4. The very act of placing contrasting items side by side can imply a value judgment. Describe the value judgment McMurtry imparts in the series of *contrasts* that end paragraph 6.

Style:

1. Is the author angry? If so, how do you know? Is anger an effective motivation for writing? Defend your answer with reasons.
2. As a philosopher and professor, McMurtry uses formal terms such as "acquiescent" and "ecumenical." Do you see loaded, emotional words as well? Cite examples. Do these vocabularies clash, or do they succeed together?
3. In portraying a Ministry of Truth removing dangerous words like "freedom" from the dictionary, George Orwell showed us in his novel *1984* the relationship of vocabulary to power. Examine the business JARGON which in paragraphs 6 and 8 McMurtry shows taking over academia. How much similarity do you see between the two settings? Between the Big Brother of Orwell's novel and the "Big Buyer" of paragraph 6?

Ideas for Discussion and Writing:

1. Think of someone you know who is well "educated." Describe this person to the class. What can she or he think or do that others cannot? Does his or her "education" bring advantages? Name them. Does it also bring problems, as McMurtry says in paragraph 12? Name them.
2. Using your own value system, rank these possible outcomes of "education" from a high of 1 to a low of 5:
   speaking other languages
   becoming rich

enjoying the arts

learning to think independently

gaining power over others

Now share your ranking with class members. Defend your view, but also listen to those who see things differently.

3. Would a dictator prefer to have a population of educated or uneducated citizens? Give all your reasons why or why not.

4. In what ways has the "tough new international marketplace" changed your country? Your province? Your school? The lives of your parents? The career you intend to enter? Is it true that "the free market . . . is the way of the world, and the necessity of the future for all" (par. 2)? If so, what are you doing to ensure your own future under this system?

5. **PROCESS IN WRITING:** *Think of the* contrast *which McMurtry suggests in paragraph 6 between a "graduate" and a "product" of school. Now draw a line down the middle of a page. Write "graduate" at the top of one column, and "product" above the other, then fill the spaces with notes. Looking these notes over, draw lines from left to right to connect* contrasting *ideas or examples. From this rough outline take your points. Decide whether to arrange them by "halves" or "point by point," then write a fast discovery draft. The next day look it over. Does every generalization have an example? If not, add. Is every* contrast *accompanied by transition words such as "but," "on the other hand," "however" and "although"? If not, add. Now edit for things like grammar and spelling. Finally, read your good version aloud to the class; answer any questions, not just with "credibility" but with "truth."*

Note: See also the Topics for Writing at the end of this chapter.

Topics for Writing

Chapter 5: Comparison and Contrast

Compare and/or contrast one of the following pairs. (See also the guidelines that follow.)

1. Audio tapes and CDs
2. Night life in English Canada and night life in Quebec
3. Renting and owning your own home
4. The classical music fan and the rock music fan
5. The pessimist and the optimist
6. Morning people and night people
7. The newspaper and a television newscast
8. The authoritarian parent and the permissive parent
9. Driving a motorcycle and driving a car
10. A wedding and a funeral
11. City people and country people
12. Writing on paper and using a word processor
13. Community college and university
14. A newborn and an elderly person
15. Using credit and using cash
16. Large families and small families
17. Canadian football and American football
18. The miser and the spendthrift
19. The cuisine of my first country and of my second country
20. Abortion and euthanasia
21. A tabloid and a serious newspaper
22. A Macintosh computer and an IBM-compatible computer
23. A desktop computer and a notebook or subnotebook computer
24. A fax and a phone call
25. A voice phone and a vision phone
26. College or university and the school of hard knocks
27. Home cooking and restaurant cooking
28. Telephoning and writing a letter
29. Canadian films and American films
30. Single parents and married parents

Note also the Process in Writing topic after each selection in this chapter.

Process in Writing: Guidelines

Follow at least some of these steps in writing your essay of comparison and contrast (your teacher may suggest which ones).

1. *Spend enough time with the topic list to choose the item that best fits your interest and experience.*

2. *Draw a line down the middle of a blank page. Brainstorm: jot down notes for subject "A" on the left and for subject "B" on the right. Now join related items with lines, then take stock of what you have: Is A better than B? Is it worse? Similar? Opposite? Or what? Express their relationship to each other in a thesis statement.*

3. *Now choose either "halves" or "separate points" to organize your argument, depending on the nature and size of your subject, then work your notes into a brief outline.*

4. *Write a rapid first draft, double-spaced, not stopping now to revise or edit.*

5. *Later analyze what you have produced: Does it follow your outline? If not, is the new material off-topic, or is it a worthwhile addition, an example of "thinking in writing"? Revise accordingly.*

6. *In your second draft cut all deadwood. Sharpen word choice. Add any missing examples. Strengthen* TRANSITIONS.

7. *Try your prose aloud before writing the good copy. If you have used a computer, save the essay on disk in case your teacher suggests further revision.*

Uniphoto/Canapress Photo Service

"Too many do not see our beauty as beauty, our music as music, our language as language, our thoughts as thoughts, for we are different from the sky creatures."

—*Margaret Laurence, "A Fable—For the Whaling Fleets"*

CHAPTER

6

ANALOGY AND RELATED DEVICES

In a way, it's like. . . .

One student wrote this memory of his Toronto childhood:

> I heard and felt a rumbling from the ground, looked up and saw a huge red metallic monster with a tail on the end approach us. "Run, run," I said, "before it eats us." My mother reassured me that no fear was necessary. The monster slowly rolled up beside us, opened its mouth, and we went in.

As adults, we know that monsters have not roamed the shores of Lake Ontario for millions of years, and that they were not red but probably green! We also know that monsters and streetcars have little in common. Yet who would say that this *analogy* does not clearly express the child's first encounter with a streetcar? It may even help us, as adults, to view with new eyes something that we have taken for granted.

In this chapter Basil Johnston describes another monster — the weendigo of Native American legend that eats humans who wander outside at night. In its new version the weendigo consumes not humans but pine, spruce, cedar and the wildlife that lives there. Though we know the forest industry is not staffed by monsters but by decent men and women trying to make a living, we cannot help but see, through Johnston's eyes, the "monstrous" destruction of clear-cutting.

In the last chapter we discussed how two items from the same category — say, two cities — can be explained logically through comparison and contrast. By seeing how Toronto and New York are alike or unlike, we gain a clearer understanding of both. An *analogy*, though, brings together two apparently *unlike* items from *different* categories (such as a monster and a modern industry). Instead of using the two to explain each other, it more often uses one as a device to explain the other. It is not the monsters we investigate but the monstrous aspects of the streetcar or the forest industry.

In the last chapter we speculated whether, instead of comparing two cities, we could compare a city and an anthill. To those of us who live in chambers along the corridors of apartment buildings or who each day crowd into holes in the ground to take the subway, the similarities may be all too clear. We see right away that such an argument is hardly logical, for the very good reason that people are not insects. Yet the analogy may be a fresh, thought-provoking way to express aspects of city life.

Topics that are unfamiliar or abstract almost cry out for analogies to explain them. Thus in the eighties, the term "computer virus" swept the world. These electronic "diseases" "contaminate" computer programs, "spreading" an "epidemic" of "contagion." The "outbreaks" of various "strains" — with names like "Leprosy," "Cancer" and "Anthrax," not to mention "Holocaust" and "Armageddon" — can "infect" programs, erase memory or even attack hardware. Of course "antiviral" software to "vaccinate" against infection has been developed, with brand names like "Flu Shot +," "Data Physician," "Antidote," "Virus RX," "ViruSafe" and "Vaccine 1.0." In addition, "safe computing practices" have been recommended to avoid infection by viruses such as "PC AIDS" (*TIME* magazine).

Now in the nineties the world of computers has seized on another analogy to depict another new subject: the "Information Highway." One issue, alone, of *PC Computing* used the terms "octane," "roadside assistance," "on-ramp," "detour," "rest stop," "tollbooth," "dead end," "rut," "U-turn," "fast lane" and "hotrods for the Information Super-highway." The "hotrods," of course, are the computers for sale.

What makes such analogies powerful is not so much their originality as their breadth — for example the heavy borrowing of vocabulary from the one item to portray the other. The further you develop such links between your two items — such as a destructive computer program and a virus — the better the analogy.

Yet even a brief statement, such as "A destructive computer program is like a virus," can have value. As a *simile* it is not much of an argument in itself, but is a vivid statement that can be used in support of another argument. While a *simile* states that one thing is *like* another, a *metaphor* states that one thing *is* another ("A destructive computer program is a virus"). Both devices occur often in poetry and in fiction, and of course in essays. This chapter's last selection, Félix Leclerc's description of his boyhood home, contains a steady stream of similes and metaphors that convey a vividly poetic sense not only of the place but also of the author's feelings about it. Though nothing objective has been proven, a message has certainly been given.

Note: For more examples of analogy and related devices, see these essays in other chapters:

Analogy:
Erika Ritter, "Bicycles," p. 230
Margaret Atwood, "Canadians: What Do They Want?" p. 306
Simile, metaphor and other figures of speech:
Margaret Laurence, "Where the World Began," p. 86
Charles Yale Harrison, "In the Trenches," p. 93
Nathalie Petrowski, "The Seven-Minute Life of Marc Lépine," p. 322

Robertson Davies

The Decorums of Stupidity

Robertson Davies is one of English Canada's most celebrated novelists, though in his long career he has also been actor, playwright, journalist, essayist, scholar and educator. Born in 1913 in Thamesville, Ontario, he studied at Queen's and then at Oxford. After acting with England's Old Vic Company, he became editor of the Peterborough Examiner, *a post he graced with his polished and urbane columns, many of them about the arts. Another career as English professor followed, when in 1963 he became Master of the newly founded Massey College of the University of Toronto. Meanwhile Davies wrote a number of plays, such as* Eros at Breakfast *(1949) and* Tempest-Tost *(1951), and gathered many of his essays into books. His celebrity, though, rests on his fiction. The early "Salterton Trilogy" of novels was well received, but it is his "Deptford Trilogy," now translated into over a dozen languages, that made his international reputation:* Fifth Business *(1970, probably his best),* The Manticore *(1972) and* World of Wonders *(1975). In these novels, one event influences another until the characters are entrapped in a web of causality. Davies' production of novels has continued steadily since then, with* The Rebel Angels *(1981),* What's Bred in the Bone *(1985),* The Lyre of Orpheus *(1988) and* Murther & Walking Spirits *(1991). Our selection, from the 1960 collection* A Voice from the Attic, *is not fiction but an essay about how good books deserve to be read.*

1   Not all rapid reading is to be condemned. Much that is badly written and grossly padded must be read rapidly and nothing is lost thereby. Much of the reading that has to be done in the way of business should be done as fast as it can be understood. The ideal business document is an auditor's report; a good one is finely edited. But the memoranda, the public-relations pieces, the business magazines, need not detain us. Every kind of prose has its own speed, and the experienced reader knows it as a musician knows Adagio from Allegro. All of us have to read a great deal of stuff which gives us no pleasure and little information, but which we cannot wholly neglect; such reading belongs in that department of life which Goldsmith called "the decorums of stupidity." Books as works of art are no part of this duty-reading.

Books as works of art? Certainly; it is thus that their writers intend   2
them. But how are these works of art used?

Suppose you hear of a piece of recorded music which you think you   3
might like. Let us say it is an opera of Benjamin Britten's — *The Turn of
the Screw.* You buy it, and after dinner you put it on your record player.
The scene is one of bustling domesticity: your wife is writing to her
mother, on the typewriter, and from time to time she appeals to you for
the spelling of a word; the older children are chattering happily over a
game, and the baby is building, and toppling, towers of blocks. The
records are long-playing ones, designed for 33 revolutions of the turn-
table per minute; ah, but you have taken a course in rapid listening,
and you pride yourself on the speed with which you can hear, so you
adjust your machine to play at 78 revolutions a minute. And when you
find your attention wandering from the music, you skip the sound arm
rapidly from groove to groove until you come to a bit that appeals to
you. But look — it is eight o'clock, and if you are to get to your meeting
on time, Britten must be choked off. So you speed him up until a
musical pause arrives, and then you stop the machine, marking the
place so that you can continue your appreciation of *The Turn of the Screw*
when next you can spare a few minutes for it.

Ridiculous? Of course, but can you say that you have never read a   4
book in that fashion?

One of the advantages of reading is that it can be done in short   5
spurts and under imperfect conditions. But how often do we read in
conditions which are merely decent, not to speak of perfection? How
often do we give a book a fair chance to make its effect with us?

△△

Further Reading:

Robertson Davies,
> *A Voice from the Attic*
> *Fifth Business*
> *The Manticore*
> *World of Wonders*

Structure:

1. In discussing "duty-reading" that is best done at high speed, how
   does paragraph 1 prepare us for the main point?
2. Where is the main point first stated?
3. Paragraph 3 develops the *analogy* upon which this essay is based: listening to music as reading a book. Books were discussed in the
   introduction, but why are they not mentioned in the analogy itself?
4. Davies closes with a standard technique: asking questions. Are these

true questions that are open to debate, or are they rhetorical questions designed to make us agree with the author?

Style:

1. Why is this essay so much shorter than others in the book? Has Davies failed to develop his point fully?
2. Why are paragraphs 1 and 3 so long while paragraphs 2 and 4 are so short?
3. What FIGURE OF SPEECH does Davies use in this sentence from paragraph 1: "Every kind of prose has its own speed, and the experienced reader knows it as a musician knows Adagio from Allegro"?
4. Is Davies entirely serious, as his dignified style would suggest? Or is humour important to his argument? Give examples.

Ideas for Discussion and Writing:

1. Is a desire to read fast like a desire to eat fast? To drive fast? To work fast? To live fast? Why is speed so highly regarded in our culture? Have you lived in another culture that encourages a slower pace? If so, which do you prefer, and why?
2. Before writing was invented, all stories and poems were of course spoken aloud. What advantages does a listener have over a reader? What advantages does a reader have over a listener?
3. Francis Bacon said, "Some books are to be tasted, others to be swallowed, and some few to be chewed and digested. . . ." Make a list of the five or ten books you have most recently read. Which did you "taste," which did you "swallow," and which did you "chew and digest"? What factors influenced your method in each case?
4. Some may see Davies' references to the wife (par. 3) as STEREOTYPING. What social factors, since the time this essay was written, have changed the way many writers depict the roles of the sexes?
5. **PROCESS IN WRITING:** *In an essay based on* analogy, *tell how you "taste," "swallow" or "chew and digest" different kinds of music. First make notes for a week, whenever you listen to music on the radio or stereo. Then put your best material into a brief outline before writing a first draft. Add plentiful examples, but cut every excess word. Read your final version aloud in class.*

Note: See also the Topics for Writing at the end of this chapter.

Margaret Laurence

A Fable — For the Whaling Fleets

*Margaret Laurence (1926–1987) was one of Canada's best-loved writers, au-
thor of* The Stone Angel *and several other important novels. (See page 86 for a
fuller biographical introduction and another of her essays.) Laurence's lifelong
reverence for nature and its life forms shines through the selection that follows, a
lyrical elegy on the whale, which in 1983 was published in Greg Gatenby's
anthology* Whales — A Celebration, *and in 1989 was reprinted in a posthumous collection of Laurence's writings,* Dance on the Earth: a Memoir.

I magine the sky creatures descending to our earth. They are very   1
different from humankind. We have known of their existence, although we cannot truly conceive of the realms in which they live. Sometimes a tiny thing has fallen to earth violently, lifeless when we found it,
like a lost bird with wings broken and useless. But the sky creatures are
not birds. They are extremely intelligent beings. Their brains, although
not as large as ours, have been developed for complex and subtle use.
They bear their young live from the mothers' bodies, as humans do,
and nourish them from the breast. Although they live in the highest
heights, we breathe the same air. Like us, they have language, and like
humankind they have music and song. They care for their young, love
them and teach them in the ways of their species. But when they loom
low over our lands in their strong air vessels, they hunt humanity with
the death sticks. At first there are only a few of them, then more and
more. There are fewer and fewer human beings. The sky creatures
make use of the dead bodies of our children, of our hunted young
women and young men, of our elders. The flesh of our dead children is
eaten by the sky creatures and their slaves. The fat from the bodies of
our loved children gives oil which is used by the sky creatures in various
ways — most of it goes to make unguents and creams for their vanity.
They do not need to hunt humans in order to survive. They continue to
slaughter us out of greed. Some of their number believe the slaying is

193

wrong. Some of them sing their songs to us, and we in return answer with our songs. Perhaps we will never be able to speak in our human languages to those who speak the sky creatures' languages. But song is communication, respectful touch and trust are ways of knowing. Too many of them, however, do not think in this manner, do not have these feelings. Too many of them hear the sounds and songs of humanity but do not sense our meanings. Too many do not see our beauty as beauty, our music as music, our language as language, our thoughts as thoughts, for we are different from the sky creatures. Our songs are lost to their ears, and soon may be lost even to our own earth, when the last of humankind is hunted and slain and consumed. If that terrifying time should come, then our love, our mirth, our knowledge, our joy in life, will disappear forever, and God will mourn, for the holy spirit that created the sky creatures and gave them the possibility of the knowledge of love, also created us with the same possibilities, we who are the earthlings, humankind.

△ △

Further Reading:

Margaret Laurence, *The Stone Angel*
Greg Gatenby, ed., *Whales — A Celebration*
Farley Mowat, *A Whale for the Killing*
Herman Melville, *Moby Dick* (novel)
J. J. Douglas, ed., *Whale Sound: An Anthology of Poems About Whales and Dolphins*

Structure:

1. What is a fable? Tell a well-known one, such as "The Tortoise and the Hare," to the class. What is its point? Who do the animals really represent? In what ways is a fable an *analogy*?
2. In Laurence's fable who are the "sky creatures"? Who are "humankind"? Who is speaking? And what is the overall *analogy* that powers the argument?
3. Name all the ways in which Laurence develops her *analogy*, showing an animal, the whale, to be like humans. Name also the problems caused by differences between the two.
4. This chapter's *analogies*, including Laurence's, are among the shortest pieces in the book. Why?
5. Laurence's fable consists of one long paragraph. Why does she not follow essay format by breaking it up?

Style:

1. Like psalms from the Bible or traditional orations by First Nations People, this fable is a prose-poem. Point out several METAPHORS and SIMILES that help create the "poetry."
2. Poetry is meant to be spoken. Read this selection aloud to the class, with expression, so both speaker and listeners can fully experience it.
3. How FORMAL or INFORMAL is Laurence's TONE? Can you imagine it better in the school cafeteria or in a holy place of worship? Support your response with examples. TONE should always match content. Does hers? Explain.

Ideas for Discussion and Writing:

1. "Some of them sing their songs to us," Laurence writes. Why are many humans so attracted to whales and touched by their plight?
2. Much less whaling is now done in the world. In the St. Lawrence River, though, the beluga are still dying of cancers brought on by chemical pollution. What could and should be done? How much more would you pay for consumer products made with less pollution?
3. First we learned to shun racism, then sexism. Is speciesism next? If the life of a whale, a grizzly bear or a bald eagle were as important to you as the life of your neighbour, what would the *effects* on our lifestyle have to be?
4. In the early nineties Maritimers and the whole nation were stunned by the disappearance of cod stocks once thought limitless. To what lengths should Canada go to reverse the loss and prevent others? Make concrete suggestions.
5. **PROCESS IN WRITING:** *Parts of Laurence's* analogy *strongly resemble descriptions by First Nations People of the arrival of Europeans ("At first there are only a few of them, then more and more. There are fewer and fewer human beings. . . .") You have just viewed humans from the perspective of whales; now view the "discoverers" of Canada from the perspective of the original Canadians. Choose a way to represent the new arrivals (as a species of animal, as aliens, as supernatural beings, or as whatever expresses the truth to you). Now write a rapid first draft of your* analogy, *comparing the new arrivals to your own group. After the draft "cools off," look it over. Have you given examples so readers can "see" your point? Have you enriched your account with FIGURES OF SPEECH? Does the TONE, FORMAL or INFORMAL, fit your content? Finally check for things like grammar and spelling as you produce the good version.*

Note: See also the Topics for Writing at the end of this chapter.

Collin Brown

A Game of Tennis*

Born in Kingston, Jamaica in 1965, Collin Brown immigrated to Canada with his parents at age seven. He is now president of The Unity Group Corporation, a Toronto firm that specializes in creating business opportunities for minorities. (He also plays tennis, the source of his analogy in the argument below.) A busy executive who thinks nothing of working late nights and weekends at the office, Brown and his "hybrid of business professionals" have created enterprises such as a greeting card manufacturer, the National Business Alliance of Canada, and an accounting service. Many more are in the works. "I thrive on people telling me 'you can't do that'," says Brown. After high school he immediately started his own business as an interior decorator, but realized it was not going to be as easy as he thought. So putting the business on hold, he attended Toronto's Centennial College to study business and marketing. Two years after his studies, he was employing over 20 people in his first company. Since then his interests have extended to real estate, finance, publishing and business development. Brown sits on numerous boards and has been involved in many initiatives for youth empowerment. His true passion, though, is motivational speaking, which allows him to help others through what he has learned. "Dare yourself to dream," he says. "If your mind can perceive it you can surely achieve it. Translate that dream into a goal and be sure that every step you take is in line with that objective. Use every obstacle as a stepping stone, look for the good in every situation, be realistic and persistent, don't stray from your goal and you will succeed." Our selection began as an interview by Toronto Star *reporter Catherine Dunphy, published on May 15, 1994. Later Mr. Brown changed the order of paragraphs and added a few more details.*

1   I grew up at Martingrove and Albion Road. It hasn't gained that negative a reputation — yet — not like its sister neighbourhood Jamestown, which is two minutes away.

2   Growing up in North Etobicoke, I had a lot of time to examine the issues of race relationships and crime versus economics. I look at this

---

*Editor's title.

issue of single parenthood and it is not rampant only in the black communities. It is prevalent in a lot of communities.

The whole circumstance is not one of race, creed, colour or anything like that. It is economic frustration that you see. The key issue here is the sense of hopelessness prevalent in so many communities today, and that is what we are here to change. 3

The issue is one of power. Unlike a lot of people out there, I'm not angry at anyone for suppressing anyone else. You know the saying, all is fair in love and war? It's like you and I go out to play a game of tennis and we bet $100 and you win. What do I do? Do I sit and complain that you won, that you took my $100? Or do I do something about it? 4

If we go back and you beat me again, and you still win, I become frustrated, and you're thinking "why even bother playing a guy I can beat anytime, every time." I'm no challenge to you, so why bother playing? That is what is happening in certain communities, not only the black community. When the power is in one place and there's no sharing, I can't win. 5

What I have decided to do, though, is practice, practice to be the best. I will learn and understand the rules of the game, then I will call you up and say I can beat you. I'll bet you $1000. I'll go to the table with something tangible. No more monkeying around. We play and I win. I beat you; you respect me. It's not an issue of domination, there's a sense of friendship involved. You don't respect someone you beat all the time. That's the bottom line. 6

When I was sitting in biology class, I was making plans to buy my own home. Everybody laughed, of course, but a few years later it was a different ball game. I bought my first house at 19 and have bought and sold many more since. I learned to look at the successes of people who had done what I wanted to do, people like Bill Cosby, who have really overcome the odds and exemplified that, hey, being wealthy and re-spected is not impossible. 7

I can tell you that I am going to be one of the wealthiest men in this country and mean it because that is my goal. Not only wealth for the sake of wealth but wealth for the sake of having the power to make the changes necessary to create more opportunities for those who need it. That essentially is my goal. 8

And I dare you to tell me I can't achieve it. 9

△△△

Further Reading:

Stephen Covey, *The Seven Habits of Highly Effective People*
Rubin "Hurricane" Carter, *The Sixteenth Round*
Lorris Elliott, ed., *Other Voices* (anthology)
Austin Clarke, *The Meeting Point* (novel)

Structure:

1. Printed interviews really have two authors — the speaker and the interviewer who often organizes and rearranges what the speaker says. In *The Toronto Star* version Brown's dream of buying a house comes *before* the analogy, but for our version Brown moved it *after*. Which position is better? Why?
2. The *analogy* of success in tennis and life came naturally to Brown, because he plays tennis. What analogy from your own life could develop the same argument?
3. How fully does Brown develop his *analogy* of practising to become "the best" at sport and career? Point out all parallels he makes.
4. Why does Brown close with a paragraph of only 11 words? Is it effective? If so, why?

Style:

1. Brown gave his recipe for success in an interview. Point out all the ways in which, as a result, its STYLE is INFORMAL and conversational. Is this TONE a good match for the subject matter? Give reasons.
2. In paragraphs 4–6 Brown seems almost to challenge you personally to tennis and a bet. To what extent does this approach involve you as you read?

Ideas for Discussion and Writing:

1. Television actor Bill Cosby was a role model for Brown's early dreams of success (paragraph 7). Who are your own role models? Choose one, and describe how she or he inspires you.
2. Brown says he is "not angry at anyone for suppressing anyone else" (paragraph 4). Are you? If so, give one example to show why. Give one concrete suggestion how your anger could be channelled to improve the situation.
3. It used to be said that the battles of England were won on the playing fields of Eton. To what extent does our society view athletics as training for competition in life, and even in war? Give examples from your own experience or observation.
4. Brown has given his recipe for success; what is yours?
5. INTERVIEW: Prepare good questions in advance, then interview a career person you know and admire (a family member, friend, neighbour, teacher, doctor, etc.) to find her or his recipe for success. Later as you play the tape back, take notes to help you put the parts in a logical order. Now write out the person's remarks, as Catherine Dunphy of the *Star* wrote those of Collin Brown. Are they in a good order? (Is there an introduction? Do examples illustrate at

the right spots? Do points increase in significance towards the end? Is there a conclusion?) Now edit punctuation and spelling. Finally, read your good version to the class.

6. **PROCESS IN WRITING:** *Does success seem to you like a ladder to climb? Or a mountain? A road to follow? A game of chance? A particular sport? Whatever analogy comes to you, freewrite on it for a few minutes to get the ideas flowing, then take stock of what you have written. Are there enough parallels between the two items to build a real analogy? If not, try again with a new comparison. If so, now write your first draft, rapidly, not stopping now to edit. When this version has "cooled off," look it over. Have you missed any steps or other areas of comparison? Add them. Have you supplied transition words like "now," "next," "suddenly," "finally," etc. to speed the action? If not, add. Finally, edit spelling and punctuation as you produce your final version.*

Note: See also the Topics for Writing at the end of this chapter.

Basil Johnston

Modern Cannibals of the Wilds

Basil Johnston is well known as a writer and as a teacher of Ojibway (Anishinabe) language, mythology and history in the Department of Ethnology of Toronto's Royal Ontario Museum. Born in 1929 on the Parry Island Reserve in Ontario, he went to the Cape Croker public school, then at the Spanish Residential School experienced the cultural dislocations of the residential school system which he would later describe in his book Indian School Days *(1988). He completed his education at Loyola College in Montreal and at the Ontario College of Education. Johnston has become a strong voice of First Nations People in Canada. Though he teaches and lectures extensively on Ojibway history, culture and language, it is his books that have reached the greatest audience:* Ojibway Heritage *(1976),* How the Birds Got their Colours *(1978),* Moose Meat and Wild Rice *(1978),* Tales the Elders Told *(1981),* Ojibway Ceremonies *(1983),* By Canoe and Moccasin *(1986) and* Tales of the Anishinaubae *(1993). Our selection is from the August 1, 1991 Toronto* Globe and Mail. *In it Johnston goes beyond his usual role of imparting Ojibway culture; in his portrait of the new "weendigo" he cuts right to the heart of modern Canadian values.*

1 Woods and forest once mantled most of this land, this continent. It was the home of the Anishinabek (Ojibway, Ottawa, Potowatomi, Algonquin), their kin and their neighbours. It was also the home of the moose, the deer, the caribou, the bear, their kindred and their neighbours. It was as well the home of the thrushes, the sparrows, the hawks, the tanagers, the ravens, the owls, their cousins and their neighbours. Mosquitoes, butterflies, caterpillars, ants, moths, their kind and their neighbours had a place therein.

2 Not only was it home, but a wellspring from which all drew their sustenance, medicine and knowledge.

3 Also dwelling in the woods and forests were weendigoes, giant cannibals who fed upon human flesh to allay their perpetual hunger. They stalked villages and camps, waiting for, and only for, the improvident, the slothful, the gluttonous, the promiscuous, the injudicious, the insatiable, the selfish, the avaricious and the wasteful, to be foolish enough to venture alone beyond the environs of their homes in winter.

But no matter how many victims a single weendigo devoured raw, he could never satisfy his hunger. The more he ate, the larger he grew, and the larger he grew, the greater his hunger. The weendigo's hunger always remained in proportion to his size.

Even though a weendigo is a mythical figure, he represents real human cupidity. What the old-time storyteller meant to project in the image of the weendigo was a universal and unchanging human disposition. But more learned people declared that no such monster ever existed, that he was a product of superstitious minds and imaginations.

As a result, the weendigo was driven from his place in Anishinabe traditions and culture, ostracized through disbelief and skepticism. It was assumed, and indeed it appeared as if, the weendigo and his brothers and sisters had passed into the Great Beyond, like many North American Indian beliefs and practices and traditions.

Actually, the weendigoes did not die out; they have only been assimilated and reincarnated as corporations, conglomerates and multinationals. They have taken on new names, acquired polished manners and renounced their craving for human flesh for more refined viands. But their cupidity is no less insatiable than their ancestors'.

One breed subsists entirely on forests. When this breed beheld forests, its collective cupidity was stirred as it looked upon an endless, boundless sea of green — as in greenbacks. They saw beyond, even into the future. Money. Cash. Deposits. Bank accounts. Interest. Reserves. Investments, securities, bonds, shares, dividends, capital gains, assets, funds, deals, revenue, income, prosperity, opulence, profits, riches, wealth, comfort.

They recruited woodsmen with axes, crosscut saws and Swede saws, sputters, shovels, cant hooks, grapples, chains, ropes, files and pikes, and sent them into the woods to fell, hue, saw, cut, chop, slash and level. The forests resounded with the clash of axes and the whine of saws as blades bit into the flesh of spruce, pine, cedar, tamarack and poplar to fill the demands of the weendigoes in Toronto, Montreal, Vancouver, New York, Chicago, Boston, wherever they now dwelt. Cries of "Timber!" echoed across the treetops, followed by the rip and tear of splintering trees, and thundering crashes.

And as fast as woodsmen felled the trees, teamsters delivered sleighload after sleighload to railway sidings and to the rivers. Train after train, shipload after shipload of logs were delivered to the mills.

Yet as fast as the woodsmen cut, as much as they cut, it was never fast enough. The quantity always fell short of the expectations of the weendigoes, their masters.

"Is that all? Should there not be more? We demand a bigger return for our risks and our investments. Only more will satisfy us. Any amount will do, so long as it's more, and the more the better."

13   The demands were met for more speed and more pulp, more logs and more timber. Axes, saws, woodsmen, horses and teamsters were replaced, and their blows and calls no longer rang in the forest. In their place, chainsaws whined, Caterpillar tractors with huge blades bulled and battered their way through the forest, uprooting trees to clear the way for automatic shearers that topped, limbed and sheared the trunks. These mechanical weendigoes gutted and desolated the forests, leaving death, destruction and ugliness where once there was life, abundance and beauty.

14   Trucks and transports operated day and night delivering cargo with a speed and quantity that the horses and sleighs could never have matched.

15   Yet the weendigoes wanted still more, and it didn't matter if their policies and practices of clear-cutting their harvest of timber and pulp resulted in violations of North American Indian rights or in the further impairment of their lives.

16   Nor does it matter to them that their modus operandi permanently defiles hillside and mountainside by erosion. They are indifferent to the carnage inflicted upon bears, wolves, rabbits, thrushes, sparrows, warblers. Who cares if they are displaced? What possible harm has been done? Nor does it seem as if these modern weendigoes have any regard for the rights of future generations to the yield of Mother Earth.

17   The new, reincarnated weendigoes are little different from their forebears. They are more omnivorous than their ancestors, however, and the modern breed wears elegant clothes and comports itself with an air of cultured and dignified respectability.

18   Profit, wealth, comfort, power are the ends of business. Anything that detracts from or diminishes the anticipated return, be it taking pains not to violate the rights of others, or taking measures to ensure that the land remains fertile and productive for future generations, must, it seems, be circumvented.

19   And what has been the result of this self-serving, self-glutting disposition? In 10 short decades, these modern weendigoes have accomplished what at one time seemed impossible; they have laid waste immense tracts of forest that were seen as beyond limit as well as self-propagating, and ample enough to serve this generation and many more to come.

20   Now, as the forests are in decline, the weendigoes are looking at a future that offers scarcity. Many others are assessing the weendigoes' accomplishments not in terms of dollars but in terms of damage — the damage they have inflicted on the environment and the climate and on botanical and zoological life.

ΔΔΔΔΔΔΔΔΔΔΔΔΔΔΔΔΔΔΔΔΔΔΔΔΔΔΔΔΔΔΔΔΔΔΔΔΔΔΔΔΔΔΔΔΔΔΔ

Further Reading:

Basil Johnston,
> *How the Birds Got Their Colours*
> *Indian School Days*

Agnes Grant, ed., *Our Bit of Truth: An Anthology of Canadian Native Literature*

Linda Jaine and Drew Hayden, eds., *Voices: Being Native in Canada*

Limits to Growth: A Report for the Club of Rome's Project on the Predicament of Mankind

Canadian Forestry Association, *Clearcutting*

M. T. Kelly, *A Dream Like Mine* (novel)

Structure:

1. Is "Modern Cannibals of the Wilds" a *fable*, like Margaret Laurence's "A Fable — for the Whaling Fleets" in this chapter?
2. Why does Johnston open by listing so many animals, birds and insects whose "home" was once most of this continent?
3. Point out the paragraph of TRANSITION where we move from the traditional weendigo to the modern one. Point out the THESIS.
4. Analyze how paragraphs 15 and 16 employ *cause and effect*.
5. Point out all the ways Johnston portrays the Canadian forestry industry as a monster and cannibal. How fully has he developed his *analogy*?

Style:

1. Where do we usually see words like "mantled" (paragraph 1), "kindred" (1), "improvident" (3) and "slothful" (3)? Describe Johnston's TONE. Compare it to that of Margaret Laurence's analogy in this chapter. Does his fit his content as well as hers fits her content?
2. Read paragraph 9 aloud to the class, so all can experience its ONOMATOPOETIC language. Which words sound like what they mean? What is the overall effect?
3. How CONCISE is Johnston's analogy? What techniques make it so?
4. Why is the METAPHOR "flesh" of paragraph 9 so appropriate to Johnston's portrayal of the weendigoes?

Ideas for Discussion and Writing:

1. Basil Johnston discusses the forest and Margaret Laurence whales. What makes the *analogy* a good tool for essays about the environment?
2. If our human forestry industry is a "cannibal," then in what sense is it "eating" us as well as trees?

3. "The more he ate, the larger he grew, and the larger he grew, the greater his hunger" (paragraph 4). What if one day the monster's "food" runs out? When our forestry industry can no longer "eat" and "grow," will it "survive"? What can we do now to either reduce its appetite or extend its food supply?

4. Defend or attack the clear-cutting that continues in British Columbia and most of Canada. Defend or attack the actions of Greenpeace, in convincing many European companies not tó buy Canadian paper made through clear-cutting.

5. Critics claim that in Canada we do not "harvest" but "mine" the forests. *Contrast* these philosophies.

6. What particularly qualifies Basil Johnston, an Ojibway, to write on this subject?

7. **PROCESS IN WRITING:** *In paragraph 16 Johnston refers to our "Mother Earth." Expand this widespread metaphor into an essay of analogy. First write the words "Earth" and "Mother" in the centre of a page, then fill the space around them with any other words they bring to mind. Connect related items with lines. Determine your main point. Now draw upon this cluster outline as you do a rapid first draft. When it has "cooled off," look it over. Do examples always help the reader "see" your point? If not, add. Does your TONE fit this important subject? If not, adjust. Is everything on topic? If not, cut. Finally, revise for things like spelling and grammar as you produce your good version.*

Note: See also the Topics for Writing at the end of this chapter.

Michael Ondaatje

Tabula Asiae*

When in 1992 Michael Ondaatje won the English-speaking world's most presti-gious literary award, the Booker Prize, for his novel The English Patient, *he gave new force to a growing pattern: writers from the margins of the old British Empire are steadily moving to the centre of English-language literature. In more than one way Ondaatje is the least "Canadian" of our major writers. He was born in 1943 in Ceylon (now Sri Lanka) to the family of eccentric aristocrats he later portrayed in his fictionalized autobiography* Running in the Family (1982). *His works are often set outside our borders and share a lyrical, often surreal, often cinematic style that suggests other places and other influences. Ondaatje moved to England in 1954 and to Canada in 1962. Here he took a B.A. and an M.A., and since 1971 has taught at Glendon College, York University, in Toronto. His first book of poetry,* The Dainty Monsters, *appeared in 1967. Then in 1969 appeared* The Man with Seven Toes, *in 1973* Rat Jelly, *and in 1979* There's a Trick with a Knife I'm Learning to Do: Poems 1963–1978. *This last won the Governor General's award, as had his 1970 book of poetry and prose,* The Collected Works of Billy the Kid. *In 1976 was published* Coming through Slaughter, *his richly poetic novel about a jazz musician in New Orleans, and in 1987 his panoramic novel of Toronto in the 1930s,* In The Skin of a Lion. *From beginnings as a poet, Ondaatje has become a major Canadian and world novelist. Our present selection is from* Running in the Family.

O n my brother's wall in Toronto are the false maps. Old portraits of Ceylon. The result of sightings, glances from trading vessels, the theories of sextant. The shapes differ so much they seem to be translations — by Ptolemy, Mercator, François Valentyn, Mortier, and Heydt — growing from mythic shapes into eventual accuracy. Amoeba, then stout rectangle, and then the island as we know it now, a pendant off the ear of India. Around it, a blue-combed ocean busy with dolphin and sea-horse, cherub and compass. Ceylon floats on the Indian Ocean

1

Tabula Asiae: Map of Asia (in Latin; apparently the words Ondaatje sees on his brother's old maps of Ceylon).

205

and holds its naive mountains, drawings of cassowary and boar who leap without perspective across imagined "desertum'° and plain.

2   At the edge of the maps the scrolled mantling depicts ferocious slipper-footed elephants, a white queen offering a necklace to natives who carry tusks and a conch, a Moorish king who stands amidst the power of books and armour. On the south-west corner of some charts are satyrs, hoof deep in foam, listening to the sound of the island, their tails writhing in the waves.

3   The maps reveal rumours of topography, the routes for invasion and trade, and the dark mad mind of travellers' tales appears throughout Arab and Chinese and medieval records. The island seduced all of Europe. The Portuguese. The Dutch. The English. And so its name changed, as well as its shape, — Serendip, Ratnapida ("island of gems"), Taprobane, Zeloan, Zeilan, Seyllan, Ceilon, and Ceylon — the wife of many marriages, courted by invaders who stepped ashore and claimed everything with the power of their sword or bible or language.

4   This pendant, once its shape stood still, became a mirror. It pretended to reflect each European power till newer ships arrived and spilled their nationalities, some of whom stayed and intermarried — my own ancestor arriving in 1600, a doctor who cured the residing governor's daughter with a strange herb and was rewarded with land, a foreign wife, and a new name which was a Dutch spelling of his own. Ondaatje. A parody of the ruling language. And when his Dutch wife died, marrying a Sinhalese° woman, having nine children, and remaining. Here. At the centre of the rumour. At this point on the map.

△ △

Further Reading:

Michael Ondaatje,
> *Running in the Family*
> *The Collected Works of Billy the Kid*
> *In the Skin of a Lion*
> *The English Patient*

Structure and Style:

1. Why is "Tabula Asiae" so short? Because it says less than other selections? Because it communicates differently? If the latter, what techniques has Ondaatje used that many authors in this book have not?

°desertum: empty land.
°Sinhalese (or Singhalese): the largest population group of Sri Lanka.

2. Ondaatje was first a poet. How CONCISE is poetry compared to PROSE? Why? Is there a sharp division between the two, or can they share some techniques? Can they ever be so alike they almost merge? Where is "Tabula Asiae" in this spectrum, and why?

3. In paragraph 1 Ondaatje describes the shape of Ceylon in early "false maps" as an "amoeba" and a "stout rectangle." Are these comparisons METAPHORS or analogies? Why?

4. In paragraph 1 Ondaatje goes on to call Ceylon a "pendant off the ear of India." What FIGURE OF SPEECH is this? Does he develop it fully enough to make it an analogy?

5. In paragraph 3 Ceylon is "the wife of many marriages." Explain how, and tell what FIGURE OF SPEECH this is.

6. In paragraph 4 the "pendant" becomes a "mirror." In what sense? And again, is this image a METAPHOR or an analogy?

7. In what sense do the "false maps" of Ondaatje's brother in Toronto constitute an *analogy* of Ceylon?

8. "Serendip" is an early name for Sri Lanka, as paragraph 3 says. In a reference dictionary, find the connection between this name and the often used word "serendipity."

Ideas for Discussion and Writing:

1. The Sri Lanka of "Tabula Asiae" — mysterious, romantic and legendary — is not at all the Sri Lanka of the encyclopedia or TV newscast. Why has Ondaatje chosen a SUBJECTIVE, poetic way to present the land of his childhood?

2. "Tabula Asiae" is a chapter of Ondaatje's autobiography *Running in the Family*. If you wrote your own, how far back in time could you begin? Who are your earliest known ancestors? When and where did they live? Do you think their homeland or their personalities helped make you who you are today?

3. Ondaatje's brother puts old maps of Ceylon on his wall in Toronto. When people change countries, should they cherish and preserve their past, as the Ondaatjes do, or forget the past while making a new life? If your family immigrated to Canada, which are you doing, and why? If English is your second language, will you retain your first? If so, how? Will you someday teach it to your children? Why or why not?

4. **PROCESS IN WRITING:** *Immigration has occurred at some point in the background of all Canadians, even "First Nations" people. Choose one of these topics:*
   — *My ancestral homeland*
   — *The arrival of my ancestor(s) in Canada*
   — *My immigration to Canada*

Select the best one for you. Focus it to fit your circumstances, knowledge and interest. Now take a page of notes, perhaps consulting a parent, grandparent, or family records. Sense the importance, even the heroic, legendary or mythic qualities you may see in this topic — then write your "discovery draft." In the next version heighten these overtones by clothing bare fact in the kinds of poetical devices Ondaatje has used in his account (see FIGURES OF SPEECH, *and especially* METAPHOR, *in the Glossary). Make each image, each word choice, reflect your overall vision of this piece of your past. Finally, test the prose by reading aloud, before doing the good copy.*

Note: See also the Topics for Writing at the end of this chapter.

Félix Leclerc

The Family House[*]

Translated from the French by Philip Stratford

Though as he got older his own music went out of style, Félix Leclerc (1914–1988), Quebec's original chansonnier, *set the example for a generation of popular singers who during the sixties and seventies were a vital force in Quebec's "Quiet Revolution." As singer Gilles Vigneault put it, Leclerc was "the father of us all." Referred to by the media simply as "Félix," honoured by the annual "Félix" music awards named after him, Leclerc spent his last years as unofficial poet laureate of Quebec, a sage to whom the public turned for words in time of crisis. When Quebec mourned the death of nationalist leader René Lévesque in 1987, it was Leclerc whose words were carved on the tomb: "The first page of Quebec's true and beautiful history has been turned. Now he takes his place among the few liberators of their people." And when Leclerc died soon after, Quebeckers mourned another fallen leader. Leclerc was born in La Tuque. After announcing, acting and writing for Radio-Canada in the thirties and early forties, he acted for several years with a theatre company. Then in 1951 he arrived in Paris, where, singing his own rough-hewn songs in music halls, he won instant acclaim as "Le Canadien." But despite his success as songwriter and singer, Leclerc viewed himself primarily as a writer. He published more than a dozen books, including poetry, plays, fables, stories and novels. Among his most widely read have been* Adagio *(1943) and* Allegro *(1944), two collections of his fables and stories written for radio;* Pieds nus dans l'aube *(1946), the autobiographical novel from which our selection comes; and his novel* Le fou de l'île *(1958), translated by Philip Stratford in 1976 as* The Madman, the Kite and the Island.

W̲e were all, brothers and sisters alike, born in a long three-storey wooden house, a house as humped and crusty as a loaf of homemade bread, as warm and clean inside as the white of the loaf.

Roofed over with shingles, harbouring robins in its gables, it looked itself like an old nest perched up there in the silence. Taking the north wind over the left shoulder, beautifully adjusted to nature, from the

[*] Translator's title.

roadside one might also have mistaken it for an enormous boulder stranded on the beach.

3   In truth it was a stubborn old thing, soaking up storms and twilight, determined not to die of anything less than old age, like the two elms beside it.

4   The house turned its back squarely on the rest of town so as not to see the new subdivision with its shiny little boxes as fragile as mushrooms. Looking out over the valley, highroad for the wild St. Maurice river, it focused as if in ecstasy on the long caravan of blue mountains over there, the ones that flocks of clouds and the oldest seagulls don't seem able to get over.

5   With its rusty sides, its black roof and its white-trimmed windows, our common cradle crouched over a heavy cement foundation sunk solidly in the ground like a ship's anchor to hold us firm, for we were eleven children aboard, a turbulent, strident lot, but as timid as baby chicks.

6   A big, robust, rough fieldstone chimney, held together by trowel-smoothed mortar, began in the cellar near the round-bellied furnace just above that drafty little iron door that sticking a mirror into you could see the stars. Like the hub of a wheel it rose through the floors distributing spokes of heat, then broke through to the outside as stiff as a sentinel with a plumed helmet and smoked there with windswept hair, close to a grey ladder lying along the roof. The grey ladder and the sooty little door, we were told, were not for human use, but for an old man in red who in winter jumped from roof to roof behind reindeer harnessed in white.

7   From top to bottom our home was inhabited: by us in the centre like the core of a fruit; at the edges by parents; in the cellars and attics by superb and silent men, lumberjacks by trade. In the walls, under the floors, between the joists, near the carpets, and in the folds of the lampshades lived goblins, gnomes, fairies, snatches of song, silly jokes and the echoes of games; in the veins of our house ran pure poetry.

8   We had a chair for rocking in, a bench for saying prayers, a sofa to cry on, a two-step staircase for playing trains. Also other fine toys that we didn't dare touch, like the two-wired bird with its long beak and the bell in its forehead that talked to the grown-ups. A flower-patterned linoleum was our garden; a hook in the wall, a bollard to tie up our imaginary boats; the staircases were slides; the pipes running up the walls our masts; and armchairs miniature stages where we learnt with the hats, gloves and overcoats of our elders how to make the same faces that we wear today but without finding them funny.

9   A vast corridor divided the ground floor lengthwise. A few rung-backed chairs made a circle in one corner; above them a row of hooks like question marks disappeared beneath the coats of visitors who came to consult Papa, the biggest timber merchant in the valley. The living

room and a bedroom for visitors stood side by side. The living room, with its black piano, its net curtains, its big blue armchair, its gold-framed pictures, a few old-style chairs upholstered in satin (particularly a spring-rocker dressed up like an old lady out of the past with tassels on the hem of her dress) gave our lives a quality of Sunday celebration. Our parents' bedroom closed its door on impenetrable secrets. In its obscurity slumbered an old dresser full of camphor-scented sheets between which my mother hid mysterious notebooks, repositories of the exact hour of our birth, the names of godfathers and godmothers, and very private family events.

To the left of the hall a smoking room served as my father's study   10
and as library for all of us. A door opened to the dining room — classroom would be more exact, for we only ate there once or twice a year. In the sewing room between the sewing machine and an enormous cupboard stood the sofa, ready to be cried on. At the back of the house, spreading the full width, was our gay and singing kitchen: the cast-iron stove with its built-in mirror, the red kitchen cupboards, the white muslin curtains hanging like fog in the narrow windows, and the patches of sunlight playing on the left of the long family table. There shone the ever-burning lamp, known to all people throughout all time as the soul of the home. There we were told of good news and bad. There Papa signed our school report cards. There in the high rocking chair we would often sit in silence to think of facts of creation discovered that day and ponder on the strange and marvellous world we had fallen into.

The first floor was lined with children's bedrooms. There were eight,   11
I think, divided between girls and boys. In the girls' rooms it was cleaner, rosier, airier than the boys'. On the walls they pinned up tiny frames, graceful silhouettes and sprigs of flowers. On ours we stuck huge vulgar calendars, of hunters waiting for game and old gents smoking rubbed tobacco.

Our room, the most spacious on the floor, looked out on the garden,   12
its black earth full as a cornucopia, and cut through with straight little paths that we walked down every evening, watering under the watching eyes of the cottontails.

We each had our own bed, a little white bed with a real straw mattress   13
and iron bedposts ending in brass knobs where we hung our clothes, our slingshots, and our hands clasped in prayer.

On the second floor a screened veranda jutted out in a bow like a   14
pilot-house. It was a veritable observation post dominating the waves of the valley like those of the sea: waves of snowstorms, waves of loggers in springtime, waves of poor families gathering wild fruit, waves of falling leaves, of showers of sunshine, of the beating of birds' wings, of paths traced by children, hunters and fishermen. On hot nights we slept there above the waves on that wooden porch which was also the

children's playroom. Soldiers, teddy bears, drums, little wooden shoes, dolls seated at table before empty china plates, all keeping good company together. A tin bridge built long ago by my eldest brother served as access to this cardboard world.

15   On the floor above, behind a bull's-eye window, stretched the attic, a long deserted dusty cage, dormitory in winter for several lumberjacks. Between the three-legged chairs and the family portraits, these men on their mattresses, devoured by fatigue, tumbled headlong each night into sleep.

16   And like the crew of a happy ship, thinking neither of arrivals nor of departures, but only of the sea that carries them, we sped through childhood all sails set, thrilled with each morning and every night, envying neither distant ports nor far cities, convinced that our ship was flying the best colours and that we carried on board all necessary potions to ward off pirates and bad luck.

17   The house we lived in was number 168, rue Claire-Fontaine.

△△

Further Reading:

Félix Leclerc,
> *The Madman, the Kite and the Island*
> *Pieds nus dans l'aube* (available only in French)

Philip Stratford, ed., *Chez nous* (anthology of writings from Quebec, translated into English)

Jacques Ferron, *Tales from an Uncertain Country* (short stories)

Structure:

1. Leclerc packs this selection with FIGURES OF SPEECH, but develops only one image so fully as to make it an *analogy*. What is it? Which paragraphs develop it?
2. What is the overall point of this selection, and where does Leclerc most openly state it?

Style:

1. Do you see twice as many METAPHORS and SIMILES here as in most of the other selections? Four times as many? Ten times as many? What effect does this concentration of figures of speech give?
2. Point out ten SIMILES, ten METAPHORS and five cases of PERSONIFICATION in this selection. Are these figures of speech well chosen to build a single dominant impression?
3. Do you imagine "The Family House" was easy or hard to translate from French to English? Is an exact translation possible? If you speak

two or more languages, how easy or hard is it to translate thoughts from one to another?

Ideas for Discussion and Writing:

1. In paragraph 8 Leclerc tells how the children imitated their elders, learning "how to make the same faces that we wear today but without finding them funny." Do you sense in "The Family House" a regret for lost childhood? Do you regret the loss of your own? Do most of us? If so, give reasons.

2. Almost everything Leclerc wrote expresses the same happiness and security that we find in "The Family House." Do happy children such as he depicts here usually become happy adults? Can unhappy children become happy adults? Give examples.

3. "Coming of Age in Putnok" is the opening of George Gabori's autobiography, while "The Family House" is the opening of Félix Leclerc's autobiographical novel. Compare the two. Which gives more facts? More feeling? More insight into the author's background and personality? Which would more strongly motivate readers to finish the book?

4. **PROCESS IN WRITING:** *Like Leclerc, depict your own childhood home in such a way as to strongly convey your feelings about it and your life there. First generate a page of* SIMILES, METAPHORS *and* SENSE IMAGES *that "show" your memories of home. Now search these notes for a common theme such as Leclerc's vision of a house as a ship. Next write a "discovery draft" to develop this analogy, using images from your notes, and new ones that come as you write. In further drafts chop out each word that does not in some way further the overall effect. Read your final version aloud, with feeling, to the class.*

Note: See also the Topics for Writing at the end of this chapter.

Topics for Writing

Chapter 6: Analogy and Related Devices

Choose either a complete topic from items 1–15, or a subject from items 16 –30 to complete. Then in an essay, extend your analogy as far as you can. (See also the guidelines that follow.)

1. Planet Earth as our mother
2. A career as marriage
3. School as a factory
4. Social classes as a prison
5. The playing field as a battlefield
6. Prejudice as a wall
7. Dancing as life
8. Music as a drug
9. White blood cells as an army
10. The public debt as a cancer
11. A career as war
12. The United States as a melting pot
13. Canada as a mosaic
14. The city as a jungle
15. Novels as dreams

16. Television as _____
17. A sports team as _____
18. Population growth as _____
19. Dating as _____
20. Old age as _____
21. Crime as _____
22. Video games as _____
23. Chess as _____
24. Marriage as _____
25. Parents as _____
26. Internet as _____
27. E-mail as _____
28. Pollution as _____
29. Money as _____
30. The United Nations as _____

Process in Writing: Guidelines

Follow at least some of these steps in writing your essay of analogy (your teacher may suggest which ones).

1. *Choose or devise a topic you really like, because motivation is the single greatest factor in writing performance.*

2. *If you complete one of the topics from 16 to 30, be sure to invent an* **analogy** *(with two items from different categories), not a* **comparison and contrast** *(with two items from the same category). Know which item is your real subject, and which one exists merely to explain the other.*

3. *Now freewrite on your topic, to achieve the spontaneity and originality that spark a good analogy.*

4. *Incorporate the best of this freewriting into your first draft. Let the ideas flow, not stopping now to revise or edit.*

5. *In your next draft add any more points of comparison that come to you (a strong analogy is fully developed). Read your prose aloud to detect awkward passages, and revise. Trim deadwood. Heighten* TRANSITIONS.

6. *Now edit for things like spelling and grammar.*

7. *Proofread your good copy slowly, word by word. If you have used a computer, save the essay on disk in case your teacher suggests further revision.*

Ronald Conrad

"It would be impossible to list all the dishonest tricks employed in used car sales. As soon as the public is alerted to one scheme, other, more elaborate frauds are used by enterprising salesmen."

—*Phil Edmonston, "Dealer Tricks"*

CHAPTER

CLASSIFICATION

There are three kinds of them . . .

Our world is so complex that without classification we are lost. To call a friend we use an alphabetized phone book. To find hamburger we head for the meat section of the supermarket. To buy a used bicycle we go right to the *classified* section of the newspaper. Putting things into categories is one of our most common methods of thought, both for good and for bad. Who would search the whole dictionary when the word in question begins with "T"? What student, *classified* into grade five, would look for the grade six *class*room?

Yet as Hitler and other racists have shown, classifying people can lead to stereotypes and stereotypes can lead to violence. Ethnic jokes may seem innocent *(Why does it take two WASPS to change a light bulb? One makes the gin and tonics while the other calls the electrician)*. But such a characterization of a group makes it harder for others to view a member of that group as an individual. If all WASPs (or all Quebeckers or Torontonians or women or Catholics or politicians or police officers) are classified as the same, we have dehumanized them. Dislike and even persecution are now possible.

Be careful, then, not to let a classification become a stereotype. For example, our society may have practical reasons to group people by age, but let's always leave room for individuals: not all teenagers drive recklessly, not all 40-year-olds are divorcing, and not all 80-year-olds are in the rocking chair. Some teenagers don't drive at all, some 40-year-olds have never married, and some people in their eighties run marathons.

Whatever its subject, your essay of classification needs at least three categories, because only two would form a comparison and contrast. And it should have no more than you can adequately develop — perhaps five or six at the most. To be logical a classification normally follows these guidelines:

Classify all items by the same principle. A study of major world religions would probably include Islam, Christianity, Judaism, Buddhism and Hinduism — but not atheism, which is the opposite of religious belief.

Do not leave out an obvious category, such as Buddhism, which has many millions of followers. On the other hand, if your neighbour forms a new religious group that attracts a dozen people to its meetings, including it as a world religion would clearly not make sense.

Do not let categories overlap. Though a classification of world religions might include Islam, Christianity, Judaism, Buddhism and Hinduism, it would not include Catholicism — because it is a subgroup of Christianity.

Classifying is not easy; it is a real exercise in logic. Keep applying the guidelines.

Also observe the main principle of any essay: *Know your purpose.* Exactly *why* are you comparing the three kinds of parents or the four kinds of teachers or the five kinds of friends? Is it because you have a vision of what a good parent or teacher or friend is, and want to share it with others? Is it because bad experiences lead you to warn against certain kinds of parents or teachers or friends? Like any argument, an essay of classification makes a point — otherwise it is "pointless." Try freewriting or brainstorming for five or ten minutes to get thoughts flowing and ideas on paper. Look these over. Let them help you decide not only what the content of your classification might be, but also its thesis. Since thinking is not easy, you need all the help you can get — and some of the best help comes from your own pen: while it is writing, you are thinking.

Note: For another example of classification, see this essay in a later chapter:

Judy Stoffman, "The Way of All Flesh," p. 250

Phil Edmonston

Dealer Tricks

He has been called "Canada's toughest customer." With a series of manuals and with television broadcasts to help ordinary people stand up against car dealers and manufacturers, Phil Edmonston has become the nation's major consumer advocate. To call him the Ralph Nader of Canada would be fitting; originally an American, Edmonston began his work as a member of "Nader's Raiders," helping the famous American consumer advocate who forced manufacturers to make safer and more reliable cars. With a law degree and experience, Edmonston then moved to Quebec, learned French, and resumed the fight. In 1974 appeared the first of his annual books, Lemon-Aid: New Car Guide, *rating all cars and exposing the "lemons." Soon were added the annual* Lemon-Aid: Used Car Guide, *a third book for vans and trucks, and the* Lemon-Aid Driver's Companion, *on car maintenance and repair. Dealers wince when customers bring in these books, quoting Edmonston on prices, on secret company memos exposing defects, and on frequency of repair ratings. In 1984* The Art of Complaining, *a manual on how to harrass companies, joined the list. The huge and craggy-featured Edmonston became a familiar face on Quebec television, giving consumer advice in his flat but fluent French, and in 1990 he was elected the first NDP Member of Parliament ever from Quebec. In his new role he continued the old tactics, harrassing vested interests; then, differing with his own party over constitutional policy, he declined to run in the next election. Today Edmonston is known nationally for his broadcasts in English, and for the Automobile Protection Association which he founded. Our selection is typical of his advice, a passage from* Lemon-Aid: Used Car Guide 1994.

Used cars and minivans are subject to the same deceptive sales practices as new cars. Some of the more common tricks involve hiding the identity of the previous owner because the vehicle was used commercially or because the vehicle had been written off as a total loss from a prior accident. It is also not uncommon to discover that the mileage has been turned back, particularly if the vehicle was part of a company's fleet. All these scams can be thwarted if you demand the name of the vehicle's previous owner as a prerequisite to purchasing it.

2   It would be impossible to list all the dishonest tricks employed in used car sales. As soon as the public is alerted to one scheme, other, more elaborate frauds are used by enterprising salesmen. Still, some of the following fraudulent practices have been used so often they have become legendary.

3   *Failing to declare full purchase price.* Used almost exclusively by small, independent dealers, the buyer is told by the salesman that he can save on sales tax by putting in a lower selling price on the contract. So, a car selling for $3000 is declared to have been purchased for only $2000. The buyer, therefore, can save as much as 9 percent of the sales tax on $1000, or about $180. But what if the car turns out to be a lemon, or the salesman has falsified the model year, mileage or mechanical condition? Generally, nothing will happen, because the salesman will then tell the hapless buyer that he will refund the full purchase price indicated on the contract, namely, $2000. If the buyer wanted to take the dealer to court, it is very unlikely, say some lawyers, that any more than the contract price could be obtained. Moreover, the purchaser could be prosecuted by the provincial tax authorities for making a false declaration to avoid paying sales tax. All this trouble just because the buyer is trying to save $180. Is it worth it?

4   *Ontario curbs sales tax cheats*
Two-thirds of Ontario's 1.2 million used car sales are made privately. Under new Ontario regulations, these 800,000 used car buyers must prove the price they paid, accept the Canadian Red Book value, or have their vehicle independently appraised. There are some common sense exceptions. For example, buyers of vehicles that have a Red Book estimated wholesale value less than $1000 can pay the retail sales tax on the purchase price they declare without an appraisal. Furthermore, vehicles that are worth more than $1000 (according to the Red Book) but are damaged or run down, can be appraised before paying the sales tax, and the tax will be calculated upon either the selling price or the appraised price, whichever is higher. Private sellers still need to buy a $20 Vehicle Transfer Package from the Ministry of Consumer and Commercial Relations. This kit contains lien information, details as to what is covered in a safety inspection, sales tax information, forms for an affidavit and bill of sale.

5   These measures have been taken to drive "curbsiders" (professional sellers posing as private individuals) from the used car business and to stop buyers from paying less sales tax than they should.

6   A spokesman for the Ontario Used Car Dealers Association estimates one car in four is sold by a curbsider. And in a recent Barrie, Ontario, survey more than 40 percent of the vehicles advertised by so-called private owners were actually dealer cars. Prior to Ontario's latest initiative,

sales tax fraud was commonplace. Ontario officials estimate they lost over $95 million in sales tax revenue annually.

In the future, most buyers will pay the Red Book value set for their vehicle. Where there is a dispute, an independent appraiser may be used. Traditional sales tax exemptions remain. For example, transactions and gifts between family members will have the sales tax rebated. Sales involving status Indians and diplomats, vehicles registered from out-of-province, and bequests for estate settlements are not subject to Ontario's sales tax.

Car dealers placing "private" want ads. Individuals sell about three times as many used vehicles as dealers. But sometimes dealers or their agents pose as private sellers in order to get a better price for their car and, more recently, to avoid the GST. This trick is on the upswing now that the GST exempts private used car transactions.

By far the most extensive use of "curbsiding" has been by groups of professional salespersons who buy hundreds of cars from dealers and auto auctions at wholesale prices and then place a number of ads in the local papers selling them as privately owned. Most new car dealers get very angry when one of these teams hits town. Unfortunately, they don't get angry enough, because they continue to sell used cars at wholesale prices to these people or use their own curbsiders. A careful buyer can spot this fraud by asking to see the vehicle's registration, the original sales contract or some routine repair orders that everyone accumulates during the ownership of a car. You can also identify a professional car dealer in the want ad section of the newspaper by checking whether one telephone number is repeated in many different ads.

"Free-exchange" privilege. Used car dealers get a lot of sales mileage out of this deceptive practice. The average consumer feels protected against getting a lemon, because the dealer offers to exchange the car for any other in stock if the buyer is not perfectly satisfied. What often happens, though, is that the dealer will not have any other cars selling for the same price and will thus demand a cash bonus for the exchange. Another possibility is that the dealer may have nothing but lemons in stock, so no matter which car is finally chosen, the buyer still gets stuck.

"Money-back" guarantee. Once again the purchaser feels safe in buying a used car with this kind of guarantee, because what could be more honest than a money-back guarantee? Dealers using this technique will often charge exorbitant handling charges, rental fees or mechanical repair costs to customers who have bought one of these vehicles and then returned it.

"50/50" guarantee. A 50/50 guarantee means that the dealer will pay one-half the repair costs over a limited period of time. This is a fair

proposition if the dealer does not insist that the vehicle be brought to his garage for repairs. What then may happen is that the dealer will inflate the repair costs to double their actual worth and write up a bill for that amount. The buyer winds up paying the full price of the warranty repairs that would probably have been much cheaper at an independent garage. The best kind of used car warranty is 100 percent with full coverage for a fixed term.

13   *"As is" cars.* Buying a car "as is" means you are aware of mechanical defects, are prepared to accept the responsibility for any damage or injuries caused by the vehicle and that all costs to fix it shall be paid by you. The courts have held that the "as is" clause is not a blank check to cheat buyers and must be, therefore, interpreted in light of the seller's true intent. That is, was there an attempt to deceive the buyer by including this clause; did the buyer really know what the "as is" clause could do to his future legal rights? It has also been held that verbal representations, "parole evidence," made by the seller as to the fine quality of the used car but never written into the formal contract may also be considered by the court. Generally, Canadian courts ignore "as is" clauses when the vehicle has been misrepresented, when a dealer is the seller or when the defects are so serious the seller is presumed to have known of their existence.

14   *Odometer tampering.* It is often too dangerous for the dealer to turn back the mileage, so independent outfits are hired to pick up the car or visit the dealership where the odometer is altered.

  Until federal and provincial laws are enforced and convictions result in severe penalties to anyone engaging in this practice (American laws allow citizens to sue for triple damages plus lawyer and court costs), the best protection from this fraud is to demand that the dealer put the mileage figure on the contract and give you the name and address of the previous owner as well as all repair receipts. When dealing with a private seller, it would be smart to demand that the same requirements be met. After all, anyone can turn back a car's mileage, no matter what the model year.

15   *Misrepresentation.* Used cars can be misrepresented in a variety of ways. A used taxi may be represented as having belonged to a little old lady. A mechanically defective car that has been rebuilt after several major accidents may have sawdust in its transmission to muffle the "clunks," a heavy oil in the motor to stifle the "clanks" and cheap retread tires to eliminate the "thumps." All these practices are fraudulent and may lead to the dealer being prosecuted for civil or criminal fraud. The best protection against this type of dirty trick is a complete verification by an independent mechanic before completing the sale.

Used car sellers, both dealers and private individuals, will often find ingenious ways to turn a client away from making an inspection of the vehicle before purchasing it.

First, the dealer will often tell the purchaser, "it's already been thoroughly inspected," or assure him that "we'll take care of anything that goes wrong," or give him a written warranty. Other ploys used to dissuade a buyer from having the car independently inspected are:

- claiming the car cannot be moved without tags (actually, all dealers have "demo" tags for just this purpose)
- blaming lack of insurance ("demo" tags provide insurance coverage)
- offering a free inspection by the dealer's own mechanic
- allowing too short a time to have the vehicle properly checked
- demanding a large, nonrefundable penalty if the sale is cancelled.

These tactics are warning signs that indicate the seller does not want to disclose the true condition of the vehicle. If the seller won't let you take the car to an independent garage, don't buy.

∆ ∆

Further Reading:

Phil Edmonston,
   The Art of Complaining
   Lemon-Aid: Used Car Guide

Structure:

1. Identify Edmonston's THESIS STATEMENT.
2. What proportion of this piece is given to *examples?* Would we grasp the argument without them? Do your essays have this many? If not, *should* they?
3. Edmonston *classifies* his subject (using italicized subtitles as cues) into what seem to be nine categories. A closer look, though, shows that one of these is just background for the item after it. Which one is this? Is its presentation as a category a flaw in organization? How would you have presented it?
4. Do any of the eight actual categories overlap? Are there further categories the author has missed?

Style:

1. The METAPHOR "lemon" occurs in paragraphs 3 and 10 as well as in the title of Edmonston's annual guide. Why is it used so often to describe cars?
2. Does the METAPHOR "tricks" of the title cast the used car business as a

kind of practical joke? As a kind of game with winners and losers? Explore the connotations.

3. Describe the AUDIENCE for Edmonston's guide to used cars. What is its level of vocabulary? Of knowledge in the subject? How well has the author packaged the material so his readers will like it and understand it?

4. Is the author angry? Disgusted? Pessimistic? Or just realistic? Analyze his TONE, giving examples.

5. In the middle of paragraph 15 we read of "clunks," "clanks" and "thumps." Read this sentence aloud, with emphasis. Analyze the effect of its SENSE IMAGES.

Ideas for Discussion and Writing:

1. Why is the used car business so prone to scams?

2. Which costs less in the long run: a new car? A good used car? A cheap used car? Give your reasons.

3. Give your own ways to tell a good used car from a lemon.

4. *Contrast* the advantages and disadvantages of buying a used car from a dealer and buying it from an individual.

5. Why is the car so central to our society? Analyze the *causes.* Analyze the *effects.*

6. Edmonston shows how, in buying used cars, some Canadians try to evade tax. Do you see such tactics of the "underground economy" as good business? As legitimate protest against overtaxation? Or as criminal and immoral behaviour? Give examples and reasons.

7. **PROCESS IN WRITING:** *Write the words "used cars" in the middle of a page. Now write around them all the other words they make you think of. Connect related items with lines. From this cluster outline now rapidly draft an essay of classification entitled "Kinds of Used Cars." The next day look the draft over. Is every item classified by the same principle (for example all by age of the car, or by size, or by condition, etc.)? Are all important categories there? Do any overlap? Revise where necessary. Now add examples where your reader cannot yet "see" your point. Finally check for things like grammar and spelling as you do your good version.*

Note: See also the Topics for Writing at the end of this chapter.

W. P. Kinsella

How to Write Fiction

In the essay that follows, W. P. Kinsella tells how for years he got up at 5 a.m., ran water over his fingers so they would "make the typewriter keys work for an hour or two," then went off to his "hateful job." No longer does he sell life insurance, make pizza or even teach creative writing. When his 1982 baseball novel Shoeless Joe *sold a million copies and was made into the film* Field of Dreams, *starring Kevin Costner, Kinsella became free to indulge the two passions of his life — baseball and writing. As a boy in a log cabin in Alberta, he had imagined playmates, then put these fantasies on paper, thinking someday he would be a writer. Kinsella's publications had already begun by the time he earned an M.F.A. at the Writer's Workshop of the University of Iowa, and they have never stopped. His books of short humorous fiction about Native peoples on the reservation (such as* Born Indian, 1981), *have been widely read in Canada, but lately have attracted opposition from Native groups on grounds that Kinsella, a white, has unjustly appropriated their " voice." In America he is better known for the baseball fiction, which by now includes* The Iowa Baseball Confederacy *(1986),* Box Socials *(1992), and* The Dixon Cornbelt League *(short stories, 1993). In these works baseball is celebrated for its own sake, but is at the same time a metaphor for life — a myth of ritual heroism and purity, expressed in a blend of fact and fantasy that has been described as "magic realism." By contrast our selection, an essay from* The Globe and Mail *of April 27, 1985, is very down to earth.*

The title, of course, is a lie, as fantastical as any of my fictional creations. I cannot teach anyone how to write fiction. No one can teach anyone how to write fiction.

What I can do, in my capacity as a professional fiction writer, is to smooth the road for those people I find who show talent as storytellers, to show them a few tricks of the trade — how to market their material, how to deal with publishers, editors, agents and the like.

I can never suggest what a would-be fiction writer should write about. If you don't have a few dozen ideas for stories floating around in your head, stories that have to be told, then stick to your other hobbies and forget fiction writing.

225

4   But if you have your heart set on writing fiction, consider the following: fiction writing, I tell my students, consists of ability, imagination, passion and stamina. Let's consider each individually.

5   By "ability" I mean the ability to write complete sentences in clear, straightforward, standard English.

6   This will not pose a problem for most of the people in the Writers Union, but it is surprising how many university students are unable to write simple sentences. If you can't express yourself clearly, abandon hope unless you are prepared to take a remedial English course. I've been known to suggest to my university students that they get a Grade 5 grammar book and begin their study there.

7   "Imagination" involves the ability to create stories. Little children can create wonderful, uninhibited stories full of fanciful characters. But as the years pass, the regimens of school and community kill the storyteller that lives within each of us. To write fiction you have to dig deep and discover that storyteller.

8   Some writing instructors tell students to "write of what you know." I disagree with that. In 99 cases out of 100, writing about what you know will fill pages, but fill them with dull and uninteresting material.

9   Let's face it, for nine out of 10 of us our lives are so dull that no one would care in the least about them. The 10th person has a life so bizarre no one would believe it if it were written down. The secret of a fiction writer is to make the dull interesting by imagination and embellishment, and to tone down the bizarre until it is believable.

10   I belong to the nine. I live a very quiet life; I have a lovely wife who is a true helpmate and ultrasupportive of my career; we have a nice home on the ocean; we have the freedom to travel. In other words, we are very happy.

11   If I wrote about that I would soon be back selling life insurance, or something equally vile. People don't want to read about happy people. Conflict is an absolute must in every story or novel.

12   I think I clipped the following statement from an American Amateur Press Association publication a few years ago: "The master plot of all novels and stories is: 'An appealing character struggles against great odds to attain a worthwhile goal.'"

13   "Struggles against great odds" are the key words. Something must be at stake, and the character must take some action. What will the conflict be? What action will the appealing character take? That is up to the author. Authors spend half their time writing, and the rest looking at their story and saying, What if? What if? What if? What if I take the story this way? What if I take it that way?

14   "Passion" is an almost nebulous ingredient. It is what an author does to make you love a character. It takes very hard work to analyze it. When you find a novel or story in which you absolutely loved a character, where you had a sweet tear in your eye at the end of the story, or where

you found yourself laughing uncontrollably, read it again for pleasure. Then re-read it 10 more times for business; analyze every line to learn how that author made you laugh or cry. When you learn the secret, use it in your next story.

Never forget that fiction writers are entertainers. Fiction writing comes from the days when the cavemen were gathered around a campfire and Ugh stood up, pounded his chest and said, "Listen to me! I want to tell you a story!" If his story wasn't interesting and suspenseful, his companions soon wandered off to their caves.

Fiction writers are not philosophers, or essayists, or pushers of causes religious or otherwise. And above all they are not navel-gazers. All of these are types of non-fiction, and should never be confused with storytelling.

One important point to remember is called Valgardson's Law (after B.C. writer W. D. Valgardson): Stories or novels are not about events, but about the people that events happen to. The fact that the Titanic is sinking or a skyscraper toppling — or even that the world is ending — is not important unless you have created an appealing character who is going to suffer if the dreaded event happens.

If you want to write fiction, cut out that paragraph and paste it on the wall in front of your typewriter. It will save you weeks, months, maybe even years of struggle.

The final ingredient is "stamina." Each of the others I have described is about 5 per cent of the writing process. Stamina is the final 85 per cent. Stamina is keeping your buns on the chair and writing even when you don't feel like it. I know it's a cliché, but though inspiration is nice, 98 per cent of writing is accomplished by perspiration.

Stamina is doing as I have done — sitting down to write my 50th short story, the previous 49 having been unpublishable, knowing that number 50 will also be unpublishable, but that it will be 2 per cent better than the previous 49.

Stamina is getting up at 5 a.m., running water over your fingers, so they will make the typewriter keys work for an hour or two before you go off to your hateful job. I did that for 20 years while I beat my head against the walls of North American literature.

If your head is still full of stories and you are still determined to write them down, lots of luck. You'll need that, too.

△ △

Further Reading:

W. P. Kinsella,
   Shoeless Joe
   The Iowa Baseball Confederacy
John Gardner, *The Art of Fiction*

Structure:

1. "The title, of course, is a lie," confesses Kinsella in his first line. Does this opening command your interest? Does it lead to the topic?
2. Where does Kinsella first announce the four categories of his *classification?*
3. What pattern do you see in the way each division of the *classification* is introduced?
4. Do "ability," "imagination," "passion" and "stamina" appear in random order or in a logical progression? Explain.
5. Do any of Kinsella's categories overlap?
6. Why are paragraphs 19–21 so vivid? What gives them power?
7. Our next chapter examines *process analysis:* explaining how something is done. Would "How to Write Fiction" be at home there? How clearly and usefully has Kinsella done the job?

Style:

1. How FORMAL or INFORMAL is Kinsella's STYLE in this selection? Give evidence for your answer.
2. In saying writing is "perspiration" rather than "inspiration" (par. 19), Kinsella has used a cliché. Do you see any others?

Ideas for Discussion and Writing:

1. In his opening Kinsella implies that fiction can be a "lie." How is this true? In what ways can an invented plot and characters be more "truth" than "lie"?
2. Do you agree with Kinsella that, since most of us live dull lives, we should avoid writing about what we know (par. 8–13)? Do any of your favourite authors write about what they know?
3. Picasso once said he spent 50 years learning to paint as he could when he was a child. Is Kinsella right that "the regimens of school and community" (par. 7) kill children's imagination? If so, how? Did it happen to you? Is the process inevitable? Or might schools do something to preserve children's natural imagination? If so, what?
4. Write your own short story, following as much of Kinsella's advice as you can. Do an exploratory first draft very fast, then revise in further versions.
5. **PROCESS IN WRITING:** *Write an essay of* classification *that explains, one by one, the "ingredients" of success in writing any one of these: a particular kind of poem, a love letter, a business letter, a lab report, a letter of application for a job, or a letter to the editor. When the draft cools off, look it over. Is every category based on the same principle? Do any overlap? Is any*

major one missing? If so, revise. Now also strengthen TRANSITIONS *between the "ingredients." Sharpen word choice. Cut deadwood. Finally, edit for things like spelling and grammar as you produce the good copy.*

Note: See also the Topics for Writing at the end of this chapter.

Erika Ritter

Bicycles

Playwright, humorist and radio personality, Erika Ritter is well known to Canadians for her satirical views on urban life, and especially on what drama critic Martin Knelman called "her favourite subject — the dilemma of the modern woman whose twentieth-century political programmes and mastery of power dressing keep bumping against her nineteenth-century psyche." Born in Regina, Ritter studied literature at McGill, then drama at the University of Toronto. Though she declines the label of "feminist," her major plays, The Splits *(1978),* Automatic Pilot *(1980) and* The Passing Scene *(1982), all examine the modern urban woman and her difficulty in maintaining relationships with men. Her plays from 1975–86 were collected in* Murder at McQueen. *In 1985 Ritter became the highly successful host of CBC Radio's* Dayshift, *a talk show, but in 1987 quit and turned her attention to writing.* Urban Scrawl *(1984) and* Ritter in Residence *(1987), her books of light satirical essays, indulge in slapstick humour, puns and fantasy, yet still develop Ritter's investigation of the modern woman and of urban life in general. Our selection comes from* Urban Scrawl, *which Ritter dedicates to her mother — "who made the mistake of encouraging this kind of thing."*

1   It wasn't always like this. There was a time in the life of the world when adults were adults, having firmly put away childish things and thrown away the key.

2   Not any more. The change must have come about innocently enough, I imagine. Modern Man learning to play nicely in the sandbox with the other grown-ups. Very low-tension stuff.

3   Now, in every direction you look, your gaze is met by the risible spectacle of adults postponing adolescence well into senility by means of adult toys: running shoes, baseball bats, roller skates, and — bicycles!

4   But the attitude is no longer the fun-loving approach of a bunch of superannuated kids, and I'm sure you can envision how the evolution occurred. Jogging progressed from a casual encounter with the fresh air to an intensive relationship, attended by sixty-dollar jogging shoes and a designer sweatband. Playing baseball stopped being fun unless you had a Lacoste (as opposed to low-cost) tee-shirt in which to impress

your teammates. And where was the thrill in running around a squash court unless it was with a potentially important client?

As for bicycles — well, let's not even talk about bicycles. On the other hand, maybe we *should* talk about them, because there's something particularly poignant about how it all went wrong for the bicycle, by what declension this once proud and carefree vehicle sank into the role of beast of burden, to bear the weight of sobersided grown-ups at their supposed sport.

First, there was the earliest domestication of the North American bicycle (*cyclus pedalis americanus*) in the late Hippie Scene Era of the 1960s. This was the age of the no-nuke whole-grain cyclist, who saw in the bicycle the possibility of Making a Statement while he rode. A statement about pollution, about materialism, about imperialism, about militarism, about — enough already. You get the picture: two wheels good, four wheels bad.

Thus it was that the basic bicycle gradually evolved into a chunky three-speed number from China, bowed down under a plastic kiddie carrier, army surplus knapsacks, and a faded fender-sticker advising Make Tofu, Not War. And a rider clad in a red plaid lumber-jacket, Birkenstock sandals, and an expression of urgent concern for all living things.

Once the very act of bicycle riding had become an act of high moral purpose, it was an easy step to the next phase of the bicycle's journey along the path of post-Meanderthal seriousness.

I'm speaking of the era of the high-strung thoroughbred bicycle, whose rider had also made advances, from pedalling peacenik to a hunched and humorless habitué of the velodrome, clad in leather-seated shorts, white crash helmet, and fingerless gloves, whizzing soundlessly, and with no hint of joy, down city streets and along the shoulders of super-highways, aboard a vehicle sculpted in wisps of silver chrome. A vehicle so overbred, in its final evolutionary stages, that it began to resemble the mere exoskeleton of a conventional cycle, its flesh picked away by birds of carrion.

Having been stripped of any connection with its innocent and leisurely origins, the bicycle now no longer bore the slightest resemblance to the happy creature it once had been. And in the mid-Plastic Scene Era, another crippling blow was struck by the upscale name-brand cyclist, who came along to finish what the fanatical velodromist had refined. Namely, the complete transformation of an ambling and unhurried mode of transit into a fast, nerve-wracking, expensive, and utterly competitive display of high speed, high technology, and high status.

The Upscale Cyclist was looking for a twelve-speed Bottecchia that matches his eyes, something that he'd look trendy upon the seat of, when riding to the office (the office!), and he was ready to pay in four figures for it.

12   Not only that, he was also prepared to shell out some heavy bread for those status accessories to complete the picture: the backpack designed by the engineers at NASA, the insulated water-bottle to keep his Perrier chilled just right, the sixteen-track Walkman that would virtually assure him the envy of all his friends.

13   So much for the cyclist. What of his poor debased mount?

14   Not surprisingly, amongst the breed of bicycle, morale is currently low, and personal pride all but a thing of the past. And yet . . . and yet, there are those who say that *cyclus pedalis americanus* is an indomitable creature, and that it is the bicycle, not its rider, who will make the last evolution of the wheel.

15   In fact, some theorize that the present high incidence of bicycle thievery, far from being evidence of crime, is actually an indication that the modern bicycle has had enough of oppressive exploitation and man's joyless ways, and is in the process of reverting to the wild in greater and greater numbers.

16   There have always remained a few aboriginal undomesticated bicycles — or so the theory goes — and now it is these free-spirited mavericks, down from the hills at night, who visit urban bikeracks, garages, and back porches to lure tame bicycles away with them.

17   Costly Kryptonite locks are wrenched asunder, expensive accoutrements are shrugged off, intricate gear systems are torn away, and lo — look what is revealed! Unadorned, undefiled *cyclus* in all his pristine glory, unfettered and unencumbered once more, and free to roam.

18   A wistful fantasy, you might say? The maundering illusions of someone who's been riding her bicycle too long without a crash helmet? I wonder.

19   Just the other day, there was that piece in the paper about a bicycle that went berserk in a shopping centre, smashing two display windows before it was subdued. And did you hear about the recent sighting of a whole herd of riderless bicycles, all rolling soundlessly across a park in the night?

20   It all kind of gets you to thinking. I mean, do *you* know where your ten-speed is tonight?

ΔΔΔΔΔΔΔΔΔΔΔΔΔΔΔΔΔΔΔΔΔΔΔΔΔΔΔΔΔΔΔΔΔΔΔΔΔΔΔΔΔΔΔΔΔΔΔΔΔΔΔ

Further Reading:

Erika Ritter,
   The Splits
   Automatic Pilot
   Urban Scrawl
   Ritter in Residence

Structure:

1. Are the words "It wasn't always like this" a good opening? Why or why not?
2. Ritter divides the evolution of "cyclus pedalis americanus" into three stages. Identify each category of her *classification* and show where it begins and ends.
3. Have any categories of this *classification* overlapped? Have any obvious ones been left out?
4. Ritter marks each major change of subject with a transitional passage. Point out three of these.
5. Ritter closes with the device examined in our previous chapter, *analogy*. As the bicycle starts "reverting to the wild," to what is it compared? Find at least ten terms that develop the analogy.
6. At the end Ritter asks, "do *you* know where your ten-speed is tonight?" To what does she allude? Is this ALLUSION a good closing?

Style:

1. Where did you first sense the light TONE of this selection? Describe Ritter's brand of humour.
2. In paragraph 4 what device of humour has baseball players wearing "Lacoste (as opposed to low-cost)" tee-shirts?
3. Explain the word play of "the late Hippie Scene Era" (par. 6), "post-Meanderthal seriousness" (par. 8), and "the mid-Plastic Scene Era" (par. 10).
4. Is Ritter's informal style right for this selection? Point out her most COLLOQUIAL expressions.
5. In a piece so conversational, why are there also academic or even learned terms such as "risible" (par. 3), "superannuated" (par. 4) and "exoskeleton" (par. 9)? Describe the overall effect. Profile the reader at which Ritter seems to aim.
6. Paragraph 9 shows the "thoroughbred" bicycle as so overbred "that it began to resemble the mere exoskeleton of a conventional cycle, its flesh picked away by birds of carrion." What FIGURES OF SPEECH do you see here?

Ideas for Discussion and Writing:

1. Erika Ritter has been well known in Canada as playwright and radio host; does her approach to "Bicycles" reflect these other roles?
2. In paragraphs 13–20 humour turns to fantasy. Has Ritter gone too far, or is fantasy right for some essay subjects?
3. Is it true that we go too far in "improving" products such as the

bicycle? Has this happened to the car, the house, the computer, food, clothes? If so, in what ways?

4. Do you have a bicycle? Tell how it does or does not fit into one of Ritter's categories.

5. **PROCESS IN WRITING:** *Ritter* classifies *evolutionary stages of the bicycle. In an essay, either funny or serious, do the same for one of these: radios, TV sets, phonographs, computers, cars or airplanes. First generate a page of notes, to find the stages of this "evolution." Now write the discovery draft, and look it over. Do categories overlap? Is a main category missing? Is your* TONE *consistent? Do* IMAGES *help readers "see" the point? Improve these areas, then read aloud to check for style.*

Note: See also the Topics for Writing at the end of this chapter.

Mavor Moore

The Roar of the Greasepaint,
the Smell of the Caucus

*Actor, playwright and producer, Mavor Moore is also one of our most authorita-
tive commentators on the nation's arts and media. He was born in Toronto in
1919, studied at the University of Toronto, and since then has virtually lived
the history of Canada's stage, radio and television. He has produced and directed over 50 plays for the stage, and many others for radio and television; has
written librettos for musical comedies and for the opera* Louis Riel *(1967); and
for many years produced and directed the annual review* Spring Thaw. *Moore was
a founder of the Stratford Shakespearean Festival, was the CBC's chief producer
in the early days of television, was founding chairperson of the Charlottetown
Festival, and has served as chairperson of the Canada Council. In recent years,
in reaction to the spread of American programming in our media, and to governmental cutbacks of public broadcasting, Moore has emerged as a defender of the
arts in Canada. For several years his column in* The Globe and Mail *carried this
message, in a polished and concise prose, arguing that the arts are vital not only
to the nation's cultural survival but even to its sovereignty. In our selection,
from the August 2, 1986* Globe, *Moore turns his attention to the politicians
and their own use of the media arts.*

The distaste with which many politicians approach theatre has been
matched only by their eagerness to embrace it. The similarities are
too obvious, too close to the knuckle and too damaging. Both deal in
drama, ritual, scenarios, role-playing, speeches, spell-binding and persuasion. But theatre is supposed to be for fun, politics for real. Theatre
is illusion, deception, fakery, a trick of sound and light. Isn't it? Politics
is substance, honesty, actuality, natural light. Isn't it?

Throughout history, governors — like soldiers, lawyers, priests and
priestesses, physicians, police, academics and many laborers — have
worn costumes, carried "props," and produced ceremonies. When occasion demanded, rulers have not hesitated to hire hairdressers and
ghost writers, musicians and decorators to improve their god-given
presence. But this is called pomp, and is not to be confused in the

public mind with the duplicity that characterizes theatre. The thing is perfectly clear to any self-respecting politician. Or is it?

3   Then came radio to provoke this ambivalence more sharply. In the twenties and thirties, radio was the perfect way to reach the whole electorate simultaneously and a foolproof way to fudge the difference between illusion and reality: you cannot see who is speaking. If, before, few voters had actually met a candidate, now most of them became close friends of the candidate's voice. Actors' techniques of faking sincerity were suddenly in great demand.

4   One of the earliest political crises in Canadian broadcasting arose from campaign use of unidentified actors, reading from scripts, who posed as "real voters" — a practice that many advertisers still find blameless. An unprepossessing Canadian expatriate, Father Charles Coughlin, convinced millions of Americans that he was the voice of God.

5   Soon after the Second World War came television. Like radio, it offered widespread simultaneous coverage; but since seeing is believing, television had even greater potential for persuasion. Once we persuaded ourselves that the most vivid evidence of reality is what appears through this prism, it became television fare that largely determined our perceptions.

6   The manipulation of "reality" became not only a temptation but politically mandatory; if you failed to take advantage of the new mass medium, your rivals were sure to seize it. The techniques for managing impressions may have been more complex than those of stage or radio, but the stakes were higher. The simulation of artlessness had to be even more clever.

7   This realization led to wholesale intimacy between politicians and "consultants." In times gone by, I myself have coached a prime minister, assorted Cabinet ministers and a rogues' gallery of notables in how to outwit the camera. I know speech teachers who have patiently exercised nominees out of a low accent into a high, or vice versa — all in the interest of plain dealing. But this is only the beginning.

8   Every time a politician goes on television, his or her public relations team springs into action: experts to choose the setting, select the wardrobe, see that the tinted hair behaves, the make-up is *comme ci* and the lights *comme ça*. If spectacles are worn, they should be casually removed at some point, as if barely necessary for such sharp eyes — but contact lenses are best: one to read the TelePrompTer and one to glance at the script occasionally to indicate that there is no TelePrompTer.

9   You must have noticed, also, how the script, written by a battery of the ablest wordsmiths influence can buy, is always held loosely in the speaker's hands to show who owns it. But the owner really doesn't need it. The words come straight from the heart. If the prompter breaks down, another take is always possible.

Perhaps, of course, the public will eventually see through it all. But at   10
the moment politicians may have to accept an unwontedly inferior
status. When it comes to promoting causes on television, raising support
for the United Appeal or teaching the public its moral duty in war and
peace, it's obvious whom the people trust: not our political, religious or
educational leaders, but our entertainers.

Television inclines us to believe entertainers, who normally show little   11
ambition to take over the real world, and to mistrust politicians, who
attempt the tricks of entertainers to achieve power. The illusionist comes
across as more honest than the realist.

Doubtless this has chilling implications for the future of government.   12
But it may explain why some democracies would sooner elect actors
who learn politicking than politicians who bridle at acting. If, that is,
they notice much difference between the two.

△△△

Further Reading:

Mavor Moore, *Six Plays by Mavor Moore*
B. W. Powe, *The Solitary Outlaw*
Brian Fawcett, *Cambodia: A Book for People Who Find Television
    Too Slow*
George Orwell, *1984* (novel)
Jerzy Kosinski, *Being There* (novel)

Structure:

1. What does a good title do? What does Moore's do? To what old
   saying does it allude, and how does it twist that saying to imply
   Moore's point?
2. Moore *classifies* media manipulation by leaders into technologically
   different periods. Which paragraphs discuss the first? The second?
   The third? Why is the section on television longest?
3. Are Moore's categories *classified* by the same principle? Are they mutually exclusive? Has he left any out?
4. While arranging the parts of his argument into a classification,
   Moore also uses other devices. Does his essay depict politicians
   through *comparisons* or through *contrasts* to actors? And are these arranged by "halves" or "point by point"? Defend your answer with
   examples.

Style:

1. In paragraph 7 Moore admits that he himself has "coached" a "rogues'
   gallery of notables in how to outwit the camera." How frequently

does he colour his argument with emotionally loaded words such as these? Give examples.

2. In paragraph 5 Moore calls television a "prism." Analyze what this METAPHOR implies about television as a medium.

Ideas for Discussion and Writing:

1. How do you, the AUDIENCE, react when in paragraph 7 Moore tells of having "coached" politicians in the art of the actor? Through aiding the very activity he criticizes, has the author lowered his credibility, or in documenting his experience does he raise it?

2. Does Moore imply that modern leaders are less honest than the earlier ones of paragraph 2? Or have the media of radio and television simply made the art of "illusion" easier to practice?

3. What powers did radio give politicians (par. 3–4)? What powers did television add, and why are they greater (par. 5–12)?

4. Do you believe you can judge a public figure through television? Or in our electronic age is the phrase "seeing is believing" obsolete? Defend your view with examples.

5. Some critics say television helps those already in power, as during election campaigns when the wealthiest party can buy the most television time. Others say TV has a democratizing effect, as when the CBC offers election debates equally to each major party. What is your view? Defend it with examples.

6. Name entertainers who "promote causes on television." Do you believe Moore's concept that we trust our entertainers more than our "political, religious or educational leaders" (par. 10)?

7. **PROCESS IN WRITING:** *Write an essay classifying the leaders of Canada's main political parties. First choose a principle: will you divide them by ideology (as in left, centre and right), by degree of effectiveness or of honesty or of experience or of skill with media, or what? Now do a page of brainstorming. Looking at your results, try a thesis. Write a fast discovery draft, then the next day look it over: does it make sense? Are your divisions mutually exclusive? Have you left any out? If so, revise. Has the actual argument contradicted your thesis? If so, revise either the argument or the thesis. Does at least half the draft consist of examples? If not, add. Finally edit for correctness before doing your good copy.*

Note: See also the Topics for Writing at the end of this chapter.

Topics for Writing

Chapter 7: Classification

Develop one of the following topics into an essay of classification. (See also the guidelines that follow.)

1. Neighbours
2. Roommates
3. Salespersons
4. Parents
5. Marriages
6. Parties
7. Music lovers
8. Teachers
9. Classmates
10. Bosses
11. Sports fans
12. Crime
13. Taxes
14. Moviegoers
15. Television watchers
16. Dancers
17. Sound systems
18. Enemies
19. Junk mail
20. Houses
21. Computer printers
22. Coaches
23. Drivers
24. Prejudice
25. Sexism
26. Restaurants
27. Pets
28. Hair styles
29. Board games
30. Gamblers

Note also the Process in Writing topic after each selection in this chapter.

Process in Writing: Guidelines

Follow at least some of these steps in writing your essay of classification (your teacher may suggest which ones).

1. *Write a short outline, since the logic of classifying is difficult. Once you have chosen the principle on which to classify your topic, decide on the categories. Then ask: Do all relate to the same principle? If not, revise. Do any categories overlap? If so, revise. Is an obvious category missing? Add it.*

2. *Write your thesis statement. Make it a significant point worth discussion.*

3. *Now arrange the categories in some climactic order that supports your thesis: smallest to largest, least important to most important, worst to best, etc.*

4. *Write a rapid first draft, double-spaced, not stopping now to revise or edit.*

5. *When this draft has "cooled off," look it over. Does it follow the outline? If not, do the changes make sense? Does every part support the thesis? If not, revise the parts, the thesis, or both.*

6. *In your second draft sharpen word choice. Add missing IMAGES or examples. Heighten TRANSITIONS. Cut deadwood.*

7. *Now as you produce the good copy, edit for spelling and grammar. If you have used a computer, save the essay on disk in case your teacher suggests further revision.*

H.A. Roberts/Comstock Inc.

"In our early 20s, the lung capacity, the rapidity of motor responses and physical endurance are at their peak. This is the athlete's finest hour."

—*Judy Stoffman, "The Way of All Flesh"*

CHAPTER

8

PROCESS ANALYSIS

Here's how it's done. . . .

Think of the last time you bought something in kit form and tried to follow the directions for assembly. Maybe you were lucky and everything went together perfectly. More likely, though, you were sweating to make out diagrams that were too small, terminology you did not know, and vague directions that left out steps or got them in the wrong order. With the bicycle or the computer desk or the bookcase lying in parts on the floor, you wondered if you would *ever* get it together. And when you did, there were parts left over.

In today's world we buy unassembled products of many kinds, no matter how unclear the directions. We also make things from scratch, following how-to-do-it books and magazines that give directions on everything from growing vegetables to building a house. In an age of mass production, we may crave the satisfaction of doing something ourselves. Or, living in a weak economy, we may need to save money. But whatever our motivation, do we still have the skills to do all these things our grandparents knew how to do?

Writing that tells us *how* can be called *process analysis*. Sometimes we write an essay that explains what we could call a *directional* process analysis. It is a sort of *narrative*, taking our readers from the beginning to the end of a task, usually in the strict time order required to grow tomatoes, tune up a car or paint a room, not to mention the many other things people do. It includes every step, for each is vital to the success of the project. And if it is written for the amateur, it includes all the details right down to the spacing and depth of seeds in the soil, the choice of motor oil, or the size of paint brush.

Have you ever eaten something so good that you asked for the recipe? A highly experienced cook has a hard time explaining. Instead of giving quantities, temperatures and measurements of time that we can actually apply, this skilled practitioner will say things like "add some yeast" or "now put in a little salt" or "take it out of the oven when it's done." The writer of recipes in a book, though, puts his or her own experience in the background and thinks instead about what the *audience* needs to know. The result is a set of directions so exact that, even if we know little about cooking, the product will usually turn out.

When you are writing directions, on whatever topic, this is the main challenge: keeping your audience in mind. If the subject is your area of expertise, you'll try to take short cuts, leaving out details that you think every reader knows. But remember your own experience with the kit in the middle of the floor. Explain! And when you write from expertise you'll tend to fill your essay with technical terms. But think of the last time you tried to understand Revenue Canada's directions on your income tax form. If you accurately judge your reader's level of knowledge and write accordingly, your directions will stand a much greater chance of working. Follow the example of Dian Cohen, who in this chapter explains a task that most people of student age have not yet tried: investing in commodities. To cover the subject she does need a few specialized terms, but note how carefully she defines each one so that, no matter how slight our knowledge of economics, we can follow.

Another kind of process analysis could be called *informational,* for it satisfies not our practical needs but our curiosity. We may enjoy learning how satellites are launched, how airplanes are hijacked, how stockholders are swindled, how liquor is distilled, how the Second World War was won or how a heart is transplanted — knowing we will never do these things ourselves. Of course not every detail is given in this kind of armchair reading: only as many as it takes to inform and interest the reader. In this chapter Judy Stoffman tells all about aging, a process we do not try to perform, and which in fact most of us resist. Though we need no *directions,* Stoffman knows this is a topic of vital interest to everyone, so she explains in clear detail how it happens.

Sometimes a writer will use process analysis not to instruct or inform, but as a means to other ends. When Stephen Leacock tells us "How to Live to Be 200," he advises us to eat cement — a strange way to reach the goal — until we see that his goal is not longevity but laughs.

Whether you aim to help the reader accomplish a task, to satisfy the reader's curiosity, or even just to entertain, your process analysis will work only if you realize *why* you are writing it: Are you giving directions? Then follow all the advice above, so your reader's efforts will be successful. Are you just explaining something that occurs, like Stoffman's topic of aging? Then above all, interest the reader with a multitude of examples, as she does. Are you even just going for laughs, like Leacock? Then do anything that is fun. But even then, you may find yourself making a serious point — like Leacock who advises us to enjoy life.

Note: For more examples of process analysis, see these essays in other chapters:

Stuart McLean, "The Shocking Truth About Household Dust," p. 122
Mordecai Richler, "1944: The Year I Learned to Love a German," p. 142
W. P. Kinsella, "How to Write Fiction," p. 225
Mavor Moore, "The Roar of the Greasepaint, the Smell of the Caucus," p. 235

Stephen Leacock

How to Live to Be 200

During his lifetime Stephen Leacock became the world's best-known humorist writing in English, a Canadian successor to the American writer Mark Twain. Though he was for decades Canada's favourite author, Leacock has gradually slipped into neglect. Born in England in 1869, at age 6 he came with his family to Ontario. He studied at Upper Canada College, the University of Toronto, and the University of Chicago, where in 1903 he received a Ph.D. That year McGill hired him to teach economics and political science, and from 1908 till his retirement in 1936, he served as head of his department. He died in 1944. Leacock wrote over 60 books, many on academic subjects, but of course it is for his books of humour that he is remembered. The best-loved have been Literary Lapses *(1910),* Nonsense Novels *(1911),* Sunshine Sketches of a Little Town *(1912),* Arcadian Adventures with the Idle Rich *(1914), and* My Remarkable Uncle and Other Sketches *(1942). Our selection, from a later version of* Literary Lapses, *is vintage Leacock: through exaggeration and incongruities, it reduces to absurdity a topic that many people, today as in Leacock's time, take seriously.*

1   Twenty years ago I knew a man called Jiggins, who had the Health Habit.

2   He used to take a cold plunge every morning. He said it opened his pores. After it he took a hot sponge. He said it closed the pores. He got so that he could open and shut his pores at will.

3   Jiggins used to stand and breathe at an open window for half an hour before dressing. He said it expanded his lungs. He might, of course, have had it done in a shoe-store with a boot stretcher, but after all it cost him nothing this way, and what is half an hour?

4   After he had got his undershirt on, Jiggins used to hitch himself up like a dog in harness and do Sandow exercises. He did them forwards, backwards, and hind-side up.

5   He could have got a job as a dog anywhere. He spent all his time at this kind of thing. In his spare time at the office, he used to lie on his stomach on the floor and see if he could lift himself up with his knuckles. If he could, then he tried some other way until he found one that

he couldn't do. Then he would spend the rest of his lunch hour on his stomach, perfectly happy.

In the evenings in his room he used to lift iron bars, cannon-balls, heave dumb-bells, and haul himself up to the ceiling with his teeth. You could hear the thumps half a mile. 6

He liked it. 7

He spent half the night slinging himself around the room. He said it made his brain clear. When he got his brain perfectly clear, he went to bed and slept. As soon as he woke, he began clearing it again. 8

Jiggins is dead. He was, of course, a pioneer, but the fact that he dumb-belled himself to death at an early age does not prevent a whole generation of young men from following in his path. 9

They are ridden by the Health Mania. 10

They make themselves a nuisance. 11

They get up at impossible hours. They go out in silly little suits and run Marathon heats before breakfast. They chase around barefoot to get the dew on their feet. They hunt for ozone. They bother about pepsin. They won't eat meat because it has too much nitrogen. They won't eat fruit because it hasn't any. They prefer albumen and starch and nitrogen to huckleberry pie and doughnuts. They won't drink water out of a tap. They won't eat sardines out of a can. They won't use oysters out of a pail. They won't drink milk out of a glass. They are afraid of alcohol in any shape. Yes sir, afraid. "Cowards." 12

And after all their fuss they presently incur some simple old-fashioned illness and die like anybody else. 13

Now people of this sort have no chance to attain any great age. They are on the wrong track. 14

Listen. Do you want to live to be really old, to enjoy a grand, green, exhuberant, boastful old age and to make yourself a nuisance to your whole neighbourhood with your reminiscences? 15

Then cut out all this nonsense. Cut it out. Get up in the morning at a sensible hour. The time to get up is when you have to, not before. If your office opens at eleven, get up at ten-thirty. Take your chance on ozone. There isn't any such thing anyway. Or, if there is, you can buy a Thermos bottle full for five cents, and put it on a shelf in your cupboard. If your work begins at seven in the morning, get up at ten minutes to, but don't be liar enough to say that you like it. It isn't exhilarating, and you know it. 16

Also, drop all that cold-bath business. You never did it when you were a boy. Don't be a fool now. If you must take a bath (you don't really need to), take it warm. The pleasure of getting out of a cold bed and creeping into a hot bath beats a cold plunge to death. In any case, stop gassing about your tub and your "shower," as if you were the only man who ever washed. 17

So much for that point. 18

19   Next, take the question of germs and bacilli. Don't be scared of them. That's all. That's the whole thing, and if you once get on to that you never need to worry again.

20   If you see a bacilli, walk right up to it, and look it in the eye. If one flies into your room, strike at it with your hat or with a towel. Hit it as hard as you can between the neck and the thorax. It will soon get sick of that.

21   But as a matter of fact, a bacilli is perfectly quiet and harmless if you are not afraid of it. Speak to it. Call out to it to "lie down." It will understand. I had a bacilli once, called Fido, that would come and lie at my feet while I was working. I never knew a more affectionate companion, and when it was run over by an automobile, I buried it in the garden with genuine sorrow.

22   (I admit this is an exaggeration. I don't really remember its name; it may have been Robert.)

23   Understand that it is only a fad of modern medicine to say that cholera and typhoid and diphtheria are caused by bacilli and germs; nonsense. Cholera is caused by a frightful pain in the stomach, and diphtheria is caused by trying to cure a sore throat.

24   Now take the question of food.

25   Eat what you want. Eat lots of it. Yes, eat too much of it. Eat till you can just stagger across the room with it and prop it up against a sofa cushion. Eat everything that you like until you can't eat any more. The only test is, can you pay for it? If you can't pay for it, don't eat it. And listen — don't worry as to whether your food contains starch, or albumen, or gluten, or nitrogen. If you are a damn fool enough to want these things, go and buy them and eat all you want of them. Go to a laundry and get a bag of starch, and eat your fill of it. Eat it, and take a good long drink of glue after it, and a spoonful of Portland cement. That will gluten you, good and solid.

26   If you like nitrogen, go and get a druggist to give you a canful of it at the soda counter, and let you sip it with a straw. Only don't think that you can mix all these things up with your food. There isn't any nitrogen or phosphorus or albumen in ordinary things to eat. In any decent household all that sort of stuff is washed out in the kitchen sink before the food is put on the table.

27   And just one word about fresh air and exercise. Don't bother with either of them. Get your room full of good air, then shut up the windows and keep it. It will keep for years. Anyway, don't keep using your lungs all the time. Let them rest. As for exercise, if you have to take it, take it and put up with it. But as long as you have the price of a hack and can hire other people to play baseball for you and run races and do gymnastics when you sit in the shade and smoke and watch them — great heavens, what more do you want?

ΔΔΔΔΔΔΔΔΔΔΔΔΔΔΔΔΔΔΔΔΔΔΔΔΔΔΔΔΔΔΔΔΔΔΔΔΔΔΔΔΔΔΔΔΔΔΔΔΔ

Further Reading:

Stephen Leacock,
> *Sunshine Sketches of a Little Town*
> *Literary Lapses*
> *My Remarkable Uncle and Other Sketches*

Robertson Davies, *Stephen Leacock*
D. Staines, *Stephen Leacock: A Reappraisal*

Structure:

1. This essay has two main parts. Where do they join? How do they differ?
2. We begin with Jiggins. How is his story organized? How does his death in paragraph 9 lead into the argument?
3. Are Leacock's health tips given in order of application?
4. What is our first clue that Leacock's *process analysis* is meant not to instruct but to entertain?

Style:

1. Leacock writes "eat" ten times in paragraph 25. Read the passage aloud. Is this repetition accidental? What effect does it have? In which other paragraph does Leacock exploit repetition?
2. Paragraph 25 states, "That will gluten you, good and solid." What effect does the word "gluten" have in this sentence?
3. Reduction to absurdity is a comic device Leacock often uses, as in the "bacilli" as insects to swat or as a favourite dog run over by a car. Where else in this essay has he reduced an idea to total absurdity?

Ideas for Discussion and Writing:

1. Do you have the "Health Habit," like Jiggins, or do you prefer comfort and luxury, like our narrator? Give reasons.
2. Update Leacock's argument for our times. Which kinds of "Health Mania" would you drop? Which would you keep? Which might you add?
3. **PROCESS IN WRITING:** *Write a process analysis of how to reach old age in good health. First brainstorm or freewrite. Then do a rapid "discovery draft," double-spaced. When it has "cooled off," analyze it: Are the steps in order? Are the instructions clear? Have you supplied examples? Revise accordingly. Now sharpen word choice as well. Heighten transitions. Cut deadwood. Finally, test the prose aloud before writing a good version.*

Note: See also the Topics for Writing at the end of this chapter.

Judy Stoffman

The Way of All Flesh

Judy Stoffman is book review editor of The Toronto Star, *though in her career as journalist she has written and edited for numerous other newspapers and magazines. Born in Hungary, she came at age ten to Canada, where she grew up in Vancouver. Stoffman studied English literature at the University of British Columbia and at Sussex University, England, where she earned an M.A.; she studied also in France. Her future seemed decided as early as grade two: when a teacher read out to the class her composition on recess, Stoffman knew she wanted to be a writer. "I love the research and dread the writing," she says. "Before I start writing I have a kind of stage fright and from talking to other writers I know they have it too, but they persist because when the words finally start to flow there is an exhilaration nothing else can give." Our selection appeared in 1979 in* Weekend Magazine. *Before writing it Stoffman did thorough research: she read ten books on aging and interviewed three gerontologists, a family doctor and a sex therapist. "Then," she says, "I tried to synthesize what I had learned, while exploring my own deepest fears." Looking back at her 1979 essay, Stoffman calls it "pretty accurate in terms of my own subsequent experience of aging." Though she looks aging "squarely in the eye," with no attempt to "prettify it," she sees no cause for gloom. Writing the piece gave her "a renewed commitment to enjoy each day to the fullest," and she recommends the same perspective to those reading it.*

1   When a man of 25 is told that aging is inexorable, inevitable, universal, he will nod somewhat impatiently at being told something so obvious. In fact, he has little idea of the meaning of the words. It has nothing to do with him. Why should it? He has had no tangible evidence yet that his body, as the poet Rilke said, enfolds old age and death as the fruit enfolds a stone.

2   The earliest deposits of fat in the aorta, the trunk artery carrying blood away from the heart, occur in the eighth year of life, but who can peer into his own aorta at this first sign of approaching debility? The young man has seen old people but he secretly believes himself to be the exception on whom the curse will never fall. "Never will the skin of my neck hang loose. My grip will never weaken. I will stand tall and

walk with long strides as long as I live." The young girl scarcely pays attention to her clothes; she scorns makeup. Her confidence in her body is boundless; smooth skin and a flat stomach will compensate, she knows, for any lapses in fashion or grooming. She stays up all night, as careless of her energy as of her looks, believing both will last forever.

In our early 20s, the lung capacity, the rapidity of motor responses   3
and physical endurance are at their peak. This is the athlete's finest hour. Cindy Nicholas of Toronto was 19 when she first swam the English Channel in both directions. The tennis star Bjorn Borg was 23 when he triumphed at Wimbledon for the fourth time.

It is not only *athletic* prowess that is at its height between 20 and 30.   4
James Boswell, writing in his journal in 1763 after he had finally won the favors of the actress Louisa, has left us this happy description of the sexual prowess of a 23-year-old: "I was in full glow of health and my bounding blood beat quick in high alarms. Five times was I fairly lost in supreme rapture. Louisa was madly fond of me; she declared I was a prodigy, and asked me if this was extraordinary in human nature. I said twice as much might be, but this was not, although in my own mind I was somewhat proud of my performance."

In our early 30s we are dumbfounded to discover the first grey hair at   5
the temples. We pull out the strange filament and look at it closely, trying to grasp its meaning. It means simply that the pigment has disap-peared from the hair shaft, never to return. It means also — but this thought we push away — that in 20 years or so we'll relinquish our identity as a blonde or a redhead. By 57, one out of four people is completely grey. Of all the changes wrought by time this is the most harmless, except to our vanity.

In this decade one also begins to notice the loss of upper register   6
hearing, that is, the responsiveness to high frequency tones, but not all the changes are for the worse, not yet. Women don't reach their sexual prime until about 38, because their sexual response is learned rather than innate. The hand grip of both sexes increases in strength until 35, and intellectual powers are never stronger than at that age. There is a sense in the 30s of hitting your stride, of coming into your own. When Sigmund Freud was 38 an older colleague, Josef Breuer, wrote: "Freud's intellect is soaring at its highest. I gaze after him as a hen at a hawk."

Gail Sheehy in her book *Passages* calls the interval between 35 and 45   7
the Deadline Decade. It is the time we begin to sense danger. The body continually flashes us signals that time is running out. We must perform our quaint deeds, keep our promises, get on with our allotted tasks.

Signal: The woman attempts to become pregnant at 40 and finds she   8
cannot. Though she menstruates each month, menstruation being merely the shedding of the inner lining of the womb, she may not be ovulating regularly.

9   Signal: Both men and women discover that, although they have not changed their eating habits over the years, they are much heavier than formerly. The man is paunchy around the waist; the woman no longer has those slim thighs and slender arms. A 120-pound woman needs 2,000 calories daily to maintain her weight when she is 25, 1,700 to maintain the same weight at 45, and only 1,500 calories at 65. A 170-pound man needs 3,100 calories daily at 25, 300 fewer a day at 45 and 450 calories fewer still at 65. This decreasing calorie need signals that the body consumes its fuel ever more slowly; the cellular fires are damped and our sense of energy diminishes.

10   In his mid-40s the man notices he can no longer run up the stairs three at a time. He is more easily winded and his joints are not as flexible as they once were. The strength of his hands has declined somewhat. The man feels humiliated: "I will not let this happen to me. I will turn back the tide and master my body." He starts going to the gym, playing squash, lifting weights. He takes up jogging. Though he may find it neither easy nor pleasant, terror drives him past pain. A regular exercise program can retard some of the symptoms of aging by improving the circulation and increasing the lung capacity, thereby raising our stamina and energy level, but no amount of exercise will make a 48-year-old 26 again. Take John Keeley of Mystic, Connecticut. In 1957, when he was 26, he won the Boston marathon with a time of 2:20. In 1979, fit and 48, he was as fiercely competitive as ever, yet it took him almost 30 minutes longer to run the same marathon.

11   In the middle of the fourth decade, the man whose eyesight has always been good will pick up a book and notice that he is holding it farther from his face than usual. The condition is presbyopia, a loss of the flexibility of the lens which makes adjustment from distant to near vision increasingly difficult. It's harder now to zoom in for a closeup. It also takes longer for the eyes to recover from glare; between 16 and 90, recovery time from exposure to glare is doubled every 13 years.

12   In our 50s, we notice that food is less and less tasty; our taste buds are starting to lose their acuity. The aged Queen Victoria was wont to complain that strawberries were not as sweet as when she was a girl.

13   Little is known about the causes of aging. We do not know if we are born with a biochemical messenger programed to keep the cells and tissues alive, a messenger that eventually gets lost, or if there is a 'death hormone,' absent from birth but later secreted by the thymus or by the mysterious pineal gland, or if, perhaps, aging results from a fatal flaw in the body's immune system. The belief that the body is a machine whose parts wear out is erroneous, for the machine does not have the body's capacity for self-repair.

14   "A man is as old as his arteries," observed Sir William Osler. From the 50s on, there's a progressive hardening and narrowing of the arteries

due to the gradual lifelong accumulation of calcium and fats along the arterial walls. Arteriosclerosis eventually affects the majority of the population in the affluent countries of the West. Lucky the man or woman who, through a combination of good genes and good nutrition, can escape it, for it is the most evil change of all. As the flow of blood carrying oxygen and nutrients to the muscles, the brain, the kidneys and other organs diminishes, these organs begin to starve. Although all aging organs lose weight, there is less shrinkage of organs such as the liver and kidneys, the cells of which regenerate, than there is shrinkage of the brain and the muscles, the cells of which, once lost, are lost forever.

For the woman it is now an ordeal to be asked her age. There is a fine tracery of lines around her eyes, a furrow in her brow even when she smiles. The bloom is off her cheeks. Around the age of 50 she will buy her last box of sanitary pads. The body's production of estrogen and progesterone, which govern menstruation (and also help to protect her from heart attack and the effects of stress), will have ceased almost completely. She may suffer palpitations, suddenly break into a sweat; her moods may shift abruptly. She looks in the mirror and asks, "Am I still a woman?" Eventually she becomes reconciled to her new self and even acknowledges its advantages: no more fears about pregnancy. "In any case," she laughs, "I still have not bad legs." 15

The man, too, will undergo a change. One night in his early 50s he has some trouble achieving a complete erection, and his powers of recovery are not what they once were. Whereas at 20 he was ready to make love again less than half an hour after doing so, it may now take two hours or more; he was not previously aware that his level of testosterone, the male hormone, has been gradually declining since the age of 20. He may develop headaches, be unable to sleep, become anxious about his performance, anticipate failure and so bring on what is called secondary impotence — impotence of psychological rather than physical origin. According to Masters and Johnson, 25 percent of all men are impotent by 65 and 50 percent by 75, yet this cannot be called an inevitable feature of aging. A loving, undemanding partner and a sense of confidence can do wonders. "The susceptibility of the human male to the power of suggestion with regard to his sexual prowess," observe Masters and Johnson, "is almost unbelievable." 16

After the menopause, the woman ages more rapidly. Her bones start to lose calcium, becoming brittle and porous. The walls of the vagina become thinner and drier, sexual intercourse now may be painful unless her partner is slow and gentle. The sweat glands begin to atrophy and the sebaceous glands that lubricate the skin decline; the complexion becomes thinner and drier and wrinkles appear around the mouth. The skin, which in youth varies from about one-fiftieth of an inch on the eyelids to about a third of an inch on the palms and the soles of the 17 feet, loses 50 percent of its thickness between the ages of 20 and 80. The woman no longer buys sleeveless dresses and avoids shorts. The girl who once disdained cosmetics is now a woman whose dressing table is covered with lotions, night creams and makeup.

18   Perhaps no one has written about the sensation of nearing 60 with more brutal honesty than the French novelist Simone de Beauvoir: "While I was able to look at my face without displeasure, I gave it no thought. I loathe my appearance now: the eyebrows slipping down toward the eyes, the bags underneath, the excessive fullness of the cheeks and the air of sadness around the mouth that wrinkles always bring. . . . Death is no longer a brutal event in the far distance; it haunts my sleep."

19   In his early 60s the man's calves are shrunken, his muscles stringy looking. The legs of the woman, too, are no longer shapely. Both start to lose their sense of smell and both lose most of the hair in the pubic area and the underarms. Hair, however, may make its appearance in new places, such as the woman's chin. Liver spots appear on the hands, the arms, the face; they are made of coagulated melanin, the coloring matter of the skin. The acid secretions of the stomach decrease, making digestion slow and more difficult.

20   Halfway through the 60s comes compulsory retirement for most men and working women, forcing upon the superannuated worker the realization that society now views him as useless and unproductive. The man who formerly gave orders to a staff of 20 now finds himself underfoot as his wife attempts to clean the house or get the shopping done. The woman fares a little better since there is a continuity in her pattern of performing a myriad of essential household tasks. Now they must both set new goals or see themselves wither mentally. The unsinkable American journalist I. F. Stone, when he retired in 1971 from editing *I. F. Stone's Weekly*, began to teach himself Greek and is now reading Plato in the original. When Somerset Maugham read that the Roman senator Cato the Elder learned Greek when he was 80, he remarked: "Old age is ready to undertake tasks that youth shirked because they would take too long."

21   However active we are, the fact of old age can no longer be evaded from about 65 onward. Not everyone is as strong minded about this as de Beauvoir was. When she made public in her memoirs her horror at her own deterioration, her readers were scandalized. She received hundreds of letters telling her that there is no such thing as old age, that some are just younger than others. Repeatedly she heard the hollow reassurance, "You're as young as you feel." But she considered this a lie. Our subjective reality, our inner sense of self, is not the only reality. There is also an objective reality, how we are seen by society. We receive our revelation of old age from others. The woman whose figure is still trim may sense that a man is following her in the street; drawing abreast, the man catches sight of her face — and hurries on. The man of 68

may be told by a younger woman to whom he is attracted: "You remind me of my father."

Madame de Sévigné, the 17th-century French writer, struggled to rid herself of the illusion of perpetual youth. At 63 she wrote: "I have been dragged to this inevitable point where old age must be undergone: I see it there before me; I have reached it; and I should at least like so to arrange matters that I do not move on, that I do not travel further along this path of the infirmities, pains, losses of memory and the disfigurement. But I hear a voice saying: 'You must go along, whatever you may say; or indeed if you will not then you must die, which is an extremity from which nature recoils.'"

Now the man and the woman have their 70th birthday party. It is a sad affair because so many of their friends are missing, felled by strokes, heart attacks or cancers. Now the hands of the clock begin to race. The skeleton continues to degenerate from loss of calcium. The spine becomes compressed and there is a slight stoop nothing can prevent. Inches are lost from one's height. The joints may become thickened and creaking; in the morning the woman can't seem to get moving until she's had a hot bath. She has osteoarthritis. This, like the other age-related diseases, arteriosclerosis and diabetes, can and should be treated, but it can never be cured. The nails, particularly the toenails, become thick and lifeless because the circulation in the lower limbs is now poor. The man has difficulty learning new things because of the progressive loss of neurons from the brain. The woman goes to the store and forgets what she has come to buy. The two old people are often constipated because the involuntary muscles are weaker now. To make it worse, their children are always saying, "Sit down, rest, take it easy." Their digestive tract would be toned up if they went for a long walk or even a swim, although they feel a little foolish in bathing suits.

In his late 70s, the man develops glaucoma, pressure in the eyeball caused by the failure of the aqueous humour to drain away; this can now be treated with a steroid related to cortisone. The lenses in the eyes of the woman may thicken and become fibrous, blurring her vision. She has cataracts, but artificial lenses can now be implanted using cryosurgery. There is no reason to lose one's sight just as there's no reason to lose one's teeth; regular, lifelong dental care can prevent tooth loss. What can't be prevented is the yellowing of teeth, brought about by the shrinking of the living chamber within the tooth which supplies the outer enamel with moisture.

Between 75 and 85 the body loses most of its subcutaneous fat. On her 80th birthday the woman's granddaughter embraces her and marvels: "How thin and frail and shrunken she is! Could this narrow, bony chest be the same warm, firm bosom to which she clasped me as a child?" Her children urge her to eat but she has no enjoyment of food now. Her mouth secretes little saliva, so she has difficulty tasting and swallowing. The loss of fat and shrinking muscles in the 80s diminish the body's capacity for homeostasis, that is, righting any physiological imbalance. The old man, if he is cold, can barely shiver (shivering serves to restore body heat.) If he lives long enough, the man will have an enlarged prostate, which causes the urinary stream to slow to a trickle. The man and the woman probably both wear hearing aids now; without a hearing aid, they hear vowels clearly but not consonants; if someone says "fat," they think they've heard the word "that."

26   At 80, the speed of nerve impulses is 10 percent less than it was at 25, the kidney filtration rate is down by 30 percent, the pumping efficiency of the heart is only 60 percent of what it was, and the maximum breathing capacity, 40 percent.

27   The old couple is fortunate in still being able to express physically the love they've built up over a lifetime. The old man may be capable of an erection once or twice a week (Charlie Chaplin fathered the last of his many children when he was 81), but he rarely has the urge to climax. When he does, he sometimes has the sensation of seepage rather than a triumphant explosion. Old people who say they are relieved that they are now free of the torments of sexual desire are usually the ones who found sex a troublesome function all their lives; those who found joy and renewal in the act will cling to their libido. Many older writers and artists have expressed the conviction that continued sexuality is linked to continued creativity: "There was a time when I was cruelly tormented, indeed obsessed by desire," wrote the novelist André Gide at the age of 73, "and I prayed, 'Oh let the moment come when my subjugated flesh will allow me to give myself entirely to. . . .' But to what? To art? To pure thought? To God? How ignorant I was! How mad! It was the same as believing that the flame would burn brighter in a lamp with no oil left. Even today it is my carnal self that feeds the flame, and now I pray that I may retain carnal desire until I die."

28   Aging, says an American gerontologist, "is not a simple slope which everyone slides down at the same speed; it is a flight of irregular stairs down which some journey more quickly than others." Now we arrive at the bottom of the stairs. The old man and the old woman whose progress we have been tracing will die either of a cancer (usually of the lungs, bowel or intestines) or of a stroke, a heart attack or in consequence of a fall. The man slips in the bathroom and breaks his thigh bone. But worse than the fracture is the enforced bed rest in the hospital which will probably bring on bed sores, infections, further weakening of the muscles and finally, what Osler called "an old man's best friend": pneumonia. At 25 we have so much vitality that if a little is sapped by illness, there is still plenty left over. At 85 a little is all we have.

And then the light goes out.   29

The sheet is pulled over the face.   30

In the last book of Marcel Proust's remarkable work *Remembrance of*   31
Things Past, the narrator, returning after a long absence from Paris,
attends a party of his friends throughout which he has the impression
of being at a masked ball: "I did not understand why I could not
immediately recognize the master of the house, and the guests, who
seemed to have made themselves up, in a way that completely changed
their appearance. The Prince had rigged himself up with a white beard
and what looked like leaden soles which made his feet drag heavily. A
name was mentioned to me and I was dumbfounded at the thought
that it applied to the blonde waltzing girl I had once known and to the
stout, white-haired lady now walking just in front of me. We did not see
our own appearance, but each like a facing mirror, saw the other's."
The narrator is overcome by a simple but powerful truth: the old are
not a different species. "It is out of young men who last long enough,"
wrote Proust, "that life makes its old men."

The wrinkled old man who lies with the sheet over his face was once   32
the young man who vowed, "My grip will never weaken. I will walk with
long strides and stand tall as long as I live." The young man who believed
himself to be the exception.

△ △

Further Reading:

Gail Sheehy, *Passages*
Margaret Laurence, *The Stone Angel* (novel)
Roch Carrier, *No Country without Grandfathers* (novel)
Ernest Hemingway, *The Old Man and the Sea* (novella)
William Shakespeare, *King Lear*
Michel Tremblay, *Albertine, in Five Times* (theatre)

Structure:

1. "The Way of All Flesh" is a striking example of chronological order
   used to organize a mass of information. Point out at least ten words,
   phrases or sentences that signal the flow of time.
2. Does Stoffman's *process analysis* tell us how to do something, how
   something is done by others, or how something happens?
3. How long would this essay be if its examples were all removed? How
   interesting would it be? How convincing?
4. What means of logic underlies paragraphs 14 and 16?
5. What effect do we feel when the last paragraph refers to the first
   paragraph?

Style:

1. Why are paragraphs 29 and 30 so short?
2. How heavily does Stoffman rely on statistics? What do they do for her argument?
3. How heavily does Stoffman rely on quotations? In fact, is this selection a research essay? Why or why not?
4. In a desk-size dictionary, find the origins of the word "gerontologist" (par. 28). How is it related to the words "geriatrics," "Geritol," "gerontocracy," "astrology" and "zoology."

Ideas for Discussion and Writing:

1. Does Stoffman's essay frighten or depress you? If so, is this effect a failure or a success on her part?
2. Is Stoffman's essay too one-sided? If she wrote another called "The Joy of Aging," recommend at least five points she could make.
3. Paragraph 21 contrasts our "subjective" and "objective" realities. Which is more vital to your own self-image? Why?
4. Is compulsory retirement at 65 good for the person? For the company? For society? When would you choose to retire? Why? What standard other than age might you apply?
5. **PROCESS IN WRITING:** *Write a* process analysis *on one of these topics:*
   — How to stay physically fit past 30
   — How to feel worthwhile in old age
   — How to help parents and grandparents be happy in old age
   First fill a page with brief notes, then scan and sort to choose your points and the order in which they will appear. After a rapid first draft, add more TRANSITIONS *to speed the chronology of your process. Are there enough* IMAGES*? Enough concrete examples? Share a draft with class members; do they think they could actually follow your directions? If not, clarify weak points. Finally, read your good copy aloud, slowly and clearly, to the whole class.*

Note: See also the Topics for Writing at the end of this chapter.

Dian Cohen

The Commodities Game[*]

Dian Cohen represents the invasion by women of an area traditionally domi-
nated by men — economics. Owner of Dian Cohen Productions Ltd.; a director
of major corporations including Noranda, PanCanadian Petroleum, Royal In-
surance, CP Ltd. and Monsanto Canada; frequent financial commentator on
Canadian radio and television; syndicated newspaper and magazine columnist;
writer of feature articles for magazines such as Canadian Business, Saturday
Night, Vancouver Magazine *and others; author of books on economics (* The
Next Canadian Economy, *1984;* Money, *1987;* No Small Change, *1992;*
Making It in a New Economy, *1992); and twice winner of the National*
Business Writing Award, Cohen is known for commentary that goes right to the
point. As business author Lyman MacInnis put it, "Dian Cohen is one of those
rare individuals — an economist who speaks and writes in understandable
language." These qualities are clearly demonstrated in our selection, from her
book on personal money management entitled, appropriately enough, Money.

**If you bet on a horse, that's gambling. If you bet you can make
Three Spades, that's entertainment. If you bet cotton will go up
three points, that's business. See the difference?**
— Blackie Sherrode

If gold is the bedrock of financial security, then commodities, with
their promises of huge trading profits, are the will-o'-the-wisps dancing
seductively above it. Yes, it is possible to lose money in gold, if you really
work at it, and it is also possible to make a bundle in commodities
trading. But over the long term, gold is literally safer than money in the
bank, whereas in the commodities game, 85% of the players are losers,
while only 15% are winners — about the same odds as horse-racing or
gambling. This fact doesn't have to keep you out of commodities. But
you have to remember that commodity trading is a technique — a tool
— to help you reach your financial goals.

---

*Editor's title.

2   Commodities are basic goods produced by primary producers. They are the raw materials consumed by secondary producers such as manufacturers. The most common examples of commodities include precious metals, like gold, silver, and platinum; other metals such as copper and nickel, produced by mine owners; agricultural goods such as wheat, corn, oats, soybeans, pork bellies (from which bacon is made), produced by farmers; and materials such as lumber and plywood, produced by sawmills.

3   There are three principal players involved in commodities markets: the producer, the consumer, and the commodities investor, or speculator. The attraction of commodities trading is the tremendous leverage that is possible. You don't put very much money down — 5% to 10% of the purchase price is average. In addition, there is no interest charged on the balance as there is with stock margins. With this kind of leverage, a very small change in the price of the commodity has great effect on your profit or loss.

4   If you purchased $10,000 worth of a stock from your broker, and put up the full $10,000, then a $1,000 move in the value of that stock would increase or decrease your investment by 10%. If you margined the stock at 50%, and thus put up only $5,000, then the $1,000 gain or loss would be 20%. That's leverage. But if you put up only $500 for a $10,000 purchase, as with the commodities market, then a $1,000 move up would show a 200% gain, while a movement downward would lose you *double* your money. That's really leverage!

5   You don't actually buy the commodities, and though you have the right, you are not obligated to take delivery of them. You are trading *contracts* to buy or sell the commodities in the future. What you are assuming is that at some point in a specific period in the future, the price of the commodity will have changed. If you feel it will be higher then than it is now, you contract to buy; if you feel it will be lower, you contract to sell.

6   How do you contract to sell something you don't own? When you make the contract, you are not required to deliver until the future date specified. That gives you plenty of time to get the commodity. In practice, you will never have to, since your plan is to offset that contract before delivery is required. Offsetting is a procedure by which your contract to deliver a commodity is cancelled. You do this by selling what you have bought, or by buying what you have sold. When you are in a "long" position, that is, you own a contract to *buy* a commodity, you offset this by obtaining another contract to *sell* the same commodity. If you start out by buying someone else's contract to sell it, you are in a "short" position and must buy a contract, to offset your position.

7   There are a number of commodity futures exchanges which operate in a similar manner to stock exchanges. There is the Chicago Board of

Trade, which deals chiefly in grains, plywood, broilers (chickens), and silver; the Comex in New York, dealing only in metals; the Chicago Mercantile, which handles eggs, pork bellies, cattle, and lumber; the London Terminal Market, dealing in cocoa and sugar; and the London Metal Exchange for copper and silver. There are several others, including the Winnipeg Commodity Exchange which handles, among other things, canola and gold. These exchanges regulate the contracted amounts so that they are the same for all traders. This eliminates opportunities for big-time speculators to edge out the little guys. It also makes offsetting possible. The exchanges record and report the price during each day of trading. Unlike stocks, commodity futures prices are allowed to move only so far each day. This is to prevent trading activity from causing massive price moves. Once the price of a commodity future has moved to its permissible daily limit, no trading can take place outside that limit. It can still take place within the limit, however, and the next day it can move to a new limit. This regulates the futures market, but if spot prices — that is, the price at which the commodity is being bought and sold in the present — are extremely volatile, you may not be able to buy or sell your futures contract until the limited price movements catch up to the spot prices.

Consumers and producers of commodities are also active traders. Chocolate manufacturers, for example, trade in cocoa bean futures as a hedge against changes in the world price of cocoa, though they seldom take delivery. Nor are they as much interested in making money on the trade as they are in maintaining a uniform price for cocoa beans for manufacturing purposes. Thus, if world prices go up, and they hold a futures contract at a lower price, they can sell that contract, take their profit, and apply it to their operations back at the plant.

Producers hedge as well. The cocoa bean producer might be unsure of what his beans will bring on the market a year from now, and he would like to be assured of a reasonable price. So, he sells a contract at a price that will provide him with a profit, and insures him against a drop in world prices. Then he watches the market carefully, and hedges where he can.

How do you compete against these insiders? They may know chocolate, but like you, they don't know which way the price is going. All any of you can do is make an informed guess. Say a manufacturer calculates that to make his profit six months from now he needs to be able to buy cocoa at that time for 30 cents a pound. He will buy a contract to take delivery at that price on a specific date.

But the effect of that transaction is to establish the two sides of an argument. The buyer says that in six months time cocoa will be worth 30 cents a pound or higher. The seller says it will be worth 30 cents or lower. It will certainly be one or the other, and that's where the speculator enters the picture. He backs one or the other by placing what is, in effect, a side bet with another speculator.

12 Some people feel that since they do not produce anything, speculators must make their money on the misfortunes of those who do produce. Others feel that speculators are essential to trading, since they will often take risks that others won't. Suppose a farmer wants to sell his eggs for future delivery, and needs to make 40 cents a dozen to cover his costs and make a profit. He may find that none of the users around will pay him more than 35 cents. He would be losing money, and obviously wouldn't sell. Enter the speculator. He is betting that sooner or later a user will have to give in to the farmer's required price. He buys the eggs now at the 40-cent price, in the hope that when the users give in, the price will be 40 cents or higher. In that way, speculators serve a useful function in the market place.

13 Another theory says that speculators tend to drive prices up or down out of all proportion to reality. For example, in the above case, the speculators may drive the price up to 50 cents. The farmer will see that the speculators are way off base, and rush in to sell, thereby getting more than he could otherwise expect. Other farmers will see what is happening and rush in too. This action will tend to drive prices down. Of course, the ideal theory holds that if all buyers and sellers are fully knowledgeable, the market will always find its proper level. But since people are never fully knowledgeable, especially about the future, the market sometimes does get out of whack with reality. Therein lies the challenge of commodity trading.

14 So, how does an amateur who knows little or nothing about a particular industry get involved in commodities trading? Very carefully.

15 In order to trade successfully in the commodities market, you must know when the price of a commodity is going to move up or down, and that's not easy. The best available knowledge about a commodity and its market is essential. Your broker might help. Watching what other traders are doing will give some indications as well. For example, if the further you look into the future, the progressively lower the price of a commodity gets, then the market, strangely enough, is tending to rise. Conversely, if the furthest futures price is progressively higher than the closest price, the market is tending to fall. These indicators are more clearly seen when a market is about to change from being a discounted (lower future price) to a premium (higher future price) market.

16 Qualifying as a bona fide trader depends on the amount of money you have, and the tolerance threshold of your broker. Most houses won't touch you unless you have a net worth of $50,000 or more. But you can find brokers who will make transactions for you, even if you don't have more than $2,000 to trade. The best rule of thumb to follow is *never* put up more than you can afford to lose.

The cost of the commodity you wish to trade depends on the com- 17
modity, and on the exchange's policy that is in effect at that time. A
contract for 5,000 bushels of wheat, or 40,000 pounds of cattle, costs
about $1,500. A contract for 25,000 pounds of copper costs $1,300. The
amount of money you stand to make also depends on the contract. A
two-cent-per-bushel move upward in wheat will make you $100 — more
than enough to cover the $65 commission. A one-cent-a-pound rise in
copper amounts to $250, again more than enough to cover the $80
commission.

Like all highly-leveraged transactions, commodity trading is risky for 18
speculators. But that's also why there are generous rewards. Commodities
should be avoided unless the rest of your investment portfolio is in
good shape, and you are prepared to lose everything you put into
commodities. It is purely and simply highly-leveraged risk taking.

△ △

Further Reading:

Dian Cohen,
Money
No Small Change
Making It in a New Economy

Structure:

1. Cohen prefaces her selection with an EPIGRAPH. Did it catch your attention? Does it lead to the subject?
2. Point out all *comparisons and contrasts* that in paragraph 1 introduce
   the subject.
3. Cohen's *process analysis* is both informational and directional. Identify passages that give background information. Identify other passages that tell us how to play "the commodities game." Would the
   directions be clear without the background?
4. Cohen's paragraphs are unusually well organized, and are long
   enough to develop their point. Identify at least five paragraphs
   that open with a topic sentence, and that clearly develop the point
   in it.
5. Why is paragraph 14 so much shorter than all the others?

Style:

1. This selection is part of Cohen's book *Money*, an introduction to
   personal finance and investment. How does she tailor her specialized topic to a general audience? How does she deal with new words?
   With new concepts?

2. Identify all the FIGURES OF SPEECH that in paragraph 1 introduce Cohen's subject.

Ideas for Discussion and Writing:

1. How clear and complete are Cohen's directions? If you had the money, could you begin the *process* today?
2. Does this selection entice you to play "the commodities game" or does it warn you away? Point out two or three passages that help you decide.
3. In paragraph 12 Cohen writes, "Some people feel that since they do not produce anything, speculators must make their money on the misfortunes of those who do produce. Others feel that speculators are essential to trading, since they will often take risks that others won't." Which side do you take? Defend your answer with examples.
4. Canadians are said to be conservative money-under-the-mattress savers instead of aggressive speculators. Is this view truth or STEREO-TYPE? Defend your answer with examples of people you know.
5. To some people "profit" is an obscene word, while to others it is the foundation of our whole way of life. Examine the profit motive: name ways in which it helps our society; name other ways in which it hurts our society.
6. **PROCESS IN WRITING:** *Today many Canadians invest in mutual funds. Consult an agent who sells them, or someone you know who invests in them. Take notes. From these decide your focus, and whether to do an* informational *or a* directional *process analysis. Now write a short outline to set the order of your process, then do a first draft, double-spaced. Perhaps the act of writing has uncovered steps you had neglected; add them. In your next draft make sure to define technical words your audience may not know, and add any missing transitions between steps. Does a point lack a good example? Add it. Is a passage off-topic or a phrase or word unnecessary? Cross it out. Finally, test your prose aloud before writing the good copy.*

Note: See also the Topics for Writing at the end of this chapter.

June Callwood

Making a Difference

One of the nation's most prolific journalists, June Callwood is also one of its leading social activists. In her long career she has never held a full-time job, yet as a freelance writer she has published thousands of newspaper and magazine articles, was from 1983 to 1989 a Globe and Mail *columnist, has ghostwritten the "autobiographies" of people as varied as Charles Mayo, Barbara Walters, Otto Preminger and Bob White, and has published many widely read books of her own, such as* The Law Is Not for Women *(with Marvin Zuker, 1976),* A Full Life *(1982),* Emotions *(1986),* Twelve Weeks in Spring *(1986),* Jim: A Life with AIDS *(1988) and* Sleepwalker *(1990). Her passionate social concerns underlie not only her articles and books, but also her other work as champion of the underdog. Siding with the weak and the poor, Callwood has helped to found over two dozen benevolent organizations, among them Digger House (a shelter for homeless youth in Toronto), Nellie's (a haven for battered women), Jessie's (a refuge for pregnant teenagers), and in 1987 Casey House (a residential treatment centre for people with AIDS). She also helped to found the Canadian Civil Liberties Association in 1965, and, as a writer, has fought strongly against censorship. Callwood holds many honorary doctorates and other awards, and is a director of numerous organizations. Our selection, from the April 1989 issue of* Homemaker's Magazine, *is vintage Callwood: practical directions for bringing about change in society.*

About a year ago, newspapers were full of a story about a woman, 1 new to Canada, who had been beaten by her husband. Many people who read about it felt sympathy for the friendless stranger hiding in a women's shelter, facing an uncertain future.

A widow of small means, a woman with grown children, called some 2 friends. "We should do something about this," she said.

"You're right," one of her friends replied. "You should." 3

"Oh dear," she replied. "Me?" 4

"Why not?" the friend said. 5

The next day, news stories about the case included a few lines about 6 a new fund that had been established. The public was informed that donations to help the battered woman could be sent to a bank, and an address was given. The widow had done three things: after consulting her bank manager, she opened an account in the woman's name with a donation of her own; then she called the media to tell of the existence of the fund; and then she contacted the police officer in charge of the case and asked him to give the woman her name and telephone number.

7   The assaulted woman gratefully called and they met for coffee. Over the next few weeks her benefactor raised enough money to help the woman get resettled and became the newcomer's companion, assisting her to find her way around the city.

8   "I feel very good about this," she told everyone. "I've learned a lot."

9   What she meant by that was her visits to a women's shelter where she talked to women fleeing from violence, and her indignant discoveries about how the welfare system works. Her experiences had changed her comfortable view of society and she was telling her friends about it, her opinions given weight because she was the only one among them with firsthand knowledge. She didn't seem to notice that she had changed greatly. She had been a warm, sympathetic woman who believed herself to be hopelessly ineffective; she had discovered instead that she was a warm, sympathetic woman who was capable and resourceful. The difference in her was pronounced; there was a new firmness in her voice and bounce in her walk.

10   Hannah Arendt, philosopher and writer, was absorbed much of her life with an effort to understand the nature of good and evil. In her book, *Eichmann in Jerusalem,* (Penguin, 1977), a study of the trial of Adolf Eichmann, the Nazi who bore a major responsibility in the Holocaust, she directed her considerable intellect to an analysis of evil. Her conclusion was that evil thrives on apathy and cannot exist without it; hence, apathy *is* evil.

11   When injustice encounters inertia, it uses that passivity exactly as if it were approval. In the absence of protest, evil is nourished and can flourish. The nature of goodness, therefore, bears a keen relationship to intervention. Individuals who seek to save their souls, or serve their consciences, or find meaning in their lives, or who wish to attain the quiet splendor of moral growth, are obliged to participate in their society.

12   The American feminist Gloria Steinem advises women, for the sake of their health, to do something outrageous every day. For instance, today a woman might write to the president of her favorite supermarket and ask him (certainly it will be a man) to list all the branches in her area with a woman manager because she wishes to shop where a woman is in charge. Tomorrow she might write to her bank president with the same reasonable request. By the third day she'll be combustible with plenty of ideas of her own.

13   Nietzsche said that people wait all their lives for an opportunity to do good in their own way. Such patience is rarely rewarded. Moments

when a useful contribution can be made by taking action almost never wear a name tag. Instead, they always look like "someone else's responsibility — not my business."

In moments when they are dissatisfied with themselves, most people yearn for a chance to do a redemptive good deed. They fantasize about taking leadership to get a much-needed crosswalk for the neighborhood, or throwing themselves into good works. The problem is: how to start. 14

First, no one should shrink from the healthy element of selfishness that nourishes selflessness. While seeking to better their society, it is reasonable for people also, and not incidentally, to hope to improve their self-worth. It is a motive not to be derided or denied. Elevating self-esteem by behaving admirably has an ancient and honorable tradition, so long as self-liking is not so abysmally low that beneficiaries are obliged to be eternally grateful and respectful. 15

Altruism is the expression of the individual's best self, the god in the machinery.° Instead of waiting shyly to be asked, some people simply seize an opportunity. One woman who visited a geriatric facility seven years ago noted that some of the aged were too weak to lift a spoon. Since then, twice a day she feeds a meal and chats to lonely people. Another woman read about children on ventilators who live in a hospital. She enrolled as a volunteer and goes twice a week to see a little girl she takes for walks in the corridor, reads to, and for whom she entertainingly describes the caprices of her cat. Another woman dropped in at Nellie's, a Toronto hostel for women, and asked what she could do. The staff person was dealing with an emergency at the time and asked her to get herself a cup of coffee and wait. Later, when she went in search of the volunteer, she found her scrubbing the stairs. 16

Another woman, a welfare recipient, was incensed that a developer had his eye on some green space where children played. She went to City Hall and persevered through polite evasions and pointed snubs until she found a civil servant and an alderman who listened. What she began snowballed into a noisy community meeting that resulted in saving the playground. 17

Making a difference starts with having a spunky attitude. The first thing to get out of the way is expectation that virtue always triumphs: in truth, most attempts to confront and defeat misdeeds are only partially successful or else seem to be outright failures. It doesn't matter; nothing is wasted in the universe. Even an effort that apparently goes nowhere will influence the future. Though the system looks untouched, it has a fatal crack in it. The next assault, or the one after that, will bring it down. At the very least, someone, somewhere, has learned a lesson and will be more thoughtful. 18

°the god in the machinery: In classical drama, a god put onstage through some mechanical device, to intervene in a perplexing situation.

19   Victory, though highly desirable, is the second-best outcome of wading into a controversy on behalf of others. The real triumph is the act of making a stand and taking on the battle. It matters when someone makes an attempt to improve the quality of life for the neighborhood, the society, the world. Even if contaminated soil continues to be dumped in the nearby lake, or the school board still won't accept a child in a wheelchair, or better street lighting is denied, something has been achieved; someone cared enough to fight.

20   Real defeat isn't failure to attain the objective: it's not trying. Most people, as theatre critic Walter Kerr once put it, live half-lives halfheartedly. They cast themselves in the role of spectator, whatever the provocation to take action. The excuses are that no effort of theirs would succeed, or that in any case they don't know what to do, or they might look foolish, or what they do might make matters worse. "Innocent bystander" is an oxymoron. People who do not intervene when something is amiss give tacit permission for injustice to continue.

21   Becoming an activist takes practice, which can start on a small scale — like a beginner's slope for skiers-to-be. People can rehearse by responding to minor acts of tyranny: a racial insult, for instance; a clerk being high-handed with someone too intimidated to protest. The very young are powerless to challenge wrongdoing and therefore must tolerate it, but futile hand-wringing is unsuitable and unbecoming in an adult.

22   In recent years, so many people have taken up slingshots against corporate and government Goliaths° that the paths are blazed for newcomers. Expertise abounds in where and how to apply pressure. Umbrella groups have been established in such fields as environment and disarmament; libraries list them in catalogues. Many communities have information centres that provide the location of such specialized services as daycare advocacy specialists or ratepayers groups. The National Action Committee on the Status of Women knows the field of women's issues and Tools for Peace or Oxfam Canada can give the latest information about what's happening in Nicaragua.

23   A critical step, in short, is information-gathering. It makes no sense to waste enthusiasm and indignation by plunging blindly into a fight. Do as the 19th-century Prussian military strategist Carl von Clausewitz always advised: secure your base, gather informed cohorts, study the terrain: knowledge is power.

24   A few years ago a group of young mothers decided their neighborhood would benefit from a parent-child drop-in centre. A friendly lawyer helped them incorporate and then they applied for tax-deductible status in order to launch a fund-raising campaign. A year later, when they

---

°Goliath: In the Bible, a giant Philistine killed by the young David with a sling (I Samuel 17).

were negotiating a lease for storefront space, they approached the government for help — and discovered that there was an underused parent-child drop-in centre only two blocks from their own site.

Duplication is an inexcusable waste in a country that sorely needs the energy and acumen of people who hold ideals of conduct. No effort to achieve social improvement should be launched without research of regulations and the historical background, analysis of the need, consultation with experts, collection of statistical data where appropriate. **25**

Before launching Nellie's 15 years ago, for instance, the founders counted the number of beds available in Toronto for homeless men (approximately 800), and the number available for homeless women (approximately 20). They enlisted the support of the police, who acknowledged that there was no place for women who needed to escape family violence. The municipality had no choice but to give support. **26**

Similarly, Jessie's, a Toronto centre established seven years ago for pregnant teenagers and teenaged parents, was the work of a task force that included some 25 representatives from every agency dealing with teenaged mothers — children's aid societies, public health, maternity homes, the YWCA, hostels, community centres, clinics, parent-child drop-in centres. By the time the task force presented the provincial government with a proposal that had been almost three years in the making, the authority behind the recommendations was too persuasive to fail. Jessie's now is backed by the Ministry of Community and Social Services, the Ministry of Health and the Toronto Board of Education, plus a host of foundations, corporations and private donors. **27**

Success is no fluke. When the government changes its mind about allowing a logging road through a park, when officials do an about-face concerning schooling for learning-disabled children, those desirable outcomes are the consequence of a hundred meetings, most of them tiring and frustrating, where people with good information plan strategy and put together briefs. Often the catalytic force is one event or one person whose life has been touched by loss, but the movement that results depends for its power on attracting the most creditable expertise the community can provide. **28**

A well-informed team, making thought-out moves, is invincible. Often the opposition is frayed and fragmented in comparison. It whines, obfuscates, denies. Positive-minded, fair-speaking citizenry, equipped with clear, well-researched proposals, has a distinct advantage. **29**

When Bruce Porter, a Toronto activist in the field of housing, was battling adults-only apartment buildings in Ontario, he assembled a group of low-income mothers and took them to the legislative hearings. One after another, they told stories of being homeless with their children. The media, adjusted to ho-hum reports read by executive directors, leapt into life and interviewed the mothers for television, radio and **30** newspaper headlines. It was no coincidence that restrictions on adults-only buildings soon afterwards passed into Ontario law.

31   Such ingenuity is often rewarded. A handful of people who wanted to start a women's hostel in a small community were frustrated for four years by a town council that maintained that the area had no battered women. Someone had a bright idea. She contacted the *wives* of councillors and asked them to the next meeting. Enough of them came, and were impressed enough by the police reports and other statistics, to shake up a smug council.

32   People fear being ridiculous more than they fear disaster. It takes courage to go against the stream. Never mind. If the path has heart in it, it's the right one and you're right to be on it. Moreover, you'll enjoy yourself.

△△△

Further Reading:

June Callwood,
   Portrait of Canada
   Emotions
   Twelve Weeks in Spring
   Jim: A Life with AIDS

Structure:

1. What common technique of opening does Callwood use? How well does it work here?
2. What proportion of this essay is *examples*? Do you use as many? Would your papers improve if you did? How do we find more examples for arguments?
3. Where is Callwood's THESIS STATEMENT?
4. Where does the introduction end and the *process analysis* of "making a difference" begin? What are its main steps and where does each begin?
5. In what passages does *cause and effect* logic strengthen the process analysis?

Style:

1. Are Callwood's vocabulary, level of argument, and general approach right for her intended *audience*, the readers of *Homemaker's Magazine?* Give reasons for your answer. Describe the reader to which the author is reaching out.
2. In paragraph 15 Callwood writes of "selfishness that nourishes selflessness." Explain how this PARADOX works.

Ideas for Discussion and Writing:

1. Why does Callwood aim this essay at women? Is her argument feminist? Is there overlap: would her advice help men too?

2. Gloria Steinem says that "to do something outrageous every day" (paragraph 12) is good for women's health. Can you give reasons why?

3. Do you read self-help books? If so, name your favourites. Is this essay at all like them? Does it inspire? Do you believe Callwood that you can "enjoy yourself" more (paragraph 32) through helping others? Respond with examples.

4. Attack or defend the idea of paragraphs 18 and 19 that trying is more important than winning. What are the implications of your own view for sports? School? Business? Politics?

5. "In the absence of protest, evil is nourished and can flourish," says paragraph 11. Describe a time when you just stood by as something bad happened. Now describe another time when you took action against an "evil." Tell the *effects*.

6. Are you satisfied with our society, or would you change things? If so, name some. Tell why. Choose one and tell how you would apply Callwood's instructions. Is her *process analysis* clear and detailed enough to show the way?

7. **PROCESS IN WRITING:** *Explore number 6 more fully in writing. First put at the top of a page the name of the thing you would change in society (in your school, neighbourhood, community or nation). Now brainstorm: fill the page with ideas, notes, reactions. Looking these over, produce a mini-outline, then write a rapid first draft of your* process analysis, *explaining how you personally could go about effecting the change. Draw as much as you wish from Callwood's techniques, using quotation marks where needed. The next day look over your instructions. Are they clear? Are all steps given? Do examples "show" how? Do transitions like "next," "then" and "finally" link the parts? Do you inspire readers by showing the good* effects *of this action, as Callwood does? Now check for things like grammar and spelling as you produce your best version. Finally, plan when you might put your own* process analysis *into action.*

Note: See also the Topics for Writing at the end of this chapter.

Captain Thomas James

Our Mansion House*

In May of 1631 Captain Thomas James (1593–1635) sailed with his crew from Bristol, England, in search of the fabled Northwest Passage. Such a route would speed merchant sailors to the Orient, to make their fortunes in trade without the danger and expense of sailing around Cape Horn. James never found the passage, for it did not exist. But in the process of looking, he explored and mapped the west coast of Hudson Bay. He and his crew also beached their ship, built shelter, and spent a harrowing winter encamped on Charlton Island, at the south end of the sea which was later named for him: James Bay. After a desperate struggle against pack ice, the men escaped Hudson Bay the next summer and arrived home in October, their ship "broken and bruis'd." King Charles I welcomed the captain of this failed but heroic expedition and commanded him to write his story. Our selection comes from The Dangerous Voyage of Capt. Thomas James, in His Intended Discovery of a North West Passage into the South Sea, *published in 1633 (our text follows the spelling, capitalization and punctuation of the revised 1740 edition). In this passage James tells how he and his men built the shelter that saved their lives.*

1   When I first resolv'd to build a House, I chose the warmest and convenientest Place, and the nearest the Ship withal. It was among a Tuft of thick Trees, under a South Bank, about a slight Shot from the Sea Side. True it is, that at that Time we could not dig into the Ground, to make us a Hole, or Cave, in the Earth, which had been the best Way, because we found Water digging within two Foot; and therefore that Project fail'd. It was a white light Sand; so that we could, by no Means, make up a Mud-Wall. As for Stones, there were none near us; moreover, we were all now cover'd with the Snow. We had no Boards for such a Purpose; and therefore we must do the best we could, with such Materials as we had about us.

2   The House was square, about 20 Foot every Way; as much namely, as our Main Course° could well cover: First, we drove strong Stakes into

---

*Editor's title.
°Main Course: a large sail, the lowest on a square-rigged mast.

the earth, round about: which we wattel'd° with Boughs, as thick as might be, beating them down very close. This our first Work was six Foot high on both Sides, but at the Ends, almost up to the very Top. There we left two Holes, for the Light to come in at; and the same Way the Smoke did vent out also. Moreover, I caus'd at both Ends, three Rows of thick Bush Trees, to be stuck up, as close together as possible. Then at a Distance from the House, we cut down Trees; proportioning them into Lengths of 6 Foot, with which we made a Pile on both Sides, 6 Foot thick, and 6 Foot high; but at both Ends, 10 Foot high, and 6 Foot thick. We left a little low Door to creep into, and a Portal before that, made with Piles of Wood, that the Wind might not blow into it. We next fasten'd a rough Tree aloft over all: Upon which we laid our Rafters; and our Main Course over them again, which lying thwartways over all, reach'd down to the very Ground, on either Side. And this was the Fabrick of the Outside of it. On the Inside, we made fast our Bonnet Sails° round about. Then we drove in Stakes, and made us Bedstead Frames; about 3 Sides of the House, which Bedsteads were double, one under another, the lowermost being a Foot from the Ground: These, we first fill'd with Boughs, then we laid our spare Sails on that, and then our Bedding and Cloaths. We made a Hearth, in the Middle of the House, and on it made our Fire: Some Boards we laid round about our Hearth, to stand upon, that the cold Damp should not strike up into us. With our Waste Cloaths, we made us Canopies and Curtains; others did the like with our small Sails. Our second House was not past 20 Foot distant from this, and made for the Wattling much after the same Manner, but it was less,° and cover'd with our Fore-Course°: It had no Piles on the South Side; but in Lieu of that, we pil'd up all our Chests, on the Inside: And indeed the Reflex of the Heat of the Fire against them, did make it warmer than the Mansion House. In this House, we dress'd our Victuals; and the subordinate Crew did refresh themselves all Day in it. A third House, which was our Store-house, about 29 Paces off from this; for fear of firing. This House was only a rough Tree fasten'd aloft, with Rafters laid from it to the Ground, and cover'd over with our new Suit of Sails. On the Inside, we had laid small Trees, and cover'd them over with Boughs; and so stored up our Bread, and Fish in it, about 2 Foot from the Ground, the better to preserve them. Other Things lay more carelessly.

°wattel'd (wattled) with Boughs: Wattling is the process of weaving small branches or twigs into a framework of larger ones to produce a wall, roof or fence.
°Bonnet Sails: a bonnet sail is an additional strip of canvas laced to the bottom of a foresail or jib.
°less: smaller.
°Fore-Course: on a square-rigged ship, the bottom sail of the mast nearest the bow.

3   Long before *Christmas,* our Mansion House was cover'd thick over with Snow, almost to the very Roof of it. And so likewise was our second House; but our Storehouse all over; by Reason we made no Fire in it. Thus we seem'd to live in a Heap, and Wilderness of Snow; forth of our Doors we could not go, but upon the Snow; in which we made us Paths middle deep in some Places; and in one special Place, the Length of ten Steps. To do this, we must shovel away the Snow first; and then by treading, make it something hard under Foot: The Snow in this Path, was a full Yard thick under us. And this was our best Gallery for the sick Men; and for mine own ordinary Walking. And both Houses and Walks, we daily accommodated more and more, and made fitter for our Uses.

△△△

Further Reading:

Captain Thomas James, *The Dangerous Voyage of Capt. Thomas James.* . . .
H. P. Biggar, ed., *The Voyages of Jacques Cartier*
Joe Armstrong, *Champlain*
Samuel Hearne, *Journey from Prince of Wales's Fort in Hudson's Bay to the Northern Ocean.* . . .

Structure:

1. In his *process analysis* how closely does Captain James follow the chronological order in which his "Mansion House" of Charlton Island would have been built?
2. Point out at least ten time signals (such as "next" or "then") which direct and speed the process analysis.
3. Does James omit any main steps of his process analysis? Any minor steps?
4. Do the short accounts of building the second and third shelters just dilute the focus, or do they contribute?

Style:

1. Clearly our language has changed since the time of Captain James. How do you react to the aspects of his STYLE listed below? Which seem weaker than their replacements in contemporary English? Which seem stronger?
   A. Very long sentences joined with many commas, semicolons and colons
   B. Much more capitalization, almost always of nouns
   C. Variant spellings
   D. Shortened suffixes (as in "resolv'd," of sentence 1)
   E. Very long paragraphs

F. A preference for short words (Hold the text at arm's length to judge the "look" of the page. Now do the same with any recent selection in this book, to compare the proportion of short and long words.)

2. Captain James dedicated his book to King Charles I, saying "Your Majesty will please to consider, That they were rough Elements, which I had to do withal; and will vouchsafe to pardon, if a Seaman's Stile be like what he most converseth with." Do you view James' STYLE as deliberately crafted, or is it really like a sailor's plain speech? Does he just pretend humility or really apologize? Do *you* consider a plain style inferior?

Ideas for Discussion and Writing:

1. How easy or difficult would it be to follow James' directions?
2. Later in the book some crew members die of scurvy, drowning or cold. All narrowly escape death as rocks, pack ice and icebergs grind their little ship. Were the planners of this expedition wrong? Did the possible gain justify the cost in misery and human life?
3. **PROCESS IN WRITING:** *Think of something you have made (a radio, an outfit, a painting, a piece of furniture, etc.). Decide whether to just tell how you made it, or to give your reader actual directions. First take a page of notes. Now draft a process analysis in chronological order. If these are directions, scrutinize them to see if they are clear and complete, then revise accordingly. Have you used terms new to your audience? Have you added time signals to move the process along? Have you used full sentences rather than recipe language? Have you read aloud to revise wordiness and repetition? Finally, if a diagram will help, add it to your good copy.*

Note: See also the Topics for Writing at the end of this chapter.

Topics for Writing

Chapter 8: Process Analysis

Tell your reader how to perform one of these processes. (See also the guidelines that follow.)

1. Enjoy winter
2. Find a summer job
3. Survive driving in city traffic
4. Avoid date rape
5. Choose a computer
6. Gain self-confidence
7. Choose your style in clothing
8. Survive eating at the school cafeteria
9. Choose an apartment
10. Get along with roommates
11. Update your wardrobe
12. Break off a romance
13. Survive as a homeless person
14. Have a successful job interview
15. Play a sport that is not known in Canada
16. Make friends in school
17. Choose a life partner
18. Study better in less time
19. Choose a sound system
20. Stop smoking
21. Get along with a new step-parent and step-brothers and sisters
22. Keep from being laid off
23. Decorate a room on a small budget
24. Choose a musical instrument
25. Eat better for less
26. Learn to dance
27. Avoid debt
28. Get along without owning a car
29. Communicate through E-mail
30. Avoid criminal attack in the big city at night

Process in Writing: Guidelines

Follow at least some of these steps in writing your essay of process analysis (your teacher may suggest which ones).

1. *Spend time deciding which topic most appeals to you, so your motivation will increase your performance.*

2. *Visualize your audience (see step 6 below), and choose the level of terminology accordingly.*

3. *Fill a page with brief notes. Scan and sort them to choose the steps of your process analysis, and their order.*

4. *Write a rapid first draft, double-spaced, not stopping now to revise or edit. If you do notice a word that needs replacing or a passage that needs work, underline it so you can find and fix it later.*

5. *When this draft has "cooled off," look it over. Are all steps of the process given? Do* TRANSITIONS *introduce them? In technical topics like those on computers or E-mail, have you defined terms that may puzzle your audience? Revise accordingly.*

6. *Now share the second draft with a group of classmates. Do they believe they could actually follow your directions? If not, revise.*

7. *If you have consulted books or periodicals to write this paper, follow standard practice in quoting and in documenting your sources. Remember that plagiarism is a serious offence.*

8. *As you produce your good copy, edit for spelling and grammar, then proofread word by word. If you have used a computer, save the essay on disk in case your teacher suggests further revisions.*

H.A. Roberts/Comstock Inc.

"To think about thermonuclear war in the abstract is obscene. To think about any kind of warfare with less than the whole of our mind and imagination is obscene. This is the worst treason."

—*Kildare Dobbs, "The Scar"*

CHAPTER

⟨9⟩

ARGUMENTATION AND PERSUASION

Therefore. . . .

So far the essays in this book have taken many paths in developing their subject. They have narrated events, they have described, they have explained, and some have entertained. But you have surely realized that in one way or another, whatever else they do, almost all the selections have tried to make a point. After all, an essay without a point is "pointless." The very use of a thesis statement implies a main idea or opinion. In this final chapter, we now focus more closely on how the writer makes that point. The process takes two complementary forms: *argumentation* and *persuasion.*

Argumentation

This word has a broad set of meanings, but here we will consider it the writer's attempt to convince the reader *through logic.* This stance implies respect: it considers the reader a mature individual capable of independent thought. It assumes the reader will also respect the thoughts of the writer, if those thoughts are presented in a logical way. In summary, the writer and reader are *partners:* since the writer does not play on the reader's emotions, the reader considers the argument with a more open mind. If the logic makes sense, the reader may be convinced. Argumentation through logic takes two opposite forms, *deduction* and *induction*. Let's look at each.

Deduction

Deduction accepts a general principle as true, then applies it to specific cases. For over two thousand years logicians have expressed this process in a formula called the *syllogism*. Here's a well-known example:

> **Major premise: All men are mortal.**
> **Minor premise: Socrates is a man.**
> **Conclusion: Socrates is mortal.**

This chain of reasoning is about as foolproof as any: since no human in the history of the world has yet lived much longer than a century, we feel safe in assuming that no one ever will; therefore "all men are mortal." And since all historical records about Socrates portray him as a man — not, say, as a rock or horse or tree — we accept the minor premise as well. Logic tells us that if both the major and minor premises are true, then the conclusion will inevitably be true as well.

But now let's look at a syllogism whose logic is not as clear:

> **Major premise: Progress is good.**
> **Minor premise: The automobile represents progress.**
> **Conclusion: The automobile is good.**

At first glance the argument may seem all right: it certainly reflects values common in our society. But let's examine the major premise, the foundation on which all the rest is built: is it true that "progress is good"? Well, how do we know until we define "progress"? Is it more jobs? More production? More cars? Higher sales? More consumption? A rising stock market? Or are all these the opposite of "progress" because our natural resources are dwindling, our highways are choked with traffic, our lakes and forests are dying of acid rain, the greenhouse effect is already disrupting our climate, and around the world two species of life per hour are becoming extinct? Our values will determine our response.

If we cannot agree on what "progress" is, how can we say that it is "good"? And how could we go on to our minor premise, saying that "the automobile represents progress"? How could we build even further on this shaky foundation, claiming in our conclusion that "the automobile is good"? Within its own framework the argument may be "valid" (or logical). But only those who accept the original premise will view the conclusion as true. Those who do not will reject it as false.

And that is the problem with deduction: not always can we agree on premises. Five hundred years ago society ran on deduction: the King or the Church or our parents told us what to believe, and we simply applied those principles to any case that came up. But in the 20th century many of us dislike being told what to think. Not only do many people now question systems of belief such as Marxism or codes of religion, but scientists even question the previously accepted "laws" of nature. How is a person to know what is true? It is therefore no coincidence that most contemporary essays argue not through deduction but through induction.

Induction

We have discussed how deduction applies a general rule to explain particular cases. Induction is the opposite: it first observes particular cases, then from them formulates a general rule. This is the basis of the scientific way, the procedure that enables humans to conquer disease, multiply food production and travel to the moon. It can produce faulty results, just like deduction, but the open mind required to use it appeals to our modern sensibilities. Let's take an example.

> **After a summer in the factory Joan thought she could afford a car, so the week before school began she bought a sporty red three-year-old Japanese model. Speeding around town with the stereo turned up was so much fun that she didn't mind the $350-a-month payments. But when the insurance company hit her for $2500 as a new driver, her savings took a dive. Each month she found herself paying $100 for gas and $150 for parking. A fall tuneup set her back $200, and new tires $400. Then came the repairs: $250 for brakes, $350 for a clutch, and $225 for an exhaust system. In desperation Joan took a part-time job selling shoes. That helped her bankbook but took her study time. Two weeks after exams, holding a sickly grade report in her hand, Joan decided to sell the car. Nobody could have told her to, since, like most people, she likes to make up her own mind. But the long string of evidence did the teaching: now Joan knows, through *induction*, that as a student she cannot afford a car.**

Induction is not infallible. Conceivably Joan's next car might never need a repair. Next year insurance might somehow drop from $2500 to, say, $75. Gas stations might sell premium for 10¢ a litre, and on Boxing Day a good tire might cost $1.99. Anything is possible. But Joan feels that the consistency of her results — the steady high cost of her car ownership — will *probably* not change. Likewise, the scientist believes that her or his years of research have yielded results that will not be disproven by the very next experiment. But in all humility both writer and scientist must consider the new principle not a fact, not an unchangeable law, but simply an idea with a very high probability of being true.

Finally, suppose that Joan analyzes her experience in an essay. If she sets up her paper as most essayists do, we will read her thesis statement near the beginning — even though the principle it states is the *result* of the evidence still to come. This positioning is not a flaw of logic: Joan simply *introduces* the main idea so we can see where we are going, then tells us how she arrived at it, letting her evidence lead inductively toward the main point which will be restated at the end. You will find this pattern at work in several of this chapter's inductive essays, for example the one by Margaret Atwood.

You will also find that, although deduction and induction represent opposite methods of logic, sometimes both are used in the same argument — as in the essay by Wendy Dennis. This does not necessarily mean weakness in logic either. Another link between these opposites is that most principles which we accept as true, and upon which we base our own deductions, originated in someone else's induction. (Newton arrived inductively at his theory of gravity, through evidence such as the famous apple that fell on his head; almost all of us now believe Newton and his theory without waiting for an apple, or anything else, to fall on our own heads.) Similarly, a conclusion we derive from our own induction could become the premise of someone else's deduction—a link in an ongoing chain of logic. To keep this chain from breaking, the individual has a double task: to check over any links provided by others, then to make her or his own link as strong as possible.

Persuasion

We have just seen how *argumentation* seeks to convince through logic. But, whether deductive or inductive, is logic enough? Now let's look at the complementary approach of persuasion, which attempts to convince through emotion. A century of inductive research into psychology has shown that we humans are seldom rational. Even when we think we are "reasoning," we are often building arguments merely to justify what we thought or felt already. It is possible to write an argumentative essay with enough restraint to be almost purely logical. But to most people the effort is difficult and unnatural, requiring a great deal of revision, and the result may seem cold and uninviting to those who have not spent years reading the almost pure argumentation of scholarly journals. Most professional writers would say that a little feeling and a little colour can help an essay. But how do we take this approach without slipping into dishonesty? Let's look now at the major techniques of *persuasion* — both their uses and abuses.

Word choice: Is a person "slim," "thin" or "skinny"? Is a governmental expenditure an "investment," a "cost," a "waste" or a "boondoggle"? Is an oil spill an "incident," an "accident," a "mistake," a "crime" or an "environmental tragedy"? Essayists tend to choose the term that reflects their feeling and the feeling they hope to encourage in the readers.

While deliberate choice of words is one of the central tasks of all writers, including essayists, let's not abuse the process. Bertrand Russell once quipped, "I am firm; you are stubborn; he is pig-headed." If too many of your word choices follow the model of "pig-headed," you will alarm an alert reader and unfairly overwhelm a careless one.

Example: Although examples form the basis of logical induction, they can also add colour and feeling to a persuasive essay. Choose vivid ones. An attempt to show old people as active may be helped by the example of your grandmother who skis. But avoid dubious cases like that of the man in Azerbaijan who is said to have ridden a horse at age 155.

Repetition: Although we try to cut accidental repetition from our writing (as in the case of one student who used the word "tire" 55 times in an essay about, you guessed it, tires), intentional repetition can build feeling. Stephen Leacock builds emphasis by using the word "eat" over and over in paragraph 25 of his essay (see p. 248), and in paragraphs 14-17 of her selection (see p. 313–314) Joy Kogawa builds feeling by starting a whole string of sentences with the contraction "it's."

Hyperbole (exaggeration): A humorist can exaggerate and get away with it, as Stephen Leacock does when he tells us "How to Live to Be 200." By contrast, an essay that is objective in tone should stay strictly with the truth. In her factual investigation of child abuse, Michele Landsberg writes that in one country girls only 13 and 14 years old "work 17-hour days at their sewing machines." While these numbers are shocking, if she had claimed the children worked 24 hours a day we would refuse to believe her, because no one can go without sleep at all.

Analogy and figures of speech: You have seen in Chapter 6 how we can suggest a point by comparing one thing with another from a different category: prose with music, a monster with the forestry industry, or a house with a ship at sea. Analogies, and their shorter cousins similes and metaphors, are powerful tools of persuasion; avoid abusing them through name-calling. Think twice before casting a political party as a dinosaur, entrepreneurs as piranhas, or police officers as gorillas. Remember, above all, that neither analogies nor figures of speech are logical proof of anything.

Irony: When in Chapter 4 Naheed Mustafa covers herself with the traditional *hijab* in order to be free, when in Chapter 8 Judy Stoffman describes the once-young athlete dying of old age, and when in this chapter Rita Schindler "thanks" her son's assailants for not killing him — we feel the power of irony. A writer can use this device for a lifetime without exhausting its emotional power; yet irony lends itself less easily to abuses than do many tools of persuasion, for both its use and its appreciation demand a certain exercise of intelligence.

Appeal to authority or prestige: Opponents of nuclear weapons love to quote Albert Einstein on their dangers; after all, since his discoveries made this hardware possible, he should know. We also invite our reader to believe what a famous economist says about money, what a judge says about law, or what an educator says about education. This approach appeals to our reader's ethical sense: he or she believes these people know the facts and tell the truth. But avoid the common abuse of quoting people on matters outside their competence — Wayne Gretzky on baseball, Hulk Hogan on communism, a disgraced politician on honesty, or a convicted murderer on religion.

Fright: You can be sure that a frightened reader is an interested reader, for fright is personal: what you say in your essay could be important! Avoid cheap effects, though. Frighten a reader only with facts that really are scary (such as the number of times computer error nearly launched a Third World War).

Climax: Whatever your argument, don't trail off from strong to weak. After a good introduction, drop to your least important or least dramatic point, then progress upward to your strongest. This very rise produces an emotion in the reader, like that of the concertgoer who thrills to the final chords of the "Hallelujah Chorus."

Playing Fair in Argumentation and Persuasion

We have looked at some abuses both of argumentation and of persuasion. Now read the following communication, an actual chain letter that arrived one day in the mail. What attempts does it make at *deduction* or *induction*? Are they logical? What attempts does it make at *persuasion*? Are they fair? (For your information, the person who received this letter did not send it on. So far he has not died or lost his job — but then, neither has he won a lottery!)

KISS SOMEONE YOU LOVE WHEN YOU GET THIS LETTER
AND MAKE SOME MAGIC

This paper has been sent to you for good luck. The original copy is in New England. It has been around the world nine times. The luck has sent it to you. You will receive good luck within four days of receiving this letter, provided you send it back out. THIS IS NO JOKE. You will receive it in the mail. Send copies to people that you think need good luck. Don't send money as fate has no price. Do not keep this letter. It must leave your hands within 96 hours. An R.A.F. officer became a hero. Joe Elliot received $40,000, and lost it because he broke the chain. While in the Philippines, Gene Welch lost his wife six days after receiving this letter. He failed to circulate the letter. However, before her death she had won $50,000.00 in a lottery. The money was transferred to him four days after he decided to mail out this letter. Please send twenty copies of this letter and see what happens in four days. The chain came from Venezuela and was written in South America. Since the copy must make a tour of the world you must make copies and send them to your friends and associates. After a few days you will get a surprise. This is true even if you are not superstitious. Do note the following: Constantine Dias received the chain in 1953. He asked his secretary to type twenty copies and send them out. A few days later he won a lottery of $2,000,000. Aria Daddit, an office employee, received the letter and forgot that it had to leave his hands within 96 hours. He lost his job. Later, finding the letter again, he mailed out twenty copies. A few days later he got a better job. Dalen Fairchild received the letter and not believing, threw it away. Nine days later he died. PLEASE SEND NO MONEY. PLEASE DON'T IGNORE THIS. IT WORKS!

Note: No essay in this chapter adopts a stance of pure logic to the exclusion of emotion, or of pure emotion to the exclusion of logic. The nine essays represent different proportions of both elements, and are arranged in approximate order from most argumentative to most persuasive.

For more examples of argumentation and persuasion, see these essays in other chapters:

Martin Hocking

Capping the Great Cup Debate

Few scientists could be better equipped to investigate the subject of our selection than Martin Hocking. With a Ph.D. in organic chemistry from the University of Southampton (1963), experience as a research chemist in industry, then extensive research and publication as associate professor of chemistry at the University of Victoria, Hocking has become a prominent voice in his field. He has advised government on scientific issues; has taught industrial and environmental chemistry for many years; holds eight patents in the fields of monomers, process chemistry and medicine; and has published over 60 scientific papers. It was his comparative analysis published in the journal Science *which in 1991 sparked debate on the environmental effects of paper cups and foam cups. Hocking concluded that, contrary to public opinion, foam was better. Some scientists questioned his emission figures and his view of paper mill energy use; others commended his open revealing of data sources, a practice not all scientists follow, and the relevance of his "cradle-to-grave" scope: from logging the raw resources to discarding the old cups in landfills. Then Hocking adapted his article for a general audience; on 16 February 1991* The Globe and Mail *published our selection.*

1 The polystyrene foam cup has long suffered contempt from an environmentally aware public that assumes paper cups are ecologically friendlier. It's easy to understand why: paper cups are made out of a wood product, a renewable resource, and therefore would seem to be the proper conservationist choice.

2 In fact, foam cups are proving to be the environmentally better choice.

3 For one thing, people overlook the fact that logging necessary for the paper industry has adverse effects on the landscape that range from the construction of roads to clear-cutting practices that typically increase the likelihood of flood and drought in immediate watershed areas.

4 In addition, a review of other factors does not support the use of paper. A comparative analysis of paper versus polystyrene conducted by us at the University of Victoria leads to the inevitable conclusion that foam cups are better from a range of standpoints.

5 Here are the principal findings of the analysis:

286

Hydrocarbons

The extraction and delivery of oil and gas hydrocarbons have a sig-   6
nificant impact on sensitive ecosystems. A polyfoam cup is made entirely from hydrocarbons, but a similar amount of hydrocarbons are
also used to produce a paper cup.

Paper cups are made from bleached pulp, which in turn is obtained   7
from wood chips. Although bark, some wood waste, and organic residues
from chemical pulping are burned to supply part of the energy required
in papermaking, fuel oil or gas is used to provide much of the rest. Even
more petroleum is needed if the paper cup has a plastic or wax coating.

Inorganic chemicals

In the making of paper cups, relatively small amounts of sodium   8
hydroxide or sodium sulphate are needed for chemical pulping makeup
requirements, since the recycling of these in the kraft pulping process
is quite efficient. But larger amounts of chlorine, sodium hydroxide,
sodium chlorate, sulphuric acid, sulphur dioxide and calcium hydroxide are normally used on a once-through basis to the extent of 160 to
200 kilograms per metric ton of pulp.

The total non-recycled chemical requirement works out to an average   9
of about 1.8 grams per cup.

Polystyrene is far superior to wood pulp for cup construction; only   10
about one-sixth as much material is needed to produce a foam cup.
Chemical requirements for the polystyrene foam cup are small because
several of the stages in its preparation use catalysts that nudge the
process along without being consumed themselves.

Alkylation of benzene with ethene (ethylene) also uses aluminum   11
chloride catalytically to the extent of about 10 kilograms per metric ton
of ethylbenzene produced.

The spent aluminum chloride is later neutralized with roughly the   12
same amount of sodium hydroxide. Further small amounts of sulphuric
acid and sodium hydroxide are also consumed to give a total chemical
requirement of about 33 kilograms per metric ton of polystyrene.

This works out to 0.05 grams per cup, or about 3 per cent of the   13
chemical requirement of the paper cup.

Utility consumption

In terms of energy consumption, polystyrene cups also appear to   14
come out ahead. One paper cup consumes about 12 times as much steam,
36 times as much electricity, and twice as much cooling water as one polystyrene foam cup, while producing 58 times the volume of waste water.

The contaminants present in the waste water from pulping and bleach-   15
ing operations are removed to varying degrees, but the residuals (with
the exception of metal salts) still amount to 10 to 100 times those
present in the waste-water streams from polystyrene processing.

Air pollution

16   The wholesale price of a paper cup is about 2.5 times that of polyfoam since it consumes more in terms of raw materials and energy. But their respective purchase prices are not so closely linked to the environmental costs of productions and recycling or final disposal. Air emissions total 22.7 kilograms per metric ton of bleached pulp compared to about 53 kilograms per metric ton of polystyrene.

17   On a per-cup basis, however, this comparison becomes 0.23 grams for paper versus 0.08 grams for polyfoam.

Emissions

18   In terms of mass, the 43 kilograms of pentane employed as the blowing agent for each metric ton of the foamable beads used to make polystyrene foam cups is the largest single emission to air from the two technologies.

19   Pentane's atmospheric lifetime is estimated to be seven years or less, about a tenth that of the chlorofluorocarbons formerly used in some foamable beads. Unlike the chlorofluorocarbons, pentane would tend to cause a net increase in ozone concentrations, both at ground level and in the stratosphere.

20   However, its contributions to atmospheric ozone and as a "greenhouse effect" gas are almost certainly less than those of the methane losses generated from disposal of paper cups in landfill sites.

21   If the six metric tons of paper equivalent to a metric ton of polystyrene completely biodegrade anaerobically in a landfill, theoretically the paper could generate 2,370 kilograms of methane along with 3,260 kilograms of carbon dioxide.

22   Both are "greenhouse gases" that contribute to global warming.

Recycling

23   The technical side of recycle capability with polystyrene foam is straightforward. All that is required is granulation and washing, followed by hot-air drying and re-extrusion of the resin for re-use. Though recycled resin may not be used in food applications, this only partially limits the many possible uses for recycled polystyrene products.

24   Such uses are in packaging materials, insulation, flotation billets, patio furniture and drainage tiles.

25   An improved collection infrastructure is all that is needed to make this option a more significant reality and convert this perceived negative aspect of polyfoam use to a positive one.

26   Paper cups use a non-water soluble hot melt or solvent-based adhesive to hold the parts together.

27   For this reason, cups are technically excluded from paper recycling programs because the adhesive resin cannot be removed during repulping.

If the paper is coated with a plastic film or wax, this too prevents recycling, at least for renewed paper products. 28

Final disposal

Polystyrene is relatively inert to decomposition when discarded in landfill. However, there is also increasing evidence that disposal of paper to landfill does not necessarily result in degradation or biodecomposition, particularly in arid regions. 29

In wet landfills, where degradation occurs, the paper cup produces methane, a gas which has five to 20 times greater global-warming effect than carbon dioxide. Water-soluble fragments of cellulose from the decomposition also contribute biochemical oxygen demand to leachate (any water that percolates through the land-filled waste) from the landfill. 30

Leachate may be treated to remove contaminants to control environmental impact on discharge, or may be lost to surface waters or underground aquifers (a porous rock layer that holds water) to exacerbate the oxygen demand in these raw water sources. 31

Thus, as a result of our analysis, it would appear that polystyrene foam cups are the ecologically better choice. 32

At the very least, they appear to be no worse than paper in one-use applications, contrary to the instinctive consumer impression. 33

ΔΔΔΔΔΔΔΔΔΔΔΔΔΔΔΔΔΔΔΔΔΔΔΔΔΔΔΔΔΔΔΔΔΔΔΔΔΔΔΔΔΔΔΔΔ

Further Reading:

Peeter Kruus, *Chemicals in the Environment*

Structure:

1. How does the opening prepare us for Hocking's argument?
2. Identify the THESIS STATEMENT.
3. Hocking's argument is a model *comparison and contrast* of paper and foam cups, organized *point by point*. Identify each of these major points.
4. Find three passages where Hocking reasons through *cause and effect*.
5. Do the subtitles help? Have you tried subtitles yourself?

Style:

1. What *audience* does Hocking write for in this condensation of a scientific journal article? Are the many technical terms a barrier to these readers? Are they to you? Why or why not?

Argumentation and Persuasion:

1. Written by a scientist, "Capping the Great Cup Debate" is the most *argumentative* essay of this chapter. Can you find any passage at all that appeals to *emotion* rather than *reason*? Does all the logic reduce your interest in this essay, or does the quality of thought increase it?

2. As the introduction to this chapter suggests, science is based on *induction*. In saying "A comparative analysis . . . leads to the inevitable conclusion that foam cups are better. . . ." (paragraph 4), scientist Martin Hocking in fact labels his argument as *inductive*. Is he right? How fully does he base his conclusion on evidence? Does he successfully avoid reasoning from prior values or assumptions?

3. How much of this argument consists of *examples*? How many are numeric (statistics)?

4. *Comparison and contrast, cause and effect,* massive *examples* and *process analysis* all help Hocking make his point. Do you think he planned to use these all, or did some just appear as he wrote? How fully *should* we organize before writing?

Ideas for Discussion and Writing:

1. Did you think paper cups were better for the environment? Do you still, or did Hocking change your mind? Tell why.

2. "Think globally, act locally," say conservationists. Consider the pollution caused by disposable pens, lighters, razors, towels and tissues, plastic wrap, diapers, paper plates — and cups, whether paper or foam. What "acts" could you perform to help "globally"?

3. Name one act you already perform to reduce pollution.

4. Is science outside the realm of values? Or are scientists responsible for the good and bad effects of their discoveries? Defend your view with examples, including Hocking.

5. Which is more important to you right now, the economy or the environment? Which will seem more important by the time you have grandchildren? What implications can you *deduce* from your answer?

6. **PROCESS IN WRITING:** *At the library, read and take notes on how vitamin C affects humans, making sure your evidence comes from the work of scientists, not health faddists. Let this collected evidence lead to your* THESIS: *whether or not taking large doses of vitamin C improves our health. Now write your argument of induction, using any form(s) of organization that work, but basing your argument very heavily on evidence. (Your teacher may advise whether to document informally or use full MLA style.) Proofread any quotations word for word against the originals, and be sure to enclose them, even short phrases of two or three words, in quotation marks. Now read your draft aloud. Does its* STYLE *promote thought or feeling? Replace any loaded or very* INFORMAL *words with more* OBJECTIVE *ones. State your conclu-*

sion *clearly. Finally, edit for things like spelling and grammar as you produce the good version.*

Note: See also the Topics for Writing at the end of this chapter.

Kildare Dobbs

The Scar *

Kildare Dobbs was born in Meerut, Uttar Pradesh, India in 1923, was educated in Ireland, then during the Second World War spent five years in the Royal Navy. After the war he worked in the British Colonial Service in Tanganyika and, after earning an M.A. at Cambridge, came in 1952 to Canada. Dobbs has been a teacher, editor for Macmillan, managing editor of Saturday Night, *and book editor of* The Toronto Star. *He was one of the founders, in 1956, of the* Tamarack Review. *He is also the author of several books, among them* Running to Paradise *(essays, 1962, winner of the Governor General's Award);* Canada *(an illustrated travel book, 1964);* Reading the Time *(essays, 1968);* The Great Fur Opera *(a comic history of the Hudson's Bay Company, 1970);* Pride and Fall *(short fiction, 1981);* Anatolian Suite *(travel, 1989); and* Ribbon of Highway *(travel, 1992). Our selection is from* Reading the Time. *It is about an event Dobbs did not witness, yet the vivid details with which he supports his argument recreate all too clearly what that event must have been like.*

1   This is the story I was told in 1963 by Emiko Okamoto, a young Japanese woman who had come to live in Toronto. She spoke through an interpreter, since at that time she knew no English. It is Emiko's story, although I have had to complete it from other sources.

2   But why am I telling it? Everyone knows how terrible this story is. Everyone knows the truth of what von Clausewitz said: "Force to meet force arms itself with the inventions of art and science." First the bow-and-arrow, then Greek fire, gunpowder, poison-gas — and so on up the lethal scale. These things, we're told, should be considered calmly. No sweat — we should think about the unthinkable, or so Herman Kahn suggests, dispassionately. And he writes: "We do not expect illustrations in a book of surgery to be captioned 'Good health is preferable to this kind of cancer.' Excessive comments such as 'And now there is a lot of blood' or 'This particular cut really hurts' are out of place. . . . To dwell on such things is morbid." Perhaps the answer to Herman Kahn is

---

*Editor's title.

that if surgeons hadn't dwelt on those things we wouldn't now have anaesthetics, or artery forceps either, for that matter.

To think about thermonuclear war in the abstract is obscene. To think about any kind of warfare with less than the whole of our mind and imagination is obscene. This is the worst treason. 3

Before that morning in 1945 only a few conventional bombs, none of which did any great damage, had fallen on the city. Fleets of U.S. bombers had, however, devastated many cities round about, and Hiroshima had begun a program of evacuation which had reduced its population from 380,000 to some 245,000. Among the evacuees were Emiko and her family. 4

"We were moved out to Otake, a town about an hour's train-ride out of the city," Emiko told me. She had been a fifteen-year-old student in 1945. Fragile and vivacious, versed in the gentle traditions of the tea ceremony and flower arrangement, Emiko still had an air of the frail school-child when I talked with her. Every day, she and her sister Hideko used to commute into Hiroshima to school. Hideko was thirteen. Their father was an antique-dealer and he owned a house in the city, although it was empty now. Tetsuro, Emiko's thirteen-year-old brother, was at the Manchurian front with the Imperial Army. Her mother was kept busy looking after the children, for her youngest daughter Eiko was sick with heart trouble, and rations were scarce. All of them were undernourished. 5

The night of August 5, 1945, little Eiko was dangerously ill. She was not expected to live. Everybody took turns watching by her bed, soothing her by massaging her arms and legs. Emiko retired at 8:30 (most Japanese people go to bed early) and at midnight was roused to take her turn with the sick girl. At 2 a.m. she went back to sleep. 6

While Emiko slept, the *Enola Gay*, a U.S. B-29 carrying the world's first operational atom bomb, was already in the air. She had taken off from the Pacific island of Iwo Jima at 1:45 a.m., and now Captain William Parsons, U.S.N. ordnance expert, was busy in her bomb-hold with the final assembly of Little Boy. Little Boy looked much like an outsize T.N.T. block-buster but the crew knew there was something different about him. Only Parsons and the pilot, Colonel Paul Tibbets, knew exactly in what manner Little Boy was different. Course was set for Hiroshima. 7

Emiko slept. 8

On board the *Enola Gay* co-pilot Captain Robert Lewis was writing up his personal log. "After leaving Iwo," he recorded, "we began to pick up some low stratus and before very long we were flying on top of an under-cast. Outside of a thin, high cirrus and the low stuff, it's a very beautiful day." 9

Emiko and Hideko were up at six in the morning. They dressed in the uniform of their women's college — white blouse, quilted hat, and 10 black skirt — breakfasted and packed their aluminum lunch-boxes with white rice and eggs. These they stuffed into their shoulder bags as they hurried for the seven-o'clock train to Hiroshima. Today there would be no classes. Along with many women's groups, high school students, and others, the sisters were going to work on demolition. The city had begun a project of clearance to make fire-breaks in its downtown huddle of wood and paper buildings.

11   It was a lovely morning.

12   While the two young girls were at breakfast, Captain Lewis, over the Pacific, had made an entry in his log. "We are loaded. The bomb is now alive, and it's a funny feeling knowing it's right in back of you. Knock wood!"

13   In the train Hideko suddenly said she was hungry. She wanted to eat her lunch. Emiko dissuaded her: she'd be much hungrier later on. The two sisters argued, but Hideko at last agreed to keep her lunch till later. They decided to meet at the main station that afternoon and catch the five-o'clock train home. By now they had arrived at the first of Hiroshima's three stations. This was where Hideko got off, for she was to work in a different area from her sister. "Sayonara!" she called. "Goodbye." Emiko never saw her again.

14   There had been an air-raid at 7 a.m., but before Emiko arrived at Hiroshima's main station, two stops farther on, the sirens had sounded the all-clear. Just after eight, Emiko stepped off the train, walked through the station, and waited in the morning sunshine for her streetcar.

15   At about the same moment Lewis was writing in his log. "There'll be a short intermission while we bomb our target."

16   It was hot in the sun. Emiko saw a class-mate and greeted her. Together they moved back into the shade of a high concrete wall to chat. Emiko looked up at the sky and saw, far up in the cloudless blue, a single B-29.

17   It was exactly 8:10 a.m. The other people waiting for the streetcar saw it too and began to discuss it anxiously. Emiko felt scared. She felt that at all costs she must go on talking to her friend. Just as she was thinking this, there was a tremendous greenish-white flash in the sky. It was far brighter than the sun. Emiko afterwards remembered vaguely that there was a roaring or a rushing sound as well, but she was not sure, for just at that moment she lost consciousness.

18   "About 15 seconds after the flash," noted Lewis, 30,000 feet high and several miles away, "there were two very distinct slaps on the ship from the blast and the shock wave. That was all the physical effect we felt. We turned the ship so that we could observe the results."

19   When Emiko came to, she was lying on her face about forty feet away from where she had been standing. She was not aware of any pain. Her first thought was: "I'm alive!" She lifted her head slowly and looked about her. It was growing dark. The air was seething with dust and

black smoke. There was a smell of burning. Emiko felt something trickle into her eyes, tasted it in her mouth. Gingerly she put a hand to her head, then looked at it. She saw with a shock that it was covered with blood.

She did not give a thought to Hideko. It did not occur to her that her sister who was in another part of the city could possibly have been in danger. Like most of the survivors, Emiko assumed she had been close to a direct hit by a conventional bomb. She thought it had fallen on the post-office next to the station. With a hurt child's panic, Emiko, streaming with blood from gashes in her scalp, ran blindly in search of her mother and father.

The people standing in front of the station had been burned to death instantly (a shadow had saved Emiko from the flash). The people inside the station had been crushed by falling masonry. Emiko heard their faint cries, saw hands scrabbling weakly from under the collapsed platform. All around her the maimed survivors were running and stumbling away from the roaring furnace that had been a city. She ran with them toward the mountains that ring the landward side of Hiroshima.

From the *Enola Gay*, the strangers from North America looked down at their handiwork. "There, in front of our eyes," wrote Lewis, "was without a doubt the greatest explosion man had ever witnessed. The city was nine-tenths covered with smoke of a boiling nature, which seemed to indicate buildings blowing up, and a large white cloud which in less than three minutes reached 30,000 feet, then went to at least 50,000 feet."

Far below, on the edge of this cauldron of smoke, at a distance of some 2,500 yards from the blast's epicentre, Emiko ran with the rest of the living. Some who could not run limped or dragged themselves along. Others were carried. Many, hideously burned, were screaming with pain; when they tripped they lay where they had fallen. There was a man whose face had been ripped open from mouth to ear, another whose forehead was a gaping wound. A young soldier was running with a foot-long splinter of bamboo protruding from one eye. But these, like Emiko, were the lightly wounded.

Some of the burned people had been literally roasted. Skin hung from their flesh like sodden tissue paper. They did not bleed but plasma dripped from their seared limbs.

The *Enola Gay*, mission completed, was returning to base. Lewis sought words to express his feelings, the feelings of all the crew. "I might say," he wrote, "I might say 'My God! What have we done?'"

Emiko ran. When she had reached the safety of the mountain she remembered that she still had her shoulder bag. There was a small first-aid kit in it and she applied ointment to her wounds and to a small cut in her left hand. She bandaged her head.

Emiko looked back at the city. It was a lake of fire. All around her the burned fugitives cried out in pain. Some were scorched on one side only. Others, naked and flayed, were burned all over. They were too many to help and most of them were dying. Emiko followed the walking wounded along a back road, still delirious, expecting suddenly to meet her father and mother.

28   The thousands dying by the roadside called feebly for help or water. Some of the more lightly injured were already walking in the other direction, back towards the flames. Others, with hardly any visible wounds, stopped, turned ashy pale, and died within minutes. No one knew then that they were victims of radiation.

29   Emiko reached the suburb of Nakayama.

30   Far off in the *Enola Gay*, Lewis, who had seen none of this, had been writing, "If I live a hundred years, I'll never get those few minutes out of my mind. Looking at Captain Parsons, why he is as confounded as the rest, and he is supposed to have known everything and expected this to happen. . . ."

31   At Nakayama, Emiko stood in line at a depot where riceballs were being distributed. Though it distressed her that the badly maimed could hardly feed themselves, the child found she was hungry. It was about 6 p.m. now. A little farther on, at Gion, a farmer called her by name. She did not recognize him, but it seemed he came monthly to her home to collect manure. The farmer took Emiko by the hand, led her to his own house, where his wife bathed her and fed her a meal of white rice. Then the child continued on her way. She passed another town where there were hundreds of injured. The dead were being hauled away in trucks. Among the injured a woman of about forty-five was waving frantically and muttering to herself. Emiko brought this woman a little water in a pumpkin leaf. She felt guilty about it; the schoolgirls had been warned not to give water to the seriously wounded. Emiko comforted herself with the thought that the woman would die soon anyway.

32   At Koi, she found standing-room in a train. It was heading for Otake with a full load of wounded. Many were put off at Ono, where there was a hospital; and two hours later the train rolled into Otake station. It was around 10 p.m.

33   A great crowd had gathered to look for their relations. It was a nightmare, Emiko remembered years afterwards; people were calling their dear kinfolk by name, searching frantically. It was necessary to call them by name, since most were so disfigured as to be unrecognizable. Doctors in the town council offices stitched Emiko's head-wounds. The place was crowded with casualties lying on the floor. Many died as Emiko watched.

34   The town council authorities made a strange announcement. They said a new and mysterious kind of bomb had fallen in Hiroshima. People were advised to stay away from the ruins.

Home at midnight, Emiko found her parents so happy to see her that they could not even cry. They could only give thanks that she was safe. Then they asked, "Where is your sister?" [35]

For ten long days, while Emiko walked daily one and a half miles to have her wounds dressed with fresh gauze, her father searched the rubble of Hiroshima for his lost child. He could not have hoped to find her alive. All, as far as the eye could see, was a desolation of charred ashes and wreckage, relieved only by a few jagged ruins and by the seven estuarial rivers that flowed through the waste delta. The banks of these rivers were covered with the dead and in the rising tidal waters floated thousands of corpses. On one broad street in the Hakushima district the crowds who had been thronging there were all naked and scorched cadavers. Of thousands of others there was no trace at all. A fire several times hotter than the surface of the sun had turned them instantly to vapour. [36]

On August 11 came the news that Nagasaki had suffered the same fate as Hiroshima; it was whispered that Japan had attacked the United States mainland with similar mysterious weapons. With the lavish circumstantiality of rumour, it was said that two out of a fleet of six-engined trans-Pacific bombers had failed to return. But on August 15, speaking for the first time over the radio to his people, the Emperor Hirohito announced his country's surrender. Emiko heard him. No more bombs! she thought. No more fear! The family did not learn till June the following year that this very day young Tetsuro had been killed in action in Manchuria. [37]

Emiko's wounds healed slowly. In mid-September they had closed with a thin layer of pinkish skin. There had been a shortage of antiseptics and Emiko was happy to be getting well. Her satisfaction was short-lived. Mysteriously she came down with diarrhoea and high fever. The fever continued for a month. Then one day she started to bleed from the gums, her mouth and throat become acutely inflamed, and her hair started to fall out. Through her delirium the child heard the doctors whisper by her pillow that she could not live. By now the doctors must have known that ionizing radiation caused such destruction of the blood's white cells that victims were left with little or no resistance against infection. [38]

Yet Emiko recovered. [39]

The wound on her hand, however, was particularly troublesome and did not heal for a long time. [40]

As she got better, Emiko began to acquire some notion of the fearful scale of the disaster. Few of her friends and acquaintances were still alive. But no one knew precisely how many had died in Hiroshima. To this day the claims of various agencies conflict. [41]

According to General Douglas MacArthur's headquarters, there were 78,150 dead and 13,083 missing. The United States Atomic Bomb Casu- [42]

alty Commission claims there were 79,000 dead. Both sets of figures are probably far too low. There's reason to believe that at the time of the surrender Japanese authorities lied about the number of survivors, exaggerating it to get extra medical supplies. The Japanese welfare ministry's figures of 260,000 dead and 163,263 missing may well be too high. But the very order of such discrepancies speaks volumes about the scale of the catastrophe. The dead were literally uncountable.

43   This appalling toll of human life had been exacted from a city that had been prepared for air attack in a state of full wartime readiness. All civil-defence services had been overwhelmed from the first moment and it was many hours before any sort of organized rescue and relief could be put into effect.

44   It's true that single raids using so-called conventional weapons on other cities such as Tokyo and Dresden inflicted far greater casualties. And that it could not matter much to a victim whether he was burnt alive by a fire-storm caused by phosphorus, or by napalm or by nuclear fission. Yet in the whole of human history so savage a massacre had never before been inflicted with a single blow. And modern thermonuclear weapons are upwards of 1,000 times more powerful and deadly than the Hiroshima bomb.

45   The white scar I saw on Emiko's small, fine-boned hand was a tiny metaphor, a faint but eloquent memento.

△ △

Further Reading:

Kildare Dobbs, *Reading the Time*
John Hershey, *Hiroshima*
Jonathan Schell, *The Fate of the Earth*
Lesley Choyce, *December Six/The Halifax Solution: An Alternative to Nuclear War*
Ernie Regehr and Simon Rosenblum, eds., *The Road to Peace*

Structure:

1. Identify Dobbs' THESIS STATEMENT, the principle from which his argument is deduced. In what very direct way does the rest of this selection teach us to apply that principle?
2. "The Scar" is mostly a *narrative*, in fact two parallel narratives. How do the stories of Emiko and of Captain Lewis complement each other? How does each focus differently on nuclear war?
3. Dobb's argument is a short essay enclosing a long narrative. Where does each part join the next? And what is the strategy behind this plan?

Style:

1. In his log Captain Lewis writes "it's a very beautiful day" (par. 9), and in paragraph 11 Dobbs adds "It was a lovely morning." What effect do these pleasant words have in the context of the situation? What literary device underlies their power?
2. Captain Lewis writes in his log, "There'll be a short intermission while we bomb our target" (par. 15). Do these words seem peculiar? If so, why?
3. In referring to the first operational nuclear bomb as "Little Boy" (par. 7), what does Dobbs add to the force of his narrative?
4. Paragraphs 23, 24, 27 and 36 are filled with gruesome details that show the effects of "Little Boy." Does this help Dobbs' argument? Do these details spur the reader to oppose nuclear weapons? Or, in their dreadfulness, do they move the reader to drop the subject and think of other things?
5. What qualifies the SYMBOL of Emiko's scar to close the essay?

Argumentation and Persuasion:

1. Dobbs' argument is *deductive*, based on his opening premise that "To think about thermonuclear war in the abstract is obscene. To think about any kind of warfare with less than the whole of our mind and imagination is obscene. This is the worst treason" (par. 3). Identify five passages where he shuns abstraction to dwell on the CONCRETE and personal experience of nuclear war. Does he apply his own thesis by using "the whole of [his] mind and imagination"?
2. Point out three passages where Dobbs shows Captain Lewis' abstract view of nuclear war to be "obscene." Does the *contrast* between Lewis' bird's-eye view and Emiko's ground-level view develop Dobbs' premise?
3. Does Dobbs make his point mostly through *argumentation* or *persuasion*? To what extent does he *argue* through objective logic, fact, and example? To what extent does he *persuade* through IRONY, loaded words, fright or other appeals to emotion?
4. In the closing, why does Dobbs shift from specific examples to generalizations and statistics (par. 42–44)?

Ideas for Discussion and Writing:

1. Albert Einstein, discoverer of the mathematics behind the atomic bomb, said that if he had foreseen the results of his work, he would have chosen to be a shoemaker. Do you consider Einstein and the scientists who worked on "Little Boy" responsible for the carnage in Hiroshima? Or should the scientist pursue abstract truth and leave the application to others?

2. The Cold War and the arms race between East and West are said to be over. Can we stop dreading nuclear weapons now? Or might new nations or terrorists obtain and use them? And what might we do to help prevent this?

3. According to the Washington, D.C. research group World Priorities, in 1986 when the arms race was still in full swing, the world was spending an average of $162 per person annually on the military but only 6¢ per person on peacekeeping. What is your response? How much better are we doing now?

4. In her 1993 book *A Matter of Survival: Canada in the 21st Century,* the Canadian economist Diane Francis states, "Already a global government has formed through the auspices of the United Nations and the G-7 process." Will a true global government prevent war? To what extent should Canada function as the "police" of a "global government" through its UN peacekeeping missions? Defend your view with examples.

5. **PROCESS IN WRITING:** *Politicians often state that one letter received from a citizen is worth a thousand votes. Decide whether you think Canada should spend more or less on the military. Now write to the Minister of Defence, arguing your point* deductively. *Apply your premise to a specific example or examples, such as tanks, fighter planes, destroyers, military bases, etc. As you look over your "discovery draft," see whether you have specialized in either argumentation or persuasion. If your treatment seems too extreme, modify it in your second draft with a dose of the other approach, to produce a combined treatment like that of Dobbs. In your final draft edit for conciseness (the best letters to politicians are short). Finally, you need no stamp to mail a letter to any member of Parliament.*

Note: See also the Topics for Writing at the end of this chapter.

Bonnie Laing

An Ode to the User-Friendly Pencil

"Anyone can write," says Bonnie Laing, "it's the rewrites that kill you." She gave her own essay three drafts on the very computer whose behaviour she describes below. When it "stops dead" she plans to acquire a faster model like the ones she uses at work. Laing is a freelance advertising copywriter, who has also written speeches and press releases for government. She regularly publishes essays and fiction as well; her humorous articles have appeared in Toronto Life, The Toronto Star *and* Canadian Living, *and her short fiction in* Fiddlehead, Quarry *and* Montreal. *In 1992 was published* The Marble Season, *a collection of her short stories about French-English relations in the East End of Montreal where she grew up. She also writes plays; since 1990 summer theatres across Canada have produced her comedy* Peggy *and* Grace. *Laing says that after completing an Honours B.A. in English at Queen's, she spent two years as a hippie in England. But once arrived in Toronto, she quickly entered advertising. As a "social marketer" of food and other "lifestyle products," Laing needs a keener sense of audience than even the essayist; in producing "target-specific" text, she says, you have to keep asking yourself "Who is this person I'm writing for?" Although she did have publication in mind, the audience of "An Ode to the User-Friendly Pencil" was herself: she vented her frustrations, felt better, then found that others liked the piece too. On April 29, 1989, The Toronto* Globe and Mail *published it.*

R ecently I acquired a computer. Or perhaps I should say it acquired me. My therapist claims that acknowledging the superior partner in a destructive relationship is the first step toward recovery. I should point out that prior to this acquisition, my idea of modern technology at its best was <u>frozen waffles</u>. My mastery of business machines had advanced only as far as <u>the stapler.</u>

I was persuaded to make this investment by well-meaning friends who said the word-processing capacity of a computer would (a) make me a better writer (b) make me a more productive writer and (c) make me a richer writer. I pointed out that Chaucer was a pretty good writer even though he used a quill, and Dickens managed to produce 15 novels and numerous collections of short stories without so much as a typewriter.

But I have to admit that option C got to me, even if I couldn't figure out how spending $3,000 on a piece of molded plastic was going to make me wealthier.

3   To date, my association with the computer has not been too successful. It has proved to be very sensitive to everything but my needs. At the last breakdown (its, not mine) the service man commented that it should have been called an Edsel, not an Epson, and suggested an exorcist be consulted. Needless to say, I am not yet in a position to open a numbered Swiss bank account.

4   But they say hardship teaches you who your friends are. And so, my computer experience has forced me to spend a lot more time with an old friend, the pencil. Its directness and simplicity have proven to be refreshing. In fact, the more I wrestled with my microchips (whatever they are), the more convinced I became that the pencil is superior to the computer. Allow me to cite a few examples.

5   To start with the purchase decision, you don't have to ask for a bank loan to buy a pencil. Since most pencils are not manufactured in Japan, you don't feel you're upsetting the nation's balance of trade by buying one.

6   In fact, pencils are constructed in part from that most Canadian of natural resources — wood. By buying pencils you create employment and prosperity for dozens of people in British Columbia. Well, a few anyway.

7   Of course, like most people I rarely *buy* a pencil, preferring to pick them up free from various places of employment, in the mistaken belief that they are a legitimate fringe benefit. It's best not to make that assumption about office computers.

8   Operationally, the pencil wins over the computer hands down. You can learn to use a pencil in less than 10 seconds. Personally, at the age of 2, I mastered the technology in 3.2 seconds. To be fair, erasing did take a further 2.4 seconds. I've never had to boot a pencil, interface with it or program it. I just write with it.

9   Compared to a computer, a pencil takes up far less space on a desk and it can be utilized in a car, bathroom or a telephone booth without the aid of batteries. You can even use one during an electrical storm. Pencils don't cause eye strain and no one has ever screamed, after four hours of creative endeavor, "The - - - - pencil ate my story!"

10   Pencils are wonderfully singleminded. They aren't used to open car doors, make the morning coffee or remind you that your Visa payment is overdue. They're user-friendly. (For the uninitiated, see comments on vocabulary.)

11   Of course, the technologically addicted among you will argue that the options of a pencil are rather limited. But the software of a pencil is both cheap and simple, consisting of a small rubber tip located at one end of the unit. A pencil is capable of producing more fonts or type-faces than any word processor, depending on the operator's skill.

Its graphic capability is limited only by the operator's talent, an element referred to as the Dürer or Da Vinci Factor. Backup to a pencil can usually be found in your purse or pocket. Although a pencil has no memory, many of us who write badly consider that to be an advantage.   12

But it's in the area of maintenance that the pencil really proves its superiority. Should a pencil break down, all you have to do to render it operational again, is buy a small plastic device enclosing a sharp metal strip, a purchase that can be made for under a dollar. A paring knife, a piece of broken glass or even your teeth can be used in an emergency. For the more technically advanced, an electronic pencil sharpener can be obtained, but I should point out that these devices don't run on electrical power but by devouring one-third of the pencil.   13

You never have to take a pencil to a service department located on an industrial site on the outskirts of Moose Factory. Neither do you have to do without them for two weeks before discovering that the malfunction is not covered by the warranty and that the replacement part is on a boat from Korea.   14

What finally won me over to the pencil was its lack of social pretension. For instance, very few people suffer the nagging doubt that their intelligence is below that of a pencil. No one has ever claimed that a pencil put them out of a job. And the pencil has not created a whole new class of workers who consider themselves superior to, let's say, crayon operators. At parties, you meet very few people who will discuss pencils with a fervor normally found only at student rallies in Tehran. Fewer people boast about being 'pencil literate.'   15

Of course, the pencil is not without its flaws. It has a nasty habit of hiding when most needed. If located beside a telephone, it will break spontaneously if a caller wishes to leave a message. Those aspiring to be professional writers should note that editors are unreasonably prejudiced against submissions in pencil.   16

But a pencil won't argue with you if you wish to write more than 50 lines to the page. It won't insist on correcting your whimsical use of grammar, and it won't be obsolete 10 seconds after you mortgage your first-born to buy one. Just in case you remain unconvinced, I ask you, can you imagine chewing on a computer while balancing your cheque book? And what do computer operators use to scratch that place in the middle of the back where they can't reach? The defence rests.   17

ΔΔΔΔΔΔΔΔΔΔΔΔΔΔΔΔΔΔΔΔΔΔΔΔΔΔΔΔΔΔΔΔΔΔΔΔΔΔΔΔ

Further Reading:

Bonnie Laing, *The Marble Season*
Heather Menzies, *Women and the Chip*
Henry David Thoreau, *Walden*

Structure:

1. Laing begins her whole essay of *contrast* with a series of shorter contrasts. In paragraph 1 identify each, and tell how it prepares us for the argument that follows.
2. Identify Laing's THESIS STATEMENT.
3. Identify the sentence of TRANSITION that moves us from Laing's introduction to the body of her argument.
4. Laing's argument is an exceptionally clear *comparison and contrast.* Does she proceed "point by point" or by "halves"?
5. The body of Laing's argument has four parts (par. 5–7, 8–12, 13–14, and 15). To organize her first draft she gave each part a heading, then later removed it. Restore those headings, labelling each division of her argument.
6. What techniques of closing do the final two paragraphs apply?

Style:

1. In paragraph 2 Laing dismisses her computer as a $3000 "piece of molded plastic." Point out five more IMAGES chosen to further her point of view.
2. In paragraph 4 Laing spends "a lot more time with an old friend, the pencil." Point out three other examples of PERSONIFICATION in her essay.
3. In paragraph 11 the pencil's "software" is its eraser. What device of humour has Laing used here?
4. In paragraph 8 Laing states, "I've never had to boot a pencil, interface with it or program it. I just write with it." Point out all the elements of repetition in this passage, and their effects. Are these effects accidental or deliberate?

Argumentation and Persuasion:

1. Laing's essay is a *comparison and contrast* as clearly organized and developed as any in the "Comparison and Contrast" chapter of this book. How well does the pattern lend itself to her *argumentative* and *persuasive* purpose? May essayists use any pattern that supports their purpose?
2. Is Laing's argument *deductive* or *inductive?* If it is deductive, point out its major and minor premises. If it is inductive, point out five major pieces of evidence that lead to the conclusion.
3. To what extent is this essay based on *argumentation?* To what extent on *persuasion?* Defend your answer with examples.
4. Laing's TONE is rich in IRONY. Point out every example of it in paragraph 15. What is the overall effect?

Ideas for Discussion and Writing:

1. Are you a technophobe, like Laing, or do you rejoice in high technology? Defend your answer with examples.

2. Do you now write with a computer? If so, tell all the contrasts you have personally experienced between "high-tech" and "low-tech" writing. Give specific examples.

3. The American philosopher Henry David Thoreau, who left town life for a cabin by Walden Pond, wrote "Our life is frittered away by detail. . . . Simplify, simplify." Has high technology simplified or complicated your life? Defend your view with examples.

4. **PROCESS IN WRITING:** *Choose one high-tech invention that you have used, and write an* inductive *essay that praises or condemns it. First freewrite on your subject for at least five minutes — automatically, never letting your user-friendly pencil stop — then look over what you have produced in order to learn your point of view. Now take more notes, gathering examples. Arrange these in order from least to most important, and from this rough outline write a draft. In the second draft adjust your tone: Is the whole argument serious and objective? Is it* argumentative? *Or is it more like Laing's essay: humorous, subjective, and therefore* persuasive? *Whichever it is, be consistent. Now read your essay aloud to family members or classmates, revise any part that fails to work on your audience, then write the final version.*

Note: See also the Topics for Writing at the end of this chapter.

Margaret Atwood

Canadians: What Do They Want?

Margaret Atwood is the nation's most celebrated writer, both at home and abroad. Born in Ottawa in 1939, she spent much of her childhood in the northern wilderness, where her father did biological research. After studies at the University of Toronto and at Radcliffe, Atwood published several books of poetry that explored the inability of language to express reality, and the alienation of women in society. Then her feminist vision emerged in fiction such as The Edible Woman *(1969),* Surfacing *(1972),* Life before Man *(1979),* Bodily Harm *(1981),* Cat's Eye *(1988) and* The Robber Bride *(1993). It was* The Handmaid's Tale, *though (1985), which became an international sensation and was made into a feature film. It portrays a future America devastated by nuclear pollution and ruled by a right-wing theocracy that reduces women to slaves. Like slaves of American Civil War times fleeing north to freedom, the narrator flees towards Canada.*

Atwood is a prolific essayist as well. She wrote our selection for the American political journal Mother Jones, *which in 1982 wished to know why many Canadians were anti-American. Atwood had a great many answers for them. Would she today? Rereading her argument in new times, we sense how far Canada has gone towards economic and cultural integration with its giant neighbour. With NAFTA now a fact, are Atwood's arguments of 1982 obsolete, a mere historical record? Is North America's continuing integration merely the new wisdom and realism of our time? Or was Atwood prophetic? Are Canadians losing their national sovereignty? Are they rushing towards cultural and even political assimilation by the nation which Atwood called an "empire"? These questions have never been more worth asking than now.*

1   Last month, during a poetry reading, I tried out a short prose poem called "How to Like Men." It began by suggesting that one start with the feet. Unfortunately, the question of jackboots soon arose, and things went on from there. After the reading I had a conversation with a young man who thought I had been unfair to men. He wanted men to be liked totally, not just from the heels to the knees, and not just as individuals but as a group; and he thought it negative and inegalitarian of me to have alluded to war and rape. I pointed out that as

far as any of us knew these were two activities not widely engaged in by women, but he was still upset. "We're both in this together," he protested. I admitted that this was so; but could he, maybe, see that our relative positions might be a little different.

This is the conversation one has with Americans, even, uh, *good* Americans, when the dinner-table conversation veers round to Canadian-American relations. "We're in this together," they like to say, especially when it comes to continental energy reserves. How do you *explain* to them, as delicately as possible, why they are not categorically beloved? It gets like the old Lifebuoy ads: even their best friends won't tell them. And Canadians are supposed to be their best friends, right? Members of the family?

Well, sort of. Across the river from Michigan, so near and yet so far, there I was at the age of eight, reading *their* Donald Duck comic books (originated, however, by one of *ours*; yes, Walt Disney's parents were Canadian) and coming at the end to Popsicle Pete, who promised me the earth if only I would save wrappers, but took it all away from me again with a single asterisk: Offer Good Only in the United States. Some cynical members of the world community may be forgiven for thinking that the same asterisk is there, in invisible ink, on the Constitution and the Bill of Rights.

But quibbles like that aside, and good will assumed, how does one go about liking Americans? Where does one begin? Or, to put it another way, why did the Canadian women lock themselves in the john during a '70s "international" feminist conference being held in Toronto? Because the American sisters were being "imperialist," that's why.

But then, it's always a little naive of Canadians to expect that Americans, of whatever political stamp, should stop being imperious. How can they? The fact is that the United States is an empire and Canada is to it as Gaul was to Rome.

It's hard to explain to Americans what it feels like to be a Canadian. Pessimists among us would say that one has to translate the experience into their own terms and that this is necessary because Americans are incapable of thinking in any other terms — and this in itself is part of the problem. (Witness all those draft dodgers who went into culture shock when they discovered to their horror that Toronto was not Syracuse.)

Here is a translation: Picture a Mexico with a population ten times larger than that of the United States. That would put it at about two billion. Now suppose that the official American language is Spanish, that 75 percent of the books Americans buy and 90 percent of the movies they see are Mexican, and that the profits flow across the border to Mexico. If an American does scrape it together to make a movie, the Mexicans won't let him show it in the States, because they own the distribution outlets. If anyone tries to change this ratio, not only the

Mexicans but many fellow Americans cry "National chauvinism," or, even more effectively, "National socialism." After all, the American public prefers the Mexican product. It's what they're used to.

8   Retranslate and you have the current American-Canadian picture. It's changed a little recently, not only on the cultural front. For instance, Canada, some think a trifle late, is attempting to regain control of its own petroleum industry. Americans are predictably angry. They think of Canadian oil as *theirs*.

9   "What's mine is yours," they have said for years, meaning exports; "What's yours is mine" meaning ownership and profits. Canadians are supposed to do retail buying, no controlling, or what's an empire for? One could always refer Americans to history, particularly that of their own revolution. They objected to the colonial situation when they themselves were a colony; but then, revolution is considered one of a very few home-grown American products that definitely are not for export.

10   Objectively, one cannot become too self-righteous about this state of affairs. Canadians owned lots of things, including their souls, before World War II. After that they sold, some say because they had put too much into financing the war, which created a capital vacuum (a position they would not have been forced into if the Americans hadn't kept out of the fighting for so long, say the sore losers). But for whatever reason, capital flowed across the border in the '50s, and Canadians, traditionally sock-under-the-mattress hoarders, were reluctant to invest in their own country. Americans did it for them and ended up with a large part of it, which they retain to this day. In every sellout there's a seller as well as a buyer, and the Canadians did a thorough job of trading their birthright for a mess.

11   That's on the capitalist end, but when you turn to the trade union side of things you find much the same story, except that the sellout happened in the '30s under the banner of the United Front. Now Canadian workers are finding that in any empire the colonial branch plants are the first to close, and what could be a truly progressive labor movement has been weakened by compromised bargains made in international union headquarters south of the border.

12   Canadians are sometimes snippy to Americans at cocktail parties. They don't like to feel owned and they don't like having been sold. But what really bothers them — and it's at this point that the United States and Rome part company — is the wide-eyed innocence with which their snippiness is greeted.

13   Innocence becomes ignorance when seen in the light of international affairs, and though ignorance is one of the spoils of conquest — the Gauls always knew more about the Romans than the Romans knew about them — the world can no longer afford America's ignorance. Its ignorance of Canada, though it makes Canadians bristle, is a minor and

relatively harmless example. More dangerous is the fact that individual Americans seem not to know that the United States is an imperial power and is behaving like one. They don't want to admit that empires dominate, invade and subjugate — and live on the proceeds — or, if they do admit it, they believe in their divine right to do so. The export of divine right is much more harmful than the export of Coca-Cola, though they may turn out to be much the same thing in the end.

Other empires have behaved similarly (the British somewhat better,   14 Genghis Khan decidedly worse); but they have not expected to be *liked* for it. It's the final Americanism, this passion for being liked. Alas, many Americans are indeed likable; they are often more generous, more welcoming, more enthusiastic, less picky and sardonic than Canadians, and it's not enough to say it's only because they can afford it. Some of that revolutionary spirit still remains: the optimism, the 18th-century belief in the fixability of almost anything, the conviction of the possibility of change. However, at cocktail parties and elsewhere one must be able to tell the difference between an individual and a foreign policy. Canadians can no longer afford to think of Americans as only a spectator sport. If Reagan blows up the world, we will unfortunately be doing more than watching it on television. "No annihilation without representation" sounds good as a slogan, but if we run it up the flagpole, who's going to salute?

We *are* all in this together. For Canadians, the question is how to   15 survive it. For Americans there is no question, because there does not have to be. Canada is just that vague, cold place where their uncle used to go fishing, before the lakes went dead from acid rain.

How do you like Americans? Individually, it's easier. Your average   16 American is no more responsible for the state of affairs than your average man is for war and rape. Any Canadian who is so narrow-minded as to dislike Americans merely on principle is missing out on one of the good things in life. The same might be said, to women, of men. As a group, as a foreign policy, it's harder. But if you like men, you can like Americans. Cautiously. Selectively. Beginning with the feet. One at a time.

△ △

Further Readings:

Margaret Atwood,
> *The Handmaid's Tale*
> *Surfacing*
> *Bodily Harm*

Al Purdy, ed., *The New Romans* (essays)

Pierre Berton, *Hollywood's Canada: The Americanization of Our National Image*

Richard Rohmer, *Exxoneration* (novel)
Donald Creighton, *Takeover* (novel)
Al Hurtig, *The Betrayal of Canada*

Structure

1. Does the opening ANECDOTE attract your interest? Does it prepare you for Atwood's subject?
2. How do the beginning and end work together? What pattern of development do both exploit?
3. What proportion of her argument does Atwood give to *examples*? Has she enough? Too many?
4. Why did Atwood's original AUDIENCE need her "translation" in paragraph 7, which *compares* American control of Canada with an imagined Mexican control of America?

Style:

1. How FORMAL or INFORMAL is Atwood's TONE? Give examples.
2. Why does Atwood close on a series of sentence fragments? Read the last paragraph aloud, to feel and analyze the effects.

Argumentation and Persuasion:

1. Through evidence, Atwood leads us *inductively* not just to one conclusion but to two related ones. The first is that America is an "empire." What is the second?
2. If Atwood is arguing *inductively*, why does she state as early as paragraph 5 that "the United States is an empire and Canada is to it as Gaul was to Rome"? Can an inductive argument introduce its conclusion before the evidence? If so, how do we distinguish such an arrangement from *deduction*?
3. Point out at least seven *examples* used inductively as evidence that America is an "empire." Do these also explain the anti-Americanism Atwood was asked to investigate?
4. To what extent is Atwood's essay *argumentative*, based on fact and reason? To what extent is it *persuasive*, based on emotion? Defend your answer with examples.
5. One of Atwood's trademarks as a writer, whether in poetry, fiction or essays, is heavy IRONY. Point out the most dramatic examples you see here. To what extent do they increase the *persuasion* that we feel?

Ideas for Discussion and Writing:

1. Does this essay, written for an audience of Americans, communicate to Canadians?

2. In paragraph 13 Atwood writes that "empires dominate, invade and subjugate — and live on the proceeds. . . ." Do you agree that America is an "empire"? If so, in what ways does it dominate, invade and subjugate Canada? Argue through specific examples.

3. How much American influence do you see in these aspects of Canadian life?

Computer software	Interest rates
Eating habits	Language
Fashions	Pollution
Film distribution	Popular music
Foreign policy	Television programming
Hockey	Textbooks

4. Atwood claims in paragraph 13 that Americans are "ignorant" of Canada. Attack or defend her view *inductively*, citing your own experiences with Americans.

5. Tell the similarities and/or differences that you see between Americans and Canadians as individuals. Cite examples.

6. When Atwood wrote this essay, "continentalism" was a bad word to many Canadians, but now the North American Free Trade Agreement (NAFTA) institutionalizes the concept. Even if resources such as gas and oil begin to run out, Canada may reduce export to America only in proportion to reductions in its own domestic use of resources. Have advantages of NAFTA justified this decrease of Canadian sovereignty? Argue with examples.

7. **PROCESS IN WRITING:** *You have probably studied NAFTA in other courses, and have heard a great deal about it in the media. Will it strengthen or weaken our nation? Brainstorm to produce a page of notes, especially examples, in no particular order. Now group your evidence into subtopics, and let them lead inductively to your conclusion. Base a first draft on this rough outline, but whenever the act of writing uncovers a new idea, consider adding it. When this draft has "cooled off," check and adjust your organization. Does every example lead to the same overall conclusion? Are there enough examples? Are there transitions between them? Now check the* TONE: *whether you lean more towards argumentation or persuasion, are you consistent enough to avoid confusing your audience? Finally, test your prose aloud before writing the final version.*

Note: See also the Topics for Writing at the end of this chapter.

Joy Kogawa

Grinning and Happy[*]

With three published books of poetry to her credit — The Splintered Moon *(1967),* A Choice of Dreams *(1974) and* Jericho Road *(1977)* — Joy Kogawa *had become a respected minor poet. But in 1981 she created a sensation with her first novel.* Obasan *represented a new step for Kogawa as a writer and as a person: in it she explored her own past and one of the most dubious events of Canadian history. Born in Vancouver in 1935, Kogawa was a child during World War Two when the federal government classified Japanese Canadians as "enemy aliens." Her parents' house in Vancouver was seized, and the family was moved first to a relocation camp in Slocan, B.C., then to the sugar-beet fields of southern Alberta, which are the setting of our selection from the novel. Our narrator is modelled after Kogawa herself, Stephen is the narrator's brother, Obasan is the narrator's silent and suffering aunt, and "Aunt Emily" is modelled after Muriel Kitagawa, a Japanese-Canadian activist whose letters Kogawa studied in the National Archives in Ottawa. These same characters returned in Kogawa's 1992 sequel* Itsuka, *about the struggle of Japanese-Canadians to gain redress for the wrongs described in* Obasan. *The book got mixed reviews, especially in comparison to* Obasan, *which remains one of the best Canadian novels of all time.*

1   There is a folder in Aunt Emily's package containing only one newspaper clipping and an index card with the words "Facts about evacuees in Alberta." The newspaper clipping has a photograph of one family, all smiles, standing around a pile of beets. The caption reads: "Grinning and Happy."

2   **Find Jap Evacuees Best Beet Workers**
Lethbridge, Alberta, Jan. 22.

3   **Japanese evacuees from British Columbia supplied the labour for 65% of Alberta's sugar beet acreage last year, Phil Baker, of Lethbridge, president of the Alberta Sugar Beet Growers Association, stated today.**

---

*Editor's title.

"They played an important part in producing our all-time record crop of 363,000 tons of beets in 1945," he added.

Mr. Baker explained Japanese evacuees worked 19,500 acres of beets and German prisoners of war worked 5,000 acres. The labour for the remaining 5,500 acres of Alberta's 30,000 acres of sugar beets was provided by farmers and their families. Some of the heaviest beet yields last year came from farms employing Japanese evacuees.

Generally speaking, Japanese evacuees have developed into most efficient beet workers, many of them being better than the transient workers who cared for beets in southern Alberta before Pearl Harbor. . . .

Facts about evacuees in Alberta? The fact is I never got used to it and I cannot, I cannot bear the memory. There are some nightmares from which there is no waking, only deeper and deeper sleep.

There is a word for it. Hardship. The hardship is so pervasive, so inescapable, so thorough it's a noose around my chest and I cannot move any more. All the oil in my joints has drained out and I have been invaded by dust and grit from the fields and mud is in my bone marrow. I can't move any more. My fingernails are black from scratching the scorching day and there is no escape.

Aunt Emily, are you a surgeon cutting at my scalp with your folders and your filing cards and your insistence on knowing all? The memory drains down the sides of my face, but it isn't enough, is it? It's your hands in my abdomen, pulling the growth from the lining of my walls, but bring back the anaesthetist turn on the ether clamp down the gas mask bring on the chloroform when will this operation be over Aunt Em?

Is it so bad?

Yes.

Do I really mind?

Yes, I mind. I mind everything. Even the flies. The flies and flies and flies from the cows in the barn and the manure pile — all the black flies that curtain the windows, and Obasan with a wad of toilet paper, spish, then with her bare hands as well, grabbing them and their shocking white eggs and the mosquitoes mixed there with the other insect corpses around the base of the gas lamp.

It's the chicken coop "house" we live in that I mind. The uninsulated unbelievable thin-as-a-cotton-dress hovel never before inhabited in winter by human beings. In summer it's a heat trap, an incubator, a dry sauna from which there is no relief. In winter the icicles drip down the inside of the windows and the ice is thicker than bricks at the ledge. The only place that is warm is by the coal stove where we rotate like chickens on a spit and the feet are so cold they stop registering. We eat cloves of roasted garlic on winter nights to warm up.

15   It's the bedbugs and my having to sleep on the table to escape the nightly attack, and the welts over our bodies. And all the swamp bugs and the dust. It's Obasan uselessly packing all the cracks with rags. And the muddy water from the irrigation ditch which we strain and settle and boil, and the tiny carcasses of water creatures at the bottom of the cup. It's walking in winter to the reservoir and keeping the hole open with the axe and dragging up the water in pails and lugging it back and sometimes the water spills down your boots and your feet are red and itchy for days. And it's everybody taking a bath in the round galvanized tub, then Obasan washing clothes in the water after and standing outside hanging the clothes in the freezing weather where everything instantly stiffens on the line.

16   Or it's standing in the beet field under the maddening sun, standing with my black head a sun-trap even though it's covered, and lying down in the ditch, faint, and the nausea in waves and the cold sweat, and getting up and tackling the next row. The whole field is an oven and there's not a tree within walking distance. We are tiny as insects crawling along the grill and there is no protection anywhere. The eyes are lidded against the dust and the air cracks the skin, the lips crack, Stephen's flutes crack and there is no energy to sing any more anyway.

17   It's standing in the field and staring out at the heat waves that waver and shimmer like see-through curtains over the brown clods and over the tiny distant bodies of Stephen and Uncle and Obasan miles away across the field day after day and not even wondering how this has come about.

18   There she is, Obasan, wearing Uncle's shirt over a pair of dark baggy trousers, her head covered by a straw hat that is held on by a white cloth tied under her chin. She is moving like a tiny earth cloud over the hard clay clods. Her hoe moves rhythmically up down up down, tiny as a toothpick. And over there, Uncle pauses to straighten his back, his hands on his hips. And Stephen farther behind, so tiny I can barely see him.

19   It's hard, Aunt Emily, with my hoe, the blade getting dull and mud-caked as I slash out the Canada thistle, dandelions, crab grass, and other nameless non-beet plants, then on my knees, pulling out the extra beets from the cluster, leaving just one to mature, then three hand spans to the next plant, whack whack, and down on my knees again, pull, flick flick, and on to the end of the long long row and the next and the next and it will never be done thinning and weeding and weeding and weeding. It's so hard and so hot that my tear glands burn out.

20   And then it's cold. The lumps of clay mud stick on my gumboots and weight my legs and the skin under the boots beneath the knees at the level of the calves grows red and hard and itchy from the flap flap of the boots and the fine hairs on my legs grow coarse there and ugly.

21   I mind growing ugly.

I mind the harvest time and the hands and the wrists bound in rags   22
to keep the wrists from breaking open. I lift the heavy mud-clotted
beets out of the ground with the hook like an eagle's beak, thick and
heavy as a nail attached to the top of the sugar-beet knife. Thwack. Into
the beet and yank from the shoulder till it's out of the ground dragging
the surrounding mud with it. Then crack two beets together till most of
the mud drops off and splat, the knife slices into the beet scalp and the
green top is tossed into one pile, the beet heaved onto another, one
more one more one more down the icy line. I cannot tell about this
time, Aunt Emily. The body will not tell.

We are surrounded by a horizon of denim-blue sky with clouds clear   23
as spilled milk that turn pink at sunset. Pink I hear is the colour of
llama's milk. I wouldn't know. The clouds are the shape of our new
prison walls — untouchable, impersonal, random.

There are no other people in the entire world. We work together all   24
day. At night we eat and sleep. We hardly talk anymore. The boxes we
brought from Slocan are not unpacked. The King George/Queen
Elizabeth mugs stay muffled in the *Vancouver Daily Province*. The camera
phone does not sing. Obasan wraps layers of cloth around her feet and
her torn sweater hangs unmended over her sagging dress.

Down the miles we are obedient as machines in this odd ballet without   25
accompaniment of flute or song.

"Grinning and happy" and all smiles standing around a pile of beets?   26
That is one telling. It's not how it was.

∆ ∆

Further Reading:

Joy Kogawa,
  Obasan
  Itsuka
Barry Broadfoot, *Years of Sorrow, Years of Shame: The Story of Japanese
  Canadians in World War II*
Ken Adachi, *The Enemy That Never Was: A History of the Japanese Can-
  adians.*
Ann Sunahara, *The Politics of Racism: The Uprooting of Japanese Canadians
  During the Second World War*

Structure:

1. Why does Kogawa "frame" her argument by citing the newspaper
   article in both her opening and closing?
2. How does the device of *contrast* help organize this selection?
3. What percentage of *examples* has Kogawa reached in the content of
   this selection?

4. How important is *description* to the success of this passage?
5. Most THESIS STATEMENTS are placed early in an argument; why is Kogawa's put in the very last line?

Style:

1. Until *Obasan*, Kogawa was best known as a poet. What poetical qualities do you see in her PROSE?
2. To what extent does Kogawa communicate by SENSE IMAGES? Cite one case each of appeals to sight, hearing, touch, taste and smell.
3. The poet Kogawa fills her prose with FIGURES OF SPEECH. Point out three good SIMILES and three good METAPHORS.
4. In paragraphs 14 through 17, how many times does the contraction "it's" appear at or near the beginning of a sentence? Is the *repetition* accidental or deliberate? What is its effect?
5. How many words long is the first sentence of paragraph 19? How many times does it use the word "and"? Is this run-on sentence accidental or deliberate? What is its effect?

Argumentation and Persuasion:

1. As a member of a persecuted minority, Kogawa's narrator rejects a *deductive* stance; she shuns the official "telling" of the newspaper article, and instead produces her own eyewitness "telling." Point out at least ten pieces of evidence that lead *inductively* to her own conclusion that the newspaper's version of the truth is "not how it was."
2. Does Kogawa rely more on *argumentation* or on *persuasion*? To what extent does she communicate through reason, and to what extent through emotion?
3. Analyze Kogawa's tools of *persuasion*: point out at least five loaded words, five SENSE IMAGES and five FIGURES OF SPEECH that build emotion. Identify one case of deliberate repetition, and one of extreme sentence length, which both build emotion. Does all this persuasion put you on guard? Or does it convince you?

Ideas for Discussion and Writing:

1. How often are you, like Kogawa's narrator, caught between two or more views of the truth? Cite a recent case. Did you act *deductively*, accepting a view already held by yourself or others, or did you move *inductively* to a new conclusion?
2. The narrator and her family are Canadian citizens of Japanese descent, removed by our federal government from the coast of British Columbia during World War II for fear they would betray Canada to the enemy, Japan. (Not a single case of such betrayal was ever found.)

Many families were separated and their property taken. Attack or defend these official actions against citizens like Kogawa's fictional family. Have such acts occurred in Canada before? Since? Can you imagine them happening in future to any group you belong to?

3. During the war the Canadian government confiscated an island off British Columbia, compensating its Japanese-Canadian owner with $2000. Two generations later his granddaughter, a university student, estimated the worth of this property at 200 million dollars. In 1988 the Canadian government officially apologized to the Japanese-Canadians and offered each survivor of the epoch $21,000. Has the wrong been righted? Attack or defend our government's actions.

4. You are the student in question 3 above. Write to the prime minister, arguing either *deductively* or *inductively* that the island be restored to the heirs of its original owner. *Or* you are the present owner. Write to the prime minister, arguing either *deductively* or *inductively* that your island should not be seized and given to descendants of the man who once owned it.

5. **PROCESS IN WRITING:** *Name a group that you think has been badly treated by Canadian society (for example the handicapped or disabled, the elderly, native peoples, farmers, immigrants, refugees, single parents, etc.). Take notes, then write an* inductive argument *giving the evidence that led to your belief. In a further draft fine-tune the balance of* argumentation and persuasion. *Now share this version with a small group of classmates, and apply their best advice. At home, read aloud to detect wordiness and awkwardness. Edit. Finally, read your good version aloud to the whole class, and be prepared to defend your view.*

Note: See also the Topics for Writing at the end of this chapter.

Rita Schindler

Thanks for Not Killing My Son

All we know about Rita Schindler is what she herself says in her letter. It was a student who noticed "Thanks for Not Killing My Son" in the "Have Your Say" feature of the December 30, 1990 Toronto Star. *He tore it out and brought it to his writing teacher, exclaiming what a fine argument it was. The teacher agreed. By the time the editor of this book tried to reach Ms. Schindler, though,* The Star *had discarded her address. None of the many Schindlers listed in the Toronto phone book knew her, and the hospital mentioned in her letter would not divulge information. The publisher even talked with a detective agency. Finally, though, the Copyright Board of Canada gave permission to reprint the letter, as it can do in such cases. We sincerely believe that Ms. Schindler would want her eloquent and highly principled argument made available to more persons of her son's generation. If you happen to know her, please show her this book and ask her to contact the publisher, who will direct her to the government office where her author's fee is waiting.*

1   I hope you will print my letter of gratitude to the strangers who have affected our lives.

2   Sometime between 1:30 p.m., Dec. 8, and 1 a.m., Dec. 9, a young man was viciously attacked — beaten and kicked unconscious for no apparent reason other than walking by you on a public sidewalk.

3   He was left lying in a pool of blood from an open head wound — in the Victoria Park-Terraview area. He was found around 1 a.m. and taken to Scarborough General Hospital where ironically his mother spent 48 hours in labor before giving him birth, 23 years earlier.

4   His mother is angry of course, but thankful for the following reasons.

5   First of all — his eye socket was shattered and hemorrhaging but his eyesight will not be affected. Thank you.

6   His ear canal was lacerated internally from a tremendous blow to the side of his head. The cut could not be stitched and the bleeding was difficult to stop. But his eardrum seems to be undamaged — thank you.

7   He required numerous stitches to his forehead, temple and face but your boots didn't knock one tooth out — thank you. His head was

swollen almost twice its size — but Mom knew that his brain was intact — for he held her hand for six hours as he lay on a gurney, by the nurses station, I.V. in his arm — his head covered and crusted with dried blood — waiting for x-ray results and the surgeon to stitch him up.

So, thank you for this eyesight, his hearing and his hands which you could have easily crushed. 8

His hands — human hands — the most intricately beautiful and complex instruments of incredible mechanism — the result of billions of years of evolution — and you people used yours to beat another human being. Five guys and two girls to beat one person. Who do I thank? Did you know he was a talented young musician with a budding career — and that playing his keyboards and piano mean more to him than my words can say. 9

And when his friends were talking about revenge, I heard him say, "No, I don't want someone else's mother to go through what mine has." That's who you were kicking in the head. And so — I thank you for not causing the most horrible and devastating thing that can happen to any parent — that is — the untimely tragic loss of a child — at any age. 10

You could have kicked him to death but you only left him to die, thank you. A person found him and called for help. 11

I am his mother — and I have been given a second chance — thanks to you. 12

I hope that someday you'll have children and love them as much as I love mine — but I wouldn't wish on your child what you did to mine. 13

Rita Schindler
Scarborough

∆∆∆

Further Reading:

Anthony Burgess, *A Clockwork Orange*

Structure:

1. Schindler's argument is cast as a letter. For what *audience* is it meant? The youths who attacked her son? All the readers of *The Toronto Star*? How well does her "letter" work as an essay?
2. Schindler organizes her letter by examining in turn each injury inflicted on her son. Point out each. What proportion of the letter's content is given to these *examples*? Are they needed to make the point?
3. After all her ironic "thanking," Schindler ends more literally: "I wouldn't wish on your child what you did to mine." Is her closing weak because it drops the IRONY, or strong because it caps the point?

Style:

1. Six of Schindler's paragraphs have only one sentence. Give reasons. Is this style effective?
2. How CONCISE is this selection? Try to find one passage of deadwood that could have been cut.
3. How FORMAL or INFORMAL is Schindler's TONE? Give examples. Does the tone fit the content? Why or why not?

Argumentation and Persuasion:

1. "You could have kicked him to death, but you only left him to die, thank you," writes the victim's mother in paragraph 11. Her letter of "thanks" is *persuasion* as strong as any in this book. Explain the IRONY of Schindler's "thanking" her son's attackers.
2. Find and explain at least ten more IRONIES in this selection.
3. The author might have called her son's attackers "thugs," "goons" or worse. Would this openly *persuasive* mode be more effective than the "thanks" she gives? Defend your answer with reasons.
4. In addition to *irony*, the introduction to this chapter lists *repetition, fright* and *climax* as techniques of persuasion. How does Schindler use each? Respond with examples.
5. Does Schindler make her point *deductively* (through an innate rejection of violence) or *inductively* (through the many examples she cites, leading to her point)? Can an argument go both ways at once? Would this be a failure of logic?

Ideas for Discussion and Writing:

1. Does Schindler attempt only to heap shame on her son's attackers, or do you also detect, for example in the closing, a desire for reconciliation?
2. When his friends desired revenge, the son said, "No, I don't want someone else's mother to go through what mine has" (paragraph 10). What would *you* have said? Defend your answer with reasons.
3. How much do techniques of nonviolent resisters such as Mahatma Gandhi and Martin Luther King have in common with the responses of Rita Schindler and her son? Is their way ultimately weaker or stronger than the way of those who defend themselves through violence? Give examples.
4. Is there violent crime at your school or campus? If so, give examples. Defend or attack the "zero tolerance" policy of some school boards that permanently expel students who commit violent offences. Are there other solutions that would work?
5. Are public forums such as the letters to the editor column or elec-

tronic bulletin boards good vehicles for promoting our own ideas? Do others actually read and heed what we say?

6. **PROCESS IN WRITING:** *Read the crime news in your newspaper or hear it on radio or TV. Choose one violent act that provokes your anger or concern. Consider how, like Rita Schindler, you can respond to it through IRONY to persuade your audience to take your side. Make notes, look them over, then write a rapid first draft of a letter to the perpetrator, to the public, or to both. The next day look it over. Will it startle and persuade the audience by meaning the opposite of what it says? (Remember Schindler's "thanking" the attackers, or in Chapter 5 Russell Baker's "criticising" Toronto, or in Chapter 8 Stephen Leacock's "advice" on how to live to be 200.) Is the ironic TONE consistent? Is the letter concise, like Schindler's? If not, revise. Finally, fix things like spelling and grammar. When you have produced your good draft, send it as a letter to the editor of the newspaper you read. Or, if you are wired up, send it from your computer to an appropriate "bulletin board" on the Internet. Check either for responses. Collect them, then show them, with the original letter, to the class.*

Note: See also the Topics for Writing at the end of this chapter.

Nathalie Petrowski

The Seven-Minute Life of
Marc Lépine*

Translated from the French by Ronald Conrad

Nathalie Petrowski, columnist for La Presse *and* Le Devoir, *is one of Quebec's favourite print journalists. Her writings are quirky, often humorous, often personal, usually satirical and sometimes very biting. In her* Devoir *column of December 16, 1989 she had a special challenge: ten days before, a 25-year-old man had walked into an engineering class at the University of Montreal's École Polytechnique, shouted at the women students "You're all a bunch of feminists, and I hate feminists," ordered the men to leave — then lifted his rifle and shot the women. Six died. During the next minutes of terror (seven according to Petrowski; twenty according to later reports) he roamed the building, shooting as he went. Altogether he gunned down 27 students, killing 14, all women. Then Marc Lépine turned the weapon on himself and died too. The nation felt a shock wave of anger and remorse, for not only was this the worst one-day mass murder in the country's history, but its selectivity seemed to express a general sexism in society. In the next days, as the flag over Parliament flew at half-mast, citizens learned that Lépine's father had beat him and mistreated the mother, that the parents had divorced, and that the boy, though intelligent, had problems in school both academically and socially. He loved war movies, and from a paratrooper uncle learned to handle firearms. Now on December 6 of every year, ceremonies across the nation honour the 14 young women, training for a profession still dominated by men, who were killed by a man whose suicide note blamed feminists for ruining his life. The essay that follows (originally entitled "Pitié pour les salauds") has a special poignancy, for Nathalie Petrowski wrote it in shock, as she and the nation first struggled to see meaning in the event. (Note: See also "Our Daughters, Ourselves," by Stevie Cameron, on the same subject.)*

1   **P**ardon if I insist, pardon if I don't just mourn and forget, but it's stronger than I am, for a week I can't stop thinking about Marc

---

*Editor's title.

Lépine. A psychoanalyst would say I'm identifying with the aggressor. But I'd say that inside every aggressor, every villain, there hides a victim.

I think of Marc Lépine to block out all the talk that just confuses things: Rambo, television, violence towards women, pornography, abortion, and firearms in display windows.

I think of Marc Lépine, still wondering what happened and exactly when the hellish countdown of his act was unleashed. Was it the morning of December 6, was it November 21 when he bought his rifle or September 4 when he applied for the firearm permit? Was it the day of his birth, the first time his father beat him, the day his parents divorced, the week when he suddenly quit all his courses, the night a girl didn't want to dance with him? What about all the hours, the days, the weeks, the years that passed before the bomb inside him went off?

Still, journalists have told us everything: where he lived, the schools he went to, the names of teachers and students he knew. We know how much he paid for his rifle and how he loved war movies. But once all this has been said, nothing has been said.

We know nothing of the ache that consumed him, of the torture inside him. We know nothing of the evil path he slipped into smiling the cruel smile of the angel of destruction, no longer himself, knowing only that he was put on earth to destroy.

I think of Marc Lépine but equally of Nadia, his sister who was beaten, too, for singing out loud in the morning, Nadia who came from the same family but didn't fall prey to the same madness. Why Marc and not Nadia, why Marc and not another? That's what I ask myself when facts only deepen the mystery, when social criticism only confuses things.

No one remembers him from grade school, or from Sainte-Justine Hospital where he spent a year in therapy with his mother and sister. Until last week Marc Lépine did not exist. He was an unknown quantity, a number, an anonymous face in the crowd, a nobody who no one would even look at or give the least warmth, the slightest affection. In a few moments he went from a nothing to one of a kind, a pathological case who the experts claim in no way represents the society where he was born and grew up.

For a week I've been talking with these experts, hoping to understand. For a week all I've seen is that there is no one answer, there are a thousand. For a week I've dealt with the official and professional voices who keep their files under key, who keep repeating that there's no use wanting to know more, that Marc Lépine is dead, that he can no longer be healed or saved, that it's too late to do anything at all. Sometimes their excuses and justifications sound like lies.

But I refuse to hear the silence of death that falls like snow, the shameful silence that freezes my blood. Somewhere deep in the ruins of our private space we hide the truth, we try to protect ourselves saying that families — ours, his, the victims' — have been traumatized.

10   Forget about the past, say the authorities, let's move on and not let Marc Lépine's act dictate our choices. Yet the surest way to let this act dictate our choices is to hide it, to let it become a medical, psychological and criminal secret, to push it into the smallest hollow of our collective memory till it's erased and we can say it never existed at all.

11   In this province where memory is reduced to a slogan on a licence plate°, we want to forget Marc Lépine like we forget all events that can disturb us and make us think. Though I know nothing of Marc Lépine's story, I've met enough young people in the high schools and colleges to know that chance as well as reasons, randomness as well as all the wrong conditions in one person's life, caused this act. His tragic destiny looks more and more like a tangle of shattered hopes, of frustrated dreams, of hopeless waits on a long and cold road without a single hand extended to help, and no guardrail.

12   Marc Lépine died the evening of December 6, but unlike his victims, he had died long before. In the end his life lasted just seven minutes. Before and after, he was forgotten.

13   So pardon my pessimism, but I cannot help believing that somewhere, at this moment, there are other Marc Lépines who won't ask for anything because they don't even know what to ask for — other children turned into monsters by abusive fathers and impersonal school systems, by a society so intent on excellence that every day it hammers the nail of Defeat further in, and plants seeds of frustration and violence in the fragile spirits of its children.

14   Though nothing can be done now for Marc Lépine, something can still be done for the others, whose inner clock has already begun the terrible countdown. It would be a mistake to forget them.

Δ Δ Δ Δ Δ Δ Δ Δ Δ Δ Δ Δ Δ Δ Δ Δ Δ Δ Δ Δ Δ Δ Δ Δ Δ Δ Δ Δ Δ Δ Δ Δ Δ Δ Δ Δ Δ Δ Δ Δ Δ Δ Δ Δ Δ

Further Reading:

Nathalie Petrowski, *Il Restera toujours le Nebraska* (novel; available only in French)

Louise Malette and Marie Chalouh, eds,. *Polytechnique, 6 décembre* (writings on the Montreal Massacre; available only in French)

Elliott Leyton, *Hunting Humans* (book on multiple murders)

Camilo José Cela, *Pascal Duarte's Family* (novel, Spain)

Gabriel García Márquez, *Chronicle of a Death Foretold* (novella, Colombia)

Anne Hébert, *The Torrent* (novella)

°Quebec licence plates bear the motto "Je me souviens" ("I remember"); Quebeckers consider this a reference to their history, and especially the Conquest.

Structure:

1. Where is Petrowski's THESIS STATEMENT?
2. Tragic events leave people asking "why?" Point out all the reasons that Petrowski examines to explain this event. To what extent is her essay constructed through *cause and effect?*
3. How does paragraph 6 use *comparison and contrast?*
4. What often-used technique of conclusion gives force to the closing?

Style:

1. In paragraph 1 and elsewhere, Petrowski groups sentences together with commas. Do you view this as faulty punctuation, or is it a way for Petrowski to express feelings about this subject? Are we ever justified in breaking rules of punctuation and sentence structure?
2. Identify all the FIGURES OF SPEECH in paragraph 9. What do they contribute?
3. What feeling does paragraph 3 convey in its flurry of questions?

Argumentation and Persuasion:

1. It seems natural that, as a journalist, Petrowski select *induction* for her logic. What difficulties does she have, though, obtaining the evidence she needs to draw a conclusion?
2. Point out five techniques of *persuasion* that Petrowski uses (consult the list in our chapter introduction). Which one has the most impact? How *persuasive* is the essay as a whole? Does Petrowski's TONE fit her subject?

Ideas for Discussion and Writing:

1. After murdering 14 engineering students because they were women, Marc Lépine also killed himself. But in what sense had he "died long before" (par. 12)? In what sense did his life last only "seven minutes" (par. 12)?
2. In her essay "Our Daughters, Ourselves," Stevie Cameron mourns Lépine's victims. Petrowski opens her own essay with the belief that "inside every aggressor, every villain, there hides a victim." Can we and should we view Marc Lépine, the killer, as himself a victim? If so, a victim of who or what?
3. In its issue covering the Montreal Massacre, *Maclean's* reported that in Canada one of every four women is harrassed sexually at some time in life, and that a million women are abused each year by their husbands or partners. It also quoted a study by Rosemary Gartner who found that "as women move into nontraditional roles, they run

a significantly higher risk of being killed." Do you see any relationship between this information and the act of Marc Lépine? Explain.

4. On that day, Lépine carried one of the most popular rifles in Canada, a .223-calibre Sturm, Ruger semiautomatic, with two 30-clip magazines holding shells with expanding slugs. Are firearms a danger in your city or town? Attack or defend the sale of arms, including handguns, over the counter. What would be lost or what would be gained through stiffer gun laws?

5. What concrete steps might have been taken, and by whom, to help Marc Lépine before it was too late?

6. **PROCESS IN WRITING:** *Lépine used a rifle, but handguns are the weapon of choice for shootings. At the library, gather information on the role of handguns in crime in Canada. Research also our current regulations for their sale and use. Now decide your* THESIS: *whether Canada should end, severely limit, or continue to permit the sale of handguns to civilians. List your reasons. From this short outline write a fast discovery draft of your essay, developed mainly through* argumentation, *not stopping now to fix things like spelling or punctuation. The next day look it over. Is every point backed by a reason or example? Does your evidence lead clearly to your conclusion? (Remember that many essayists will change a conclusion or even a thesis when writing gives them new ideas.) Finally edit for correctness as you produce your final version.*

Note: See also the Topics for Writing at the end of this chapter.

Stevie Cameron

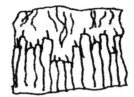

Our Daughters, Ourselves

Her full and varied experience has made Stevie Cameron one of the nation's most authoritative journalists and social commentators. For many years she reported for The Toronto Star *and the Ottawa* Journal, *and was editor, parliamentary reporter and columnist with* The Ottawa Citizen. *In 1984 she joined* The Citizen's *special investigative reporting unit, where her exposés revealed corruption in both the Trudeau and Mulroney governments. These studies led in 1989 to her book* Ottawa Inside Out: Power, Prestige and Scandal in the Nation's Capital. *In 1994 appeared another book,* On the Take, *an exposé of the Mulroney government's alleged misdeeds. Cameron has also written for the Toronto* Globe and Mail, *and is well-known to television viewers as an investigator for the CBC's* Fifth Estate. *It was on December 9, 1989 that her article "Our Daughters, Ourselves" appeared in* The Globe. *Three days earlier had occurred one of the worst crimes in Canadian history: a 25-year-old man had murdered 14 engineering students in Montreal because they were women, and had left a suicide note blaming feminists for ruining his life. (See a fuller account of the Montreal Massacre in the introduction to Nathalie Petrowski's essay "The Seven-Minute Life of Marc Lépine," also in this chapter.) While Cameron's lyrical and devastating essay is directed at the 14 young women who had aimed at a profession dominated by men, it also examines the context of this crime — the problems of sexism routinely faced by all daughters of our society. Cameron's elegy aroused such public response that The Canadian Research Institute for the Advancement of Women later named it best feminist article of the year, and on the first anniversary of the murders* The Globe *printed it again.*

They are so precious to us, our daughters. When they are born we see their futures as unlimited, and as they grow and learn we try so hard to protect them: This is how we cross the street, hold my hand, wear your boots, don't talk to strangers, run to the neighbors if a man tries to get you in his car.

We tell our bright, shining girls that they can be anything: firefighters, doctors, policewomen, lawyers, scientists, soldiers, athletes, artists. What we don't tell them, yet, is how hard it will be. Maybe, we say to ourselves, by the time they're older it will be easier for them than it was for us.

3   But as they grow and learn, with aching hearts we have to start dealing with their bewilderment about injustice. Why do the boys get the best gyms, the best equipment and the best times on the field? Most of the school sports budget? Why does football matter more than gymnastics? Why are most of the teachers women and most of the principals men? Why do the boys make more money at their part-time jobs than we do?

4   And as they grow and learn we have to go on trying to protect them: We'll pick you up at the subway, we'll fetch you from the movie, stay with the group, make sure the parents drive you home from babysitting, don't walk across the park alone, lock the house if we're not there.

5   It's not fair, they say. Boys can walk where they want, come in when they want, work where they want. Not really, we say; boys get attacked too. But boys are not targets for men the way girls are, so girls have to be more careful.

6   Sometimes our girls don't make it. Sometimes, despite our best efforts and all our love, they go on drugs, drop out, screw up. On the whole, however, our daughters turn into interesting, delightful people. They plan for college and university, and with wonder and pride we see them competing with the boys for spaces in engineering schools, medical schools, law schools, business schools. For them we dream of Rhodes scholarships, Harvard graduate school, gold medals; sometimes, we even dare to say these words out loud and our daughters reward us with indulgent hugs. Our message is that anything is possible.

7   We bite back the cautions that we feel we should give them; maybe by the time they've graduated, things will have changed, we say to ourselves. Probably by the time they're out, they will make partner when the men do, be asked to join the same clubs, run for political office. Perhaps they'll even be able to tee off at the same time men do at the golf club.

8   But we still warn them: park close to the movie, get a deadbolt for your apartment, check your windows, tell your roommates where you are. Call me. Call me.

9   And then with aching hearts we take our precious daughters to lunch and listen to them talk about their friends: the one who was beaten by her boy friend and then shunned by his friends when she asked for help from the dean; the one who was attacked in the parking lot; the one who gets obscene and threatening calls from a boy in her residence; the one who gets raped on a date; the one who was mocked by the male students in the public meeting.

10   They tell us about the sexism they're discovering in the adult world at university. Women professors who can't get jobs, who can't get tenure. Male professors who cannot comprehend women's stony silence after sexist jokes. An administration that only pays lip service to women's

issues and refuse to accept the reality of physical danger to women on campus.

They tell us they're talking among themselves about how men are 11 demanding rights over unborn children; it's not old dinosaurs who go to court to prevent a woman's abortion, it's young men. It's young men, they say with disbelief, their own generation, their own buddies with good education, from "nice" families, who are abusive.

What can we say to our bright and shining daughters? How can we 12 tell them how much we hurt to see them developing the same scars we've carried? How much we wanted it to be different for them? It's all about power, we say to them. Sharing power is not easy for anyone and men do not find it easy to share among themselves, much less with a group of equally talented, able women. So men make all those stupid cracks about needing a sex-change operation to get a job or a promotion and they wind up believing it.

Now our daughters have been shocked to the core, as we all have, by 13 the violence in Montreal. They hear the women were separated from the men and meticulously slaughtered by a man who blamed feminists for his troubles. They ask themselves why nobody was able to help the terrified women, to somehow stop the hunter as he roamed the engineering building.

So now our daughters are truly frightened and it makes their mothers 14 furious that they are frightened. They survived all the childhood dangers, they were careful as we trained them to be, they worked hard. Anything was possible and our daughters proved it. And now they are more scared than they were when they were little girls.

Fourteen of our bright and shining daughters won places in engi- 15 neering schools, doing things we, their mothers, only dreamed of. That we lost them has broken our hearts; what is worse is that we are not surprised.

△ △

Further Reading:

Doris Anderson, *The Unfinished Revolution*
Jane Gaskell, *Gender Matters from School to Work*
Jesse Vorst, ed., *Race, Class, Gender: Bonds and Barriers*
Margaret Atwood,
    Bodily Harm (novel)
    The Handmaid's Tale (novel)
Manuel Puig, *Boquitas pintadas* (novel, Argentina; available only in
    Spanish)

Structure:

1. How well does Cameron's title reflect the essay that follows?
2. In opening with the word "They," what strategy does Cameron use?
3. Identify the THESIS STATEMENT.
4. Is Cameron's *chronological order* a good choice for showing what happens to the daughters of our society? Give reasons.
5. To what extent does *comparison and contrast* help organize the essay? Cite passages based on it.

Style:

1. Paragraph 3 asks five questions in a row. Why? What is their overall effect?
2. What FIGURE OF SPEECH is the term "dinosaurs" in paragraph 11?

Argumentation and Persuasion:

1. Cameron's many examples lead through *induction* to her conclusion. Cite those which best show why the mothers, at the end, are "not surprised."
2. Stevie Cameron wrote "Our Daughters, Ourselves" in the heat of reaction to the Montreal Massacre — the murder of 14 women engineering students by a male who blamed feminists for his problems. Though her examples do argue through logic, her appeals to emotion are so deep that this selection is one of the most *persuasive* in the book. Point out examples of all these techniques of *persuasion*:
   A. Repetition
   B. Figures of speech
   C. Irony
   D. Fright
   E. Climax
3. In what ways does this elegy to a generation of daughters transcend PROSE to become POETRY?

Ideas for Discussion and Writing:

1. Do you feel safe on campus? Downtown at night? Home alone? If not, tell why. Is your feeling related at all to your gender? If so, give examples to show why.
2. If your family has both sisters and brothers, have the parents protected the sisters more, as Cameron suggests in paragraphs 4, 5 and 8? If so, give examples. Is such protection needed in today's society? Tell why or why not.
3. Rita Schindler's letter in this chapter describes a near-fatal attack on

a male victim, her son. What *comparisons*, if any, would you make with the violence towards women discussed by Cameron? What *contrasts*?

4. Nathalie Petrowski's essay in this chapter reflects on the life of Marc Lépine who murdered the 14 women engineering students mourned by both Petrowski and Cameron. Do you view Lépine as a victim of our society, like those he himself killed? Tell why or why not. If so, what factors ultimately *caused* the violence?

5. Marc Lépine thought women should not be engineers. Are employees in the field you intend to enter mostly male or mostly female? Why? What pressures have you felt, if any, to choose according to your gender? Give examples.

6. Are you "surprised" or "not surprised" at the act of Marc Lépine? Tell why, giving examples.

7. **PROCESS IN WRITING:** *Either read today's newspaper or think about recent news you have read or heard. Choose a crime of violence, with a victim either female or male, and decide whether you are "surprised" or "not surprised." Now write either "surprised" or "not surprised" in the centre of a blank page, and around it add other words that explain why. Connect related items with lines, then from this cluster outline devise your THESIS. Now incorporate the material into a fast discovery draft which, like Stevie Cameron's essay, uses emotion to persuade. The next day look it over. Are there enough persuasive elements like deliberate repetition, figures of speech, irony and fright to move the reader? Do examples help the reader "see" your point? Do they show "why"? Do transitions such as "because," "therefore" and "since" highlight causes and effects? Do your points rise to a climax? If not, revise. Finally, check for things like spelling and grammar as you produce your final draft.*

Note: See also the Topics for Writing at the end of this chapter.

Wendy Dennis

A Tongue-Lashing for Deaf Ears

Wendy Dennis has been a teacher, an editor and now a freelance writer. Born in 1950, she has lived in Toronto all her life. After attending York University and the University of Toronto, she taught high school English for seven years, then, "terminally bored with that line of work," discovered a deeper interest while attending Ryerson Polytechnic University's journalism program. Since then she has published extensively in magazines such as Maclean's, Cosmopolitan, Toronto Life, City Woman, Homemaker's, Chatelaine, Ontario Living *and* New Woman. *She has also contributed to the CBC radio program* Later the Same Day. *Then in 1992 she created a sensation with her book* Hot and Bothered: Sex and Love in the Nineties. *Response was so intense that on her book tour Dennis appeared on hundreds of television talk shows and radio interviews in three countries. Dennis sometimes writes in an analytical, objective, argumentative vein, but says her readers respond with more letters when she takes the personal, subjective, persuasive approach of our selection. Though "A Tongue-Lashing for Deaf Ears" dates from some time ago, it remains one of her favourites. "It was a joy to write that piece," she says, "because I was so angry and frustrated." She suggests to other writers that "the best place to start is with something you have felt or observed strongly, because the thinking will follow naturally from the writing." Her essay appeared in 1981 in the "Podium" column of* Maclean's.

1   The last time I went to the movies and got stuck beside a motor-mouth whose IQ bore an uncanny resemblance to his shoe size, I vowed, like Peter Finch in *Network*, that I was mad as hell and I wasn't going to take it anymore. That night I dreamt that my own rage-twisted face was projected in cinemascopic grandeur on the screen, while my Charlton Heston voice boomed hideous warnings in Dolby sound at foolish would-be noisemakers. No longer would I smile sweetly and apologize for the unusual craving I had to follow the plot without a Howard Cosell play-by-play; no longer would I stand miserably by while some pimply-faced prefect with a flashlight solemnly asked the buffoon on my right to please stop belching through the love scenes. It was time to retaliate.

I considered my options carefully. I thought of Nancy Reagan, who 2 reportedly sleeps with "a tiny little gun" beside her bed, and had to admit that her solution, like the First Lady herself, possessed a certain clean elegance. But I didn't require a lethal weapon. A canister of tear gas maybe? Or a branding iron? Perhaps one of those guns they use to stun cattle before transforming them into the neat little cellophane packages you find under the red lights at supermarkets. I liked the poetic justice of that. Stun the beast and call four of those scrubbed choirboys theatres inevitably hire as ushers to deposit him under the marquee, where he would symbolize the long-overdue revolt of the Silent Movie Majority.

Noisy invasion of public spaces by yahoos is hardly a new problem 3 but, unless my experience has been atypical, it seems to be nearing epidemic proportions. And the brutes are branching out. No longer content merely to destroy the sweet holy silence of the movie houses, like nasty malignant cells, they're now everywhere — and they're out for blood. I see them on subway platforms, where their infernal amplified radios bring demented stares to other passengers' faces but never seem to rouse the offenders from their somnambulant stupor. I've pulled up beside roving packs of them at red lights, where they stare like zombies, blithely unaware that the decibel level of their tape decks is precipitating anxiety attacks in passers-by for miles. I've come face to face with them as close to home as a campsite in Algonquin Park and as far away as a surf-washed beach in Bali; recently I've even encountered them at live theatre. All of which convinces me there's something awry in the land.

But to blame it entirely on a lapse in good manners is, I think, to 4 miss the whole point. It has to do with something much larger and scarier than rudeness. What brought it all home to me was an incident that occurred in a Grade 12 English class I was teaching a few years ago. While we discussed a movie everyone had seen, I saw a wonderful opportunity to interject a few comments about my pet obsession — the invasion of movies by morons. Before I could sermonize, one of the boys said, "I know just what you're going to say and it bugs me too." Delighted I'd be preaching to the converted, I tried to continue, but he interrupted me again: "It really burns me when I go to the movies with my friends and we're horsing around and some jerk turns around and asks us to be quiet." When my berserk ravings had melted into a whimpering whine, I was struck by an overwhelming sadness — the kind of sadness one feels when a familiar touchstone has been lost. Here was someone I knew to be quite normal, sometimes even thoughtful, explaining how people who requested quiet in movies constituted an invasion of *his* rights. There was no doubt about it — something was certainly rotten.

I blame television. Though TV is a convenient whipping boy, what 5 else could have so warped that boy's perception of what a movie ought to be? Like the tube he switches on for company the moment he gets home, the movie screen is just supposed to be there — several dollars worth of objective background noise for *his* performance. Add to that insidious ethic a healthy dose of egocentricity, and you begin to understand the value system of the radio-schleppers too. If they travel in hermetically sealed vacuum-packed capsules of indifference, so must everyone else. Sadly then, all the reliable approaches to solving such a problem, like asking the offenders to quieten down, no longer work. What's worse, it has been my experience that *any* approach tends to evoke obscene remarks or the verbal equivalent of two longs and a short. Perhaps soon the home video revolution will keep them safely locked up and they will venture into the public domain only spasmodically to cart away armloads of tapes from the corner video outlet. Until then, however, this travesty demands a little noisemaking from the rest of us.

6   Now I've never been one to shirk a struggle, but I'll admit this one is getting me down. I'm weary of paying to see a film and getting a rumble instead. I'm tired of cowardly theatre managers who won't throw the bums out. But most of all I'm sick of this rabid Canadian disease of deferential politeness — even to neanderthals who deserve nothing better than to have their eyes burned out with projector bulbs. I figure we've got one chance only. If, in a few short years, the nonsmokers could make us feel like social lepers for lighting up in public, maybe we can do the same to the noise polluters. Is anybody out there listening?

△ △

Further Reading:

Environmental Health Directorate, *Noise Hazard and Control*
Anthony Burgess, *A Clockwork Orange* (novel)

Structure:

1. Is the opening good? Do its *examples* draw you into the essay?
2. What percentage of Dennis' argument consists of *examples*? What would we lose without them? Which is your favourite and why?
3. Paragraph 5 blames the epidemic of noisemaking on television and "egocentricity." Why does Dennis wait so long to name these *causes*? What is the *effect* of waiting?
4. Point out all the *comparisons* and *contrasts* which paragraph 6 uses to power the closing.
5. Why does Dennis save her question "Is anybody out there listening?" for the very last line.

Style:

1. Dennis states in her first sentence that she is "mad as hell." What other COLLOQUIALISMS or SLANG does she use? Would FORMAL language be better or worse in this essay?
2. In paragraph 3 noise polluters are "like nasty malignant cells." Point out five more SIMILES or METAPHORS in this selection.
3. The term "yahoos" (par. 3) is an ALLUSION to the semi-human monsters of *Gulliver's Travels.* To what does "the Silent Movie Majority" of paragraph 2 allude? How do allusions foster CONCISENESS?

Argumentation and Persuasion:

1. Dennis keeps showing how noise pollution has increased. Point out all the evidence in paragraphs 1, 3 and 4 that leads *inductively* to this view.
2. In never questioning her view that others *should* be quiet in the movie house and other public places, Dennis also reasons *deductively.* Put this view into the major premise of a syllogism, then add Dennis' minor premise and conclusion.
3. In this essay of persuasion, how much does Dennis also use *argumentation?* Find three passages that rely on logic.
4. Dennis hints as early as her violent title that she will specialize in *persuasion.* Point out at least five of her persuasive techniques, giving examples.

Ideas for Discussion and Writing:

1. If Wendy Dennis is angry, why does she also use humour, as in paragraph 1? Is anger a good reason for writing? How can it help — or harm? What does it do for Dennis' argument?
2. Has Dennis gone too far in so heavily favouring *persuasion* over *argumentation?* Has her shoot-from-the-lip approach put you off, or has it convinced you?
3. If you, too, hate noise in public places, give examples from experience. Or if you are one of the "noise polluters," is Dennis just trying to ruin your legitimate fun? Explain why you should be allowed to talk in "the sweet holy silence of the movie houses" or play your radio on the beach.
4. Have you noticed the "rabid Canadian disease of deferential politeness" that Dennis laments in closing? Are we too tolerant of those who violate social norms? Or of foreign countries that violate our national norms? If so, give examples.
5. **PROCESS IN WRITING:** *What is your own "pet obsession"? In an essay mostly of persuasion, denounce the thing you hate, and, like Dennis, pro-*

pose a solution. First write the name of your "obsession" in the middle of a page, then near it write other words that it calls to mind. Connect related items with lines, then apply the best of this cluster outline as you write the first draft. In your next draft add more tools of persuasion: *loaded words,* SENSE IMAGES, FIGURES OF SPEECH, *and examples that support your view. But don't go overboard; respect both the intellect and emotions of your audience. Do* TRANSITIONS *speed your prose? Has deadwood been cut? Do the points rise to a climax? Finally read your good version to the class, with expression, and be ready to answer questions.*

Note: See also the Topics for Writing at the end of this chapter.

Topics for Writing

Chapter 9: Argumentation and Persuasion

Develop one of the following topics into an essay of argumentation and/or persuasion, choosing the side you wish to take. (See also the guidelines that follow.)

1. It (is/is not) important for New Canadians to pass their first language on to their children.
2. Television has been a (good/neutral/bad) influence on my life.
3. Compulsory retirement at 65 should be (continued/abolished).
4. Canadian foreign aid should be (directed where it is needed most/directed where it will serve Canadian foreign policy and trade).
5. Car insurance (should/should not) cost the same for males and females.
6. My neighbourhood is becoming (safer/more dangerous).
7. The minimum driving age should be (lowered/maintained/raised).
8. Racism in Canada is (decreasing/continuing/increasing).
9. The NAFTA free trade agreement will (decrease/increase) job opportunities in the career I hope to enter.
10. Most Canadians watch far more foreign TV programming, especially American, than Canadian; should our government increase the Canadian content required on television channels?
11. Official censorship of films should be (abolished/continued/increased).
12. It is (beneficial/destructive) to family life for stores to open on Sundays.
13. The minimum drinking age should be (decreased/maintained/increased).
14. Canada should (decrease/maintain/increase) its level of immigration.
15. The police in my town or city are (ineffective/effective).
16. Use of cars in the centre of cities should be (abolished/reduced/maintained).
17. Capital gains (should/should not) be taxed.
18. Canada Post (should/should not) be privatized.
19. Food in the school cafeteria is (terrible/fair/mediocre/good/excellent).
20. The school library is (terrible/fair/mediocre/good/excellent).
21. The school computer facilities are (terrible/fair/mediocre/good/excellent).

22. Futurists predict increasing droughts around the world. Should Canada, which has a great many lakes, ever export this resource in large quantities?
23. Television commercials aimed at children are (beneficial/neutral/destructive).
24. The great majority of films shown in Canadian theatres are foreign, mostly American. Should theatres be required to show a higher percentage of our own films?
25. Adopted children (should/should not) be told who their birth parents are.
26. "Streaming" of students in the high schools should be (abolished/reduced/maintained/increased).
27. Companies (should/should not) be held liable for their own pollution.
28. Knowing (French/Spanish/Chinese) (will/will not) be important in my future career.
29. Computerization in society (decreases/increases) freedom of the individual.
30. There (is/is not) life in outer space.

Process in Writing: Guidelines

Follow at least some of these steps in writing your essay of argumentation and/or persuasion (your teacher may suggest which ones).

1. *Choose a good topic, then go to either 2 or 3 below.*

2. *DEDUCTION: Do you already know your point of view because of a moral or intellectual principle you hold? First examine that principle, the foundation of your argument: Is it extreme, or is it reasonable enough (and clear enough) that your* AUDIENCE *can accept it? If the latter, proceed. Make notes, then write a rapid and double-spaced first draft showing how the principle supports your point.*

OR

3. *INDUCTION: Did experience or observation teach you the point you wish to make? First generate a page of notes. Then put these experiences or observations into the order that led you to your conclusion. Now transfer this argument to a rapid, double-spaced first draft.*

4. *You have probably organized your draft through a pattern we studied in an earlier chapter.* Cause and effect *is a natural for either deduction or induction, and so is* comparison and contrast *(in this chapter see Margaret Atwood for the former and Bonnie Laing for the latter). You have surely used* examples, *perhaps* narrating *or* describing *them. You might also have* classified *your subject, or cast your logic in a* process analysis. *Apart from* analogy, *which appeals more to emotion than to logic, all the approaches we have studied so far can serve deduction or induction. Use whatever works. If your first draft makes partial use of a major pattern, consider revising to extend the pattern and strengthen its effect.*

5. *As you look over your first draft, add any missing examples, especially if your argument is inductive (the more evidence, the better). Heighten your logic with signals such as "however," "therefore," "as a result" and "in conclusion."*

6. *Now judge how* argumentative *or* persuasive *your approach has been so far. Does your cold logic need a little colour and life? If so, add it, consulting pages 282-284 on techniques of persuasion. Or do your emotional appeals, like those of Wendy Dennis in this chapter, dominate your argument? Do they even encourage the audience not to think? If so, revise towards a more blended stance in your second draft.*

7. *Now cut all deadwood. Check for details of spelling and grammar. Do your good copy, then proofread it word by word. If you have used a computer, save the essay on disk in case your teacher suggests further revision.*

GLOSSARY

Abstract Theoretical, relying more on generalities than on specific facts. Abstract writing tends to lack interest and force, because it is difficult to understand and difficult to apply. *See also* the opposite of abstract, CONCRETE.

Allegory In poetry or PROSE, a passage or an entire work that has two levels of meaning: literal and symbolic (*see* SYMBOL). Like a parable, an allegory draws such numerous or striking parallels between its literal subject and its implied subject that, without ever stating "the moral of the story," it leads us to perceive a moral or philosophical truth. An allegory, however, is longer and more complex than a parable. It also differs from an analogy in that it does not openly identify and compare the two subjects.

Allusion An indirect reference to a passage in literature or scripture, an event, a person, or anything else with which the reader is thought to be familiar. An allusion is a device of compression in language, for in a few words it summons up the meaning of the thing to which it refers, and applies that meaning to the subject at hand. Critics of big government, for example, will often allude to Big Brother, the personification of governmental tyranny in George Orwell's novel *1984.*

341

Anecdote A short account of an interesting and amusing incident. An anecdote can be a joke or a true story about others or oneself and is often used as an example to introduce an essay, close an essay, or illustrate points within an essay.

Audience The reader or readers. One of the essayist's crucial tasks is to match the level and strategy of an argument with the needs and qualities of the particular audience that will read it. *See* the section "Who is my audience?" on page 6 in this book's introductory essay, "The Act of Writing."

Bias words Terms which, either subtly or openly, encourage strong value judgements. SUBJECTIVE language is a vital ingredient of much good writing, especially in description and in persuasion; to avoid it altogether would be both impossible and undesirable. The important thing is to avoid blatantly loaded language in an essay: words like "Commie," "slob," "cretin," "Newfie" or "ex-con" will inflame an uncritical reader and offend a critical one. Note that many bias words are also SLANG.

Cliché A worn-out expression that takes the place of original thought: "to make a long story short," "sadder but wiser," "bite the bullet," "hustle and bustle," "by hook or by crook," "as different as night and day," and "hit the nail on the head." All clichés were once fresh, but like last year's fad in clothing or music, have lost their appeal and may even annoy.

Climax In an essay, the point at which the argument reaches its culmination, its point of greatest intensity or importance. The closing of an essay is normally a climax; if it is not, it may give the impression of trailing feebly off into nothingness.

Colloquial Speech-like. Colloquial expressions like "cop," "guy," "kid," "nitty gritty" and "okay" are often used in conversation but are usually avoided in essays, especially FORMAL essays. Although they are lively, colloquialisms are often inexact: "guy," for example, can refer to a person or a rope, and "kid" can refer to a child or a goat. *See also* SLANG.

Conciseness The art of conveying the most meaning in the fewest words. A concise essay does not explain its topic less fully than a wordy one; it just uses words more efficiently. Concise writers get straight to the point and stay on topic. They are well enough organized to avoid repeating themselves. They give CONCRETE examples rather than pages of ABSTRACT argument. They use a short word unless a long one is more exact. And most concise writers, to achieve these goals, revise extensively.

Concrete Factual and specific, relying more on particular examples than on abstract theory. Concrete language makes writing more forceful, interesting and convincing by recreating vividly for the reader what the writer has experienced or thought. SENSE IMAGES, ANECDOTES, FIGURES OF SPEECH and CONCISENESS all play a part in concrete language and are generally lacking in its opposite, ABSTRACT language.

Deduction A kind of logic that accepts a general principle as true, then uses it to explain a specific case or cases. *See* "Deduction," p. 280, and its opposite, "Induction," p. 281.

Dialogue The quoted conversation of two or more people. Normally a new paragraph begins with each change of speaker, to avoid confusion as to who says what. A certain amount of dialogue can lend colour to an essay, but heavy use of it is normally reserved for fiction and drama.

Economy See CONCISENESS.

Epigram A short, clever, and often wise saying. The best-known epigrams are proverbs, such as "What can't be cured must be endured" and "To know all is to forgive all."

Epigraph A short introductory quotation prefixed to an essay or other piece of writing.

Essay Derived from the French term *essai*, meaning a "try" or "attempt," the word "essay" refers to a short composition in which a point is made, usually through analysis and example. While most essays are alike in being limited to one topic, they may vary widely in other ways. The *formal essay*, for example, is objective and stylistically dignified, while the *familiar essay* is subjective, anecdotal and colloquial.

Euphemism A polite expression that softens or even conceals the truth: "pass away" for "die," "senior citizens" for "old people," "low-income neighbourhood" for "slum," "gosh darn" for "God damn," "perspire" for "sweat," "eliminate" for "kill," and "de-hire" or "select out" for "fire." Euphemisms are becoming more and more common in uses ranging from personal kindness to advertising to political repression.

Fiction Imaginative literature written in PROSE. Consisting mainly of novels and short stories, fiction uses invented characters and plots to create a dramatic story; most essays, by contrast, rely on literal fact and analysis to create an argument. There is of course an area of overlap: some fiction is very factual and some essays are very imaginative.

Figures of speech Descriptive and often poetic devices in which meaning is concentrated and heightened, usually through comparisons:

A. **Simile**: A figure of speech in which one thing is said to be *like* another. ("With its high buildings on all sides, Bay Street is like a canyon.")

B. **Metaphor:** A figure of speech, literally false but poetically true, in which one thing is said to *be* another. ("Bay Street is a canyon walled by cliffs of concrete.")

C. **Hyperbole**: Exaggeration. ("The office buildings rise miles above the city.")

D. **Personification**: A figure of speech in which a non-human object is described as human. ("At night the empty buildings stare from their windows at the street.")

Formal Formal writing is deliberate and dignified. It avoids partial sentences, most contractions, colloquial expressions and slang. Instead its vocabulary is standard and its sentences are often long and qualified with dependent clauses. In general it follows the accepted rules of grammar and principles of style. *See also* INFORMAL.

Hyperbole *See* FIGURES OF SPEECH.

Image In literature, a mental picture triggered by words. Because they strongly stimulate thought and feeling, yet take little space, well-chosen images are vital ingredients of writing that is CONCRETE and has CONCISENESS. *See also* SENSE IMAGES.

Induction A kind of logic that derives a general principle from the evidence of specific examples. *See* "Induction," p. 281, and its opposite, "Deduction," p. 280.

Informal Informal writing resembles speech and, in fact, is often a representation of speech in writing. It may contain partial sentences, many short sentences, contractions, COLLOQUIAL expressions and sometimes SLANG. *See also* FORMAL.

Irony A manner of expression in which a statement that seems literally to mean one thing in fact means another. "That's just great!" is a literal statement when said by a dinner guest enjoying the fondue but is an ironic complaint when said by a driver who has backed into a tree. In a larger sense, *irony of situation* is a contrast between what is expected to happen and what does happen. It is this that creates our interest in the national leader who is impeached, the orphan who becomes a millionaire, or the evangelist convicted of tax fraud. Irony is a powerful tool of argument and especially of SATIRE.

Jargon Technical language or language that seeks to impress by *appearing* difficult or technical. Specialized terms can hardly be avoided in technical explanations: How could two electricians discuss a radio without words like "capacitor," "diode" and "transistor"? But these same words may need definition when used in an essay for the general reader. Other jargon uses technical-sounding or otherwise difficult words to seem important. An honest essayist will try to avoid "input," "output," "feedback," "interface," "knowledgeable," "parameters" and other ugly words of this sort when writing for the general reader.

Juxtaposition The deliberate placing together of two or more thoughts, IMAGES or other elements that emphasize each other, usually by contrast.

Metaphor *See* FIGURES OF SPEECH.

Neologism A newly invented word. Some new terms are accepted into our standard vocabulary. For example, a word like "laser" tends to become standard because it is needed to label a new and important invention. Most newly minted words are nuisances, though, for they are meaningless to the great majority of readers who do not know them.

Objective The opposite of SUBJECTIVE. In objective writing the author relies more on hard evidence and logical proof than on intuitions, prejudices or interpretations.

Onomatopoeia A poetical device in which language sounds like what it means. Some onomatopoetic words, such as "boom," "bang" and "crash," are out-and-out sound effects; others, such as "slither," "ooze" and "clatter," are more subtle. Onomatopoeia can be achieved not only through word choice but also through larger aspects of style. A series of short sentences, for example, gives an impression of tenseness and rapidity.

Paradox A statement that seems illogical but that in some unexpected way may be true. The Bible is full of paradoxes, as in "Blessed are the meek, for they shall inherit the earth."

Personification *See* FIGURES OF SPEECH.

Prose Spoken or written language without the metrical structure that characterizes poetry. Conversations, letters, short stories, novels and essays are all prose.

Pun A play on words. A pun is based either on two meanings of one word or on two words that sound alike but have different meanings.

Often called the lowest form of humour, the pun is the basis of many jokes. (Why did the fly fly? Because the spider spider.)

Quotation   The words of one person reproduced exactly in the writing or speech of another person. A well-chosen quotation can add force to an argument by conveying the opinion of an authority or by presenting an idea in words so exact or memorable that they could hardly be improved upon. Quotations should be reproduced exactly, and of course should be placed in quotation marks and attributed to their source.

Reduction to absurdity   A technique of SATIRE in which the subject is belittled through being portrayed as absurd. A favourite device of humorists.

Sarcasm   Scornful and contemptuous criticism, from the Greek word *sarkazein* ("to tear flesh").

Satire   Humorous criticism meant to improve an individual or society by exposing abuses. In TONE, satire can range from light humour to bitter criticism. Its chief tools are wit, IRONY, exaggeration, and sometimes SARCASM and ridicule.

Sense images   Descriptive appeals to one or more of the reader's five senses: sight, hearing, touch, taste and smell. Sense images are vital in helping the reader to experience, at second hand, what the writer has lived in person. CONCRETE language has many sense images; ABSTRACT language does not.

Simile   *See* FIGURES OF SPEECH.

Slang   Racy, unconventional language often limited to a certain time, place or group. Slang is the extreme of colloquial language, terminology used in conversation but hardly ever in an essay except for dialogue or special effects. One reason to avoid a slang term is that not everyone will know it: expressions like "swell," "square" and "far out" have gone out of use, while expressions like "bug juice," "croaker," "jointman" and "rounder" are known to only one group — in this case, convicts. *See also* COLLOQUIAL.

Stereotype   An established mental image of something. Most stereotypes are of people and are based on their sex, race, colour, size or shape, economic or social class, or profession. Jokes about mothers-in-law, "Newfies," absent-minded professors, woman drivers or short people are all examples of stereotyping. While they may provoke humour, stereotypes are anything but harmless: they hinder recognition of people's individuality and they encourage prejudices which, at their extreme, can result in persecution like that of the Jews in Nazi Germany.

Style In general, the *way* something is written, as opposed to *what* it is written about. Style is to some extent a matter of TONE — light or serious, INFORMAL or FORMAL, ironic or literal. It is also a matter of technique. Word choice, FIGURES OF SPEECH, level of CONCISENESS, and characteristics of sentence structure and paragraphing are all ingredients of style. Although a writer should pay close attention to these matters, the idea that one deliberately seeks out "a style" is a mistake that only encourages imitation. An individual style emerges naturally as the sum of the writer's temperament, skills and experience.

Subjective The opposite of OBJECTIVE. In subjective writing the author relies more on intuitions, prejudices or interpretations than on hard evidence and logical proof.

Symbol One thing that stands for another, as in a flag representing a country, the cross representing Christianity, or a logo representing a company. Symbols appear frequently in poetry, drama, fiction and also essays.

Thesis statement The sentence or sentences, usually in the introduction, which first state the main point and restrict the focus of an essay.

Tone The manner of a writer toward the subject and reader. The tone of an essay can be light or serious, INFORMAL or FORMAL, ironic or literal. Tone is often determined by subject matter; for example an essay about cocktail parties is likely to be lighter and less formal than one about funerals. An innovative writer, though, could reverse these treatments to give each of the essays an ironic tone. The identity of the reader also influences tone. An essay for specialists to read in a technical journal will tend to be more OBJECTIVE and serious than one written for the general reader. The main point for the writer is to choose the tone most appropriate to a particular essay, then maintain it throughout.

Transition A word, phrase, sentence or paragraph that moves the reader from one part of the essay to the next. Transitions even as short as "next," "then," "as a result," "on the other hand," "in conclusion" or "finally" are crucial not only to moving the argument along, but also to pointing out its logic.